Allison Ireland

Babel and Babylon

Babel and Babylon

· · · · · · · · · · · · ·

Spectatorship in American Silent Film

Miriam Hansen

Harvard University Press
Cambridge, Massachusetts
London, England
1991

Library of Congress Cataloging-in-Publication Data

Hansen, Miriam, 1949–
    Babel and Babylon : spectatorship in American silent film / Miriam
Hansen.
        p.   cm.
    Includes bibliographical references and index.
    ISBN 0-674-05830-5
    1. Silent films—United States—History and criticism.   2. Motion
picture audiences—United States—History.   3. United States—Social
life and customs—1865–1918.   4. Feminism and motion pictures.
    I. Title.
PN1995.75.H36   1991
791.43'0973'09041—dc20

90-41808
                                                                                                       CIP

For Arthur E. and Ruth Bratu

Acknowledgments

· · · · · · · · · · · ·

This book has evolved in various places and stages and is therefore indebted to many institutions, colleagues, and friends. The first drafts and outlines were written in 1981–82, during my affiliation with the Whitney Humanities Center, Yale University, where I enjoyed the critical comments of Peter Brooks, John Hollander, and my colleague in Film Studies, Donald Crafton. The actual writing of the book began in 1985–86, thanks to an Andrew Mellon Faculty Fellowship at Harvard University. During that time a number of people have helped me develop a clearer vision of the project. I am particularly grateful to Daniel Aaron, Kathryne Lindberg, Alfred Guzzetti, Richard Allen, and Inez Hedges for stimulating conversations and readings of the emerging manuscript.

Rutgers University supported my work in important ways. I received several faculty grants, including a fellowship at the Center for the Critical Analysis of Contemporary Culture in 1988–89. For valuable discussions and new perspectives, I wish to thank the group of CCACC fellows, in particular Jackson Lears, Linda Zerilli, and the director, George Levine. Thanks also go to my friends and colleagues in English and other departments who supplied ideas, suggestions, and criticisms: Richard Poirier, William Walling, Alan Williams, E. Ann Kaplan, Sandy Flitterman-Lewis, Victoria de Grazia, and, above all, Emily Bartels.

I have benefited greatly from participating in the Columbia University Seminar on Cinema and Interdisciplinary Interpretation. That seminar, which meets once a month at the Museum of Modern Art, offered probably the single highest concentration of early film historians in this country, including Eileen Bowser, Charles Musser, Tom Gunning, Robert Sklar, Janet Staiger, Roberta Pearson, William Uricchio, and Richard Koszarski. I also wish to acknowledge my debt to the staff of the Museum's Film Department, and especially to Peter Williamson for invaluable information concerning his reconstruction of *Intolerance*.

Over the years a number of friends have advanced this book with their intellectual and emotional support, critical comments, and sustained debate. I am particularly grateful to Heide Schlüpmann, Gertrud Koch, Hauke Brunkhorst, KD Wolff, Alexander Kluge, and Berndt Ostendorf, and to Martin Christadler, who first worked through *Intolerance* with me in a collaborative article of 1974. On this side of the Atlantic, I am much indebted to Eric Rentschler, Philip Rosen, Mary Ann Doane, Anne Friedberg, Lynne Kirby, Patrice Petro, Serafina Bathrick, Alice Kaplan, Jane Gaines, Charles Musser, Angus Fletcher, and to Harold Bloom without whose advice and encouragement the book would not have its present shape.

Lindsay Waters has nurtured this book with unflagging interest and faith. Ann Louise Coffin McLaughlin edited the manuscript with gentle rigor and genuine curiosity. Thanks also to Joyce Jesionowski for most of the frame enlargements and to Christine Gledhill for illustrations and editorial suggestions on the Valentino part. Cynthia Scheinberg performed the crucial task of clearing up last-minute questions and organizing me into actually completing the manuscript. Finally, my special thanks go to Tom Gunning, who read this manuscript at various stages and who generously shared his ideas, expertise, and passion for early cinema.

An earlier version of Chapter 12 appeared in *Cinema Journal* 25.4 (Summer 1986), and parts of Chapters 8 and 10 were published in *The South Atlantic Quarterly* 88.2 (Spring 1989).

Contents

Introduction: Cinema Spectatorship and Public Life   1

I   *Rebuilding the Tower of Babel: The Emergence of Spectatorship*   21

1   A Cinema in Search of a Spectator: Film-Viewer
      Relations before Hollywood   23

2   Early Audiences: Myths and Models   60

3   Chameleon and Catalyst: The Cinema as an Alternative
      Public Sphere   90

II *Babel in Babylon: D. W. Griffith's* Intolerance (1916)   127

4   Reception, Textual System, and Self-Definition   129

5   "A Radiant Crazy-Quilt": Patterns of Narration
      and Address   141

6   Genesis, Causes, Concepts of History   164

7   Film History, Archaeology, Universal Language   173

8   Hieroglyphics, Figurations of Writing   188

9   Riddles of Maternity   199

10 Crisis of Femininity, Fantasies of Rescue   218

III   The Return of Babylon: Rudolph Valentino and Female
        Spectatorship (1921–1926)   243

11   Male Star, Female Fans   245

12   Patterns of Vision, Scenarios of Identification   269

       Notes   297
       Index   367

Babel and Babylon

Introduction: Cinema Spectatorship and Public Life

The Corbett-Fitzsimmons Fight, a Veriscope "illustration" of the long-delayed bout for the heavyweight championship, premiered at New York's Academy of Music in May–June 1897 and subsequently ran in major American cities for many weeks. Approximately 100 minutes long, usually accompanied by an expert's running commentary and occasionally interrupted by vaudeville acts, the film made up one of the first full-length programs centering on motion pictures. But length was not the only unusual thing about the success of The Corbett-Fitzsimmons Fight. While the film attracted large audiences that cut across class boundaries, reviewers noted with amazement that the shows were heavily attended by women; in Chicago, according to one source, women made up 60 percent of the patronage. [1] Unlike live prizefights with their all-male clientele, the cinematic mediation of the event gave women access to a spectacle from which they traditionally had been excluded. To be sure, this access was not the same as participation in the live event, the experience was abstracted into visual terms, removed from the sensuous impact of noise, smell, and audience excitation. At one remove, however, it afforded women the forbidden sight of male bodies in seminudity, engaged in intimate and intense physical action.

Almost three decades later, following the death of Rudolph Valentino in August 1926, millions of American women went to see The Son of the Sheik, the star's last and most perverse film. In one of the early sequences of that film, the romantic hero is captured by a gang of swarthy villains, half-stripped and suspended from his wrists on the wall of an exotic ruin, then whipped, taunted, and tortured at length. Although reverse shots showing the villains as gloating spectators ostensibly disclaim the effects of the sadistic spectacle, there is no doubt for whose benefit this spectacle was really staged—for the spectator in front of the screen, the fan, the female consumer. The prolonged display of Valentino's naked torso, proven successful in previous films such as *Moran of the Lady Letty* (1922) and *Monsieur Beaucaire* (1924), had become a calculated ingredient of star packaging. Taking the fate of the matinee idol to unprecedented extremes, Valentino became an emblem of the simultaneous liberalization and commodification of sexuality that crucially defined the development of American consumer culture.

These two snapshots condense, individually and in juxtaposition, a number of issues I will explore in this book. To begin with, they both turn on the spectator, on a particular mode of spectatorship, as a fundamental category of the institution of cinema. Like other media of visual representation and spectacle, but more systematically and exclusively, the cinema focused the creation of meaning on the register of the look, on processes of perceptual identification with seeing and seen. Yet the two instances also reveal a crucial distinction: in the case of Valentino, the film anticipates a spectator, specifically a female spectator, through particular strategies of representation and address; whereas, in the case of *The Corbett-Fitzsimmons Fight*, the film's success with female audiences was more or less accidental. When, how, and to what effect does the cinema conceive of the spectator as a textual term, as the hypothetical point of address of filmic discourse? And once such strategies have been codified, what happens to the viewer as a member of a plural, social audience?[2]

The two vignettes speak of spectatorship in pronounced terms of gender and sexuality, as visual pleasure revolves around the display of bodies of the opposite sex. Yet because the bodies in question are male and the beholders female, the configuration of vision and desire seems to violate a long-standing taboo in patriarchal culture—the taboo on an active female gaze, linked to the woman's traditional position as object of spectacle. This taboo, operative in different ways in high art and popular entertainment alike, had not yet been elaborated in specifically cinematic ways when *The Corbett-Fitzsimmons Fight* was made. In the Valentino films, however, it served as a backdrop for a self-conscious and lucrative transgression. How did the cinema respond to women's massive moviegoing, and how did moviegoing change the patterns of women's lives?

What I wish to suggest with the juxtaposition of the two vignettes is that the emergence of cinema spectatorship is profoundly intertwined with the transformation of the public sphere, in particular the gendered itineraries of everyday life and leisure. The period of American film history on which I focus—roughly from the beginnings of the cinematic institution in the 1890s through the end of the silent era toward the end of the 1920s—marks a major shift in the topography of public and private domains, especially with regard to the position of women and the discourse on sexuality. What changed were not only the standards by which certain realms of experience could be articulated in public while others remained private but also the methods by which these delineations were drawn. The very fact of female spectatorship, for instance, assumes a different meaning in relation to the homosocial tradition of popular entertainments, as invoked and subverted in the boxing film, than from the perspective of the systematic appropriation of female desire by an emerging culture of consumption.

To consider the question of spectatorship under the aspect of the public sphere seems especially important in light of developments both within and beyond the discipline of cinema studies. As even film scholars have begun to notice, we are on the threshold, if not already well past it, of yet another major transformation of the public sphere: the new electronic media, in particular the video market, have changed the institution of cinema at its core and made the classical spectator an object of nostalgic contemplation (in the manner of Woody Allen's *The Purple Rose of Cairo*). This does not mean that the category of spectatorship can be dissolved in favor of cynical celebrations of corporate communication or a wide-eyed advocacy of postmodernist participation.[3] On the contrary, now that cinematic spectatorship is becoming sufficiently contaminated with other modes of film consumption, we can trace more clearly its historically and theoretically distinct contours: on the one hand, a specifically modern form of subjectivity, defined by particular perceptual arrangements and a seemingly fixed temporality; on the other, a collective, public form of reception shaped in the context of older traditions of performance and modes of exhibition.

It is no coincidence that at this historical juncture spectatorship has become a key issue in scholarly debates, especially since the mid-1970s. The shift of focus from the filmic object and its structures to the relations between films and viewers, between cinema and spectator, was a prime motor in the development of a particular direction in film theory, derived from linguistically informed paradigms of semiotics and psychoanalysis. In the writings of Christian Metz, Jean-Louis Baudry, and others, in the pages of the British journal *Screen*, the spectator was conceptualized under the poststructuralist category of the subject (as elaborated by Lacan and Althusser) and corresponding notions of ideology. Arguing from critical perspectives, mainly Marxist and feminist, film theorists advanced a systematic analysis of how the cinema, in particular classical Hollywood cinema, works to bind and realign the spectator's desire with dominant ideological positions; above all, how it simultaneously mobilizes and masks the subject's fundamental heterogeneity in such a manner as "to create within the spectator the comforting illusion that s/he is in fact a transcendental, unified subject."[4]

This approach has yielded two overlapping types of inquiry. One centers on the concept of the cinematic apparatus (a concept combining basic technological aspects, Althusser's *dispositif*, and Freudian metapsychology), in which the spectator figures as the transcendental vanishing point of specific spatial, perceptual, social arrangements, such as "the darkness of the auditorium and the resultant isolation of the individual spectator; the placement of the projector, source of the image behind the spectator's head; and the effect of the real produced by the classical fiction film."[5] Whether theorized in terms of the analogy with Plato's cave, the metaphor of the mirror stage, the principles of Renaissance perspective, or the ideological self-effacement of classical continuity conventions, the apparatus refers to the *general* conditions and relations of cinematic reception, the technologically changing yet ideologically constant parameters of the institution. By contrast, the other type of inquiry is concerned with the step-by-step solicitation of the spectator in the textual system of particular films. Relying on the linguistic concept of "enunciation" (Emile Benveniste), writers such as Raymond Bellour and Stephen Heath developed methods of textual analysis guided by the question of how positions of understanding and subjectivity are being offered to—and expected of—the film's recipient, how knowledge and authority, pleasure and identification, are organized through systematic processes of vision and narration.[6]

In either case the spectator under consideration is not to be confused with the empirical moviegoer, as a member of a social audience. Rather, psychoanalytic-semiotic film theory deals with the spectator as a term of discourse, an effect of signifying structures. Yet this does not make the spectator simply an "implied" or "ideal" reader in the sense of literary reception aesthetics. Instead, the emphasis is on the constitutive tension between the spectator inscribed by the filmic text and the social viewer who is asked to assume certain positions—on identification as a *process* which, on a temporary yet institutional basis, interweaves empirical subjects with the discourse of the Subject.[7]

Despite the theoretical recognition that there is more to reception than textually and ideologically predetermined subject positions, the spectator of film theory remains a somewhat abstract and ultimately passive entity. Although the subject of textual analysis (inasmuch as he or she is engaged in a hypothetical reading) may appear to perform a more active part than the subject of the cinematic apparatus, the concept of enunciation likewise implies that the spectator has been duped in some way, since the signifying process depends upon the gratifying illusion by which the viewing subject imagines him or herself as the enunciating author of the filmic fiction. Moreover, as feminist critics from Laura Mulvey to Mary Ann Doane have argued, classical spectatorship is fundamentally gendered, that is, structurally masculinized, which makes textually dominant routes of identification problematic for the female viewer (or for that matter any viewer who is not male and heterosexual, middle class and white). Increasingly, therefore, efforts to conceptualize a female viewer have gone beyond the psychoanalytic-semiotic framework to include culturally specific and historically variable aspects of reception. In effect, the question of female spectatorship has been a major impulse for film theory to confront empirical levels and formations of reception (such as the industry's catering to female audiences through particular stars and genres)—in other words, to take up the contradictions posed by film history. [8]

During the same decade that film theory moved into the forefront of scholarly debate—in a sense constituted itself as a movement, a new discourse—film history too made a break with the discipline's past by redefining the entire area of research. Film historians dissatisfied with the traditional surveys of pioneer inventions and great works of film art set out to revise the standard narratives—of American cinema in particular—through detailed empirical studies. Like film theory, the new historiography questioned the primacy of the filmic object, of canonized products and oeuvres, and turned its attention to the cinema as an economic and social institution, to relations between film practice and developments in technology, industrial organization and exhibition practices. The spectator enters these studies as a consumer, as a member of a demographically diverse audience. According to Robert Allen and Douglas Gomery, even the notion of a socially and historically specific audience is already an "abstraction generated by the researcher, since the unstructured group that we refer to as the movie audience is constantly being constituted, dissolved, and reconstituted with each film-going experience." [9]

This may be an extreme statement of the empiricist case (not necessarily endorsed by Allen and Gomery), but it is indicative of a self-imposed abstinency of the new film history with regard to the social and cultural dynamics of cinema consumption, with discourses of experience and ideology. We seem to be faced with a gap between film theory and film history, between the spectator as a term of cinematic discourse and the empirical moviegoer in his or her demographic contingency. The question, then, is whether the two levels of inquiry can be mediated at all; whether and how the methodologies and insights of each can be brought to bear upon the other. There is no doubt that theoretical concepts of spectatorship need to be historicized so as to include empirical formations of reception. By the same token, however, a reception-oriented film history cannot be written without a theoretical framework that conceptualizes the possible relations between films and viewers.

Among a number of attempts to overcome the split between theoretical and historical-empirical directions in cinema studies, the recent recourse to cognitive psychology is of particular interest, especially if it is combined, as in the work of David Bordwell, with the project of a historical poetics of cinema. [10] As in psychoanalytic-semiotic film theory, perhaps even more so, the spectator appears primarily as a function of signifying structures, specifically, the strategies of filmic narration. But the viewer, Bordwell insists, is more than a passive victim of ideological conspiracy; the viewer is an active participant in the filmic narration, "a hypothetical entity executing the operations relevant to constructing a story out of the film's representation." Supplemented by "many sorts of particular knowledge," the viewer's "experience is cued by the text, according to intersubjective protocols that may vary." This concept of reception may seem to include a historical dimension on two counts: the somewhat vague reference to "many sorts of particular knowledge" and the "intersubjective protocols" which vary according to different paradigms and norms of narration, such as the classical Hollywood example, the art film, or different types of modernist cinema; each paradigm in turn is flexible as to its various components and, in the case of modernist types of narration, specifically concerned with foregrounding "the historicity of all viewing conventions." [11]

What kind of history can be grasped through the meshes of cognitive psychology, as a model that crucially relies on the assumption of human, if not biological, universals? (The same question of course applies to certain aspects of psychoanalysis.) It might also be of importance that, by limiting the viewer's activity to conscious and preconscious mental processes, the cognitivist approach deliberately evades the contested zone of sexuality and sexual difference. But it is equally problematic that the tension between the textually inscribed spectator and the empirical viewer seems to evaporate altogether—that nothing but the one-hundred-percent successful performance of perceptual operations expected of the viewer should qualify as spectatorship. If the viewer exists only as the formal function of the filmic address, where does this leave the female audiences of *The Corbett-Fitzsimmons Fight?* And how do we distinguish between historical acts of reception and the contemporary critic's analysis of narratorial cues?

What is eliminated with the tension between textually inscribed and empirical viewer is not merely the contingency of individual acts of reception, but rather the hermeneutic constellation in which a historical spectator makes sense of what he or she perceives, how he or she interprets the filmic narration. [12] This is less a question of the "many sorts of particular knowledge" that get called up to enable the reception of particular films than of a specific social horizon of understanding that shapes the viewer's interpretation. That horizon is not a homogeneous storage of intertextual knowledge but a contested field of multiple positions and conflicting interests, defined (though not necessarily confined) in terms of the viewer's class and race, gender and sexual orientation.

What is missing from any theory that conceptualizes the spectator as a function—or effect—of a closed, albeit flexible, system, be it the formal codes of narration or the script of Ideology, is a place for the public dimension of cinematic reception. This public dimension is distinct from both textual and social determinations of spectatorship because it entails the very moment in which reception can gain a momentum of its own, can give rise to formations not necessarily anticipated in the context of production. Such formations may crystallize around particular films, star discourses, or modes of exhibition, but they are not identical with these structural conditions. Although always precarious and subject to ceaseless—industrial, ideological—appropriation, the public dimension of the cinematic institution harbors a potentially autonomous dynamic which makes even a phenomenon like the Valentino cult more than a consumerist spectacle orchestrated from above.

In this book, I approach the question of spectatorship from the perspective of the public sphere, as a critical concept that is itself a category of historical transformation. In light of the blind spots resulting from the increased specialization of both film theory and film history, the concept of the public sphere offers a theoretical matrix that encompasses different levels of inquiry and methodology. On one level the cinema constitutes a public sphere of its own, defined by particular relations of representation and reception; these depend upon processes specific to the institution of cinema, that is, the uneven development of modes of production, distribution, and exhibition, in conjunction with particular forms of film style. At the same time the cinema intersects and interacts with other formations of public life, which fall into the areas of social and cultural history. In both respects the question is which discourses of experience will be articulated in public and which remain private; how these delineations are organized, for whom, by whom and in whose interest; how the public, as a collective and intersubjective horizon, is constituted and constitutes itself under particular conditions and circumstances.

The idea of the "public"—and the concomitant distinction of public and private—has a vast history, which has been taken up by various traditions of social and political thought; in the American tradition, for instance, by writers like John Dewey, C. Wright Mills, Hannah Arendt, and Richard Sennett. More recently it has been of concern to social and women's historians, particularly in studies of mass and consumer culture.[13] Although I draw on some of this work, I rely primarily on the German debate on the public sphere, initiated by Jürgen Habermas' 1962 publication of *The Structural Transformation of the Public Sphere*.[14] This debate not only offers the most elaborated theoretical framework on the topic so far but also implies a number of significant trajectories because of the contexts in which it was elaborated: discussions on the conditions of culture under advanced capitalism in the tradition of the Frankfurt School, in particular Horkheimer and Adorno's *Dialectic of Enlightenment*; the development of the German New Left and of the "alternative movements" of the 1970s (including the women's movement), which, adopting a concept from Oskar Negt and Alexander Kluge, defined themselves as "oppositional" or "counter public spheres"; and, finally, the conception of the cinema in terms of the public sphere in Kluge's writings, films, and media politics.

Unlike sociological attempts to conceptualize the "public" in typological and functionalist terms, or traditional political theory's efforts to ground it in idealized versions of the Greek polis, Habermas sets out to reconstruct the public as a fundamentally historical category, linked to the emergence of bourgeois society under liberal capitalism. He complicates "the standard dualistic approaches to the separation of public and private in capitalist societies"[15] by establishing the "public sphere" as a fourth term, distinct from the Hegelian trinity of family, state, and civil society, terms which in turn participate in the dialectic of private and public. Habermas traces the constitution of the bourgeois public sphere in the informal association of private persons vis-à-vis and in opposition to the "sphere of public violence" (the state, the realm of the "police"). The forms of civil interaction that define this new type of association—equality, mutual respect, general accessibility, and potential openness to all subjects and subject matter—are based on an autonomy grounded in the private realm, that is, civil society and its property relations (commodity circulation and social labor) and, at the core of that realm, the intimate sphere of the nuclear family. Yet, as the public emerges as an arena in which social status is suspended, it brackets economic laws and dependencies, thereby suppressing the material conditions of its historical possibility. Its very claim to expressing and representing a discourse of general, "merely" or "purely" human concern depends upon the assertion of separateness from the sphere of economic necessity, competition, and interest.

What distinguishes such an assertion from earlier formations of public life, for instance in the Greek polis, is that it is subtended by a specific form of subjectivity, rooted in the sphere of familial intimacy. This subjectivity is articulated through the symbolic matrix of culture, especially writing, reading, and literary criticism—activities which challenge the interpretive monopoly of church and state authorities. As culture emerges in the modern sense, as a commodity that pretends to exist for its own sake, it functions as the "ready topic of a discussion through which an audience-oriented (*publikumsbezogene*) subjectivity communicated with itself."[16] In the rehearsal of critical self-reflexivity and intersubjective argument, cultural discourse (*Räsonnement*)—as it unfolds in the eighteenth-century institutions of the French salons, the English coffeehouses, book clubs, and the press—prepares the ground for political emancipation and the rise to hegemony of the bourgeois public sphere. At the same time, this mutual empowerment of politics and culture depends upon the idealization of its source, the nuclear family, as the mainstay of a private autonomy whose economic origin and contingency are denied. The identity of propertyowner and patriarchal head of the family provides the linchpin for the fictive unity of the bourgeois public sphere. As this sphere disintegrates, the idea of humanity collapses into the ideology that naturalizes the subjectivity of a particular class as "generally human."

Habermas' concept of the public sphere has a dual function: as a *historical* category, it offers a model for analyzing fundamental changes in relations among economy, society, and state, and in the conditions and relations of cultural production and reception; once institutionalized, the idea of the public becomes a *normative* category which, though never fully realized, is effective as a standard for political critique.[17] As a regulative principle, then, the emphatic sense of the public outlives its Enlightenment origins; it overlaps with the dimension that Habermas, in his later work, has theorized as the ideal of undistorted, domination-free communication. (In a similar, even more partisan way, Richard Sennett reconstructs the eighteenth-century public sphere as a model for the "conditions under which human beings are able to express themselves forcefully to each other.")[18]

Much as the emphatic connotation of the public seems indispensable—

especially in light of scientistic claims that would use the notions of public and private as "purely" descriptive tools—the oscillation between a historical and a normative concept of the public is problematic for at least two reasons. For one thing, the history of the public sphere subsequent to its early bourgeois formations can be conceived only in terms of disintegration and decline—which obviously poses problems for dealing with the cinema and other modern mass media. Another, perhaps more fundamental, problem concerns the relationship between idea and ideology in the conceptualization of the public sphere. Are the contradictions between idea and ideology an effect of historical decline, or does this decline reveal the ideological inscription of the bourgeois public sphere from its inception, in its very constitution?

The latter problem is of particular significance for the place of women in relation to the public sphere. As feminist historians have begun to demonstrate, the bourgeois public sphere was gendered from the start—as an arena of virtuous action, and civilized interaction, for the "public man." By contrast, a "public woman" was "a prostitute, a commoner, a common woman."[19] Habermas himself notes a gender discrepancy in the constituencies of the literary and the political public (whose symbiosis, is crucial to his argument). Although women and social dependents make up the majority of the *reading* public, which mediates familial subjectivity with public discourse, they are excluded from the *political* public sphere by virtue of both law and brute fact.[20] Despite his persistent critique of the bourgeois family (the denial of its economic origin, the ideological fusion of propertyowner and paternal authority), the sexual imbalance that sustains the fiction of "private autonomy" remains marginal to Habermas' theory; his basic conception of the public sphere is gender-neutral. However, as Joan Landes argues in her study on the French Revolution which revises Habermas' framework from a feminist perspective, "the exclusion of women from the bourgeois public was not incidental but central to its incarnation." Hence, "the bourgeois public is essentially, not just contingently, masculinist, and . . . this characteristic serves to determine both its self-representation and its subsequent 'structural transformation.'" Not only was one of its founding acts the suppression of an actively female and feminist public sphere, that of the prerevolutionary *salonnières,* but the masculinization of public life also involved a restriction of women's activities to the domestic space, and the concomitant alignment of the familial sphere with a new discourse of an idealized femininity.[21]

The assymetries of gender also complicate the disintegration of the bourgeois public sphere, precipitated in Habermas' analysis by the antagonism of classes inherent in the development of industrial capitalism, the supersession of a liberal market by monopolistic practices, and the shift from cultural discourse to cultural consumption. For Habermas, the industrial dissemination of cultural products is structurally incompatible with the possibility of public discourse: "the web of public communication unraveled into acts of individuated reception, however uniform in mode."[22] Like Horkheimer and Adorno before him, Habermas does not simply blame the commodification of art as such; on the contrary, the capitalist market is the very condition of the notion of aesthetic autonomy, the emancipation of art from feudal and sacral contexts. The crucial distinction is that the early literary market gave rise to a public discourse that emphatically defined itself as separate from private economic interest, whereas under advanced capitalism that tension collapses altogether. Cultural products are designed for mass consumption; they are not just also commodities, but "commodities through and through."[23] Yet Habermas' own observation concerning the gender discrepancy of literary and political publics suggests that the distinction was perhaps not as absolute; that the logic of consumption already invaded—as well as enabled—classical forms of public life. And with women increasingly being perceived as the subject of consumption, the repressed gender subtext of the bourgeois public sphere returns—with the emergence of qualitatively different types of publicity such as the cinema, with relations of representation and reception no longer predicated on the exclusionary hierarchies of literary culture.

The historical emergence of competing types of public sphere that cannot be explained in terms of the bourgeois model is the point of departure of Negt and Kluge's study, *The Public Sphere and Experience* (1972), which presupposes a familiarity with Habermas' book.[24] More skeptical than Habermas, Negt and Kluge question the distinction between Enlightenment idea and ideology in the conception of the bourgeois public sphere. The very principles of generality and abstractness underlying its claims to self-representation, they argue, sanctioned the exclusion of large areas of social reality, in terms of participants (women, workers, social dependents) and subject matter (the material conditions of social production and reproduction, including sexuality and child-rearing). Furthermore, Negt and Kluge observe, Habermas' conceptual grounding of the public sphere in the historical emergence of a reading public turns into a heuristic limitation when he dismisses any nonbourgeois public formations as mere variants of, respectively, a "plebeian" ("illiterate") or a "postliterary" public sphere.[25] In addition to the bourgeois model, therefore, they introduce two other *types* of public sphere—the notion of the so-called "public spheres of production"

(*Produktionsöffentlichkeiten*), which refers to industrial and commercial contexts such as factory "communities" or the media of consumer culture, and the notion of a "proletarian" or "oppositional" public sphere.

The industrial-commercial forms of publicity, in Negt and Kluge's analysis, no longer pretend, like the bourgeois model, to a separate sphere above the marketplace, although they still graft themselves upon the remnants of the former for a semblance of coherence and legitimacy. As an immediate branch of production and circulation, they tend to include, as their "raw material," areas of human life previously considered private. Hence they relate more directly—and more comprehensively—to human needs and qualities, if only to appropriate and desubstantialize them. However, even in the capitalist re/production of such needs, Negt and Kluge contend, a substantially different function of the "public" comes into view: that of a "social horizon of experience," the experience in particular of those excluded from the dominant space of public opinion.[26] Unlike Habermas, who focuses on the structural possibility of public discourse, Negt and Kluge emphasize questions of social constituency, of concrete needs, interests, and power. The political issue is whether and to what extent a public sphere is organized from above—by the exclusive standards of high culture or the stereotypes of commodity culture—or by the experiencing subjects themselves, on the basis of their context of living (*Lebenszusammenhang*).

As a counterconcept to the bourgeois public sphere, but also in opposition to the industrial-commercial variants, Negt and Kluge call this alternative type of public sphere "proletarian," a term that epitomizes the historical subject of alienated labor and experience. Historically, they assert, rudimentary and ephemeral instances of a "proletarian" public sphere have already emerged—their examples include English Chartism, Italian Maximalism, and certain moments in the October revolution—in the fissures, overlaps, and interstices of nonlinear historical processes.[27] As a discursive construction, they insist, it could be derived from its negation, that is, from hegemonic efforts to suppress, destroy, isolate, split, or assimilate any public formation that suggests an alternative organization of experience.

It is important to note here that the concept of "experience" (*Erfahrung*) underlying this argument is explicitly opposed to an empiricist sense of the word, to notions of perception and cognition based on stable subject-object relations and directed toward instrumental uses in science and technology. Negt and Kluge assume instead a rather complex theory of experience in the tradition of Adorno, Kracauer, and Benjamin: experience as that which mediates individual perception with social meaning, conscious with unconscious processes, loss of self with self-reflexivity; experience as the capacity to see connections and relations (*Zusammenhang*); experience as the matrix of conflicting temporalities, of memory and hope, including the historical loss of these dimensions.[28] The emphasis on the discursive organization of experience, rather than the perspective of class struggle, makes it possible to adapt their theory of the public sphere to feminist concerns, notwithstanding their own idealizations of a feminine, that is, maternal, mode of production.[29]

For Kluge, as a filmmaker and media politician, the cinema is one of the key institutions in which competing types of public life intersect. Although indebted to left-modernist media theory (Eisenstein, Vertov, Brecht, Benjamin, Enzensberger), Kluge has long since abandoned the epithet "proletarian" or even "oppositional" in conjunction with the public sphere. Instead he returns to an emphatic notion of public life, defined by such principles as *openness* (the etymological root of the German word for public, *öffentlich*), freedom of access, multiplicity of relations, communicative interaction, and self-reflection.[30]

But how can the cinema, which by its very technology has eliminated the conditions of participation, interaction, and self-representation (such as, according to Sennett, distinguished the eighteenth-century theater), be considered public in the emphatic sense? In an interesting revision of Benjamin's essay, "The Work of Art in the Age of Mechanical Reproduction" (1935–36), Kluge suggests that the historically significant watershed is not between the cinema and the "classical arts" but, between the cinema and television or, specifically in West Germany, the entire fleet of the privately owned, "new" electronic media. In light of recent upheavals affecting the European media map, he concludes that "the cinema belongs to the classical public sphere."[31] Benjamin's statement that film precipitated the disintegration of the "aura," Kluge observes, is hyperbolic. While aspects of the classical aura did disappear with the invention of cinema, new forms of auratic experience have entered the movie theater as a result of the particular relationship between film and audience—the structural affinity between the film on the screen and "the film in the spectator's head." Like Benjamin himself, Kluge tries to salvage the experiential possibilities of the disintegrated aura for a secularized, public context: an element of reciprocity ("to invest a phenomenon with the capability of returning the gaze"), of intersubjectivity and memory. Thus the reciprocity between the film on the screen and the spectator's stream of associations becomes the measure of a particular film's use value for an alternative public sphere: a film either exploits the viewer's needs, perceptions, and wishes or it encourages their autonomous movement, fine-tuning, and self-reliance.[32]

Such a possibility requires a third term—the other viewer, the audience as collective, the theater as public space, part of a social horizon of experience. This aspect distinguishes Kluge's notion of spectatorship, as the process that organizes experience in and through the cinema, most clearly from the directions in film theory and film history. Kluge conceives of the spectator in the plural even at the level of discursive construction (the textually inscribed subject, the consumer targeted by the industry), as a position addressed not to the empirical viewer as socially contingent individual, but to an audience endowed with historically concrete contours, conflicts, and possibilities. While the trope of the film in the spectator's head no doubt encompasses psychoanalytic dimensions, it is doubly contextualized both within a particular public sphere—constituted by an ad hoc social audience, a particular site, phase, and mode of exhibition—and by the public horizon, which is produced and reproduced, appropriated and contested, in the cinema as one among a number of cultural institutions and practices. Most important, in its dependence on both individual psychic processes and an intersubjective horizon, cinema spectatorship for Kluge essentially includes a moment of unpredictability. It is this unexpected, almost aleatory, component of collective reception that makes the viewing "public" (*Publikum*) a public sphere (*Öffentlichkeit*) in the emphatic sense. [33]

A conceptual framework developed primarily in relation to the European public sphere cannot simply be applied to an American context. No doubt significant differences exist, and it could be argued that the idea of the public as an autonomous dimension never acquired that much normative weight in a country where it did not arise to delegitimize the *cultural* power of feudal social structures and an absolutist state. Yet there are important parallels, especially with regard to the gender subtext of the bourgeois public sphere, the hierarchic segregation of public and private as male and female domains. Moreover, the capitalist foundation of modern forms of public life makes it impossible to conceive of them as independent national developments. Indeed, for the process of transformation (in Habermas' terms, the disintegration of the bourgeois public sphere), the American "culture industry" emerges as the hegemonic model—and material cause—for the direction of mass-cultural production and reception in European countries and elsewhere.

The distinction between different types of public life that Negt and Kluge propose throws into relief the specific circumstances that favored the emergence of this hegemonic model in the United States, such as, on the most obvious level, the contradictions of an immigrant, ethnically and racially segregated society. If, for instance, we were to limit our notion of the public to the period's discourse on "the problem of the public," the cinema could not even be considered in those terms—nor could the institutions of working-class ethnic and black culture which the cinema in part absorbed and largely displaced. For Progressive Era intellectuals such as Walter Lippmann, who criticized the function and ideology of "The Public," the concept itself remained uncontested, more or less synonymous with "public opinion." The alternative for Lippmann was not a wider, more hetero-geneous and inclusive notion of public life but, rather, the legitimation of an elite of experts and leaders exempt from the sphere of public argument.[34]

More effectively, the cinema was excluded from dominant notions of the public by the legal discourse surrounding the question of censorship. Shortly after the opening of *The Birth of a Nation* in February 1915, the Supreme Court handed down a unanimous decision (Mutual Film Corpora-tion v. Industrial Commission of Ohio) by which moving pictures were denied the constitutional protection of freedom of speech and press. "It cannot be put out of view," the Court wrote, that their exhibition is "a business pure and simple, originated and conducted for profit, like other spectacles, not to be regarded . . . as part of the press of the country or as organs of public opinion."[35] Whether because of a puritanical reservation against spectacle or on the grounds of the essentially private motivation of its economic existence, the cinema was refused First Amendment protection—recognition of a "public" status. This decision capped numerous efforts on local and state levels, from about 1908 on, to establish control over the mushrooming exhibition of motion pictures—precisely because the dominant forces discerned in it the incipient formation of an alternative public sphere.

In the struggle over control, the industry resorted to a number of strat-egies to assert the cinema's public status; recourse to the forms and names of bourgeois culture was one of them. It is part of D. W. Griffith's histori-cal significance that he approached the problem of the cinema as public not just defensively, by trying to legitimize an industrial enterprise and low-class entertainment with the cultural trappings of a bourgeois public sphere. With all his cultural anachronisms and personal political invest-ments, he understood that the cinema offered the possibility of a new, different kind of public sphere, a chance to close the gap perceived by his Progressive contemporaries between a genteel literary culture and the encroachment of commercialism. As I suggest in my reading of *Intolerance* (1916), he envisioned such an alternative public sphere through the project of a new American hieroglyphics, the conception of film as a new universal, written language. This can be seen as an effort to extend the idea of a prepolitical reading public (in Habermas' sense) to the masses of the uprooted and downtrodden who populated the nickelodeons. At the same time, Griffith's vision of a new public sphere tried to exorcise the psychosexual forces unleashed by the very development that had enabled him to have his vision: the contradictory dynamic of consumption and female subjectivity which crucially determined the structural transformation of public life in, through, and around the cinema.

In what follows, then, I pursue the question of film spectatorship through exemplary moments in the history of American cinema, specifically the silent period. First I trace the emergence of the category of the spectator as a historical construction that does not necessarily coincide with the invention of cinema. Rather, it is linked to the paradigmatic shift from early to classical cinema during the decade, roughly, between 1907 and 1917. This shift is defined by the elaboration of a mode of narration that makes it possible to anticipate a viewer through particular textual strategies, and thus to standardize empirically diverse and to some extent unpredictable acts of reception.

I consider the creation of this classical spectator from a variety of perspectives, beginning with the different organization of film-viewer relations in early cinema. These differences are located on the level of textual conventions of representation and address and on the level of exhibition practices, which are embedded in the public sphere of late-nineteenth century popular, commercial entertainments. In Chapter 2, I discuss the emergence of spectatorship from the angle of audience composition, specifically the vexed question of the legendary symbiosis between the nickelodeon (the first independent exhibition outlet for films) and its immigrant working-class clientele. Among other things, I argue that the gentrification efforts that set in on the heels of the nickelodeon boom were designed to elevate a temporarily quite class-specific motion picture audience to the level of the upwardly mobile mass public of commercial entertainments, in particular vaudeville and amusement parks like New York's Coney Island. In this process, the elaboration of classical methods of spectator-positioning appears as the industrial response to the problems posed by the cinema's availability to ethnically diverse, socially unruly, and sexually mixed audiences. The ideological objective of constructing a unified subject of—and for—mass-cultural consumption, of integrating empirically diverse audiences with this goal, was troped in the ambiguous celebration of film as a new universal language, as a historically unique chance to "repair the ruins of Babel."

Although the metaphor of Babel refers to the normative aspect of the institution, the positioning of the spectator as the subject of a universal film language, it also implies the connotation of futility. With it emerges the possibility that this positioning is more than just an expression of the circular logic of consumption, but that there remains, even in the ceaseless repetition of this process, a margin of autonomous interpretation and reappropriation. In Chapter 3, I delineate such a margin in the dynamics of public reception, particularly in exhibition practices that lag behind the mass-cultural standards of production and distribution. These exhibition practices emphasize the value of the show as live performance over the projection of the film as uniform product, thus providing the structural conditions for locally specific, collective formations of reception. I suggest, therefore, that the cinema might have functioned as a potentially autonomous, alternative horizon of experience for particular social groups, such as immigrant working-class audiences and women across class and generational boundaries.

In Part II, the methodological focus is narrowed to a close reading of a single film, Griffith's *Intolerance*, a film that dramatizes the tension between spectatorship and reception on the threshold of classical codification. I discuss the "failure" of the film with contemporary audiences as an aspect of Griffith's attempt to put the universal language analogy into practice, to ordain a new idiom of visual self-evidence that would be not only equal but superior to verbal languages. With its protostructuralist narration—the accelerated intercutting of narratives from four different periods of history—*Intolerance* conflicted with classical norms of linearity, character-based causality, and closure already formulated by 1916. But even on the level of individual sequences, the film impedes classical routes of viewer identification by its peculiar organization of vision and space, its systematic refusal to allocate the spectator a place within the diegesis, that is, the fictional world of film.

I consider this idiosyncratic conception of film-viewer relations part of Griffith's inscription of the cinema with a particular variant of the universal language myth—the discourse on hieroglyphics in the tradition of the American Renaissance. As a "hieroglyphic" text par excellence, marked by graphic and stylistic heterogeneity, *Intolerance* projects something like a public reading space, asking the viewer to participate in a collective process of deciphering and interpreting. This invitation may smack of a patrician, if not paternalistic dispensation; but it also suggests, at a crucial juncture in the formation of the institution, an alternative conception of spectatorship, an appeal to the viewer to engage in an intersubjective process rather than merely identify with and through predetermined spectatorial positions.

What disturbs the ingenuity of the film's design and complicates the fiction of hieroglyphic self-evidence is an excessive textuality; this I link to the film's obsession with a crisis of femininity. I trace this countercurrent both through structures of gendered vision and in the film's violent and ambiguous figurations of the single woman—the spinster, the bereft mother, the murderer, the prostitute. While the film's guiding emblem of the Woman Who Rocks the Cradle still invokes the nineteenth-century ideology of domesticity, the doctrine of a separate female sphere, the modernity of *Intolerance* lies in its recognition that the boundaries between public and private are irrevocably blurred, no longer capable of containing the real or projected expressions of female desire.

The historical basis of much of Griffith's fear and fascination was the female consumer who, especially after World War I, became the primary target of Hollywood publicity and products. In Part III I discuss the contradictions posed by this development—the industry's massive catering to women viewers in a medium that increasingly depended, for the kinds of pleasure it offered the viewer, on a patriarchal organization of vision along the axis of sexual difference. Reopening the focus of investigation halfway, this part deals with a single star, Valentino, and the contradictions of female spectatorship that erupted around him. As a scandal that simultaneously promoted his stardom, Valentino's career became a function of the discourse on female sexuality, compounded by the transgressive appeal of his ethnic otherness and deviant masculinity. I pursue this configuration on the levels of star publicity and of the particular scenarios of vision and identification that structure his films. The conflict between short-term marketing interests and a long-range patriarchal orientation of the institution made Valentino a catalyst for major changes in gender roles and relations, a figure oscillating between stereotypes of romantic love and visions of erotic reciprocity. Whatever the ideological inscription of his films, their spectacular reception gave rise to a female subculture as distinct as the nineteenth-century cult of domesticity. This subculture, if more short-lived, was also more threatening for it challenged the sexual economy of the relations of representation and reception and temporarily derailed the consumerist appropriation of female desire into the dynamics of public life.

The title of this book, *Babel and Babylon*, has one reference point in the conflation of the universal language myth with the polymorphously perverse phantasmagoria of Griffith's Babylon. No doubt it was also inspired by the popular reputation of Hollywood as Babylon—the Whore, rather than the ideal civilization. Kenneth Anger's trivia classic, *Hollywood Babylon*, opens with a still of the Babylonian set of *Intolerance*. Exposing the seamy sides of the studio era, Anger allocates Valentino a central place in that tradition. [36] The juxtaposition of Babel and Babylon is programmatic to my approach to the question of spectatorship in the sense that it highlights a tension, at least during the silent era, between the cinema's role as a universalizing, ideological idiom and its redemptive possibilities as an inclusive, heterogeneous, and at times unpredictable horizon of experience.

Rebuilding the Tower of Babel:
The Emergence of Spectatorship

. . . .

I

A Cinema in Search of a Spectator:
Film-Viewer Relations before Hollywood

1

From its inception in 1895–96, cinema was defined as the projection of films upon a fixed screen before a paying public. But the film spectator, as distinct from a member of an empirically variable audience, did not come into existence until more than a decade later. As a concept, a structural term, the spectator emerged along with the set of codes and conventions that has been analyzed as the classical Hollywood cinema. Specifically, classical cinema offered its viewer an ideal vantage point from which to witness a scene, unseen by anyone belonging to the fictional world of the film, the diegesis. With the elaboration of a type of narration that seems to anticipate—or strategically frustrate—the viewer's desire with every shot, the spectator became part of the film as product, rather than a particular exhibition or show. As reception was thus increasingly standardized, the moviegoer was effectively invited to assume the position of this ideal spectator created by the film, leaving behind, like Keaton in *Sherlock Jr.*, an awareness of his or her physical self in the theater space, of an everyday existence troubled by social, sexual, and economic discrepancies.

The classical mode of narration and address began to be formulated around 1909, although it can be discerned as early as 1907.[1] During the early and mid-teens, respective innovations in framing, editing, and mise-en-scène were normalized on a wide scale and came to complement each other more systematically. By 1917 the classical system "was complete in its basic narrative and stylistic premises."[2] As film historians have emphasized in recent years, classical cinema did not simply arise from the inventions of a few solitary pioneers, inventions that, as traditional film histories would have it, were fused into an art by the genius of Griffith. The emergence of the classical system was a complex process intertwining developments in modes of production, distribution, and exhibition, including the beginning of a journalistic discourse on the new medium. Nor can the rise of the classical system be described as a linear evolution of techniques, let alone a gradual perfecting of a natural "film language." On the contrary, the transition involved a paradigmatic shift from one kind of cinema to another—a shift, above all, in the conception of the relations between film and spectator.

This view of film history maintains that "primitive" or early cinema has to be considered as much a paradigm in its own right as its classical successor, a mode of representation relatively elaborated in its technical and stylistic options.[3] More than a chronological distinction, the concept of early cinema implies a paradigmatic otherness in relation to later practices—even though certain *elements* of the classical continuity system (such as the point-of-view shot) appeared earlier. Moreover, "primitive" devices lingered well into the mid-teens, and were often used along with classical conventions; they made a most spectacular return, on the threshold to classical cinema, with Griffith's *Intolerance* (1916). As Tom Gunning contends, the kinds of fascination prevalent in early cinema did not disappear from film history but persisted underground—in the tradition of avant-garde filmmaking and as a component of certain genres (such as the musical).[4] They also could be traced in the development of the star cult, both in its general aesthetics of display and in the erotic personae of individual stars such as Valentino.

Early films, although they lacked the mechanisms to create a spectator in the classical sense, did solicit their viewer through a variety of appeals and attractions and through particular strategies of exhibition. In the attempt to reconstruct early film-spectator relations, however, we confront the methodological problem of measuring them against the later norm: either heuristically, by focusing on modes of reception that have disappeared from subsequent film history, or conceptually, by drawing upon methods of formal analysis developed primarily in the study of classical cinema. If recent historiography has taught us to avoid evolutionary models and metaphors, we should also resist a kind of inverse teleology which would idealize early cinema in its paradigmatic otherness.[5] Still, a modicum of teleological bias is almost inevitable: not only can we not escape viewing early cinema from the perspective of the fully developed institution (with its own semblance of teleology), but any reconstruction of historical relations of reception—as textual, psychic, and social configurations—is bound up with the writer's own critical subjectivity and historical contingency. Because I am interested in formations of spectatorship primarily in terms of their function as public horizons, as structural conditions for the articulation and reflection of experience, I will seek to elucidate early film-spectator relations less in an abstract opposition to the classical norm than in their multiplicity and complexity, in their uneven makeup and development.

An Excess of Appeals

The invention of film both challenged and undercut historically available modes of reception. While the receptive behavior rehearsed in traditional branches of entertainment, popular or "legitimate," no doubt fostered the desire and disposition required for the consumption of films, it was not quite adequate to the new medium. As a perceptual technology advertised for the "illusion of lifelike movement," film had been prepared for by realistic directions in the theater as well as screen entertainments like the magic lantern and stereopticon shows.[6] But as cinema, as a particular type of social and aesthetic experience, the reception of films was without institutional precedent. The "proper" relations among viewer, projector, and screen, the peculiar dimensions of cinematic space, were part of a cultural practice that had to be learned.

A celebrated document of this learning process is Edwin S. Porter's short film *Uncle Josh at the Moving Picture Show* (Edison, 1902), a remake of a British import, Robert Paul's *The Countryman's First Sight of the Animated Pictures* (1901).[7] The country rube was a stock character in vaudeville, comic strips, and other popular media, and early films seized upon the encounter of supposedly unsophisticated minds with city life, modern technology, and commercial entertainment as a comic theme and as a way of flaunting the marvels of that new urban world (compare *Rube and Mandy at Coney Island* [Porter/Edison, 1903]). In *Uncle Josh at the Moving Picture Show* the country rube is a naive spectator who mistakes the representations on the screen for reality. Initially standing in a box to the left of a stage and screen, Uncle Josh is shown watching three different films which successively appear on the screen during this brief one-shot film: *Parisian Dancer, The Black Diamond Express,* and *The Country Couple.* Besides being clips from earlier Edison films (the major departure from the British source), the films-within-the-film represent a selection of popular genres: a dance film, a scenic view showing a train (rushing toward the camera at an oblique angle, as in the well-known Lumière film or Biograph's *Empire State Express* [1896]), and a sexually suggestive knockabout comedy.

Uncle Josh's transactions with each film demonstrate particular misconceptions about the nature of the cinematic illusion; they also highlight different components of spectatorial pleasure. Thus, seeing the Parisian dancer, Uncle Josh jumps onto the stage and attempts to dance with her, expressing a need for participation, mimesis, and reciprocity. His expectations are thwarted by the screen, the barrier between absence and presence, which teases the viewer—as does the dancer's skirt—by concealing what it promises to reveal. But, as the second film suggests, this barrier also functions as a shield, protecting the viewer from the impact of the perceptual thrills it affords. Like the legendary early spectators who fled from their seats at the sight of oncoming trains or waves, Uncle Josh withdraws in terror from *The Black Diamond Express*, returning to the safe distance of his initial place. Not accidentally, it is the final film, a larger-than-life depiction of a "country couple," which agitates him beyond control. As he watches the rube's unmistakable advances toward the woman, Uncle Josh most acutely feels the structural exclusion of the cinematic spectator from the space observed—a primal scene par excellence. [8] Now altogether infantilized, he assaults and tears down the screen. Aiming at the paternal rival, he gets embroiled instead with the projectionist *behind* the screen, the hidden author of the illusion. By transgressing the boundaries between theater space and the space of illusion, Uncle Josh ends up destroying the latter.

With his deviant and excessive behavior in relation to the projected images, the spectator-within-the-film becomes himself a spectacle, an object displayed to someone else's view, for someone's viewing pleasure. As a comic allegory, then, the film implies certain lessons for the spectator *of* the film: lessons concerning the spatial arrangement of cinema, especially

Figure 1.1

Figure 1.2

the role of the fixed screen; lessons of sexual economy, in particular regarding the image of the woman; and lessons in film history.

By 1902 the viewers of *Uncle Josh* were no longer likely to repeat the naive
behavior of those legendary viewers who had become part of the novelty of
motion picture screenings, whether in Paris, Berlin, or at Koster and Bial's
Music Hall in New York. The comic appeal of the film thus turns on an

underlying assertion of "progress," with respect to representational techniques and to the development of a mode of reception appropriate to the cinema. In its formal construction, *Uncle Josh* belongs to the tradition of the primitive tableau, a one-shot scene presenting an extended action from a singular (usually frontal) viewpoint and long-shot (stage) distance.[9] Stylistically, however, the film is more complex than any one of the films projected within its mise-en-scène; what is more, by quoting these films, it marks them as earlier and more "primitive." For one thing, *Uncle Josh* displays a sense of narrative progression and closure which, in the projected films, is rudimentary at best. Moreover, by juxtaposing diverse genres and representational styles, the film subsumes them into a larger whole, at once more comprehensive and more advanced than the fragments quoted. Thus, even at this early stage the cinema's sense of its own, albeit brief, history is inscribed with a tendency toward subsumption and integration characteristic of the later institution.

A similar tension is at work in the relations *Uncle Josh* sets up with its viewer, on the thematic as well as structural level. The viewer addressed by *Uncle Josh* is certainly not yet the classical spectator. Instead, he or she was likely to have been seated, like Uncle Josh, in a vaudeville theater—which, prior to 1906, was the predominant exhibition site for films, at least in urban areas. Given this setting, the comic effect is predicated on an alleged cultural disparity between the spectator-in-the-film and the spectator-of-the-film, which suggests a particular social dynamic of identification. While distanced from Uncle Josh's experience of the projected films—because they are quoted, because they give occasion to his misbehavior—the viewer is expected to recognize the films, or types of film, along with the kinds of fascination experienced by him- or herself not too long ago. For even as they are ridiculed as naive and literalizing, Uncle Josh's transactions with each film spell out distinct aspects of spectatorial pleasure—mimetic-narcissistic, kinesthetic, voyeuristic. Like the style of the individual films shown, these pleasures are marked as regressive, partial, and disorienting, inappropriate to the receptive attitude expected from the viewer *of* the film. The narrative clearly articulates a pressure for these pleasures to become integrated, subordinated to a more mature mode of reception; but it can do so only by negative example. What had yet to be developed was the matrix of integration: a mode of narration that would grant the viewer fictional presence and identification on the very condition of his or her perceptual absence, the segregation of film and theater space.

Uncle Josh's confusion seems to result less from the unique and unprecedented appeal of film than from an *excess of appeals*; less from a lack than an

overdetermination of models of receptive behavior. As Alan Williams has
pointed out, the celebration of cinema as a unique invention concealed from
the start the heterogeneity of the medium's origins, its fundamental character of *"bricolage."*[10] Just as it borrowed inventions from other areas of technology (such as the bicycle and the sewing machine), early cinema relied for its
subject matter and representational strategies on a vast repertoire of commercial amusements that flourished around the end of the century. The
Wild West, minstrel and magic shows, the burlesque, the playlet, the dance
number, pornographic displays, acrobatics, and animal acts—all supplied
the cinema with subject matter, performance conventions, and viewer
expectations; so did the magic lantern and the stereopticon shows with their
configuration of projected image, darkened theater space, and sound
accompaniment.[11]

In a rather basic sense, early film-spectator relations were determined—
and overdetermined—by the contexts in which films were first exhibited:
vaudeville and variety shows, dime museums and penny arcades, summer
parks, fair grounds, and traveling shows. These institutions provided not
only the locations and occasions for film exhibition, but also a particular
format of programming, the *variety format*. Whatever the number and status
of films within a given program—initially perhaps up to eight short films
filling a twenty-minute slot—their sequence was arranged in the most random manner possible, emulating the overall structure of the program in its
emphasis on diversity, its shifting moods and styles of representation. As an
entrepreneurial and aesthetic principle, the variety format shaped reception
even after 1905–06, when the cinema found an exhibition outlet of its own,
the nickelodeon. It persisted well into the teens, when the introduction of
the feature film enforced a major change in exhibition practices and
audience behavior.[12]

The rapid succession of seemingly unrelated films and live performances
encouraged a mode of reception incompatible with that mandated by the
traditional arts—a tendency toward "distraction" or "diversion" that notably
Siegfried Kracauer and, following him, Walter Benjamin valorized as a practical critique of bourgeois culture.[13] If the traditional arts required an
extended contemplation of and concentration upon a singular object or
event, the variety format promised a short-term but incessant sensorial
stimulation, a mobilization of the viewer's attention through a discontinuous series of attractions, shocks, and surprises. This type of reception
was perceived very early as a specifically modern form of subjectivity,
reflecting the impact of urbanization and industrialization upon human
perception. A 1911 survey by the Russell Sage Foundation compared the

variety format to "the succession of city occurrences," describing it as equally "stimulating but disintegrating."[14] More than a mere reflection of urban life and industrial technology, the principle of short-term and excessive stimulation had been elaborated by the media of an emerging consumer culture from about the mid-nineteenth century on, whether in advertising and shop-window displays or in a whole range of consumption-oriented spectacles—from the World Fairs and Pan-American Expositions, through the Panoramas and Dioramas, to amusement parks like Coney Island.[15]

The diversion experienced by viewers of early cinema was thus predicated on an excessive supply of visual sensations, at once modernist bricolage and ideological mirage. The variety format not only provided a convenient structure for adapting as many existing traditions as possible, it seems also to have encouraged the production of diversity, in a sense literalizing the root of diversion. This is most strikingly the case in the degree of heterogeneity among genres or types of early film—a heterogeneity which, as we saw from Uncle Josh's predicament, was something of a mixed blessing, inasmuch as it gave rise to diverging and deviant viewer responses.

Diversity and Display

While many of the films, especially before 1903, were modeled on familiar acts and vernacular iconography, the transposition of these into a new medium emphasized distinctions between genres rather than, as in later classical practice, making them variants of a relatively homogeneous mode of representation known as cinema. Fictional genres were derived largely from vaudeville acts, such as comic skits and sight gags, dances, erotic scenes, highlights from popular plays and operas, and melodramatic episodes; they were also reenactments of historical events and tall tales of the Wild West, tableaux from Passion Plays, and trick films in the tradition of the magic shows. Interspersed with these—and proportionally predominant—were films depicting non-acted, ostensibly unstaged scenes that could be categorized as documentaries: news films or actualities (events from the Spanish-American and Boer wars, parades, prizefights, sensational murders, executions, or disasters); views of everyday life, work, and leisure in the Lumière style; and a large number of travelogues and scenics (exotic locales, panoramas of buildings, landscapes, and exhibitions), the genre most closely affiliated with the tradition of the stereopticon.[16]

Imposing the later distinction between documentary and fictional genres upon primitive diversity, however, is problematic in several respects. Many actualities involved reconstructions—such as the notorious examples of

Spanish-American War films shot on a New York rooftop or bathtub recreations of naval battles—yet not necessarily with the intent to deceive; as a subgenre, dramatic reenactments of current events were considered legitimate. Though occasional complaints were heard early on, the standard of authenticity by which all such films would be rejected as "fake pictures" evolved with the classical paradigm and became one of the war cries in the campaign against primitive modes. [17] While the boundaries between documentary reality and mise-en-scène may have been relative, they seem to have mattered less than the kind of fascination which connects, for instance, the "realistic imitation" of President McKinley's assassin in the electric chair in *The Execution of Czolgosz* (Porter/Edison, 1901) with historical reenactments such as *The Execution of Mary Queen of Scots* (Edison, 1895)—or the substitution trick in *Execution by Hanging* (Biograph, 1905) with the authentic footage of *Electrocuting an Elephant* (Edison, 1903). The sensationalist appeal of such films cuts across documentary and fictional modes of representation and overtly caters to sadistic impulses; later films could do this only in the guise of narrative motivation and moral truth. A distinctly different sensibility speaks from catalog descriptions like that of *Beheading the Chinese Prisoner* (Sigmund Lubin, 1900)—"the executioner displays the head to the spectators to serve as a warning for evil doers[;] [v]ery exciting"—or from the copy advertising a comedy like Porter's *Appointment by Telephone* (Edison, 1902), which has an angry wife wreck the interior of a restaurant and "horsewhip" her husband and the young lady she finds in his company: "A very fine photograph, full of action from finish to start, and a subject that will appeal to everyone."[18]

If sadism played an important part in early cinema's appeal, so did other partial pleasures that elude the fiction-documentary label. Robert Allen cites the popularity of the "local actuality" films shot in a particular city one day and shown in a local theater the next. [19] Public interest was captured by the work of the camera team and by the reproduction of scenes from people's everyday lives, the possibility of seeing oneself or someone familiar on the screen. This interest, which Allen terms "narcissistic," could also be linked to Benjamin's political assertion that "any man today can lay claim to being filmed."[20] At any rate, the viewer's investment in the screen as mirror differs from later, narratively mediated forms of identification—with characters, star images, and the look of the narrating camera—which effectively displaced interest in local and personal representation from the institution of cinema, relegating it to the private province of "home" movies.

Another aspect of primitive fascination can be gleaned from a variant of the travelogue: kinesthetic films, which convey the sensation of traveling by means of a mobile camera, or, rather, a camera carried on a car, a boat, or even an aerial balloon, though more often a vehicle moving along railway tracks. Add the darkness of a tunnel (as in *Interior N.Y. Subway, 14th Street to 42nd Street* [G. W. Bitzer/Biograph, 1905]), and the representational object is abstracted by the thrill of motion and varying speeds, the changing proportions of the passing space, the dizzying play of light and shadow. The most unsettling effect, however, may have been the viewer's inescapable consignment to the place of the invisible camera, experienced in terms of an overpowering orality—an oral fascination that seems the flipside of Uncle Josh's fear of the oncoming train. A review of a 1897 Biograph film taken by a camera riding through the Haverstraw Tunnel describes this effect in diction overwhelmed with its own helplessness:

> The spectator was not an outsider watching from safety the rush of the cars. He was a passenger on a phantom train ride that whirled him through space at nearly a mile a minute. . . . There was nothing to indicate motion save that shining vista of tracks that was eaten up irresistibly, rapidly and the disappearing panoramas of banks and fences. The train was invisible and yet the landscape remorselessly [sic] and far away the bright day became a spot of darkness. That was the mouth of the tunnel and toward it the spectator was hurled as if a fate was behind him. The spot of blackness closed around him and the spectator being flung through that cavern with the demoniac energy behind him. The shadows, the rush of invisible force and the uncertainty of the issues made one instinctively hold his breath as when on the edge of a crisis that might become a catastrophe. [21]

The genre reached its peak with Hale's Tours, a form of exhibition that premiered at the Saint Louis Exposition in 1904 and became popular in several American cities over the next two years. Designed like a railroad car, complete with conductor and simulated sways and jolts, clickety-clack and brake sounds, this theater projected scenic views taken from a moving train. While the realistic environment motivates the kinesthetic experience (and thus to some extent contains its destabilizing effect), it still betrays a distinctly primitive attitude toward the cinematic illusion, one that includes the spectator in the space and process of make-believe. [22]

Local actualities and "phantom rides" convey a fascination not only with particular moving images but also with the apparatus that produces them, reminding us that "in the earliest years . . . the cinema itself was an attraction"—in addition to being a medium for a traditional repertoire of attractions. [23] Especially during the initial novelty period (1895–1898), audiences went to exhibitions as much to marvel at the machine—the Biograph, the Vitascope—as to view the films. In subsequent years display of the apparatus continued in a less explicit, though hardly more discreet, manner. In many films the view or plot provides an occasion for demonstrating specifically cinematic techniques and possibilities: the camera's ability to traverse and mobilize space (as in the panoramas and phantom rides); its suspension of spatio-temporal laws (fast, slow, and reverse motion, multiple exposure, split screen) and its geographic ubiquity (film as a substitute for mass tourism); its manipulation of perception through magical transformations (stop-motion photography and substitution splices) and its play with scale and proportions (miniatures and matte shots); but also its capacity to witness and record, whether transient phenomena of nature, public events, incriminating situations (like illicit love), or subjects of surveillance and documentation.

A number of early films advertise the process of vision itself, the cinema's capability of bringing objects into view, whether mediated by the scopic agency of a character or put forth directly to the spectator. A British film, *Grandma's Reading Glass* (G. A. Smith, 1900), shows a boy looking at various objects—including his grandmother's eye—through a magnifying glass. These long shots alternate with close views of the respective objects in a circular mask, supposedly representing the boy's point of view; the cut has no function other than to provide the "pleasure point of the film."[24] The type of visual pleasure catered to by such magnified inserts no doubt has fetishistic implications, whatever the narrative pretext. These are most overt in films displaying partial views of the female body, as in Smith's film of the same year, *As Seen through a Telescope*, or Edwin S. Porter's *The Gay Shoe Clerk* (Edison, 1903), both of which focus on the female ankle. In the latter, the closer view shows the object in striped hose as the clerk ties the young woman's shoe and she slowly raises her skirt. This cut-in may be compositionally motivated (in that it condones the clerk's attempt to kiss her in the following shot),[25] yet it is clearly staged for the benefit of the viewer—all the more so since the angle of vision remains the same as before: frontal, rather than from the point of view of the amorous clerk.

Whether showing off the possibilities of the new medium or the object envisioned, the basic conception of early filmmaking is one of display, of demonstration, of showmanship. It is, to use Gunning's term, a "cinema of attractions," closer to the tradition of fairground and variety shows than to the classical priority of articulating a story.[26] This does not mean that early films did not also engage in storytelling; on the contrary, narrative gained considerable ground, especially after 1901. But the specificity of early cinema, its paradigmatic difference, has more to do with the "thrill of display," an exhibitionist attitude that fuels both narrative and non-narrative, both fictional and documentary forms. Accordingly, the "cinema of attractions" implies a fundamentally different type of address than is found in later films. This address is predicated on diversity, on distracting the viewer with a variety of competing spectacles (rather than absorbing him or her into a coherent narrative by way of a unified spectatorial vantage point). But the display of diversity also means that the viewer is solicited in a more direct manner—as a member of an anticipated social audience and a public, rather than an invisible, private consumer.

Another Kind of Voyeurism

The logic of display that inspires a diversity of genres also characterizes the conception of the shot on the level of framing and editing. The type of shot considered most characteristic of the "primitive" style is the theatrical tableau, with its long-shot distance, frontal perspective, and often static and relatively noncentered composition. As in other early shot types, signification relies upon the single frame in its unity of viewpoint, whatever manipulations and transformations it may contain (or enable, as in trick films where the uninterrupted framing in fact constitutes the condition of the magical trompe l'oeil). [27] The shot is perceived as a unit of relative autonomy, as opposed to the classical conception of the shot as a part blending into a continuous narrative space. When a series of tableaux are joined in a narrative, the action depicted in the scene is usually completed before the cut; spatial and temporal connections between successive shots remain confused or unspecified. But even the shot itself is not always immediately readable. In the tableau tradition the image tends to be overloaded with visual meaning, making the viewer hover between multiple points of narrative interest (an extreme case is the department store shot in Porter's *The Kleptomaniac* [Edison, 1905] in which the lady thief goes about her business just as unnoticeable to us as to the customers within the diegesis). [28] All these traits—unity of viewpoint, unspecified spatio-temporal continuity, and noncentered composition—are not only inspired by an aesthetics of display but also require a mode of exhibition in which the sights on screen are presented as part of a larger show.

The frontality and uniformity of viewpoint is clearly the mark of a *presentational*—as opposed to representational—conception of space and address. If classical cinema was to "introduce [the spectator] into the space of the film," as Jean Mitry says regarding Méliès, in early cinema "the space . . . comes forward to present itself to the spectator within a uniformity of theatrical framing."[29] Yet, as Gunning and Musser have argued, this difference in spatial organization should not be reduced to theatricality: the magic-lantern tradition, the comic strip, the political cartoon, the proliferation of picture postcards—all are models of presentation and framing that contributed to early cinema's distinctive style.

The theatrical tableau was not the only type of shot, nor did all films keep "the spectator looking across a void into an action in a separate space."[30] Thus, the appeal of the phantom rides depended upon a specifically cinematic form of reception—the spectator's identification with the viewpoint of the camera, its mobility, and potential ubiquity.[31] The films of the "facial expression" genre may have recruited their personnel from the popular stage, but the medium-shot framing asserts a specificity not available to the theatergoer. *The Kiss* (Edison, 1896), one of the most popular early films, reenacts a highlight from a contemporary Broadway hit, *The Widow Jones*, performed by its stars, May Irwin and John C. Rice. The point of such a film is precisely the "impossible" placement of the viewer: the thrill of witnessing an intimate act from a close proximity which in "real life" would preclude that very intimacy, and which on stage would disrupt the illusion of reality. The privilege of seeing the familiar stars in peep-show vicinity blends into the familial scenario of the primal scene, as in *Uncle Josh*, though that scenario still lacks the dimension of emotional interiority. As in the phantom rides, a classical principle—the welding of the spectator's vantage point with that of the invisible camera—appears quite early, though the device is not yet endowed with narrative function, not yet assimilated in terms of causal motivation and character psychology.

The Kiss, like many early films, displays a titillating sight; at the same time it explores the mechanisms of cinematic voyeurism, in particular as distinct from theatrical forms of voyeurism. Christian Metz argues that the distinction of cinematic voyeurism is its affinity with the regime of the keyhole, the unauthorized, isolated and unilateral scopophilia of the primal scene. For him this affinity is intrinsic to the cinematic apparatus because of the opposition of absence and presence that constitutes cinematic representation— the absolute gap between filmic production and reception—and the attendant segregation between the space of the film and the space of the audience: "the filmic spectacle, the object seen, is more radically ignorant of its spectator, since he is not there, than the theatrical spectacle can ever be." Metz associates the latter with a different kind of voyeurism (also operating in domestic scenarios), one that thrives on a reciprocity of seeing and being seen, an "active complicity" between exhibitionist and voyeur. In its ceremonial self-consciousness, theatrical voyeurism retains a public, "civic" dimension; it involves the viewer as a member of a "true" audience, a "temporary collectivity." By contrast, "those attending a cinematic projection . . . are an accumulation of individuals who, despite appearances, more closely resemble the fragmented group of readers of a novel."[32]

If we take Metz's argument to refer to a distinction between competing cultural institutions and practices rather than an ontological difference between the cinematic apparatus and that of the theater, early cinema seems closer to the theatrical kind of voyeurism than to the scopic regime of classical cinema. With their emphasis on display, early films are self-consciously exhibitionist, whereas classical cinema disavows its exhibitionist quality in order to maintain the spell of the invisible gaze.[33] For one thing, the segregation of film and spectator space essential to the classical mode was not yet codified or, rather, had not yet achieved priority as an aesthetic principle. Thus, despite the technologically based gap of absence and presence (which characterized other visual illusions as well), there was still a perceptual continuity between the space on the screen and the social space of the theater, including projection and other elements of exhibition, such as music and sound effects. As long as the cinema depended for an exhibition outlet on established forms of theatrical entertainments, the screening of films in the context of a mixed program would not necessarily have diminished the audience's awareness of itself as a public, as a collective body present to the spectacles being exhibited. (This public dimension is obviously missing in what has been considered the prototype of cinematic voyeurism in Metz's sense, the kinetoscope with its isolated viewing conditions and peep-show associations.)

If early film-viewer relations had more in common with theatrical voyeurism, they did so in a necessarily eclectic, composite form. For the diverging traditions of the popular and the legitimate stage in turn involved, in the United States at least, not only a social and cultural hierarchy but also different, conflicting conventions of scenography, performance, and address, particularly with regard to standards of "realism."[34] Thus, within the institution of theater at large, defined vis-à-vis the cinema by the physical copresence of audience and performance, the scopic drive already was engaged with considerable variations, depending upon whether the spectator was intentionally absent or present to the actors, whether the aesthetic goal was diversion, spectacular effect, melodramatic catharsis, or the impression of reality. Although the cinema developed in the context of popular theatrical entertainments, which favored predominantly direct modes of address, at an early stage it also absorbed highbrow traditions of representation, among them the principle of the fourth wall.

The eclectic and ambivalent make-up of early cinema's scopic relations is most evident in one recurring practice: an actor's sudden and direct look at the camera. Whether as a comic aside or an erotic wink, such a look ruptures the illusion of a self-enclosed fictional world, by prevailing standards of theatrical realism as well as those to be developed with classical cinema. At the same time, however, the direct look at the camera already plays with the difference between two aesthetic registers: between conflicting conceptions of cinematic space, and between distinct types of voyeurism. Some films seem to be testing the boundary between the illusionist space on screen and the spectator's space in the theater rather aggressively, in the manner of the much-discussed medium close-up of the outlaw pointing his gun at the viewer at the beginning—or end—of *The Great Train Robbery* (Porter/Edison, 1903). In *The Burlesque Suicide*, an Edison film of the previous year, this kind of transgression is the whole point: within a single medium shot we see a man take a drink, look at his pistol, and raise it to his temple; then he stops, and points his finger toward the camera, laughing at the audience for having taken him seriously.[35]

The direct look at the camera became a virtual taboo in the early teens because, in the words of Frank Woods, one of the most eloquent advocates of the classical mode, "facial remarks directed at the camera destroy the illusion of reality."[36] Woods's insight is concerned less with an equivalent between representation and referent than with the spectator's willing absorption into the self-contained fictional world on screen, the diegesis. In the view of practitioners and theorists of the classical mode, such absorption crucially depends upon the spectator's ability to witness the narrative from an ideal vantage point—that of the narrating camera—unseen by any of the characters within diegetic space. The direct look at the camera by an actor or character undermines this mechanism, because it not only foregrounds the fact of filmic enunciation but jeopardizes the segregation of film and theater space and thus the spectator's position as invisible intruder.

However, Marc Vernet reminds us, the disruptive power traditionally attributed to the look at the camera is itself based on a fiction, that of the temporary alignment of actually separate and incompatible spaces: "the space of filming, the diegetic universe, and the space of the theater." While the look at the camera may momentarily disturb the classical voyeur, it also epitomizes the gap upon which the cinematic institution thrives; it stages a "failed encounter," beckoning the spectator into a nostalgic mise-en-abyme. The nostalgia Vernet observes in conjunction with particular instances of the look at the camera extends to the cinema's past symbiosis with popular entertainments, especially in genres like the musical and comedy in which the direct address invokes conventions of the music hall and burlesque.

What is invoked along with these conventions is the desire for a mythical popular audience, the ideal public: "the addressee implied by the 'look at the camera,' far from being the real individual spectator, is actually a collective addressee (the public) but also an imaginary one (the other public)."[37]

From the perspective of the established institution, with its mass audience of isolated, alienated individuals, the appeal to such an ideal public more often than not serves ideological purposes.[38] At this early stage in film history, however, the look at the camera suggests other possibilities. On one level, it no doubt asserts a link with performance conventions familiar from the popular stage; yet on another level, especially when the look occurs suddenly and unexpectedly, it seems to project a spectator not yet in place, and perhaps never in place in the classical sense—the possibility of combining the cinema's technological potential for generality with the structural conditions of a public sphere, of an intersubjective horizon for the articulation of experience.

The alternative implications of the recurring look at the camera, as of early cinema's affinity with theatrical voyeurism in general, are especially relevant to questions of gender and sexuality. As feminist film theorists from Laura Mulvey to Mary Ann Doane have elaborated, the psychic mechanisms of voyeurism and fetishism inscribed in the classical apparatus reproduce the patriarchal hierarchy that makes the woman the object and the man the agent of the look. Predicating cinematic pleasure on these mechanisms involves a *structural* "masculinization" of the spectator position, regardless of the viewer's actual gender.[39] To be sure, early cinema was no less patriarchal than its classical successor, considering that many films were inspired by the male-oriented repertoires of the peep show, the burlesque, or the concert saloon. But they still lacked the formal strategies to predetermine reception in the classical sense, the power of an indirect mode of address predicated on the regime of the keyhole and fetishistic distance.

It is no coincidence that the direct glance at the camera most often occurs in erotic films. The object of fascination is usually a woman, with an emphasis on her body (preferably ankles and legs) in various stages and suggestions of unveiling and concealing. The performer frequently participates in staging herself as spectacle through physical skills, movement, and action, as in the Serpentine and Butterfly dances or in the numerous routines of (mostly partial) disrobing. Often, as in *From Showgirl to Burlesque Queen* (Biograph, 1903) or *The Wine Opener* (Biograph, 1905), the woman's flirtatious look at the camera culminates—and thus foregrounds—the act of exhibition. Such rituals recapture metaphorically some of the self-reflexivity that Metz attributes to theatrical voyeurism: "If there is an element of triumph in this kind of representation, it is because what it exhibits is not exactly the exhibited object but, via the object, the exhibition itself."[40]

Stressing the act of exhibition in conjunction with the female body recalls the psychoanalytic concept of the "masquerade," as it has been elaborated in feminist film theory.[41] By putting the representation in quotation marks, as it were, the female performer at once enacts traditional norms of femininity (including their pornographic violation) and displays them as cultural conventions. So even when the woman is reduced to an object of prurient anticipation, the performer's glance at the camera may add a twist to an otherwise sad joke. In *What Happened on Twenty-Third Street, New York City* (Porter/Edison, 1901), for instance, a young woman's skirt is blown up as she walks across a subway grate. Set in a real location, the film shows people in the street occasionally casting a curious glance in the direction of the camera, as does the performer when she completes her turn. While her closing aside could be read as a come-on, it also asserts a modicum of distance between the performer and her objectified image—a distance that would have been of greater significance for women in the audience than for the textually inscribed spectator of male, homosocial entertainments.[42]

The foregrounding of exhibition in early erotic films conveys a sense of role-playing, a degree of interchangeability of roles within the transgressive scenario. The lure—as well as the limit—of such role-playing is thematic in a 1903 Edison film, *What Happened in the Tunnel.* A male passenger tries to steal a kiss from a young woman as the train enters the tunnel and the screen goes black; when the train emerges, he discovers with horror that he had kissed the woman's black maid. This racist and sexist joke is complicated by the fact that the man becomes the object of ridicule as the two women burst out laughing. While the figure of the prankster falling prey to his own prank is quite common in the genre of mischief comedy, the maid's direct glance at the camera suggests not only that she was not merely a prop but that she, rather than her mistress, might have authorized the substitution.[43]

A similar emphasis on role-playing and ambivalence (in Freud's technical sense referring to the coexistence and relative reversibility of opposite drives)[44] can be seen in films that feature acts of voyeurism, staging the look through a character's point of view. Films like *As Seen through a Telescope* (G. A. Smith, 1900), *Ce que l'on voit de mon sixième, Peeping Tom* (both Pathé, 1901), or *Inquisitive Boots* (Hepworth, 1905) show a nosy character peeping through some kind of device—telescope, keyhole—then cut to a view of what the character supposedly sees, usually indicating the mediated vision by means of a—circular or keyhole shape—matte; often, the alternation concludes with the voyeur being caught and punished. In an illuminating essay on what he calls the "Peeping Tom" series, Gunning discusses the difference of such early versions of the point-of-view shot from its later, classical deployment: "Rather than providing narratively significant information, or indications of character knowledge or psychology, these glimpses deliver bits of scopic pleasure, spectacle rather than narrative." The scopic pleasure thus delivered, Gunning underlines, may be mediated by the character's look but is still acknowledged and shared with the spectator. Significantly, the Peeping Toms often "perform a mocking pantomime of what they see" and communicate their delight to the viewer by directly addressing the camera.[45] Just as the voyeur can play exhibitionist to an implied audience, his or her ultimate denouement suggests a similar role reversal for the object spied upon. This display of ambivalence not only asserts the primacy of the perverse scenario as an aesthetic principle over narrative causality and closure, it also has important implications for the gendered economy of vision and concomitant arrangements of public and private.

Insofar as the "Peeping Tom" films reproduce the peep-show perspective of the kinetoscope or mutoscope parlors, with their overwhelmingly male clientele and lure of cheap pornography, they no doubt assume a patriarchal economy of vision. At the same time they register the breakdown of the hierarchic segregation of male and female spheres that crucially defined nineteenth-century demarcations of public and private. Whether in the tradition of popular cross-dressing or in response to an emerging female audience, the Peeping Tom films occasionally acknowledge the threat—and thrill—of sexual disorientation and the confusion of gender roles. In *A Search for Evidence* (Biograph, 1903), for instance, the role of voyeur is assigned to a woman who, accompanied by a male detective, tracks down her adulterous husband by peering into a succession of hotel rooms.[46] A less respectable and less motivated version of female scopophilia occurs in *The Indiscreet Bathroom Maid (La fille de bain indiscrète, Pathé, 1902).* The voyeuristic desire for a glimpse of the female body may be frustrated on the other side of the threshold as well. The most bizarre example is a British film, *Inquisitive Boots,* in which a nosy bootblack introduces us to a series of keyhole views showing, successively, a man cross-dressing in front of a mirror; a man with six toes trying to remove the surplus member with a handsaw; a woman rocking a dog in a cradle; and a couple squirting water with a syringe at the optical intruder.

Like Uncle Josh, these Peeping Toms must be read as figurations of early film-viewer relations. Like the former, they articulate the precarious nature of cinematic space, its peculiar interpenetration of public and private realms. For the psychosexual ambivalence displayed within the film invites the spectator to play a part in the scenario, to engage in a collective ritual of seeing and being seen in the tradition of the theatrical public sphere. While classical cinema eclipses this public dimension in favor of the spectator's privileged, invisible access to the most private of dramas, the Peeping Tom series "forces private dramas into the public space of corridors, and the invoked space of the place of exhibition itself."[47] Though perhaps intended as nothing more than a practical joke, the scopophilic transgression of boundaries enacts a practical critique of historical demarcations of public and private—the possibility of bringing hitherto unrepresented discourses of experience into the view of a radically inclusive, heterosocial public sphere.

However, only the more perverse examples of the Peeping Tom series celebrate a reciprocity of scopic pleasure with the spectator; others are inspired by the narrative purpose of bringing a private transgression into the light of moral censure. In *A Search for Evidence* the wife's voyeuristic excursion culminates in ascertaining her husband's guilt, rather than in a sadistic reversal of her own transgression. In a similar vein, *The Story the Biograph Told* (Biograph, 1904) stages the infringement on someone else's privacy as a legitimate function of the cinematic apparatus, complete with a public theater situation. A mischievous office boy secretly films the proprietor kissing his secretary; the film is then projected in a vaudeville show attended by the proprietor and his wife. The film within the film (which repeats the illicit action from the boy's camera angle) combines the possibility of seeing oneself (or one's philandering husband) on the screen with the spectacle of public exposure and embarrassment. Although both strands of the plot— the practical joke administered by a mischievous boy and the motif of marital infidelity exposed—are familiar staples of early cinema, *The Story the Biograph Told* already points beyond the sheer accumulation of sadistic and voyeuristic pleasures to a later conception of spectatorship as medium of moral truth and social uplift.

The difference between the early use of point of view and its later, classical function is not merely narrative motivation but a deliberate yoking together of vision and truth, a moral inscription of the gaze that has come to be associated with the name of D. W. Griffith.[48] During the transitional period this tendency is allegorized in characters who see their own fate dramatized as spectators, such as the penitent father in *A Drunkard's Reformation* (Griffith/Biograph, 1909) or the seduced country boy recognizing his own destruction in *The Vampire* (Kalem, 1913); in each case, a family is restored as a result of the vision. Although both of these films stage a personal conversion experience in response to a theatrical performance, they undoubtedly imply an analogy with the institution of cinema, considering the concurrent battle against the threat of censorship. The message of uplift becomes explicit, albeit in the form of a parody, in *Tillie's Punctured Romance* (Sennett/Keystone, 1914), when Chaplin and his moll (Mabel Normand) visit a movie theater that looks like a cross between a Salvation Army mission and a court of law. Seeing a felonious couple get caught on the screen, Mabel and Charlie's behavior hyperbolizes a conception of spectatorship radically different from the anarchic and perverse appeals their own comedy still thrived upon.

Exhibition as Public Performance

The emphasis on exhibition distinguishes early cinema's voyeuristic ceremonies from the classical model in more ways than a general aesthetics of display and flagrant exhibitionism. The lack of closure that radical formalists like Noël Burch have exalted as an aspect of primitive cinema's paradigmatic otherness is predicated upon a particular practice of exhibition: the mediation of the image on the screen by exhibitors or by personnel present in the theater—lecturers, musicians, or sound-effect specialists. As Charles Musser has shown, these mediating activities were not perceived as compensatory, in the sense of clarifying or lending support to a fledgling language of film, but explicitly continued long-standing practices of screen entertainment. For two centuries magic lantern shows had presented fictional narratives, allegorical themes as well as views of documentary interest. With the increased availability of photographic slides in the second half of the nineteenth century, the travelogue became a more prominent and elaborate genre, in many ways anticipating a mode of presentation for films. Lanternists often tried to articulate spatial continuity by arranging successive views in the manner of later editing figures (cut-ins, exterior/interior, point-of-view, and shot/reverse shots), indicating the type of relationship in the course of the lecture. [49]

Considering this tradition, it no longer seems unusual that early multishot films were often distributed in separate reels so that the exhibitor could assemble them in an order of his own choice. The most famous instance of this is the close shot of the outlaw in *The Great Train Robbery* which was shown either at the beginning or at the end of the film, depending on the exhibition context. Whatever legal and marketing strategies may have prolonged that policy of partial sales (for Edison through 1906), it assumed an exhibitor who was more of a lanternist than a projectionist, with a similar conception

of editorial control over narrative and spatial sequencing and in the juxtaposition and mixing of genres.[50] As hyperbolized in *Uncle Josh*, the early
exhibitor still had the function, as well as the status, of a master of
spectacle—a Wizard of Oz on the verge of being unmasked by Toto.

As long as the exhibitor retained this function, cinematic techniques like
editing belonged to the context of a particular presentation rather than to
the film as a finished product and mass-cultural commodity. Early exhibition
still claimed the singularity of a *live performance*, even though the films themselves were circulated on a national and international scale. That sense of
performance also derived from a whole range of other activities that outlived
the exhibitor's editorial control and persisted well into the nickelodeon
period. These can be divided into two types: activities relating to the
projected films more or less simultaneously, such as lectures, sound effects,
and music; and activities alternating with the projection of films in keeping
with the variety format, such as illustrated songs, vaudeville turns, and
occasionally, as late as 1909, magic lantern and stereopticon shows.
Although nonfilmic attractions varied in currency, status, and combination,
at least some of them could be expected as a rule, especially musical
accompaniment.[51]

As a crucial element of cinematic experience, the live portions of the
show shaped a mode of reception substantially different from that which was
to become the norm, at the latest with the advent of synchronized sound
and a standardized speed of projection. Even at a minimum, musical accompaniment gave the audience a sense of collective presence that Norman King
maintains persisted throughout the silent era: "Sound functioned *differently*
during the silent era. . . . Essentially it produced effects in the cinema that
recorded sound could not, a sense of immediacy and participation. Live
sound actualised the image and, merging with it, emphasised the present-
ness of the performance and the audience."[52] The presence of live accompaniment relating to the projected image maintained a sense of continuity
between the space/time of the theater and the illusionist world on the
screen—as opposed to the classical subordination of the former under the
absolute rule of the latter. But the priority of "the feeling of being seated in a
theatre in front of a screen" over "the feeling of being carried away by an
imaginary time-flow" is not necessarily subversive in itself (as Burch
implies).[53] More than simply a formal opposition to the classical concept of
spectatorship, exhibitions varying from time to time and place to place
allowed for locally and culturally specific acts of reception, opening up a
margin of participation and unpredictability. In this margin the cinema
could assume the function of an alternative public sphere for particular

social groups, like immigrants and women, by providing an intersubjective horizon through—and against—which they could negotiate the specific displacements and discrepancies of their experience.

Such alternative formations of spectatorship were, for obvious reasons, not as widely documented as the tendencies that prevailed, but they did leave their traces by way of negation. A different notion of cinema can be inferred, for instance, from exhibition practices that were denounced or became the object of conflicts between individual exhibitors and producers, or from efforts to minimize nonfilmic acts and activities or subordinate them to the film (music and sound effects) or transform them to become part of the product (intertitles, editing, camera narration)—in short, from the elimination of conditions around which local, ethnic, class, and gender-related experience might crystallize. This process of negation involved representational strategies aimed at suppressing awareness of the theater space and absorbing the spectator into the illusionist space on screen: closer framing, centered composition, and directional lighting; continuity editing which created a coherent diegetic space unfolding itself to an ubiquitous invisible observer; and the gradual increase of film length, culminating in the introduction of the feature film. The most important vehicle of absorption, however, was "the story," the narrative tradition that cinema adopted with such force, a commentator observed in 1909, that "the people forgot the film, forgot the screen, and forgot themselves."[54]

Narrative, Intertextuality, Genre Crossing

The rise of the story film, which began after 1901, was an important factor in stabilizing the industry—not least because the production of narratives could be planned in a way that wars and earthquakes could not. By the end of 1904 fictional narratives had displaced actualities and scenics as the dominant product of American companies, not only in the share of copyrighted titles (53 vs. 42 percent) but, more important, by the higher number of prints of individual titles sold.[55] The trick film had all but disappeared by that time (it accounted for the remaining 5 percent), its techniques being adapted by other genres. Between 1907 and 1908 the number of narrative titles increased from 67 to 96 percent, while documentaries dropped to only 4 percent of copyright entries. At the same time comedies, which had dominated the fiction film prior to 1907 began to fall behind serious drama, or melodrama; in 1908 they accounted for less than a third of narrative titles.

Historians have discussed the move to narrative in terms of a number of interrelated developments, especially the nickelodeon boom and cinema's eventual emancipation from vaudeville, but also the establishment of film exchanges and the introduction of industrial methods in film production.[56] I will limit myself to the following questions: What distinguishes primitive forms of narrative from the model developed after 1907? What kind of relations do early narratives set up with their viewer? What are the implications of the reduction of nonfictional genres and the decline of trick films and comedies? What happened to the unabashed display of visibility and other aspects of primitive fascination?

One of the basic problems narrative films confronted between 1902 and 1907 was the tension "between scenes perceived as self-contained wholes on the one hand and their potential as part of a more complex sequence on the other."[57] Films tended to be nonlinear in two opposite directions: either the narration was too elliptical, giving the viewer too little information to understand the story; or it might demonstrate spatial contiguity between shots at the cost of temporal overlap, by repeating the same action from two different views (usually interior and exterior).[58] In both cases narrative clarity was not an issue if the films were presented by an exhibitor or lecturer who would specify spatio-temporal connections, point out details, and provide dialogue and motivation for the characters' actions.

Even without such guidance, many of the most popular films succeeded because they drew upon well-known plays, novels (or, more often, their theatrical adaptations), folk- and fairy-tales, comic strips, political cartoons, and popular songs.[59] A famous instance of such primitive intertextuality is Porter's *Uncle Tom's Cabin* (Edison, 1903), based upon George Aiken's stage version of Harriet Beecher Stowe's novel, which at the time was probably the most frequently performed play in the history of American theater. The film consists of fourteen tableaux, an episodic series of highlights modeled on the condensed plays that helped gentrify the vaudeville stage. These tableaux do not provide a plot summary but assume the viewer's familiarity with play or novel; they function as "illustrations for a narrative which is elsewhere."[60] Each is introduced by a title which gives away the narrative point in advance (for example, shot 1: "Eliza Pleads with Tom to Run Away"). Some captions refer to actions that do not occur until well into the respective scene.

The reception implied by such procedures differs from the kinds of expectations raised by illusionist types of narrative (whether novelistic, dramatic, or cinematic), such as the pleasures of enigma and suspense contingent upon the reader/viewer's temporary belief that the story is taking place for the first time. Unlike later Hollywood adaptations, which by and large participate in an illusionist disavowal of intertextuality, *Uncle Tom's*

Cabin not only acknowledges the preexistent text throughout the film—it would remain incomplete and incomprehensible without it—but further solicits the viewer on the basis of his or her foreknowledge. Reception becomes a ritual of recognition or, as the case may be, initiation into an audience already familiar with the story. The specifically cinematic appeal of the film, moreover, involves types of visual pleasure germane to such non-narrative genres as actualities, scenics, and trick films. Thus, the tableau staging "The Race between the Lee and the Natchez" uses miniature boats in the style of the reenacted naval battles of the Spanish-American War (compare Porter's own news reproduction, *The Sampson-Schley Controversy*, 1901).

A distinct strain of non-narrative fascination can also be found in chase comedies like Wallace McCutcheon's *Personal* (Biograph, June 1904), plagiarized by Porter as *How a French Nobleman Got a Wife Through the New York Herald "Personal" Columns* (Edison, August 1904) and by producer Sigmund Lubin as *Meet Me at the Fountain* (November 1904).[61] Probably the most successful narrative genre from late 1903 through 1906, the chase film took the extended incident of the vaudeville stage into the streets and open spaces, thus advancing an elaboration of continuous action in cinematic terms: "With the chase film, moving pictures really began to move."[62] Beyond their kinetic appeal, most chases played for comic effect, with the frequent admixture of erotic sights. In all three versions of *Personal* a French dandy in search of an American wife finds himself pursued by a horde of women all responding to his ad. After a few shots motivating the action, the chase proceeds in typical fashion. Pursued and pursuers both enter the frame in a distance and run diagonally or in curved lines toward and past the camera; the last person's exit prompts a cut (or dissolve, as in the Lubin version) carrying the action over to the next shot until the eventual capture. Although the editing remains subordinate to the integrity of the scene (there is no crosscutting between the two groups as, for instance, in Griffith's rescue races after 1908), the length of individual shots provides ample opportunity to show leg. Indeed, the narrative seems little more than a pretext for a relentless display of awkward positions, as the women pursue their prey across fences, hedges, ditches, down the hill, and through the water. It comes as no surprise that, in the Lubin version, the day is carried by an older woman played by a female impersonator, a remnant of vaudeville's plebeian heritage, who winks at the camera in the final shot, asserting the priority of perverse mischief over narrative clarity and diegetic absorption.[63]

The tension between the call of narrative and a primitive diversity of appeals—a diversity whose common denominator was the impulse toward

151-051, 142, 120, 141, 77

151-2, 35, 233, 302, 102, 62, 101

Hansen

display—is also evident in films combining different genres, mixing stylistic trends as well as strategies of address. Porter's *The Execution of Czolgosz* (Edison, November 1901) opens with two panorama shots of Auburn State Prison, thus providing an authentic setting for the dramatic reenactment of the electrocution (which could be purchased with or without the panoramas). The execution of the President's assassin was part of a whole string of news events surrounding the Pan-American Exposition in Buffalo (at which McKinley was shot). Edison capitalized on all of them, both through a monumental display of light bulbs (including test bulbs on the reproduction of the electric chair) and by a booming output of scenics, actualities, and even a historical topical (*Martyred Presidents*). The same aesthetics of display in the end inspires the moving shot that unfolds the marvels of electricity in Porter's *Pan-American Exposition at Night* (October 1901)—a pan turning day into night by means of time-lapse photography—and the one used to authenticate another kind of spectacle in *The Execution of Czolgosz*.[64]

The hybrid appeal of longer films is even more pronounced when the narrative no longer refers to a singular incident but accommodates both documentary and comic-dramatic styles within an overall fictional framework. Porter's well-known 1903 films, *Life of an American Fireman* and *The Great Train Robbery*, exemplify this tendency, as does Biograph's *The Hold-Up of the Rocky Mountain Express* (photographed by Bitzer in 1906). The latter begins like a travel film of the kinesthetic variety, then switches to interior shots of the passenger car showing some mildly bawdy comedy with a racist touch, and culminates in a railway hold-up combining a Western theme with the violent crime genre imported from England a few years earlier. The more linear execution of the crime plot may lend *The Hold-Up* a greater degree of closure than *The Great Train Robbery*, with its loose ends and obstreporous close-up, guaranteeing a more consistent reception of the film regardless of format, site, and time of exhibition.[65] Still, the relation between narrative whole and intertextual fragments appears no less precarious than in Porter's film, inasmuch as the parts maintain a distinct style and pace of their own, displaying rather than denying their heterogeneous generic affiliations.

This tension has important implications for the quality and range of film-spectator relations as well as for the type of intertextual horizon invoked. Composite narratives like *The Hold-Up* may well be self-explanatory (that is, they no longer require commentary or audience foreknowledge of the story), yet they do not necessarily appear self-contained (by classical standards of compositional unity and closure). In preserving a stylistic heterogeneity of their component parts they invoke a larger field of intertextual bricolage of which the individual film is only a segment, as is the particular program in which it is shown. While the classical genre film relies upon the viewer's intertextual awareness primarily within the specialized category of one and the same genre and according to preexisting standards of homogeneity, the films in question mobilize intertextual awareness across genre boundaries, playing with contiguities among formally distinct types of film. In doing so these films acknowledge a diversity of viewer interests not yet subsumed under the spell of narrative and narrative forms of identification and subjectivity; they assume an interest in narrative just as polymorphous and diverse as the spectatorial pleasures it assembles.

By intersecting documentary and fictional modes the composite genre films advance a greater affinity between the cinema and the texture of experience, the kind of interaction between the film on the screen and the "film in the spectator's head" that Kluge sees as the structural condition for the cinema's functioning as a public sphere. [66] The discourse of experience, he argues, does not obey the division of labor evolved by the Hollywood system of production, its hierarchy of narrative and non-narrative genres, but tends to mix news with memory and fantasy, factuality with desire, linear causality with associational leaps and gaps. The connections and connotations enabled by primitive intertextuality, however, appear as ambivalent in an ideological sense as on the stylistic level: capitalist-imperialist in the case of the light-bulb displays that link Exposition and execution; disconcerting and politically shrewd in the case of *The "Teddy" Bears*.

If Porter had succeeded in incorporating various genres, trends, and strategies with *The Great Train Robbery* (which remained a hit well into the nickelodeon period) to the point of fashioning a national genre, the Western, he could also employ the same method of intertextual bricolage to almost contrary effect: invoking audience expectations only to frustrate and subvert them. A sophisticated example of such defamiliarization is his film *The "Teddy" Bears*, released in February 1907 and in circulation for a number of years. I will discuss this film in some detail because it seems symptomatic of a variety of issues relevant to my argument, among them the relation between genre crossing and the invocation of a specific public sphere; the transition from narratives relying on audience foreknowledge to self-sufficient narratives whose outcome was not necessarily known and which could engage the viewer through enigma, surprise, and suspense; and, finally, competing conceptions of spectatorship articulated in terms of gender, pleasure, and authority.

The first two-thirds of *The "Teddy" Bears* are an adaptation of *Goldilocks and the Three Bears*, in the tradition of the fairy tale genre developed by Méliès, G.

A. Smith, and Porter himself, notably with *Jack and the Beanstalk* (1902). Unlike the latter film, *The "Teddy" Bears* does not conclude with the ending of the original story—a rather inconclusive story to begin with—but shifts from fairy-tale to chase comedy. When Goldilocks is discovered and escapes through a window, the setting changes from studio backdrops to an outdoors location, as the bears pursue her through a sunlit snowy landscape. The mood abruptly shifts again when the film switches to the referential framework of political cartoons: a grown-up hunter dressed like Theodore Roosevelt appears on the scene, shoots the parent bears, and captures Baby Bear, leading him away on a leash.

Contemporary audiences were familiar with newspaper cartoons lampooning Roosevelt and his much publicized hunting sprees. Relying on this intertext, Porter had satirized Roosevelt as early as 1901 with *Terrible Teddy, the Grizzly King*, which featured the then vice-president-elect with his press agent, his photographer and a dead cat.[67] The particular incident dramatized in the later film—Roosevelt's refusal to shoot a bear cub on a hunting expedition in Mississippi—spawned the novelty of stuffed "Teddy Bears," which by 1906 had become a craze. The film's most explicit tie-in with that craze occurs in the first part, when the girl wanders through the cabin and peeps through a hole in one of the doors: the next shot, masked by an oval wooden frame to suggest her point of view, shows a chorus line of animated teddy bears. This enchanting turn of toys was probably accompanied by "The Teddy Bear March," a popular hit that year. (The film apparently continued its affiliation with the promotional intertext of toys: the *Moving Picture World* reports it as being shown in one of the great New York department stores probably as late as 1912.)[68]

The Goldilocks story too was a relatively recent and highly popular source. It has an antecedent in an ancient Scottish cautionary tale (in which the intruder is a female fox who gets devoured by the bears in retaliation). In an 1831 version the "vixen" becomes an angry old woman, and in Robert Southey's first printed version of 1837, the fate of the woman, after the bears make her jump out of the window, remains unknown—although the narrator hopes for the worst. In a version published in 1856, the intruder is changed into a little girl called "Silver-Hair," which became "Goldilocks" in 1904. It is not until 1878, in *Mother Goose's Fairy Tales*, that the three bears are presented as a family; in that version the ending assumes its current inconclusive form.[69]

The "Teddy" Bears offers a complex form of address, operating on at least two distinct levels. As a contemporary reviewer complained, the hunter's intervention jeopardizes the film's success as a children's film.[70] Yet, as

Figure 1.3

Figure 1.4

Musser points out, the film was obviously aimed at adults, using the nursery story as a pretext for a grim little allegory. Since the chase comedy of the middle section provides a common ground for both young and adult viewers, it also veils the discrepancy between the two positions and further increases the shock effect of the matter-of-fact, deliberate killing. Both first and third sections assume a certain foreknowledge on the part of the audience, though different in type and degree. Thus, while the Goldilocks part is more or less accessible without audience precognition of the plot, which ironically makes it the institutionally more "advanced" part of the film, the political references would be lost to a viewer unfamiliar with the hype surrounding Teddy the hunter and the spared cub. But an adequate reception of the film does not depend merely upon familiarity with these references; after all, even children—especially of families who could afford toys—may have known about the cub. The point of the film is that the juxtaposition of generically distinct frames of reference creates a moment of surprise, a glimpse of a type of narrative whose outcome need not necessarily be known. Thus, the film requires a viewer capable not only of shifting between diverse positions and referential contexts but also of getting pleasure from the disjunction, from surrendering, if only momentarily, to the authority of narration.[71]

In the fairy-tale tradition *Goldilocks* is a story about a child's encounter with nonhuman others or, rather, their respective reactions to each other's traces; it is a failed encounter. Although Goldilocks may marvel at the strange habitat, the young reader is already assured that the other is basically an extension of his or her own growing identity, defined by the structure of the nuclear family and a respect for private property. The projection of supposedly universal human qualities upon the bears does not make them equal; Goldilocks violates their private space with impunity. The reconciliation of human beings and nonhuman nature, which genuine fairy-tales still imply as a utopian promise, cannot be envisioned on such diminished terms; the humanization of the other remains merely cute. (Bruno Bettelheim sees the popularity of the story at the turn of the century as a sign of sympathy for the outsider—the lack of punishment for Goldilocks—at a time when an increasing number of people came to feel like outsiders.[72] Given the physiognomic clichés of a predominantly white and Anglo-Saxon culture, however, the perception of Goldilocks as an outsider or alien seems somewhat skewed.) Finally, as Bettelheim argues, the story mimics the itinerary of the child who gets lost in order to find him- or herself. Yet the Oedipal conflict does not get resolved, the less so since the child in question is a girl. She can neither identify with any of the familial roles she tries out (the three sets of porridge, chairs, and beds)—not even with Baby Bear's—nor is she allowed to learn from her failed experience.

Porter transposes this rather regressive scenario into the domain of newsreels and political cartoons—an adult world of imperialism, nativism, and racism, a country whose social others were immigrant, black, and working-class. By confronting the discourse of the fairy-tale domesticity with that of contemporary politics, the film connects traditionally segregated zones of experience—segregated by the abstract divisions of private and public. It highlights these seemingly independent discourses as ideologically interdependent, by supplying the nursery story with a sequel that is actually its prehistory. As the hunter reenacts the process of colonization and domestication, he simultaneously strips away the ideology of the family which had glossed over the basic inequality between humans and nonhumans in the Goldilocks story. Thrust into the "real" world, the term "bears" abruptly changes its meaning: the droll neighbors revert to mere beasts, cadavers in the snow. The hunter's brutal gesture denies them even the semblance of subjectivity that comes with the attribution of familial feelings; it prefigures Griffith's strategy toward blacks in *The Birth of a Nation.* As the authority incarnate of "Teddy Bear Patriarchy" (Donna Haraway), the hunter not only consummates the girl's Oedipal fantasy with a vengeance but also teaches her the difference between human subjects and others which the story had blurred.[73]

Yet Goldilocks is not as innocent as she acts, nor is she that blond and cute (which may confirm Bettelheim's point). Though she may cover her eyes and plead for Baby Bear's life, she is female consumer enough to accept him as her new toy, along with the stuffed bears she gets to pillage from the deserted cabin. Her desiring look at the dancing bears suggests her collu-

Figure 1.5

Figure 1.6

Figure 1.7

sion, retroactively, with the hunter's acts of violence and domestication. Moreover, the discourse of consumption has penetrated the home of the bears even before the advent of Goldilocks. The tokens of universal domesticity are projected on the bears to the point of parody—portraits on the wall, a sign reading "God Bless Our Home" above the door, the distribution of paternal and maternal roles in disciplining and, respectively, comforting the child. But the conflicts of discipline arise in the first place because Baby Bear is preoccupied with his stuffed toy bears. Whether he assumes the figurative role of domesticated slave or that of a second-generation immigrant, Baby Bear is allied with Goldilocks—and set off from his parents' generation—by the common cause of consumption.

This kind of reading may not correspond to Porter's intentions, but it does proceed from conflicts and contradictions that shaped the historical horizon of reception. However, to the extent that such a horizon can be reconstructed, it challenges the status of any single reading—especially for early films, which depended specifically upon the particular site and modality of exhibition. The connotations of the bears' otherness, for instance, probably would have varied according to the audience's ethnic and racial make-up and identification. Considering the dynamic by which ethnically diverse but white immigrants were encouraged to identify with dominant American culture at the expense of the racial other, the film's success with nickelodeon audiences might have fed on such fantasies of integration, the desire to disaffiliate oneself from the "bears." At the same time, we can imagine an alternative reception in the context of all-black exhibition outlets, of jazz accompaniment and live performances aimed at that particular audience—a subversion of racist imagery along the lines of the rhetoric of minstrelsy.[74] It is this margin of indeterminacy and alternative interpretations, the public dimension of early exhibition practices, that the implementation of classical modes of narration and address sought to minimize and regulate.

As Musser observes, *The "Teddy" Bears* is an example of a sophisticated elaboration of a mode of representation about to be transformed.[75] Stylistically the film remains squarely within the early paradigm: predominantly tableau framing, one instance of temporal overlap between shots (as Goldilocks enters the bears' bedroom), dependence of the plot on the viewer's familiarity with the stories. Yet the shift of genres through which *The "Teddy" Bears* stages its concerns relates to a more general shift that preceded the transition to the classical mode. This shift entailed the adaptation of stylistic elements of the newsreel genre (authentic locations, mobile framing, greater variety of camera distance and angle) to the narrative film, a tendency which set in around 1903. It systematically increased from 1907 on, when the production of newsfilms as a distinct genre dropped drastically, as did scenics and trick films. As the newsreel aesthetic pervaded the visual *style* of fictional narratives, "the fantasy realm of optical and erotic delights was eliminated by the constraints of visual and moral realism."[76]

Yet for quite some time conflicting styles of narration existed side by side, most strikingly in the frequent combination of artificial and natural settings—a practice that appears to have been acceptable at least until about 1909.[77] The mixture of two-dimensional painted backdrops and outdoor locations can be found not only in shifting genres or moods from one scene to the next (as in *The Hold-Up of the Rocky Mountain Express* or *Cohen's Fire Sale*) but also within a single shot, whether suggesting a greater sense of depth (by showing, for instance, a real landscape through a painted window frame) or just curiously incongruous, as in *The Hooligans of the West* (Pathé, 1907), where a cavalry crosses a real stream decorated with large artificial rocks.[78]

The persistent combination of contrasting materials, the unabashed eclecticism that does not even try to cover its tracks, often carried quite specific connotations, including the assertion of an implicit hierarchy of realist and nonrealist styles. For instance, Porter's *European Rest Cure* (Edison, 1904) opens with a panorama of the Manhattan waterfront as we accompany an American tourist on a torture trip through Europe and the Middle East. The foreign sites are all shot against grossly stylized pasteboard sets and painted drops; the canvas flutters on the scaffold of the pyramid, and a two-dimensional Sphinx lurks in the background. Although the film is a delightful parody of the travelogue, the formal distinction between domestic and foreign settings (in conjunction with a half-serious isolationist message) asserts the newsreel style as a specifically American idiom, cinematically superior to theatrical modes of representation.[79] Only a few years later "realistic" story films dealing with "American subjects" began to be marketed as the natural and universal language of film (as opposed to the artificiality of foreign imports), and the connotation of documentary authenticity became a major facet of Hollywood ideology.

The "Teddy" Bears participates in this general tendency, both in its shift from artificial to natural settings and in the way it associates them with competing modes of engaging the viewer. Thus, the tripartite movement of *The "Teddy" Bears* could be read as encapsulating available options of spectatorship at the threshold of institutional change. Goldilocks, after all, is herself depicted as a spectator when her curious gaze produces the chorus line of miniature bears. The pronounced gesture of diegetic anchoring (through point-of-view editing and the wooden mask) and Goldilocks' frustration at being unable to open that particular door suggest a link between consumer desire and the later acts of violence and domestication. Yet the neutral background and the duration of the act remove the vision from any narrative function. The shot of the dancing bears—the film's first major addition to the literary source—celebrates a type of optical delight which clearly belongs to the repertoire of early cinema, from the Peeping Tom films to the more sophisticated uses of trick photography in dream visions and magic films. [80] By assuming Goldilocks' point of view, the spectator is invited to share in the pure spectacle of pattern and movement, a spectacle which continues, in somewhat less elegant form, through the comic chase. The third part stamps such pleasures as naive, childish, and obsolete, making the spectator either sadistically complicit (by relishing the debunking of domestic ideology) or aware of a compensatory economy that binds aesthetic pleasure to social and sexual inequity.

The film's popularity with contemporary audiences suggests the former, meaning that the effect of the sudden intrusion of reality was probably closer to the crude materialism and black humor of slapstick comedy than to moral or political reflection. Nonetheless, there remains a certain moralizing, allegorizing undertone (familiar from Porter's other work, for example, *The Kleptomaniac* [1905]) in the film's construction: in the confrontation of two incompatible concepts of spectatorship and cinematic pleasure epitomized, respectively, by Goldilocks' vision of the dancing bears, and the narrative sadism personified by the paternal hunter. Porter's "ambivalent" position in film history (to paraphrase Burch) is as evident here as in his other films, perhaps even more so. By deploying a more "adult," "virile" stance against a "childish," "effeminate," regressive fantasy, *The "Teddy" Bears* seems to point toward a cinema of moral, psychological, and social realism. At the same time the film acknowledges a sense of loss entailed by the transition, all the more so since it cannot yet envision a type of narrative that would *integrate* spectacle and visual pleasure with the continuous flow of action, motivation, and meaning.

In its configuration of spectatorship *The "Teddy" Bears* accentuates a disjunction between sheer scopophilia and narratively motivated vision, between a "cinema of attractions" and a notion of cinema as a moral institution. This disjunction is marked by the opposition of "childish" and "adult" and by the terms of gender and sexuality. While Goldilocks functions as the focus of enunciation for the larger part of the film, she eventually renounces her position at the keyhole and entrusts her desire to the authority of the male narrator figure. In *Terrible Ted*, a Biograph film of the same year, the eleven-year-old hero gets to enact his fantasy, a "bad boy" version of Roosevelt adventurism culminating in the rescue of an Indian maiden, killing a bear, and a scalping massacre; he is awakened and punished by his mother only after the successful completion of these episodes. Unlike Terrible Ted, Goldilocks is not allowed to maintain her power of enunciation, to complete the scenario for herself—and for the viewer. The objects disclosed in her "primal scene" remain genderless: her *curiositas* is reduced to a *cupiditas rerum*, a desire for things, a reification of desire. [81] The hunter's discourse, on the other hand, is not yet endowed with visual subjectivity; in terms of the spectator's identification with the gaze, it merely conveys displeasure.

In terms of the relations of gender and authority, the circumscription of Goldilocks' gaze foreshadows the seeming paradox between the industry's increased catering to female audiences and the structural masculinization of the spectator position attributed to classical cinema. In terms of the implicit hierarchy of childish and mature, the configuration of spectatorship suggested here brings into play the analogy that critics like Burch or Michael Chanan, relying on Freud and Melanie Klein, have drawn between the "infancy of the cinema" and "certain infant-like characteristics" of early viewers. [82] No doubt the types of fascination current in early cinema have a greater affinity with polymorphous perversity than with genital sexuality, and their eventual integration under the rule of narrative could be compared to the Oedipal subordination of the partial drives. The ontogenetic analogy, however, short-circuits the parallel emergence of both cinema and psychoanalysis as institutions, the mediation of each by uneven historical developments. A deviant libidinal economy is certainly an important aspect of early cinema's paradigmatic otherness, but it assumes this significance only in conjunction with other factors, such as the bifurcation of popular and high culture, their institutional demarcations of gender and sexuality, or the accelerated pressures of modernization and acculturation. As we saw in the case of Uncle Josh, the childlike behavior of spectator figures was already a trope of film history, an attempt to negotiate complex institutional problems through a familiar cliché.

Narrative Perspective and Upward Mobility

Early figurations of spectatorship suggest certain positions on the part of the viewer to whom the film is addressed. These positions differ from later ones in their formal effectiveness (they are not yet sustained by consistent strategies of narration and identification), and in their social dynamic. If the naive spectator of early films is depicted as a child or childlike, or as excessive and hysterical, the adequate spectator must be mature and balanced, which means respecting the boundaries between illusion and reality along with the segregation of screen and theater spaces that regulates them. Similarly, if the spectator figure is embodied by a rube, the implied viewer is assumed to be more sophisticated and acculturated, familiar with the urban world of technology and mass entertainment. In either case the perspective offered the viewer is one of superiority in relation to the scene and subject of representation.

In an interesting essay on the development of narrative perspective, Ben Brewster traces the metaphor of spectatorship and identification in *Stella Dallas* (the novel, 1923; two film versions, 1926 and 1937) through a series of early films culminating in Griffith's *Gold Is Not All* (Biograph, 1910). The fantasy of projecting oneself, unseen, into a fictional world "up there" which claims a greater degree of reality involves a social hierarchy that asks the spectator to identify with the perspective of the "poor" looking in on the "rich." The parallel narration of *Gold Is Not All* shows a poor couple looking over a wall at a rich couple, themselves oblivious to the poor: "the rich are ignorant of the poor; the poor see the rich and envy them; the spectator knows rich and poor and knows the poor do not realise how unhappy the rich really are. Inside and outside on the screen duplicate inside and outside in the movie-house."[83] Such a perspective prefigures a key aspect of film-spectator relations after World War I and throughout the 1920s; it also provides a significant contrast with early cinema.

In the address of later films upward mobility tends to remain a consumerist fantasy, perennially promised and deferred (a discrepancy naturalized by such implicit assertions as "the poor are happier than the rich"). In early cinema, however, the angle is more often reversed: upward mobility enters film-viewer relations as already accomplished, inasmuch as spectatorial pleasure is frequently bound up with a position of social and epistemological superiority. This tendency can be observed in the particular figurations of spectatorship and on a more structural level of address, especially in comedies featuring stock characters inherited from vaudeville, the circus, or comic strips—tramps, rubes, ethnics, eccentrics, pranksters.[84] The tramp figure inspired a whole string of films around the turn of the century, ranging from *The Tramp's Dream* (Lubin, 1899) through Edison's *Happy Hooligan* and *Weary Willie* series. In *Weary Willie in the Park*, a "dirty tramp" wins a park bench previously occupied by "ladies and gentlemen" merely by sitting next to one after the other (Edison Catalogue, 1901). Lewis Jacobs comments on the appeal of this film: "Mingled with the humor here was the patent lesson that a tramp is a social outcast. If the picture flattered the audience by hinting that they were better people than Willie, it also intensified their subconscious determination never to sink to such a low condition."[85] Thus, while sharing in the sadistic pleasures occasioned by the social other as either exponent or victim, viewers could put a safe distance between themselves and a lower-class background from which many of them were at best one or two generations removed.

At this point the question of spectatorship reaches the limits of formal analysis and urges us to consider the demography of film exhibition and the social composition of early audiences. Prior to the nickelodeon period, which began in 1905, most films were shown as part of vaudeville programs, at least in urban areas. The perspective of early comedies, therefore, can be understood as part of the ideological mechanisms at work in that institution. Although vaudeville was ostensibly middle-class in admission prices, decor, and cultural pretensions and, as some managers claimed, even attracting the "carriage trade," its primary appeal was to the rising class of white-collar workers—social climbers who might have been the first or second generation in their family to aspire to a middle-class life-style and status. The comic display of class, ethnic, and racial stereotypes might have fulfilled a two-fold function for such audiences. It offered a nostalgic potpourri of older folk traditions, as derivative and eclectic as anything in vaudeville. At the same time the stereotypes provided a negative foil for a new, ostensibly middle-class identity or, rather, for an identification with a specifically American myth of success that blurred all class and ethnic distinctions. [86]

While vaudeville continued the popular tradition of direct address, it prefigured cinematic relations of reception in important ways. Unlike variety or burlesque, which encouraged vocal audience participation, the vaudeville fantasy required a relatively passive, silent, and well-behaved spectator marveling at the show from a distance. Uncle Josh's response to the projected films would have been just as inappropriate in relation to a vaudeville show. The implied spectator of *Uncle Josh at the Moving Picture Show* is neither properly theatrical nor yet classical, although the lesson points in that direction. It is a spectator oscillating between distraction and absorption, between specific memories and shared ambitions, between intersubjective experience and alienated, universalized forms of subjectivity, between a cinema relying on the social space of the theater as a public sphere and a cinema that initiates its viewers into a larger consumer culture.

The creation of the classical spectator—as a hypothetical term of cinematic discourse, as a position anticipated by strategies of narration and address—was not possible until cinema found its own exhibition outlet. In a number of ways the nickelodeon continued to resemble its vaudeville precursor, especially in the adaptation of the variety format. But it also involved a distinctly lower class of patrons and, at the same time, promised a more comprehensive and more cost-effective grasp on an emerging mass audience. In realizing this goal, the cinema actually rehearsed a scenario of upward mobility similar to that which had proven successful in vaudeville, though on a much larger scale.

Early Audiences: Myths and Models

2

Few topics in film history have generated more controversy than that of the social composition of early audiences. It has been a long cherished assumption in survey histories and journalistic views of Hollywood that the first motion picture audiences were mainly immigrant and working-class and that this was the single most important factor in shaping American cinema as an institution. The assumption is problematic because it not only underrates other influences and interests, but it also invites suspicion as one of the staples of Hollywood's ideology about itself—a myth of origin that would advertise a giant corporate enterprise as a genuinely democratic, popular culture. Over the past decade, therefore, revisionist historians have contested the presumed symbiosis of immigrant, working-class audiences and the motion picture business on, roughly, three counts: the limited duration of the nickelodeon period; the location of the theaters in areas other than working-class neighborhoods; and the development of film practice, that is, a classical mode of narration and genres and subject matter that did not necessarily reflect the traditions of working-class, ethnic culture. [1]

Most of the debates over early audiences center on the period following 1905, when the cinema found a full-time exhibition outlet in the nickelodeons. The social profile of motion picture audiences for the decade *preceding* the nickelodeon period, however, remains no less controversial and difficult to assess. Audiences were as varied as the contexts in which films were originally shown—vaudeville and variety theaters, dime museums and penny arcades, summer parks, fair grounds, and traveling shows. What the audiences had in common was a striking distance from the genteel tradition that had dominated American culture since the end of the Civil War. Eluding the control of cultural and religious arbiters, a new public sphere had emerged with a whole range of commercial entertainments that flourished toward the turn of the century. Its constituency was a heterogeneous mass audience, mostly the new urban middle class, especially upwardly mobile white-collar workers and their families, as well as the more prosperous working class—anyone who could afford the admission prices, transportation, and leisure time. Access to this new public sphere was defined primarily in economic terms (with the exception of varying degrees of racial segregation), rather than by the exclusive standards of cultural tradition and social hierarchy. Concomitantly, the ideological orientation of the new entertainment forms, especially vaudeville and amusement parks, was toward blurring any class divisions among its patrons, offering them participation in an ostensibly classless, Americanized, community of leisure. [2]

Compared to this emerging mass public, the audiences that flocked to the nickelodeons displayed a more distinct class profile. Charging a nickel or a dime, the converted theaters, storefronts, or saloons that proliferated in Midwestern and East-Coast cities after 1905 attracted not only those segments of the working class who, with some effort, could afford mainstream amusements but also millions of people who had next to no disposable income or recreation time. [3] The latter group, mostly recent immigrants and their families, had never before been considered an audience in a commercially significant sense, except by such marginal enterprises as ethnic theater, music halls, puppet shows, dime museums, or penny arcades. The nickelodeons filled this market gap with their low admission fee (a vaudeville ticket cost at least twenty-five cents) and flexible time schedule (continuous shows of variable length that could be attended on the way home from work or shopping). And, while a trip to the amusement park or a downtown theater would add transportation expenses to the ticket price, the nickelodeons tended to be spread more widely and in greater proximity to their audiences—near shopping districts, on major thoroughfares, and in working-class neighborhoods. [4]

The nickelodeons offered easy access and a space apart, an escape from overcrowded tenements and sweatshop labor, a reprieve from the time discipline of urban-industrial life. They encouraged modes of reception and viewer behavior that were closer to the traditions of working-class and immigrant culture than to the more advanced forms of commercialized leisure. The neighborhood character of many nickelodeons—the egalitarian seating, continuous admission, and variety format, nonfilmic activities like illustrated songs, live acts, and occasional amateur nights—fostered a casual, sociable if not boisterous, atmosphere. It made moviegoing an interactive rather than merely passive experience. To whatever extent and frequency this type of theater experience actually took place, the conditions that enabled it clearly deviated from the middle-class standards aspired to by other spectator pastimes, especially "high-class" vaudeville with its scaled ticket prices and sophisticated style of presentation. At the same time, moviegoing marked significant changes in the patterns of working-class culture itself—changes, specifically, from an ethnically separatist, inward-looking public sphere to a more inclusive, multiethnic one; and from a gender-segregated public sphere (like the male domain of the nineteenth-century saloons) to a heterosocial one in which women of all ages and marital status could move in relative freedom from family and social control. [5]

The nickelodeons differed from traditional working-class culture and other commercial entertainments mainly in that they exhibited a commodity that was circulated on a national and international scale. The late-nineteenth-century entrepreneurs of the amusement parks and vaudeville circuits had successfully applied the methods of mass production and mass marketing to recreation, thus subordinating communal control over leisure activities to monopolistic objectives. However, they lacked the technology of representation that would make the cinema a model of mass-cultural consumption, at least for the first half of the twentieth century. The most advanced forces in the film industry, among exhibitors and producers, both within the Edison Trust and among the rising Independents, realized the potential of the formula and sought to attract the better-paying audiences. Robert Allen has shown that in Manhattan, as early as 1908, several commodious "small-time" vaudeville houses had been converted into movie theaters, offering a mixed program of film and vaudeville acts at medium-range prices (between ten and thirty-five cents). Exhibitors in New York and other urban centers, responding to an increasingly competitive market, began to upgrade their theaters and the quality of the shows. Newly founded trade periodicals (especially *The Moving Picture World*) became a nationwide forum for such ambitions, recommending improvements in interior and exterior decoration or, more explicitly, advising against nationally slanted programs, ethnic vaudeville acts, and sing-alongs in foreign languages—but they also published articles warning against losing the cinema's "traditional" clientele. Before long, nickelodeons ceased to be the primary focus of the industry's attention; the frontier of the market lay with the "picture palace" and the feature film, with audiences who could afford higher admission fees, who had more leisure time and longer attention spans. [6]

The industry's gentrification efforts were designed to elevate motion picture audiences to the level of the upwardly mobile mass public of mainstream commercial entertainments. In other words, they were to link the relatively autonomous public sphere of the nickelodeons to the more comprehensive, less class-specific public sphere of an emerging consumer culture. In terms of its technology of representation, the cinema was more "advanced" compared to the live entertainments—that is, by a capitalist standard of the development of the productive forces. As a social horizon of experience, however, the cinema lagged behind the emerging culture of consumption to the extent that the initial marginality of the nickelodeons allowed audiences—and exhibitors often of the same background—to shape modes of reception reminiscent of older forms of working-class, immigrant culture. To the extent that these audiences also sought access to a more "modern," more affluent, American society, their dreams of upward mobility converged with the industrial objective of upgrading and expanding the market.

Theater owners and producers found some ideological support from Progressive crusaders and reformers, a group largely opposed to the motion pictures. Within two or three years nickelodeons were perceived by middle-class reformers as "the core of the cheap amusement problem," not only because they drew by far the largest crowds but also for the unprecedented hazards that lurked between the flickering screen and the darkness of the theater space.[7] Like prostitution and working-class drinking, the cinema became the site of a struggle over cultural authority. One form of intervention, headed by prominent representatives of the Christian clergy, led to the closing of movie theaters (notably in New York on December 23, 1908) and to censorship of films by municipal authorities throughout the United States. In response to these threats the Motion Picture Patents Company supported the National Board of Censorship, which was administered by the People's Institute, an organization devoted to civic reform. Another strategy on the part of reformers to regulate working-class leisure activity was to advocate the production of motion pictures in the service of moral uplift, acculturation, and the containment of class conflict.[8] The assertion that moviegoing could be redeemed for the cause of social progress, reiterated by social-work journals like *The Survey* (and endorsed in its pages by Edison), lent an added air of legitimacy to the industry's wooing of the middle class.

The industry's bid for public status also entailed the marketing of film as (high) art. For this, producers relied in part on the same methods that had helped gentrify the vaudeville stage more than a decade earlier, such as adapting successful productions from the legitimate stage in the form of condensed "playlets" and casting stage celebrities (like Sarah Bernhardt) in episodic highlights from well-known works.[9] Beyond the vaudeville model, almost all of Western tradition was called upon to testify to the cinema's cultural respectability. Between 1907 and 1911 the Vitagraph Company, for instance, produced close to fifty films drawing on literary, historical and biblical sources (*King Lear; Napoleon, Man of Destiny;* and *Salome,* for example); many of these "quality" films received special notice in the trade press.[10] The very genre of film criticism, advanced by writers like Frank Woods as an activity for the "public good," assumed the treatment of film as "art and dramatic productions instead of mere articles of merchandise."[11] Yet Woods also knew that the claim to aesthetic status required more than just a respectable source. It depended upon the development of a particular mode of narration, based on psychological motivation, on standards of "realism" and subjectivity descended, through a series of mediations, from the nineteenth-century novel.

A crucial figure in ensuring the recognition of film as an art form was D. W. Griffith, though in a more complicated way than in his mythical role as father of American film perpetuated in survey histories. Griffith's work for the Biograph Company (1908–1913) has been seen as an attempt to translate the heritage of the bourgeois novel into cinematic forms—in its development of complex forms of narration, especially parallel editing, and in its transformation of the "histrionic" acting style descended from stage melodrama toward a more psychological delineation of character, using closer camera ranges for connotations of intimacy, interiority, and individuality.[12] Yet by the end of the transitional period Griffith's particular mode of invoking the epic tradition was beginning to diverge from the institutionally more advanced forms of classical narrative. His service to the industry at this point, notably with the success of *The Birth of a Nation* (1915), was perhaps less a matter of aesthetic influence than of his public image—as "master," "artist," "genius"—which raised the prestige of the cinema as a whole. In that sense Griffith's ambition "to translate a manufacturing industry into an art and meet the ideals of cultivated audiences" was only a more genteel phrasing of Adolph Zukor's resolution "to kill the slum tradition in the movies."[13] Griffith's naive striving for cultural respectability only literalized the industry's attempts to stabilize the new public sphere that had crystallized around the cinema, among other things, by borrowing the cultural façade of a bourgeois public sphere. That public sphere, however, had been disintegrating since before the Civil War; besides, it had never possessed the same degree of autonomy—hence legitimation value—as its European prototypes.

The most effective strategy of legitimation, in the end, was the marketing of cinema as a "democratic art," the valorization of "popular" culture. This involved mythologizing the very audiences that had initially appeared to block the market's expansion. The more the nickelodeon receded from the forefront of the motion picture business, the more the discourse on its humble patrons assumed rhetorical and ideological functions. Rather than disassociate the cinema from its working-class clientele, as the industry's initial courting of the "better classes" might have implied, the long-range strategy was to submerge all class distinctions in an ostensibly homogeneous culture of consumption. The nickelodeon provided a powerful myth of origin for this ideal, a democratic—and specifically American— legitimation for capitalist practices and ideology.

Uplift, Popular Expertise, Acculturation

Beginning in 1907, the nickelodeon and its audiences became the object of attention by journalists, reformers, and sociologists. These first reports emphasized the enormous popularity of the new amusement, the diversity of the programs, and the composition of its audiences—not just their being predominantly working-class and immigrant but also the high number of women and children, with or without family. Reformers in particular noted the nickelodeon's function as a "neighborhood institution," as a social—and heterosocial—space. Jane Addams remarked that the motion picture show was decidedly "less formal" than the regular theater: "there is much more gossip and social life as if the foyer and the pit were mingled. The very darkness of the room . . . is an added attraction to many young people, for whom the space is filled with the glamour of love making."[14]

To the middle-class observer the nickelodeon seemed a strange phenomenon, offering a glimpse of cultural otherness, an opportunity to go slumming or a field to study and reform. During the first few years working-class audiences were perceived as part of the spectacle—all the more so since their naive absorption presumably made them unaware of being themselves observed. The author of an article in *Harper's Weekly* acknowledges this voyeuristic implication by troping his field trip as an illicit activity: "Let any person who desires—metaphorically speaking, of course—put himself in the shoes of a pickpocket and visit one of these five-cent theatres. . . . Having entered one of these get-thrills-quick theatres and imagined he is a pickpocket, let him look about at the workingmen, at the tired, drudging mothers of bawling infants, at the little children of the streets, newsboys, bootblacks, and smudgy urchins."[15]

The spoils of such excursions are precisely images like that, images that were to bestow a picturesque patina on the nickelodeon for decades to come. A writer rarely admitted to his or her own fascination with the phenomenon; if so, the identification was likely to be sentimental and patronizing. Michael Davis, a researcher for the Russell Sage Foundation, complains about the crudity of the illustrated songs ("set to one of three spiritual keys: the mawkishly sentimental, the patriotic, and the suggestively immoral"), only to concede: "Yet no warm-blooded person can watch the rapt attention of an audience during the song, and hear the voices swell as children and adults join spontaneously in the chorus, without feeling how deeply human is the appeal of the music, and how clearly it meets a sound popular need."[16]

As soon as they came into the purview of middle-class publicity, nickelodeons were inscribed with the rhetoric of uplift. Articles in popular journals, unless they simply condemned the cinema, abounded with clichés like "the poor man's elementary course in drama," "the academy of the working-man," "the speechless pedagogue," "a grand social worker."[17] The trade periodicals printed and reprinted some of these articles, welcome in the fight against censorship. For the most part, however, they displayed a more complex rhetoric regarding the working-class profile of motion picture audiences. On the one hand, countless reports testify to the success of gentrification efforts, commending theater after theater for being able to attract a "new class of spectators." On the other hand, the self-serving optimism of such reports suggests that on a larger scale the problem did not go away that easily. In 1911 the working class were still perceived to "constitute the great majority of the patrons of the picture," and in smaller industrial towns (like Worcester, Massachusetts), this seems to have been the case as late as 1914.[18] One mode of response was to acknowledge the presence of so-called "plain people," but to emphasize how well-behaved, how spellbound, how eager they were to be impressed by the events on screen. Just as the "dirty little dumps" had been sanitized, the behavior typical of neighborhood audiences—"the buzz and idle comment," booing and applause, the "howling of small boys"—had become a matter of "days of long ago."[19] The domestication of working-class viewing behavior, these comments imply, depended upon the exhibitor's ability to produce a "totality of effect," a type of fascination that would subdue social and cultural distinctions among viewers and turn them into a homogeneous group of *spectators*—"a tense, well knit, immobile mass of human faces, with eyes fixed alertly on the screen."[20]

At the same time some trade columnists began to tout working-class audiences as competent, expert viewers, capable of dramatic as well as moral judgment. Louis Reeves Harrison, one of the few writers who insisted that the cinema's function was to entertain (rather than uplift), defends even the notorious "small boys" for their natural sense of "discrimination between theatrical pretense and that high art which seems not to be art at all." He invokes working-class judgment in the ongoing polemic against cheap vaudeville acts.[21] With populist flourish, Harrison rejects the "highbrow" monopoly on morality in favor of critical norms derived from the principle of democracy and the "possibilities of liberty." His notion of "public taste," however, is indistinguishable from the logic of the marketplace:

> It is no easy matter to prejudge the taste of millions of men, women and children. No individual publisher or producer can do more than make a guess at it and when he guesses wrong he hates to acknowledge failure and falls back upon denunciation of what he should respect—the really keen and discriminating judgment of the whole people. . . .
> *The men of real talent and power are not engaged in damning public taste, but in studying it.*[22]

By contrast, a self-conscious and ambitious critic like Woods, writing on film for the *New York Dramatic Mirror,* insisted upon the distinction between popular demand and aesthetic judgment. Criticizing the *Moving Picture World's* campaign for the "always happy ending," he brackets "reasoning [that] savors of the commercial" (even though he takes the public to be favoring the tragic mode) and chooses to discuss "not what the public most unmistakably wants but what it ought to want."[23]

Harrison may have been on the losing side at the time, considering the industry's anxious wooing of the middle class. Yet in the long run his pronounced deference to popular expertise, his evocation of box-office democracy, became a standard argument in the ideology of consumer-oriented art, of "merely giving the people what they want." The pervasive recommendation to study "public taste" was realized in later decades by Hollywood's systematic analysis of its own market.[24] As industrial publicity began celebrating the sheer mechanisms of supply and demand as democratic art, the nickelodeon emerged as a founding myth for this ideology in survey histories. The working-class profile of early audiences became the touchstone of American cinema's manifest destiny, a token of its inherently democratic nature and vitality. Benjamin Hampton, one of the first film historians and a film producer, explains the feedback characteristic of the expanding phase of the industry: "If spectators enjoyed a film and applauded it, the nickelodeon owner scurried around and tried to get more like it, and if they grumbled as they left the show he passed on the complaints to the exchange, and the exchange told the manufacturer." Whatever the factual basis of the account, it instantly assumes teleological significance for the legitimation of dominant practices: "In this simple way, and unconsciously, the American public began to take charge of the screen."[25]

The nickelodeon also became a founding myth for historians on the left, notably Lewis Jacobs in his influential study, *The Rise of the American Film* (1939).[26] Writing under the impact of the Depression and the New Deal, Jacobs hailed the American cinema as a fundamentally progressive institution, a popular art founded upon the organic unity of business, art, and social agency. According to him, this organic tendency had manifested itself early—in a symbiotic relation between the movies and their working-class patrons. Unlike industrial apologists such as Hampton and Terry Ramsaye, Jacobs focuses on the social function of the cinema, especially for the masses of "new" immigrants. Like the reformers and social workers (whose reports he favors among his sources), he sees this function primarily as one of acculturation and integration: "Immigration was at its peak in 1902–1903, and the movies gave the newcomers, particularly, a respect for American law and order, an understanding of civic organization, pride in citizenship and in the American commonwealth. . . . More vividly than any other single agency they revealed the social topography of America to the immigrant, to the poor, and to the country folk."[27]

Whether emphasizing the opportunity to learn English or the instruction in models of social behavior, Jacobs, and many historians following him, cast the interaction of ethnically and culturally diverse viewers with the cinema as a scenario of Americanization and upward mobility, conveying the impression, as Judith Mayne puts it, "that movie houses and nickelodeons were the back rooms of the Statue of Liberty. It is as if moving pictures had a well-defined role within the melting pot of American society, and immigrants went to the moving pictures as passive subjects eager to be integrated into the mainstream of American life."[28]

The Social Theme: Representation and Address

One of the most controversial assumptions in Jacobs' study is that the cinema's social function can be located in the films themselves, on the level of content and subject matter. The "first American story films," Jacobs observes, became popular (over imported fairy-tales and magic fantasies) because their "subject matter was derived from American life," because they dealt with characters, conflicts, environments familiar to "audiences and film makers alike." This trend continues, he states, from 1908 to 1914, even though films of that period invariably "preached," that is, they had sentimental plots and moralistic endings. Yet, by dramatizing issues like poverty, crime, alcoholism, corruption, and capital-labor conflicts, by recognizing ethnic minorities and illustrating American virtues and values, films reflected—and made audiences reflect upon—contemporary "reality." They were concerned with "interpreting the working man's world."[29]

This assumption (which has become commonplace) is especially questionable for the period before the nickelodeon, before the cinema's detour, as it were, through the lower regions of the entertainment market. As I have pointed out, early films were not concerned with representing social reality, let alone with introducing immigrants to American customs. Certain films might have functioned to that effect (Porter's *Life of an American Fireman, The Great Train Robbery,* or *The Kleptomaniac,* for example), but Jacobs' claim seems incompatible with the general diversity of genres and perversity of appeals—the popularity of prank, knockabout, and chase comedies, trick films, scenics, actualities—as well as with the international character of early cinema. Moreover, these films were not yet catering to a predominantly working-class audience but rather to the broader, upwardly mobile clientele of commercial entertainments. As for the social background of early filmmakers, an affinity between manufacturers and audiences is arguable only for a later phase, notably with the Jewish immigrant producers who challenged the Edison Trust (Carl Laemmle, William Fox, and Adolph Zukor), and even then the impact of this affinity on film practice is more complicated.[30]

Jacobs' argument is more plausible for the transitional period, considering the increased output of narrative films and the concomitant reduction of primitive diversity—including broad physical comedy—after 1907. The rise of the story film, which began as early as 1901, could be described as the development of a specifically American idiom, especially with the adaptation of the "newsreel style" for fictional narratives. But the type of narrative film that mushroomed around 1907–08 was not distinguished by photographic realism or attention to social milieu. Rather, the increased demand generated by the nickelodeon boom resulted in a proliferation of "cheap melodrama," short, action-filled narratives associated with the popular stage and working-class taste.[31] Subsequent efforts toward achieving greater "realism"—especially the development of a more restrained acting style, psychological motivation of characters, attention to pictorial detail, and elimination of painted backdrops—reflected the industry's bid for a higher-class audience.

The tension between immediate market demands and long-term institutional objectives may have yielded a number of "story films with a social theme" (the linchpin of Jacobs' argument), but compared to the overall American output (not to mention foreign imports), their share is relatively small. Vitagraph, in many ways the most advanced and influential production company before World War I, released over two and a half thousand titles between 1905 and 1916. Among a sample of roughly one hundred and fifty of them, perhaps a dozen deal explicitly with poverty, slum life, or ethnic difference. Films that touch on social themes—such as *The 100 to 1 Shot* (1906; eviction), *The Mill Girl: A Story of Factory Life* (1907; sexual harassment and unfair firing practices), *The Alpine Echo* (1909; immigration), or *Jean and the Waif* (1910; exploitation of orphans)—use these themes as a pretext for melodramatic action, suspense, and sentiment, but tend to deprive them of any political implications and ethnic specificity. By and large the Vitagraph settings of the transitional period are dominated by a relatively unspecific lower middle-class milieu. (By the same token, only a few films are set in upper-class surroundings, though in the early teens there seems to be an increase proportionate to a greater emphasis on sophisticated visual style.)[32]

The extent to which films of this period might have had a specific social function is less a question of subject matter and its dramatization than of modes of representation and address—of the ways in which films solicited their viewers. The Vitagraph Company, after all, was at the forefront of the industry's wooing of the middle class, especially with its recourse to prestigious sources ("quality" films) and its introduction of longer films as early as 1909, notably *The Life of Moses*. While still reaping profits from the nickelodeon circuit, these productions were aimed at "better" audiences both at home and abroad; more than any other American company, Vitagraph cultivated European models and markets.[33] (Also, Vitagraph's cofounder, the British-born sketch artist John Stuart Blackton, was ideologically close to Edison and joined in the Trust's anti-Semitic campaign against immigrant exhibitors and distributors trying to break into production.) Hence it should not be surprising to find only a limited number of Vitagraph films that support Jacobs' argument. But what of films produced by companies with a more conservative attitude toward the market, like Biograph, or films targeting particular segments of the nickelodeon clientele, such as Universal's "Hebrew Series," or special productions by companies like Kalem, Lubin, Yankee, or Thanhouser? Such films may be marginal compared to the overall number of releases, but they exhibit a precarious relationship between representation and reception, registering as they do the transformation of a more local, ethnically conscious public sphere into the more comprehensive, all-American public sphere of mass and consumer culture.

My examples will be drawn from the genre of the "Ghetto Film" (using Patricia Erens' term), melodramas featuring the hardships of Jewish immigrant characters, mostly women, against the background of the crowded Lower East Side.[34] These films are by no means typical or statistically representative; among Biograph films from 1908 to 1912, for instance, a much higher proportion deal with Italian immigrant themes and milieu.[35] But Jewish immigrant experience has traditionally been a vortex of assimilationist desire and ideology; it thus offers a paradigmatic, if overdetermined, instance of the dialectic of ethnic image-making and image-consumption. Because Jews were involved in film production early on, they had a certain input in the shaping of their public image from which other minorities, especially blacks, were barred. Yet this modicum of personal control did not lift Jewish images above the business of representation, above commercial opportunism and the mechanisms of ideology.

Beginning with *Old Isaacs, the Pawnbroker* (Biograph, 1908), the publicity surrounding the Ghetto films emphasized the break with the anti-Semitic clichés familiar from the vaudeville stage.[36] These clichés, which had easily found their way into early films (such as *Cohen's Advertising Scheme* (Edison, 1904), *Cohen's Fire Sale* (Edison, 1907), and *Lightning Sketches* (Vitagraph, 1907), had survived most vigorously in slapstick comedy, a genre defined by caricature and exaggeration.[37] While exploiting anti-Semitic stereotypes, many of these comedies also allowed the victim to act against the grain—in settings requiring physical skills like the Far West, the Civil War, Coney Island, or prizefights—and to assert him- or herself in the new environment and vis-à-vis other ethnic groups. (This was especially true in films starring Jewish comedians, as did the Universal and Mutual series.) Melodramatic films, on the other hand, tended to dissolve anti-Semitic clichés more didactically (the pawnbroker with a family sense, money as an object of need rather than greed) or through plot strategies that rewarded the characters' striving for assimilation.

The Ghetto films dramatize conflicts between traditional values and American customs and attitudes—conflicts exacerbated by poverty, hard work, and unhealthy living conditions. True to the melodramatic genre, plots center on family separation and reunification, on dead or dying mothers, on faithless fiancés or "missing" husbands, and, above all, on generational conflicts over marriage. Before 1914 films involving broken engagements (for example, *The Ghetto Seamstress* [Yankee, 1910], *The Heart of a Jewess* [Universal, 1913], *A Passover Miracle* [Kalem, 1914]) or the conflict between romantic love and arranged marriage (*Romance of a Jewess* [Griffith/Biograph, 1908]) remain unequivocally within the pale of the

Jewish community. However, beginning with *The Jew's Christmas*, a Lois Weber-Phillips Smalley production released December 1913, the source of conflict shifts to intermarriage and the second generation's abandoning of the faith of their fathers. In postwar films of the Ghetto genre, intermarriage virtually becomes an Oedipal trope for the difficulties of assimilation, conflating romance with melting-pot ideology.

The different staging of the marriage conflict in the early Ghetto films suggests a different conception of the audience for whom the films were made and of the ways in which they were consumed. *Romance of a Jewess* tells the story of a pawnbroker's daughter who refuses the wealthy suitor procured by the *schadchen* (matchmaker) to marry a poor Jewish bookseller for love. Rejected by her father, the couple and their child live happily until the bookseller is accidentally killed and the young widow falls sick. The little girl takes the mother's locket (a gift from her own dying mother) to a pawnshop across the Ghetto. It happens to belong to the grandfather, who recognizes his kin and reconciles with his daughter on her deathbed. For the most part, *Romance of a Jewess* displays a "primitive" visual style, with tableau shots and painted backdrops; the exception are two remarkable location shots that show the girl, and the girl and her grandfather, moving through a teeming Lower East Side street. (The Biograph bulletin advertises these shots as "decidedly interesting in the fact that they were actually taken in the thickly settled Hebrew quarters of New York City.") Although it has rudi-

Figure 2.1

mentary patterns of linearity and alternation, the narration remains quite elliptical, relying on the viewer's familiarity with Jewish marriage customs. Even if the relevant information was supplied by the missing intertitles, the film addresses an audience that could empathize with the nature of the conflict—an audience probably just as familiar with the comic routines in the opening scene, which seem to have come with the setting of the pawnshop.[38]

Later critics have misread *Romance of a Jewess* as a Jewish-Gentile romance film, assuming the issue to be the bookseller's religion rather than one of class and patriarchal authority.[39] The heroine's resistance to orthodox marriage customs no doubt points in the direction of assimilation, but the conflict of romantic love versus arranged marriage is pervasive *within* the East European Jewish tradition (and remains a staple of Yiddish cinema well into the 1930s).[40] An assimilationist misreading of *Romance of a Jewess* might also be facilitated by Griffith's later film, *A Child of the Ghetto* (Biograph, 1910), in which the young Jewish heroine finds shelter in a pastoral landscape, saved by her marriage to a presumably Gentile farmer. More important than this ideological subtext, it seems to me that *Romance of a Jewess*, given its uneven mode of address, assumes an audience still differentiated in terms of class and ethnicity and defined by a particular horizon of experience.

The targeting of Jewish audiences continued well into the next decade—with special productions and films released with both English and Yiddish intertitles. It became a standard sideline for certain producers (Laemmle, for example) through the 1920s, by which time the targeted group was part of a multiethnic mass audience. The Ghetto films mark a juncture in this dual strategy, encapsulating the conflict between short-term market interests (catering to the nickelodeon clientele) and long-term objectives (wooing the middle class, blurring class distinctions). The increase of films dealing with intermarriage after 1913 did not reflect an actual increase in Jewish-Gentile marriages. On the contrary, that figure was extremely low; around 1912 it was only 1.17 percent, which scarcely exceeded that of interracial marriages at the time. But, as Erens points out, intermarriage plots enabled the producers to have it both ways, to cater to Jewish audiences and also to practice melting-pot ideology in the service of market expansion. "By including several ethnic groups within one story, producers hoped to reach wider audiences."[41] It is no coincidence that Carl Laemmle named his company "Universal."

The involvement of Jews in production undoubtedly made a difference, as can be seen by comparing *The Jew's Christmas* with *A Passover Miracle*, but the measure of authenticity was just as much a question of address, of compromises made in the interest of marketing—of the very mechanisms of representation. Although the Ghetto films hark back to the narcissistic appeal of the "local actualities" that had been so popular only a few years earlier, they go beyond such narrow "self-reflection." As fictional narratives, they dissociate the object of representation from its addressee. It is a truism that realistic modes in nineteenth-century literature and painting were seldom addressed to the lower classes they purported to represent. [42] This paradox of representation also governs the socially conscious films of the classical silent era, from *The Cup of Life* (West/Ince, 1915) to *The Crowd* (Vidor/MGM, 1928). Likewise, whatever its actual reception, the social realism advertised by Universal, Kalem, or Biograph was aimed at wider audiences beyond the Ghetto—local color to mainstream Americans, nostalgic memories to already acculturated, upwardly mobile immigrants.

A case in point is Griffith's *The Musketeers of Pig Alley* (Biograph, 1912), a film that blends the Ghetto setting with a gangster plot. To be sure, *Musketeers* already displays Griffith's stylistic and ideological signature—the preoccupation with unprotected females, an emphasis on chivalry, a desire to absorb "the city into his pastoral world."[43] But the way in which the film invokes the iconography of the Ghetto films still illustrates the more pervasive contradictions of representation and address already outlined. Shot partly on location in Lower Manhattan, *Musketeers* is known for its "crisp documentary realism," its "authentic" depiction of tenement life.[44] The action moves swiftly between the street, back alley, saloon, and living quarters. A relative lack of spatial orientation and a systematic use of off-screen space suggest rather fluid, precarious demarcations between public and private spaces. The outdoor setting is teeming with "types from city streets" (the title of Hutchins Hapgood's 1910 book)—loiterers, prostitutes, children, shoppers, a Chinese launderer, and a Jewish street-vendor similar to one in *A Child of the Ghetto*. These images recall the tradition of realist still photography, in particular Jacob Riis's *How the Other Half Lives* (1890). Yet they do so less by their presumed documentary authenticity than by the manner in which the figures seem to be frozen in carefully composed postures and gestures, merged with the environment, framed at a paternalistic distance. [45]

Against this studiedly haphazard background the protagonists are set off through acting style and more intimate camera ranges that ensure identification on the basis of individual character traits; moreover, none of the main characters display any recognizable ethnic features. The plot involves a romance centering on the character played by Lillian Gish, rivalry between her suitors and a gang warfare that results in the reuniting of the original couple and the perpetuation of gang rule. A touch of comedy takes the sting

Figure 2.2

out of working-class experience, and poverty, violence, and alienation are muted in social compromise, as the Snapper Kid (Elmer Booth) receives a payoff from off-screen (title: "links in the system"); this in turn is sanctioned by the couple's final embrace.[46]

From the opening title, "New York's Other Side," the spectator's position is assumed to be on the "right" side, removed from the social environment represented in the film. With this allusion to Riis (familiar in contemporary discourse on the urban immigrant and poor), Griffith tenders images of Ghetto life—no doubt of a haunting beauty, no doubt also ritualized and bordering on the picturesque—to be consumed from a touristic or nostalgic vantage point. At the same time he offers the viewer a way back into the film, by setting into play mechanisms of identification—with individual characters, with the narrating gaze—that point toward the illusionist voyeurism of classical cinema. From this perspective the image of the immigrant, safely relegated to the status of decor, no longer articulates any specific social experience but provides a "realistic effect" (in Barthes's sense), authenticating the narrative as a whole.[47]

Chaplin, whose reputation as a working-class comedian poses similar questions, shrewdly comments on the appropriation of the immigrant as image and metaphor in *The Immigrant* (Mutual, 1917). Charlie's survival and his marriage with a fellow immigrant (Edna Purviance) depend upon their discovery by a painter who hires them as models. Whether this ending is "realistic" or deliberately implausible, it shows an awareness of the mechanisms by which immigrant experience was being turned into an aesthetic and commercial value. But Chaplin's own persona as tramp did not escape the dialectic of mass-cultural representation and consumption either. If his early films had a radical function for immigrant working-class spectators and might have encouraged fantasies of resistance and autonomy, it was in his anarchic protest (long before *Modern Times*) against the regimentation of the industrial-capitalist workplace, the discipline of the clock, and the conveyor belt, through a subversive mimicry of processes of reification and alienation. In the measure in which Chaplin appealed to a wider audience and romanticized the tramp persona in terms of individual psychology and human sympathy, however, he facilitated his reception as "universal and timeless," as existentialist philosopher and eternal clown.[48] This does not necessarily mean that his films—or, for that matter, assimilationist Ghetto films—were always received according to the intentions of their address. Exhibition contexts still varied sufficiently to have allowed for alternative readings and thus for a certain degree of reappropriation.

A New Universal Language: Spectatorship

The dynamic of recognition, appropriation, and draining of substance that marks the filmic representation of immigrant working-class experience can also be traced in the discourse surrounding the emergence of the cinema as an institution, such as the celebration of film as a new "universal language."[49] This metaphor was used in a wide variety of contexts—by journalists and literary intellectuals, social workers and clergy, filmmakers, producers, and industrial apologists. It resonates with sources as diverse as the French Enlightenment, nineteenth-century positivism and metaphysics of progress, Protestant millennialism, and contemporary movements such as Esperanto and Progressive reform. Mobilized in part against the threat of censorship, the defense of film as a universal language plays upon the utopian vision of a means of *communication* among different people(s). At the same time it foreshadows the subsumption of all diversity in the standardized idiom of the culture industry, monopolistically *distributed* from above.[50]

The myth of a visual language overcoming divisions of nationality, culture, and class, already a topos in the discourse on photography, accompanied the cinema from the Lumières' first screening through the 1920s.[51] In its most general usage the metaphor of film as a universal language emphasized connotations of egalitarianism, internationalism, and the progress of civilization through technology (claiming that the invention of cinema not only equaled but transcended that of the printing press). In the American context, the universal language metaphor assumed a particular significance, especially with the rise of the nickelodeon, considering the cinema's appeal to recent "foreigners" unfamiliar with the English language or illiterate, hence its potential usefulness for dealing with the problems of an immigrant society. The immigrant's partiality to the new entertainment was attributed to film's nonverbal mode of signification: "the imagination is appealed to directly, and without any circumlocution."[52]

Another, specifically American variant of the universal language myth was its inscription with millennialist thought and the Babelistic tradition, resonating in the trope of a "visual Esperanto." Although these sources were neither exclusively American nor Protestant—the founder of the Esperanto movement, Ludwig Zamenhof, was inspired by Jewish millennialism—the combination of cinema and language theology seems to have been a unique response to the American situation. Not all churches were opposed to moviegoing, and a number of ministers tried to harness its popularity to religious instruction and the social gospel, welcoming film as a new, God-given universal language.[53] The best-known instance of the desire to "repair the ruins of Babel" with the aid of celluloid may be Griffith's injunction to an anonymous actress, reported by Lillian Gish, never to use the word "flicker": "She was working in the universal language that had been predicted in the Bible, which was to make all men brothers because they would understand each other. This could end wars and bring about the millennium."[54] This conviction no doubt played a part in Griffith's defense against charges of racism in The Birth of a Nation (1915) and informed the textual make-up of his subsequent project, Intolerance (1916).

In the latter film Griffith's notion of a universal film language converges with that of another prophet of motion picture millennialism, the poet Vachel Lindsay. In The Art of the Moving Picture (1915) Lindsay elaborates his vision of film as democratic art in terms of a new language of "hieroglyphics," specifically a new "American hieroglyphic" in the tradition of Emerson, Poe, and, above all, Whitman. No less transcendentally inspired than Griffith, he linked his advocacy of film hieroglyphics to the emerging idiom of modern consumer economy: "American civilization grows more hieroglyphic every day. The cartoons of Darling, the advertisements in the back of the magazines and on the bill-boards and in the street cars, the acres of photographs in the Sunday newspapers, make us into a hieroglyphic civilization far nearer to Egypt than to England."[55] Lindsay's enthusiasm for commercial picture-writing elides questions of authorship, interest, and power not unlike the consumerist script it celebrates—a script proliferating in an abundance of seemingly uncoded, transparent, and universal images.

As self-evident, irrefutable proof of the cinema's manifest destiny, the universal-language metaphor was soon adapted by industrial publicists and advertisers (most graphically in Laemmle's retroactive motivation of his choice of name for Universal).[56] By elevating immigrant working-class audiences to a symbol of divine providence, the invocation of the universal-language myth came to mask the institutional suppression of working-class behavior and experience. Social conflict, like ethnic and cultural heterogeneity, evaporated under the light rays of uplift and human brotherhood. As an "Occasional Contributor" tells the editors of a magazine in a fictive dialogue:

> "This is the marvel of motion pictures: it is art democratic, art for the race. It is in a way a new universal language, even more elemental than music, for it is the telling of a story in the simple way that children are taught— through pictures. There is no bar of language for the alien or the ignorant, but here the masses of mankind enter through the rhythm of vivid motion the light that flies before and the beauty that calls the spirit of the race. For a mere nickel, the wasted man, whose life hitherto has been toil and sleep, is kindled with wonder: he sees alien people and begins to understand how like they are to him; he sees courage and aspiration and agony, and begins to understand himself. He begins to feel himself a brother in a race that is led by many dreams."[57]

By taking class out of the working class and ethnic difference out of the immigrant, the universal-language metaphor in effect became a code word for broadening the mass-cultural base of motion pictures in accordance with middle-class values and sensibilities.

By the same logic of expansion, the rhetoric of universal language accompanied the industry's efforts to ensure American films' dominance on both domestic and world markets. The universal-language metaphor had harbored totalitarian and imperialist tendencies to begin with, even in its more egalitarian and utopian instances. After the war, when the metaphor was altogether absorbed in apologetic discourse, any possible ambiguity or tension disappeared, and the progress of civilization became synonymous with the worldwide hegemony of the American film industry.[58] Before the war, however, the universal-language argument assumed a more interesting twist in the context of the campaign against foreign competitors on the domestic market, in response to the fact that, until about 1908 U. S. exhibition was dominated by foreign, especially French, films. (This campaign was bound up, in turn, with the Trust's defense against the Independents and the campaign of both against the "state-righters," smaller distributors who depended largely on imports.) In 1910 *The Moving Picture World* launched a debate on "What Is an American Subject?" with an editorial supporting the cry for "American made pictures of American subjects." This crusade was renewed in the promotion of "American Features" (from 1913 on) when European companies threatened to corner the market with longer films. [59] In the bid to control the domestic market, the superiority of American over foreign products and styles was asserted in terms of a subsumption of the particular by the universal. Actually the "Americanization" of the cinema seems to have been less a question of treating nationally specific themes (like Indian and Western films) than of developing a particular *type* of film: "simple life stories like [*All on Account of the Milk*], without exaggerated situations and represented by clean, good looking actors, is what our people want and mean by 'an American subject.'"[60] The universal language by which American products were to transume their foreign rivals corresponded, on the level of film style, to the emerging codes of classical narrative cinema.

The celebration of film as a new universal language ultimately coincided in substance and ideology with the shift from primitive to classical modes of narration and address that occurred, roughly, between 1909 and 1916. This shift involved a transition from narratives highly dependent on extradiegetic sources—audience foreknowledge of the story, mediation through a lecturer, or sound effects—to narratives that were self-explanatory and self-contained. Toward that goal, to paraphrase Tom Gunning, the resources of cinematic discourse, of framing, editing, and mise-en-scène, were increasingly integrated with the task of narration. This task was defined by classical principles of clarity, compositional unity, and thorough motivation, principles elaborated above all in terms of effect. In contrast with primitive cinema, Kristin Thompson observes, "classical narration tailored every detail to the spectator's attention." And Eileen Bowser discerns an effort as early as 1907 on the part of filmmakers "to enlist the spectator in the narrative by the way in which it was structured," to integrate cinematic techniques in such a way as to "control the vision of the audience."[61] Thus, the transition from primitive to classical narration corresponded to a shift in the conception of the spectator—from a participant in a concrete and variable situation of reception to a term that informs the structure of the film as product.

The process by which we "got into pictures" (Burch), the paradigmatic effort to standardize reception through strategies of narration, entailed a number of developments on different levels of cinematic discourse. Films of the transitional period began to tell stories clearly defined by temporal and spatial coordinates, with cause-effect relations that center on the action and psychology of individual characters. As the individual shot increasingly became subordinated to the flow of narrative action—through devices of continuity editing such as cutting on movement and eyeline match— filmmakers elaborated ways of manipulating that flow both along the axis of time and space and through parameters of narrative knowledge. Patterns of alternation and parallel editing evolved (notably in Griffith's Biograph films, but in other films of the period as well), allowing for effects of suspense and closure. Omniscient narration gave the viewer an epistemological edge over characters, thereby encouraging emotional involvement and identification. These strategies were enhanced by changes in visual style, especially closer framing, centered composition, and directional lighting, which not only facilitated the instant reading of a scene but also helped foreground characters as the focus of narrative subjectivity. As the pantomimic acting style increasingly was modified by more restrained and naturalistic approaches that emphasized facial expression instead of broad physical gesture, characters were conceived less and less as moral or comic types but as psychologically motivated individuals with whose predicaments, aspirations, and emotions the viewer could identify. [62]

This seemingly unmediated appeal to sentiment and sympathy was one aspect of the promotion of the narrative film as universal language—a language of identification feeding on "the ambiguous myth of the human 'community'" (Barthes), which reduced all social, cultural, and historical differences to an essential humanity. [63] A writer for *The Moving Picture World* asserted in 1910:

> The motion picture brings its note of sympathy alike to the cultured and to the uncultured; to the children of opportunity and to the sons of toil. It is literature for the illiterate, for the man of limited opportunity, or of alien tongue. It knows no boundary lines of race or nation. The same stories are being flashed upon the screen to-night from Moscow to the Golden Gate.
>   . . . the thing essential is the story; the methods of production and reproduction do not interest the spectator. He goes to see, to feel, to sympathize. He is taken for the time out of the limitations of his environment; he walks the streets of Paris; he rides with the cowboy of the West; he delves in the depths of earth with swarthy miners, or tosses on the ocean with sailor or with fisherman. He feels, too, the thrill of human

sympathy with some child of poverty or sorrow; perhaps with some dainty maid in silk attire; he thrills with the touch of mother love or father tenderness. The motion picture artist may play on every pipe in the great organ of humanity.[64]

Playing on those organ pipes required more than merely presenting an action of great emotional intensity; it meant asking the spectator to view characters and events from a certain angle, to assume a certain position with regard to them, to identify simultaneously on the levels of both seeing and seen.

Classical narration crucially expanded the possibilities of placing, or "positioning," the spectator in relation to the represented events, in both figurative and literal senses of "position."[65] Early narrative films had tried sporadically to guide and interpret the viewer's perception—through allegorical tableaux, parallelism, or expository titles—though such commentary remained largely outside the narrative. Transitional films sought more consistently to ensure the spectator's perceptual placement *within narrative space*, by means of different camera set-ups and editing devices such as shot-reverse shot, the 180-degree rule, eyeline match, and point of view. Such devices were not just attempts to position the spectator in relation to particular aspects of the scene; they were part of a system that assumed the very notion of a spectator as an implicit reference point, functionally comparable to the vanishing point in Renaissance perspective.[66] This reference point was constituted as an effect of two interrelated principles of narration: internal coherence or compositional unity in relation to the spectating subject, and simultaneous absence of that subject from the narrated scene, the diegesis.

Film theorists of the 1970s (Jean-Louis Comolli, Jean-Louis Baudry, Christian Metz, and Stephen Heath, among others) have pinpointed the simultaneous deployment and masking of strategies of spectator positioning, the legendary "invisibility" of classical techniques, as cinema's prime mechanism of ideology. It not only naturalizes particular discourses and interests but, more fundamentally, it offers the viewer a position of imaginary coherence and omnipotence, the illusion of a unified, transcendental subject. Much as this analysis has been (and still needs to be) challenged on both historical and theoretical grounds, the focus on the peculiar psychic effects of classical narration, its particular enmeshing of conscious and unconscious processes, remains pertinent—not least because it resonates with observations that accompanied the historical institution of classical codes.

Whether used in a critical or an affirmative sense, terms like the "illusion of reality," the "invisibility" of technique, or the "transparency" of the new universal language were as inaccurate then as they are now. Like much of the public discourse surrounding the cinema, they are hyperbolic, rhetoric rather than "scientifically" valid description. As hyperbolic tropes, however, they capture a crucial distinction between the cinematic fantasy and other forms of theatrical experience. At the same time they register the historical perception of a paradigmatic difference between early cinema and the classical mode. That difference was less a matter of "realism," which had been a pervasive advertising claim with shifting connotations since the turn of the century, [67] than of a different relationship between film and viewer, a particular way of imbricating representation and reception. Early cinema solicited its viewer through a variety of displays, including the display of the apparatus itself; the viewer was often acknowledged as addressee. By contrast, advocates of the classical style recognized that the specifically cinematic "impression of reality" depended upon suppressing awareness of the apparatus on the viewer's part and, therefore, of the viewer on the part of the film.

Among the first to formulate this insight was the critic Frank Woods, promoter of Griffith and later his collaborator on *The Birth of a Nation* and *Intolerance*. While the writer recently quoted observed that "the methods of production and reproduction do not interest the spectator," Woods realized that they *must* not interest the spectator, if the narration was to have the desired effect: "We the spectators are not part of the picture, nor is there supposed to be a camera there making a moving photograph of the scene." [68] Woods elaborated his insight in a variety of injunctions, advising against pantomimic acting style and heavy make-up, against "facial remarks directed at the camera," against settings arranged frontally as if facing an audience— against anything that would betray an awareness of the apparatus and of the viewer as part of it. The desired effect of "naturalness" became the very condition of engaging or, more precisely, prestructuring the viewer's attention: "The camera must be made to see, as with the eyes of the spectators who are to be, all that takes place, but that which the camera sees and records should appear truthful and natural and should not bear on its face the stamp of counterfeit." [69] In other words, identification with the gaze of the narrating camera, the ideal vantage point within narrative space, depended upon the viewer's perception of this space as a self-contained, closed diegesis. [70]

Unlike some of the more popular commentators, Woods never claimed that spectators mistook the representation for the real world, but linked the impression of reality to a special "mental attitude"—"an influence akin to hypnotism or magnetism by visual suggestion." When the "sense of reality is destroyed," it is "as if a hypnotist were to snap his finger in the face of his subject and say, 'Right!'"[71] This hypnotic spell gives motion pictures an advantage over other forms of illusionist represention, especially that of the stage; therefore, Woods concludes, an aesthetics of cinema should cultivate the mechanisms by which the illusion of reality is simultaneously produced and concealed.

A few years later, when the classical paradigm was by and large elaborated, these mechanisms were explored more systematically by Harvard philosopher Hugo Munsterberg in what has to be considered the first theoretical treatise on spectatorship, *The Photoplay: A Psychological Study* (1916). Drawing on contemporary research in perceptual psychology, Munsterberg locates the cinematic illusion primarily in the mental processes of the spectator upon which it crucially depends for dimensions of depth and movement, faculties of attention, memory, imagination, and emotion. Though he exalts film's affinity with the "free play of our mental experiences," he leaves no doubt that successful reception requires an absolute surrender to the "cues" by which the filmmaker guides the viewer's involuntary attention. Like Woods, Munsterberg measures the suggestive power of a film by its paradoxical ability to mask that very operation:

> The spectator may not and ought not to be aware that the lines of the background, the hangings of the room, the curves of the furniture, the branches of the trees, the forms of the mountains, help to point toward the figure of the woman who is to hold his mind. The shading of the lights, the patches of dark shadows, the vagueness of some parts, the sharp outlines of others, the quietness of some parts of the picture as against the vehement movement of others all play on the keyboard of our mind and secure the desired effect on our involuntary imagination.[72]

If Woods still emphasizes photographic naturalism, Munsterberg insists on compositional unity as the primary condition of cinematic illusionism— "the perfect unity of plot and pictorial appearance," which guarantees the film's "complete isolation from the practical world."[73]

This may sound like a travesty of a Kantian aesthetics of autonomy, but Munsterberg's emphasis on isolation describes a crucial aspect of the transition to classical cinema: the segregation of the fictional space-time on the screen from the actual one of the theater or, rather, the subordination of the latter under the spell of the former. The absorption of the viewer into narrative space on a stylistic level corresponded to an increased derealization of the theater space—the physical and social space of the spectator. The "blotting out [of] spectatorial space" (Burch) was accomplished not only through representational strategies that enhanced the viewer's absorption in the imaginary flow on the screen; it can also be traced on the level of exhibition practices. From about 1909 on, exhibitors were urged to stream-line their shows in the interest of a "totality of effects," to reduce nonfilmic activities (especially "cheap" vaudeville acts) or to subordinate them to the film experience (like music and sound effects). The most effective step in minimizing awareness of the theater space—in particular the distractions attendant upon the variety format—was the introduction of the feature film (1912–13), which mandated prolonged attention and absorption. Thus, the relationship between the illusory space on screen and the actual theater space tended to become perceptually polarized into a dialectic of absence and presence, of mutually exclusive yet interdependent realms of consciousness.[74]

By the same logic, the segregation of film and theater space involved a differentiation between the empirical moviegoer and the spectator as a structural term anticipated by the film, the invisible linchpin of the narra-tion. It was through this segregation, as well as the implementation of classical codes, that the concept of *the spectator* emerged in the first place. During the nickelodeon period, when a specialized form of reception began to evolve, the film viewer was still referred to by the plural term "audience," or as a member of a particular social group—"workingmen," "drudging mothers," "cultivated folks." Around 1910, however, these labels were joined by the more abstract term "spectator," especially in writings con-cerned with aesthetic questions. (It is no coincidence that Woods published under the pseudonym of "The Spectator.")

In a basic sense the term "spectator" implied a shift from a collective, plural notion of the film viewer to a singular, unified but potentially universal category, the commodity form of reception. On the level of film style this shift was epitomized in the centering of narration through the unobtrusive guidance of the omniscient camera, which implicated the viewer as a tem-porarily incorporeal individual.[75] On the level of reception it marks the dynamics by which cinematic pleasure and meaning increasingly came to depend upon the viewer's identification with the position of a textually constructed spectator, upon the viewer's desire to submerge for a spell the complexities and frustrations of everyday experience into the ordered per-ceptions of a fantasmatic, mobile, yet seemingly unified self. On the level of production strategies, finally, the concept of the spectator made it possible to precalculate and standardize individually and locally varying acts of reception, to ensure consumption across class, ethnic, and cultural boundaries.

The invention of spectatorship thus marks a point in which the representational processes of cinema converge with the social and cultural developments discussed earlier, in particular the absorption and transformation of working-class, immigrant audiences. In terms of ideological effect, the creation of a spectator through classical strategies of narration was essential to the industry's efforts to build an ostensibly classless mass audience, to integrate the cinema with an emerging consumer culture. The ritual of identification rehearsed in the reception of each individual film, and from film to film, helped standardize the consumption of films; it also made the cinema a most powerful matrix of consumerist subjectivity—a symbolic form binding vision and desire with myths of social mobility and homogeneity.

Film spectatorship epitomized a tendency that strategies of advertising and consumer culture had been pursuing for decades: the stimulation of new needs and new desires through visual fascination. Besides turning visual fascination itself into a commodity, the cinema generated a metadiscourse of consumption (not unlike one of its antecedents, the nineteenth-century world fair), a phantasmagoric environment in which boundaries between "looking" and "having" were blurred. This environment beckoned the viewer with an abundance of images—and images of abundance—unavailable to the addressee, or available at best in fragmentary substitutes. As Jeanne Allen states, "a standard of living [was] promised to the viewer ideologically, but awarded only to the eye; possession was translated into spectatorship."[76]

If cinema and consumerism converged in a large-scale transformation of perception and ideology, they also shared certain methods and psychic mechanisms. The emerging "aesthetics" of the shop window, for instance, in many ways resonates with classical principles of representation and address. New technologies of transparent glass and electric lighting made it possible to capture the shopper's attention and to transfigure the mundane purpose of shopping, creating an imaginary scene that transcended the mere commodities for which it was being staged in the first place. Essential to this effect was the concealment of the very techniques used to achieve it and the derealization of the economic transaction. William Leach, quoting a decorator, observes: "the point was to 'eliminate the store.' Store merchants destroyed the older reality associated with retail selling and created a new reality that voraciously incorporated every myth and fantasy, every custom and tradition to entice people to shop and to keep them in the stores."[77] Like a freeze-frame tableau, at once fascinating and inaccessible, the shop window turns on a similar paradox as classical spectatorship, the viewer's simultaneous separation from and projection into an imaginary space.

By translating the whole world into specular terms, the cinema mobilized a desire that was by definition in excess of the specific products marketed (whether more films with the same stars or particular commodity tie-ins and fashions). If it could be satisfied by any single purchase, the flow of consumption would come to a stop. By channeling this excess into narrative form, film spectatorship provided an *aesthetic* rationale for the circularity of consumerist ideology, a circularity manifesting itself in the "double purpose of sales and 'civilization.'"[78] Individual acts of consumption were encouraged by the promise of a better standard of living, as a means to the end of belonging to an imaginary peer group that had accomplished the process of self-transformation and Americanization. The construction of such a peer group in turn involved "socializing a regionally and ethnically diversified population into a more homogeneous nation of consumers."[79] In other words, the cinema became a powerful vehicle of reproducing spectators as consumers, an apparatus for binding desire and subjectivity in consumerist forms of social identity.

Although this analysis is more than confirmed by historical development—all the more so, if in different ways, by the advent of television—it tends to duplicate the closed-circuit logic it sets out to demystify. In a less deterministic vein the invention of spectatorship could be seen as part of the strategies to stabilize the contradictions engendered by consumerism—such as the discrepancy between utopian images of abundance, exotic splendor, and sensuality deployed to create consumerist desire and the industrial-capitalist discipline of labor necessary to produce the spending power. The mobilization of the gaze in the service of consumption was just as likely to subvert this discipline—along with the gender hierarchy that traditionally excluded women from the agency of the look. In view of such accidental and potentially autonomous formations, whether of class and ethnicity (nickelodeon) or gender (female consumers/moviegoers), the codification of spectatorship offered a mechanism to regulate and contain forms of scopic desire, to channel it into scenarios of conformity and consumption.[80] However, since that desire had to be ceaselessly renewed and redefined according to the frontiers of the market, it also harbored the risk of reproducing some of the same tensions and contradictions—within and against the classical codes designed to minimize them.

I have traced the problem of the social composition of early audiences on a number of different levels: from the discourse on the nickelodeon; through questions of representation and address in the Ghetto films; to the ambiguous metaphor of film as a new universal language and the emergence of classical narration and the concept of spectatorship. During the past decade film historians have sought to explain the shift from primitive to classical cinema in terms of a combination of "generative mechanisms," such as changes in modes of production, distribution, and exhibition practice. The most comprehensive effort in this direction, *The Classical Hollywood Cinema* (1985), by David Bordwell, Kristin Thompson, and Janet Staiger, focuses on the interdependency of stylistic and economic developments, linking the elaboration of classical norms to the adaptation of industrial methods and standards of production.[81] No comparable effort has been made so far to extend this approach to the realm of reception—and perhaps for good reason.

If anything, the role of audience composition for the emergence of the classical paradigm remains controversial. Burch, who conflates his advocacy of early cinema as an alternative film practice with political claims about the proletarian nature of early audiences, assumes that the concerted strategies to "linearize the visual signifiers" around 1909–10 were motivated by the attempt "to help new middle-class patrons decipher a medium to which they were unaccustomed."[82] He ignores the fact that the primitive paradigm had been fully elaborated in the decade *before* the nickelodeon, that is, before the cinema acquired a distinct working-class profile. (Besides, some of the productions aimed at attracting the middle class from 1908 on, such as the prestigious "quality" films and first feature films, actually reverted to the nonlinear tableau style associated with early film.)[83] Critics of Burch, specifically Bordwell, Thompson, and Staiger, come close to reversing the traditional account, arguing that the emergence of the classical paradigm coincided with—or, as Staiger suggests, was prompted by—the opening up of the cinema to working-class and immigrant audiences.[84] While early films, according to Staiger, could rely on the intertextual horizon of a relatively homogeneous middle-class clientele watching films in vaudeville theaters, such a horizon could no longer be assumed, given the much larger, ethnically diverse mass audience of the nickelodeons; hence the economic need to develop a "universally" accessible mode of narration. This hypothesis to some extent explains the connection between stylistic standardization and the simultaneous specialization and expansion of film exhibition. But it seems to overrate the cultural homogeneity of vaudeville audiences and to underrate the narrative competence of working-class immigrant viewers and the hermeneutic function of the social situation of reception.

Whatever pattern of causality may or may not apply, the connection between audience composition and the emergence of the classical paradigm cannot be grasped in terms of a simple dichotomy of the middle and working classes. Early films could rely upon the intertextuality of mainstream commercial entertainments and media—rather than pure and homogeneous middle-class "culture." By the same token, working-class audiences were stratified in significant ways that ranged from unskilled factory laborers to self-employed specialists (such as carpenters, plumbers, or mechanics), and a 1911 survey lists 25 percent clerical workers.[85] Moreover, the dynamics of Americanization and upward mobility complicates economic definitions of class with cultural and ethnic distinctions, with significant variables of generation and affiliation.

The formation of a mass audience for the movies involved a process of multiple and uneven transitions, drawing on and combining different types of public sphere. In its emancipation from existing live entertainment outlets the cinema grafted itself onto surviving structures of working-class culture for some time. These in turn were transformed, rather than merely rejected, by the industry's efforts to match the mass formula with the better-paying clientele of mainstream entertainments. The conflict between immediate market interests (catering to the traditional nickelodeon clientele) and long-term institutional goals (wooing the middle class and upwardly mobile) was eventually negotiated through classical codification and the creation of a spectator. During the transitional period, however, it may well have been a source of textual ambiguity and overdetermination.

What is at stake in these debates is not just a question of competing readings of a particular historical development; it is a question of how one defines—and confines—the concept of the cinema as an institution. The revisionist focus on industrial strategies and stylistic norms tends to obscure the social and cultural dynamics of the transition, its nonsynchronous layers and accidental effects. Registering only what became functional and systematic (in the tradition of sociological functionalism and philosophical pragmatism), this focus implies a concept of the institution that tends to side with the victor—the forces of standardization, the normative side of film history. Identifying institutional development with industrial practice, albeit from a revisionist perspective, such approaches neglect configurations of *film culture* that are no longer—or not yet—the dominant focus of economic and ideological attention. They tend to discount the experiential perspective that was appropriated by the discourse of mythology: the significance of the cinema *for* working-class, immigrant audiences, however briefly they might have been the primary subject of commercial attention.

If we base our understanding of the transitional period primarily on data of industrial discourse, the nickelodeon may be nothing more than a brief interlude in the gentrification of popular entertainments and their integration into a mass and consumer culture. If we view the films of those years primarily for the ways in which they elaborate the components of the classical system, we obviously are not looking for the ways in which the aesthetic experience inside the theater might have interacted with the viewer's experience as a member of a particular social group. Such an experience was defined not only by class but also by gender, race, ethnicity, and generation, as well as by psychic processes that remain in the realm of speculation and interpretation. If we are to take the spectator seriously as a productive force, we must consider those aspects of reception that go beyond the cognitive operations required by classical narration and persist even after the cinema's conquest of the middle class.

Chameleon and Catalyst: The Cinema as an Alternative Public Sphere

3

In the previous chapter I traced the emergence of spectatorship as a *normative process*—in the codification of a mode of narration that absorbs empirical viewers into textually constructed positions of subjectivity, in the historical convergence of social and economic objectives and stylistic strategies. In the following I will turn around and trace a countercurrent, emphasizing a margin that remains between the *ideal* of spectatorship operative in production and the social and cultural forms of reception. Accordingly, I will resume an argument suggested in Chapter 1: that early cinema, because of its paradigmatically different organization of the relations of reception, provided the *formal* conditions for an alternative public sphere, a *structural* possibility of articulating experience in a communicative, relatively autonomous form. I believe that something of that order persisted even after the classical codes were elaborated and the textual inscription of the spectator had become standard practice—that there remained a significant margin between textually constructed molds of subjectivity and their actualization on the part of historical viewers.

The first section of this chapter explores the conditions of cinematic reception in terms of theater experience, as a category that has been neglected by the theoretical preoccupation with the ways in which the spectatorial subject is positioned through both textual strategies and the psycho-perceptual parameters of the cinema as apparatus. Although my discussion focuses on the transitional period—the decade between 1907 and 1917—occasionally it slips beyond that historical boundary, when, in terms of the filmic text, classical modes of narration and address were more or less fully in place. Similarly, the last two sections consider particular social audiences at particular historical junctures, yet my argument has theoretical implications for other formations of spectatorship as well, and perhaps for an alternative conception of spectatorship in general. The slip-page between historical and theoretical considerations, however, is not just a methodological problem; it marks the heuristic advantage, indeed the critical edge of conceptualizing the cinema in terms of the transformation of the public sphere.

The argument about early cinema as an alternative public sphere remains to some extent a theoretical construct, derived from the formal parameters of the film-viewing experience and a critical stance toward later, dominant forms of reception. To recall Negt and Kluge, even if there were no empiri-cal traces of autonomous public formations, they could be inferred from the force of negation, from hegemonic efforts to suppress or assimilate any conditions that might allow for an alternative (self-regulated, locally, and socially specific) organization of experience. Such efforts are amply docu-mented for the cinema—in the industrial strategies aimed at standardizing reception, such as the elimination and subordination of nonfilmic activities and the stylistic integration of narratorial agency into the film as finished product and mass-marketed commodity.

Yet in what sense can the relations of reception thus negated be called *alternative*—especially if the spectators of early cinema (in the context of vaudeville shows) were predominantly middle class? For one thing, as indi-cated at the end of Chapter 1, that assumption is itself questionable, since it is based on an economic definition of class and ignores the social and ideological dynamic of vaudeville as an institution. While the more advanced entrepreneurs promoted middle-class standards of propriety, vaudeville might still have offered a public horizon for the psychic and cultural scars of upward mobility and Americanization.[1] The question therefore needs to be modified: alternative *for whom* and at which historical juncture, in relation to which configurations of experience? Which social groups were likely to benefit from the type of public sphere that opened up with the cinema and, by the same token, became the occasion for its containment and transformation?

I share the perspective of social historians such as Roy Rosenzweig, Elizabeth Ewen, and Kathy Peiss, who have explored the significance of the cinema for social groups whose experience was repressed, fragmented, or alienated in systematic ways—the recently urbanized working class, new immigrants, and, overlapping with terms of class and ethnicity, women.[2] These groups had either no access to existing institutions of public life or, in the case of women, only in a highly regulated and dependent form; they had not previously been considered an audience in the sense of a "viewing public." The significance of the cinema for these groups emerges in relation to their exclusion from dominant formations of public discourse and their displacement—whether by migration, industrialization, urbanization, or the growing cult of consumption—from older traditions of working-class, ethnic, or gender-specific culture. At less expense than the mainstream commercial entertainments, the cinema offered an horizon that made it possible to negotiate the historical experience of displacement in a new social form—even though its own institutional development enhanced the very process of displacement.

If, as I think, the cinema allowed for the public recognition of concrete needs, conflicts, anxieties, memories, and fantasies on the part of particular social groups, this does not mean to assume an identity of interests between the industry and those groups, let alone impute an inherently democratic quality to the capitalist market model. Rather, if an alternative formation of spectatorship can be claimed, it existed both *because of* and *despite* the economic mechanisms upon which the cinema was founded, its status as an industrial-commercial public sphere. To resume Negt and Kluge's argument, as an immediate branch of capitalist production and consumption, this new type of public sphere no longer pretended, like the bourgeois model, to a separate sphere above the marketplace. Unlike the latter, which tended toward exclusion and abstraction of large parts of social experience, the industrial-commercial public spheres were, above all, indiscriminately *inclusive.* They seized upon hitherto unrepresented discourses of experience as their raw material, if only to appropriate them—as commodity—and render them politically ineffective. Yet, with neither a legitimation ideology nor experiential substance of their own, the industrial-commercial public spheres grafted themselves onto older forms of cultural practice, creating an unstable mixture which, for particular constituencies under particular circumstances, could produce the conditions of an alternative public sphere.

If such conditions took shape during the founding phase of the cinema, it was because of its voracious intertextuality, its dependence—for subject matter, genres, and modes of representation—upon popular entertainments and the fragments of bourgeois culture, and because of its indiscriminate appeal to as yet untapped audiences. A graphic example of this opportunistic mixture is *The Corbett-Fitzsimmons Fight,* described in my Introduction. The film's amazing success with women was to a large extent accidental, resulting from the temporary overlap of different types of public sphere: the homosocial world of late-nineteenth-century popular entertainments; and the maximally inclusive and homogenizing, specularized world of mass culture. As a moment in the history of consumer culture, the incident is ambiguous, considering that less than three decades later the display of Valentino's naked torso was to become a calculated ingredient in packaging the star for his female fans. As a moment in the history of the public sphere, however, the accidental transgression of the homosocial taboo functions as a critique of the gendered delimitations of public and private, suggesting that women might be able to organize their experience in other matters as well.

Whatever autonomous formations emerged in the cinema in the following decades, they did so as a historical by-product of retrospectively more systematic processes—in the seams and fissures of institutional development. This argument seems particularly relevant with regard to the political quandary surrounding the nickelodeon. Rather than pinning the question on the class make-up of its audiences or the thematic and representational make-up of the films, the alternative potential of the nickelodeon could be described as an accidental effect of overlapping types of public sphere, of "nonsynchronous" layers of cultural organization.[3] This nonsynchronism seems to characterize both the cinema's parasitic relationship to existing cultural traditions and, within the emerging institution, the uneven development of modes of production, distribution, and exhibition.

Thus, while new methods of distribution (through a rental system of exchanges) provided the basis for circulating films on a mass-market scale, filmmaking during the first few years of the nickelodeon boom "remained a cottage industry."[4] More important, while the product could be multiplied like other mass-manufactured goods, the mode of exhibition predominant in the nickelodeons lagged behind this technological-economic standard by continuing the presentational practices of early cinema and a concomitant organization of the relations of reception.

Theater Experience versus Film Experience

Early film-viewer relations differed from the classical model on the stylistic level and in the mode of exhibition. It is a mark of early cinema's specificity that its effects on the viewer were determined less by the film itself than by the particular act of exhibition, the situation of reception. The variety format not only inhibited any prolonged absorption into the fictional world on screen, but the alternation of films and nonfilmic acts preserved a perceptual continuum between fictional space and theater space. A sense of theatrical presence was also maintained by nonfilmic activities that accompanied the projected moving image and were essential to its meaning and effect upon the viewer—lectures, sound effects, and, above all, live music. Such exhibition practices lent the show the immediacy and singularity of a one-time performance, as opposed to an event that was repeated in more or less the same fashion everywhere and whenever the films were shown. Hence the meanings transacted were contingent upon *local* conditions and constellations, leaving reception at the mercy of relatively *unpredictable*, aleatory processes.

Likewise, early film-spectator relations were characterized by a *social* dimension found later only in a diminished form. Obviously certain conventions, such as sing-alongs and amateur nights, encouraged a display of collectivity which, in retrospective accounts, became a nostalgic counterimage to the isolation endemic to the classical apparatus. Yet the term "social" here refers not merely to the ad hoc viewing collective but also to the relation between the films and a particular social horizon of reception. This horizon was mobilized, for instance, by narrative films that depended on the audience's familiarity with the story (see *Uncle Tom's Cabin*) or, as in the case of *The "Teddy" Bears*, invoked such familiarity only to defamiliarize it, thus drawing attention to the contradictory construction of the public sphere. Whether by virtue of its pronounced intertextuality or its greater dependence upon the situation of exhibition, early cinema advanced a more open relationship with the area of public discourse surrounding it; this in turn allowed that discourse to be contested and interpreted in alternative ways.

The paradigmatically different organization of early cinema's relations of reception, its emphasis on theatrical presence and local variability, persisted well into the nickelodeon period. It thus briefly came to serve a more class-specific clientele than it had in the vaudeville theaters—audiences who were economically excluded from the mainstream culture of leisure and consumption and who brought their own traditions, needs, and configurations of experience to the motion picture shows. Without the middle-class veneer it had acquired in vaudeville (at least in the institutionally most advanced, gentrified type of vaudeville), the variety format in tendency reverted to its plebeian lineage, notably in the variety theater, the circus, and the road show. In this nonsynchronous mixture, the nickelodeon offered structural conditions around which older forms of working-class and ethnic culture could crystallize and responses to social pressures, individual displacement, and alienation could be articulated in a communal setting.

The relative autonomy of the nickelodeon from both a genteel high culture and the "big-time" entertainment market was short-lived and precarious. This could be seen, on the level of filmic representation, in the dynamic of recognition and appropriation of immigrant working-class experience in the Ghetto films, in the dual address of both nickelodeon and "new" audiences. Film production soon began to catch up with the demands of mass-cultural distribution. It adopted industrial methods of production and developed strategies of narration and address designed to reach the widest possible audience.[5] Exhibition practices, however, remained an area of considerable conflict, testifying to the potential of the cinema as an alternative public sphere. The first major attack of the antifilm forces in New York in December 1908, did not resort to confiscating reels of film but to closing the theaters, denying the physical space of a social and cultural formation that eluded hegemonic control. Subsequent campaigns by the trade press to eliminate nonfilmic activities like "cheap" vaudeville and sing-alongs were unmistakably directed against manifestations of class and ethnicity. The problem with such activities was not just their content but that they encouraged modes of spectatorial behavior which deviated from middle-class standards of reception—a more participatory, sound-intensive form of response, an active sociability, a connection with the other viewer.

The struggle over the way films were to be received echoed the wide-scale transformation of audience behavior that had been promoted since the mid-nineteenth century—in theaters, opera houses, concert halls, and museums. Prior to this transformation, audiences in both Europe and the United States had a sense of themselves as a public gathering, an "active force" (Richard Sennett) witnessing and participating in the performance. By the beginning of the twentieth century, Lawrence Levine writes, audiences in all areas (with the exception of sports and religion) "had become less interactive, less of a public and more of a group of mute receptors"; they had been privatized, converted "into a collection of people reacting *individually* rather than collectively." Throughout the process of transformation, the "discipline of silence" functioned as an instrument of class segregation. As Richard Sennett observes, "restraint of emotion in the theater became a way for middle-class audiences to mark the line between themselves and the working class."[6] The same principle can be seen at work in the very institutions of popular entertainment that had been segregated in the name of high culture. For the pioneers of vaudeville gentrification in the 1880s and 1890s, subduing the "gallery gods" was a major step toward middle-class propriety. Nonetheless, working-class norms of conviviality and expressivity persisted in cheap commercial entertainments such as ethnic theater and ethnic vaudeville and, with much of the same clientele, in the nickelodeons.[7] The implementation of the rule of silence in the motion picture shows not only imposed a middle-class standard of spectatorship; by suppressing a locally and regionally specific linguistic environment—foreign languages, accents, dialects—it contributed to the cultural homogenization of a mass audience.

It could be argued that the guiding interest in eliminating nonfilmic activities was the logic of classical codification, whether in the name of narrative clarity and compositional unity (Bordwell, Thompson) or the "linearization of the visual signifier" (Burch); and that the suppression of these activities was directed not so much *against* a public sphere of class and ethnic specificity but rather *toward* the creation of a larger mass-cultural audience that submerged all social distinctions under the banner of middle-class values and standards of respectability. From the perspective of institutional development this argument is no doubt cogent, but in terms of the politics of the public sphere the development appears somewhat less providential. For not all nonfilmic activities were of the same class, as it were, nor did they all disappear at the same time and for the same reasons. On the contrary, while "cheap" vaudeville acts and sing-alongs were ostracized for their plebeian implications, other devices were claimed by the discourse of uplift, and even became part of the ambition to create more complex yet generally accessible narratives. [8]

A case in point is the revival of the on-stage film lecturer around 1908–09. A direct descendent of the lanternist and initially identical with the film exhibitor, the lecturer was a staple of early film shows. In this tradition the lecturer was associated with genres like travelogues, scenics, topicals, and actualities, which by 1907 had sharply declined in favor of fictional narratives. Similarly, the lecturer had become a somewhat rare asset with the rise of the story film and the beginning of the nickelodeon boom. Yet, at the same time, the lecturer came to symbolize claims asserting the educational value of the medium, in keeping with a middle-class discourse of uplift. The reintroduction of the lecturer toward the end of 1908 thus served as a strategy in the fight against censorship and for respectability, most notably after the Mayor of New York made Sunday film showings contingent upon *their* "illustrating lectures of an instructional or educational character."[9]

There were other reasons for the revival of the lecturer, of which the bid for respectability was only one facet. The live commentary accompanying the projection of a film actually became part of the elaboration of classical narrative, a temporary solution to problems eventually resolved in a more stable and efficient manner by classical codification. Like other sound devices that supplemented the dramatic illusion on screen (such as the dubbing in of dialogue by actors behind the screen), the lecturer was considered an important means to accomplish fundamentally classical goals: narrative clarity and legibility, "totality of effect," absorption of the spectator. This supplementary function of the lecturer, Tom Gunning points out, was quite different from his earlier incarnation: "The lecturer's new role consisted in aiding spectator comprehension of, and involvement with, the more complex stories," a complexity that came with production aspiring to the status of the bourgeois drama and novel. His role was "to *narrate* rather than hype the film as the first lecturers had done."[10] In this proto-classical conception, the lecturer not only integrated the narration but, by the same logic, was supposed to integrate audience response as well. W. Stephen Bush, a professional lecturer writing for *The Moving Picture World*, recommends the use of "The Human Voice" as a strategy of crowd control, as a means to suppress and channel the very discourse that made the nickelodeon an alternative public sphere:

> As the story progresses, and even at its very beginning, those gifted with a little imagination and the power of speech will begin to comment, to talk more or less excitedly and try to explain and tell their friends or neighbors. This current of mental electricity will run up and down, *wild, irregular, uncontrollable*. The gifted lecturer will gather up and *harness* this current of expressed thought. He has seen the picture before, and convincing his audience from the start that he has the subject well in hand, all these *errant sparks* will fly toward him; the *buzz and idle comment* will cease, and he finds himself without an effort the spokesman for the particular crowd of human beings that make up his audience.[11]

While Bush's emphasis on the lecturer's cultural authority resonates with the discourse of uplift, the metaphor of electric energy points forward to the classical construction of the spectator—as a process in which the empirical viewer surrenders his or her experience to the homogenized subjectivity on screen, as if it were merely a more efficient expression of the same energy.

Yet, Noël Burch argues that, even though the lecturer was temporarily claimed by the forces of linearization, his function remained that of a supplement, adding a layer of signification external to the visual representation. Paradoxically, while aiming to clarify the narrative and enhance the viewer's absorption, the lecture effectively undermined an emerging sense of diegetic illusion; the presence of a human voice inhibited closure of the fictional world on screen and thus the perceptual segregation from theater space essential to the diegetic effect.[12] It is no coincidence that Frank Woods, the first theorist of the classical diegesis, had no use for the lecturer in his recommendations toward greater "realism." Woods anticipated a mode of narration in which the lecturer's function would be integrated with the diegetic process in the film itself.

If the lecturer eventually followed other nonfilmic activities into oblivion, it was not just because of an undoubtedly operative tendency of linearization, but because he remained adjunct to a particular show, a live performance, the local sphere of exhibition. Whether he sailed under the flag of uplift or that of narrative effect, the lecturer represented an *interpretive agency* that was both more influential and less predictable than the piano player or sound-effects personnel. During the early teens attempts were made to circumscribe this agency. Marcus Loew's theater chain set up a staff of lecturers to cover the country, to circulate with particular films; production companies sent out copy to standardize the commentary as much as possible. But such efforts were soon abandoned—as was the lecturer. By definition, the lecturer eluded the methods of mass distribution because his success depended upon interaction with local and particular audiences— upon rhetorical skills and personal involvement, upon professional experience and familiarity with the situation of reception. It is in this tradition of individual showmanship that the institution survived in certain pockets of film culture. As late as 1920 the *New York Times Magazine* reports on five "professors" still active on the Lower East Side, in theaters catering to audiences on the threshold of Americanization. Delivered in the "Yankee" language, the address of these lectures seems to have been as Janus-faced as that of the Ghetto films—promoting integration, while thriving on memories of ethnic difference: "Now and then the voice coming through the megaphone drops a Yiddish phrase, and then there are wide manifestations of delight."[13]

The ambiguous reappearances of the lecturer have to be understood in a larger context—that of the struggle for control over the film's reception between national production and distribution companies on the one hand and local exhibitors on the other. As Charles Musser has shown, early exhibitors exerted considerable influence over the meaning of films by determining the selection and sequence of scenes and the general shape of their program. This influence was curtailed with the downgrading of the exhibitor's function to that of a projectionist and the differentiation between projectionist and theater owner. The industry's growth and stabilization seemed to mandate a concentration of meaning within the film as product and commodity, and thus its increased independence from the sphere of exhibition. Developments concurrent with the elaboration of classical codes, such as the reduction of a primitive diversity of genres, the gentrification of exhibition, and the introduction of the feature film, were not simply aimed at upgrading and homogenizing the audience but became issues of control between centrally organized production companies and locally based exhibitors, in the context of the Motion Picture Patents Company's efforts to impose licensing requirements on theater owners and exchanges. With the cinema's emancipation from other entertainment outlets, exhibitors had become a dynamic force in the industry, moving into production via distribution (notably the Independents) or expanding their theaters into chains. Exhibitors cultivating the local market, however, whether as managers or independent entrepreneurs, maintained a strong sense of their contribution to the product, especially as increased competition demanded that they distinguish their presentations from those of other theaters. Many local exhibitors shared their customers' ethnic and social background, an affinity that seems more likely to have created the conditions of an alternative public sphere than the often cited affinity between audiences and producers. [14]

Exhibition practices during the transitional period continued to emphasize the value of "the show" over that of the film as circulating product. As Richard Koszarski argues, the priority of the show continued throughout the silent era, which calls into question the efficacy of the classical objective of a textually centered spectator, even at a time when classical strategies of narration and address were already fully elaborated. Thus nonfilmic activities were considered not merely as auxiliary but rather as "added attractions," advertised along with an orchestra here and a $30,000 organ there, with powder rooms, ushers, and architectural design. Roughly one-fourth to one-third of a two-hour program would be devoted to items outside the feature (which, if necessary, was cut down or projected at faster speed)—to live acts, musical performances (such as orchestral overtures or illustrated songs), news weeklies, comedy shorts, or animated cartoons. More important than the textual integrity or even narrative consistency of the featured film was the overall appeal of the entertainment mix, the "balanced program." In Koszarski's words, "the belief in a 'balanced program' was almost mystical among silent picture palace managers, who clearly saw this part of their business as closer to the work of vaudeville managers than operators of legitimate houses." This concept of the show enjoyed enormous popularity with audiences. Surveys throughout most of the 1920s suggest that only a small fraction (10 percent in one survey) of moviegoers had come to see the feature; the overwhelming majority (68 percent) had come for the "event." "Going to the movies" during the silent era, Koszarski concludes, "remained essentially a *theater experience*, not a film experience."[15]

The advent of synchronized sound drastically curtailed the initiative of the individual exhibitor. The addition of a prefabricated soundtrack was yet another step toward making the film a more "complete" product which could be distributed and consumed in more or less the same manner everywhere; and the standardized speed of projection prohibited tampering with ("improving") the feature, which had been standard practice before. Moreover, the activities surrounding the film increasingly became a promotional ritual organized from above, culminating in the 1930s with commodity tie-ups, fashion shows, give-aways, and other advertising schemes. [16] The tendency toward standardizing theater experience, however, already can be observed in the early 1920s, within the very tradition of showmanship that emphasized the exhibitor's autonomy. For the notion of a "balanced program" could go either way: continuing the emphasis on diversity inherited from the variety format, the "cinema of attractions," or streamlining the presentations to give the impression of an "organic" whole thematically centered on the weekly feature—a distinction first analyzed by Kracauer in his 1926 essay on "distraction." Whatever formula was applied (the "prologue," the "headliner," or "pure," theme-oriented spectacle), the ideal of a unified presentation raised the stakes of exhibition. As investment costs for the live aspects of the program soared, lavish presentations increasingly became the trademark of particular theater chains, either replicated locally or packaged to tour a circuit of theaters. [17]

The size and quality of the "show" depended on the size and type of theater. The picture palaces soon "became the flagships, the most profitable theatres in large regional chains," but they represented only a small portion of American movie theaters—1 percent in 1915, 5 percent between 1915 and 1933. [18] Neighborhood theaters charging lower prices continued in business, and continued to attract ethnic and working-class crowds. To be sure, on special occasions these audiences also visited the downtown theaters mingling there with the middle class and being treated as "ladies and gentlemen"; but the middle class did not reciprocate. Like the picture palaces, the smaller houses cultivated a belief in the "show," and their status among neighborhood theaters depended upon the "added attractions" that could be afforded. In contrast with the more expensive shows, the live portions of the program were often geared to particular ethnic and racial constituencies. In Chicago, for instance, Polish plays were performed side by side with cinematic entertainment, and, in Lizabeth Cohen's words, "Italian music shared the stage with American films." Furthermore, as Mary Carbine has shown, theaters catering to black audiences included jazz performances as well as acts from the black, particularly Southern, entertainment tradition. [19] While these live portions were attractions in their own right, they also shaped the way mainstream films could be received—and reinterpreted—by nonmainstream audiences.

As long as an exhibitor catered to such audiences, the show was likely to maintain a locally specific, potentially interactive and aleatory dimension. If it did so, this was not because the individual exhibitor believed in defending communal culture against the onslaught of monopolization, but because the format was profitable and competitive. Yet that same economic principle created a kind of scissors effect: the more ambitious and costly the show, the larger and less specific its intended audience.

Spaces of Transition, Pockets of Time

In what follows, I will discuss the question of an alternative public sphere from a less systematic perspective, focusing on the cinema's function for particular social groups at particular historical junctures, specifically, new immigrants and a recently urbanized working class as well as women both within these groups and across class and ethnic boundaries. Such a perspective must remain speculative, since it is difficult to know how these groups— or, for that matter, any group—received the films they saw and what significance moviegoing had in relation to their lives. Still, we can try to reconstruct the configurations of experience that shaped their horizon of reception, and ask how the cinema as an institution, as a social and aesthetic experience, might have interacted with that horizon.

The immigrant and working class have traditionally been singled out for their "symbiotic relationship" with the movies, a relationship that almost instantaneously spawned a powerful mythology. It is necessary to denaturalize that "symbiosis," by situating the cinema's appearance in immigrant life in a particular historical constellation, broadly defined by the experience of modernization and the emergence of consumerism. In doing so, I am not presuming to offer a general theory of "the immigrant experience"; I wish to suggest certain patterns and possibilities that may help explain the cinema's ambiguous ascendancy over other institutions of immigrant culture. Nor do I mean to obliterate significant distinctions among immigrant groups, especially with regard to moviegoing habits, or to underrate the importance of local and regional variations in immigrant culture and the demographics of film consumption.[20] Yet, despite such variations, and despite the separatism that governed relations among diverse ethnic groups, basic patterns of experience were shared by immigrant working-class communities across the board. This common experience was defined by the discrepancy between the types of society and economy the immigrants had left behind and the conditions they confronted in America (conditions themselves in rapid transformation) as well as by the particular strategies mobilized in dealing with that discrepancy.

Social historians have discussed the immigrant experience of that period (1893–1919) primarily under two overlapping aspects: modernization and, more recently, the emergence of a consumer economy. The former points

back to earlier phases of industrial capitalism, the latter describes a development concurrent with—and in crucial ways dependent upon—the new
wave of mass immigration. In his influential 1973 essay Herbert Gutman
describes the encounter of immigrants from premodern societies with industrial modes of production as a kind of déjà vu of the experience of first-
generation factory workers during the early decades of the nineteenth century: "American society, of course, had changed greatly, but in some ways it
is as if a film—run at a much faster speed—is being viewed for a second
time."[21] By the end of the century this experience entailed not only an
encounter with steam, machinery and electricity, with low wages, long
hours, and a punitive system of work discipline, but also a more refined
regime of the clock, linked to an increasing division and hierarchy of labor,
standardization, and the elaboration of methods of mass production.[22]
Modern factory practices were as alien to the work habits of East-European
artisans and peddlers as to those of Italian or Slavic peasants. Like earlier
instances of mass industrialization, they provoked forms of protest that
drew strength from the very subcultures that were being negated.

Immigrants experienced the effects of accelerated industrialization not
only in the factory but in all areas of everyday life—as a violent displacement and deprivation, as disorientation, alienation, shock, and loss.
Whether they came from the small-town environment of the East-European
shtetl or the rural *mezzogiorno*, arrival in urban America catapulted them into a
world without nature, a grey concrete jungle of overcrowded tenements and
filthy streets, of artificial lighting, noise, and speed. The loss of preindustrial nature went hand in hand with the loss of a communal cultural and
linguistic environment, a framework of traditional norms and values. The
world the immigrants had left behind was one of poverty and oppression,
but it was a familiar one, bounded within a closed religious worldview and a
hierarchic social order. The new world had promised a liberation from
oppressive conditions and unlimited possibilities; instead it entailed, for
first-generation immigrants at least, a reduction of space and time, a curtail-
ment of their sphere of interaction, expression, and interpretation.[23]

The loss of that horizon of experience was superimposed with new
demarcations of public and private (which themselves were undergoing a
major transformation). In a society of extended families and kinship networks, the boundaries between public and private had hardly been as pronounced and were fluid at best. Transplanted into an industrial-capitalist
economy, the immigrant family lost its role in the production process (similar to what had happened to the American family more than half a century
earlier) and was reduced to a unit of reproduction and consumption. While

the immigrant family was thus abruptly privatized, work pressures and overcrowded living conditions rendered any real privacy a luxury, putting immense strain on marital relations and relations between parents and children. At the same time immigrants were barred from most institutions of the dominant public sphere, whether by reason of language, custom, class, or lack of means and leisure time.

Yet, as Gutman admonished historians in 1973, it would be a mistake to perpetuate the notion "that the large-scale uprooting and exploitative processes that accompanied industrialization caused little more than cultural breakdown and social anomie. Family, class and ethnic ties did not dissolve easily."[24] And, as social historians have amply documented since, the very conditions of alienation not only mobilized a web of familial, social, and personal relationships but also gave rise to new forms of public life that mediated the loss of the old culture with the challenges of the new.[25] Speaking of the secular culture that emerged among Jewish immigrants from Eastern Europe, Irving Howe asserts that it "was different from the one they had left behind, despite major links of continuity," and that "it struggled fiercely to keep itself different from the one they found in America, despite the pressures of assimiliation."[26] The institutions of immigrant public life ranged from the traditional and in their own way exclusive voluntary societies and lodges (like the Jewish *landsmanshaftn*), through social clubs and educational centers to labor-related and political activities; from ethnic theaters, such as the Yiddish theater, the Italian opera and marionette theater, and ethnic vaudeville through the more casual (though no less regular) gatherings in candy stores, soda fountains, and saloons to the more anonymous and potentially dangerous encounters at the dance halls. As Roy Rosenzweig argues with regard to working-class leisure culture in Worcester, Massachusetts, such institutions constituted a local, separate, and relatively autonomous sphere which, although not overtly *oppositional*, still presented an *alternative* to dominant social norms.[27]

It is part of the cinema's ambiguous record that its success destroyed many of these institutions, especially the whole spectrum of ethnic theatrical entertainments, along with public gathering places like the candy store and the saloon.[28] As the cinema prevailed over its live competitors by virtue of the greater profit margin, it both absorbed and in crucial ways surpassed the appeal of other entertainments to immigrant audiences. The nickelodeon permitted a continuation of class and ethnically specific habits of reception because of its neighborhood character, low admission fee, and egalitarian seating structure (uniform ticket price), its informal atmosphere and interactive mode of exhibition. At the same time, moviegoing marked a departure from this tradition, opening up a less traditionally defined, qualitatively different type of public sphere.

The relation of the cinema to existing forms of immigrant public life was not just that of another institution but that of a chameleonlike creature grafting itself onto these formations. "Despite the standardized product," Kathy Peiss writes, "the experience of the movies took on the flavor of the surrounding neighborhood."[29] This observation cuts both ways. It accounts for the survival of working-class sociability and familiarity in neighborhood theaters, but it also explains the lack of these dimensions in other locations. In 1911 Mary Heaton Vorse, a Greenwich Village radical, compares motion picture audiences in Jewish and Italian areas of New York and finds a contrasting experience in a Bowery theater: "In the Bowery you get a different kind of audience. None of your neighborhood spirit here. Even in what is called the 'dago show'—that is, the show where the occasional vaudeville numbers are Italian singers—the people seem chance-met; the audience is almost entirely composed of men, only an occasional woman."[30] In this passage, as throughout her article, Vorse emphasizes the role of the audience as a productive force, crucial to supplying the films and numbers with an interpretive, intersubjective dimension. But the distinction she observes in the Bowery theater also describes an important difference between the cinematic institution and the more traditional ethnic entertainments: "the people seem chance-met."

Most institutions of immigrant public life were defined by quite strict standards of inclusion (hence also exclusion)—by origin, craft, or religious affiliation—as well as particular conventions of access, especially in terms of gender and generation. Women were excluded from traditionally male working-class entertainments such as the burlesque, concert-saloons, dime museums, or sports. Many other leisure activities, like a promenade in the park or a trip to more upwardly mobile entertainments like vaudeville and amusement parks, were available to them only in the company of men or the whole family. Although the tightly knit web of kinship relations and ethnic coherence may have provided a buffer against alienation and the pressures of adaptation, it also drove the younger generation to seek escape, particularly toward encounters with members of the other sex outside the narrow pale of family connections and ethnic community. One such escape was the visit to the dance hall, a new kind of social space, less personal but free of family surveillance, which for many served as a rehearsal ground for the styles of a heterosocial modernity.[31]

Because of its chameleonlike quality, the cinema seems to have assumed a certain threshold function, oscillating between the tradition of family-centered ethnic entertainment and the more anonymous, more modern forms of commercialized leisure. Cheaper than vaudeville or Coney Island and safer than the dance halls (and therefore less subject to parental censure), the cinema allowed for the mixing with friends, acquaintances, and even strangers. Discussing the emergence of the audience as public in eighteenth-century Paris, Sennett distinguishes two kinds of strangers: the stranger as outsider, as in the "categorizable strangeness of immigrants from another land," and "the stranger as an unknown, rather than an alien." Although he refers to ethnic stereotyping in Boston and New York around 1900 as an example of the former, the following description seems nonetheless apt for the less clearly defined gathering of strangers in American movie theaters: "the stranger as an unknown can dominate . . . the perceptions of people who are unclear about their own identities, losing traditional images of themselves, or belonging to a new social group that as yet has no clear label." The farther the theater from the neighborhood centers and the less associated with a particular immigrant constituency, the more likely it was to assemble strangers of diverse ethnic backgrounds who were not only displaced in relation to dominant forms of identity but had that displacement in common with each other—"materially alike but not cognizant of their similarities."[32] Like the new public spaces of the eighteenth-century cosmopolitan city, the cinema offered a site for experiencing diversity, for civil interaction among strangers. Yet the same conditions that enabled this public dimension also entailed its opposite, both with the increased privatization of viewing behavior and the textual homogenization of positions of subjectivity.

Neither a primeval paradise of viewer participation nor merely a site for the consumption of standardized products, the cinema rehearsed new, specifically modern forms of subjectivity and intersubjectivity at the same time that it addressed older needs and more recent experiences of displacement and deprivation. If it assumed both of these functions, it did so not only because of the liminal situation of its audiences and its own threshold status among commercial entertainments but also because of the particular kind of collectivity actualized in the individual viewing experience. Vorse describes in great detail a woman watching an Indian-trapper melodrama in a Lower East Side theater. Accompanied by a man, she was "so rapt and entranced" with the events on screen "that her voice accompanied all that happened—a little unconscious and lilting *obbligato*." Significantly, the running commentary was in German, with an Austrian accent, rendered by Vorse in English punctuated with foreign phrases. The writer's own fascination seems divided between the heteroglossic transaction behind her and the spectacle that was prompting it: "a guileless and sentimental dime novel, most ingeniously performed; a work of art; beautiful, too, because one had glimpses of stately forests, sunlight shifting through leaves, wild, dancing forms of Indians, the beautiful swift rushing of horses." But, as Vorse hastens to add, "to the woman behind it was reality at its highest. She was there in a fabled country full of painted savages. The rapidly unfolding drama was to her no make-believe arrangement ingeniously fitted together by actors and picture-makers. It had happened; it was happening for her now."[33]

Whatever we make of the radical intellectual's own kind of disavowal, she describes a spectatorial disposition that is at once absorbed and active, at once self-abandoning and very much part of the situation of exhibition. The woman's expressive behavior, in particular its linguistic distinctiveness, runs counter to the middle-class standards of silence and passivity that were becoming the mark of the cinema's respectability; yet her engagement with the narrative seems consistent with the tenets of classical illusionism. This combination challenges the conceptual coupling (notably in Brechtian film theory of the 1970s) of narrative identification with spectatorial passivity and, conversely, of an active mode of reception with a distanced awareness of the film's discursive operations.[34] What upsets these formalist opposi-tions as well is the trajectory Vorse draws between the woman's dialogue with the film and the spatial and symbolic relationship of the show with a particular social environment:

> Outside the iron city roared; before the door of the show the push-cart vendors bargained and trafficked with customers. Who in that audience remembered it? They had found the door of escape. For the moment they were in the depths of the forest following the loves of Yellow Wing and Dick. The woman's voice, so like the voice of a spirit talking to itself, unconscious of time and place, was their voice. There they were, a strange company of aliens—Jews, almost all; haggard and battered and bearded men, young girls with their beaus, spruce and dapper youngsters begin-ning to make their way.

The image of a female voice divorced from the body, abstracted from time and place yet speaking for a particular group or mode of being, is a Romantic topos, reminiscent of Wordsworth's "Solitary Reaper." The woman's voice becomes the voice of the Ghetto, as it were, because it speaks from the unconscious, because it is fueled by a common need for escape. What barely saves this rhetoric from the pitfalls of the "collective unconscious" is the configuration of the world inside and outside the movie theater, the separate yet interrelated spaces of fantasy and reality. The cinematic fantasy com-pensates for the deficiencies of the outside world: the pressures of survival and success, the experience of aliens, the loss of familiar surroundings. But the space of fantasy is no less alien, no more continuous with the traditions from which they had been dispossessed. It is no coincidence that the melodramatic conflict on screen revolves around terms of racial difference, whether advancing an identification with the white hero at the expense of the exotic, barbaric other (*"wildes und grausames Volk"*) or allowing for a fictional reconciliation of the opposition by way of an interracial romance. To whatever degree such scenarios might have served to inculcate dominant racist ideology in ethnic but white immigrants, [35] they also provide symbolic parallels with the experiential horizon of those immigrants, their own confrontation with new terms of strangeness and identity. In that sense the type of identification described by Vorse could be read as a form of reappropriation, an imaginative assimilation of foreign images to the collective experience of alienation and displacement.

In its spatial and symbolic configurations of inside and outside, of familiarity and strangeness, the cinema belongs to the social sites that Michel Foucault has characterized as "heterotopias"—"places [that] are absolutely different from all the sites that they reflect and speak about." In their irreducible heterogeneity in relation to the surrounding spaces, heterotopias are "something like counter-sites, a kind of effectively enacted utopia in which the real sites, all the other real sites that can be found within the culture, are simultaneously represented, contested, and inverted." Foucault himself lists the cinema among a number of such sites—sites of transportation such as trains or sites of temporary relaxation such as cafes and beaches. He discusses it as an example of one particular principle of the heterotopia: the capability "of juxtaposing in a single real place several spaces, several sites that are in themselves incompatible." The cinema obviously qualifies as such in the very basic sense that it is "a very odd rectangular room, at the end of which, on a two-dimensional screen, one sees the projection of a three-dimensional space."[36]

While this spatial configuration is as old as the magic lantern show and more or less typical of the cinema throughout its history, Foucault's notion of heterotopia can be taken further to describe a more specific historical experience, during the transition from early to classical cinema, on the part of particular social groups. For over half a century urban populations in Europe and the United States had been adapting to the effects of modern technology on human perception, a fundamental transformation of spatio-temporal coordinates. [37] The vast majority of immigrants arriving in American cities around the turn of the century confronted this transformation from one day to the next, without preparation—a shock which, according to autobiographical statements and social worker reports, left many stunned, disoriented, literally dis-placed. [38] Although the cinema no doubt participated in the historical upheaval of traditional coordinates of space and time, it also offered a refuge in which the violence of the transition could be negotiated in a less threatening, playful, and intersubjective manner.

The nickelodeon was a real place, located in the center or at the margin of the immigrants' world, ordinary and easily accessible. At the same time it opened up into a fantastic space, giving pleasure in the juxtaposition of diverse, often incompatible, and at times impossible sites or sights—in the very principle of disjunction that informed the variety format. The jumble of strange and familiar, of old and new, of ordinary and exotic, made the movies an objective correlative of the immigrant experience. As a writer for the *Jewish Daily Forward* observed, "our Jews feel very much at home with the detectives, oceans, horses, dogs, and cars than run about on the screen."[39] The significance of such a series is less in its individual referents than in its cheerfully avowed randomness, a surrealistic equality among its elements. This aesthetics of disjunction not only contested the presumed homogeneity of dominant culture and society in the name of which immigrants were marginalized and alienated; more important, it lent the experience of disorientation and displacement the objectivity of collective expression. It is in this sense that the notion of the cinema as a heterotopia converges with the concept of an alternative public sphere—as a medium that allows people to organize their experience on the basis of their own context of living, its specific needs, conflicts, and anxieties.

The "despatialization of subjectivity" (Mary Ann Doane) that marked the immigrants' entry into American modernity was just as much an experience of violent detemporalization. It is thus that the cinema might have functioned as a "time-place" (*Zeitort*) in Kluge's sense, a site for the actualization of different temporalities. [40] Foucault attributes this capability to heterotopias in general when he notes that they "are most often linked to slices of time." The experience of different temporalities is possible only at a certain stage of historical development: "The heterotopia begins to function at full capacity when men arrive at a sort of absolute break with their traditional time." Foucault contrasts sites concerned with the accumulation of time with a view to eternity (archives, museums, libraries) with ones that are linked "to time in its most fleeting, transitory, precarious aspect, to time in the mode of festival." As an example of the latter he cites the fairgrounds, "these marvellous empty sites on the outskirts of cities that teem once or twice a year with stands, displays, heteroclite objects, wrestlers, snakewomen, fortune-tellers, and so forth"; but he might as well have included preclassical cinema, the "cinema of attractions."[41]

Again, Foucault has to be read somewhat against the grain, read backwards through more contemporaneous historians of modernity such as Kracauer and Benjamin. Foucault tended to celebrate the ascendancy of categories of space over those of time in a somewhat ahistorical manner. Kracauer and Benjamin, however, saw in the spatialization of time a crucial moment in the historical process, itself a sign of the times. They wrote about urban spaces—streets, squares, hotel lobbies, movie theaters, arcades—as sites of a temporal crossing, as thresholds of social and political change. Thus they turned the German word for arcade, *"Passage,"* into a complex historical metaphor.[42] For both, film and photography assumed a pivotal function in the crisis that pervaded all areas of modern life, in what Kracauer called "the all-out gamble of history."[43] For Benjamin this crisis was linked to the general decline of the capability of experience, the dissociation of collective memory and individual recollection; by the same token, the emancipation of experience from cultural tradition and privilege, epitomized by film and photography, offered the historical chance to reshuffle the spatialized fragments of time, to make them "quotable" and collectively accessible.[44]

As with the transformation of spatial perception, the break with traditional temporality was exacerbated for immigrant men and women who brought preindustrial, agricultural, or artisanal rhythms of time to a country increasingly run by train schedules and the discipline of the factory clock. The enforced adaptation to the latter entailed a detemporalization, a quantification, and reification of time; it also reduced the play of memory (for Kracauer and Benjamin synonymous with the capability of experience). While immigrant organizations and personal and kinship networks worked to keep memories of the old world alive, the pressures of Americanization demanded precisely the opposite. In a study published in 1921, Chicago sociologist William Isaac Thomas condemns the prevailing concept of "quick and complete Americanization" for promoting the "destruction of memories," for preventing immigrants from living "in the light of the past" and making constructive changes on the basis of their experience.[45]

To people under the assault of the present both on their jobs and by the institutions of dominant culture, the cinema offered a "time-place" in a number of ways. With its lack of a fixed schedule and continuous admission, Rosenzweig contends, the nickelodeon provided a "refuge from the time discipline of the factory."[46] Mothers for whom family leisure activities usually meant a continuation of housework on different premises could disappear in the darkness of the movie theater for a few hours, with or without children, to vary on Horkheimer and Adorno's notorious phrase, "just as [they] used to gaze out of the window, when there were still homes and the hour after a day's work [*Feierabend*]."⁴⁷ The dimness of the theater set the stage for the viewer's surrender to the manipulations of time on screen—the duration of a panorama shot, the thrills of fast and reverse motion, the simultaneity of parallel editing—at least until filmic temporality became more firmly subordinated to the linear momentum of narrative.

If the cinema could help immigrants come to terms with competing temporalities, it also lent itself to the unceremonious actualization of memories. This capability seems linked to the affinity of film with mimetic traces in the historical experience of nature. In journalistic discourse of the period, the cinema is often ascribed a compensatory function for people who could not afford to travel. A 1908 article, for instance, emphasizes a German exhibitor's efforts to procure "scenes from the Rocky Mountains, forest views, and flowing cascades": "He would bring to the heart of the Ghetto the heart of Nature itself, and even though devoid of color and freshness and odor, he would at least suggest something of that flowering world which is farthest away from asphalt and brick."⁴⁸ But for first-generation immigrants this spatial distance translated into a temporal one: it was not that they had never seen the beauties of nature; they had lost them. As Elizabeth Ewen observes, "New York had abolished the forests forever, leaving them retrievable only in memory or in the pictorial reproductions that hung on the walls of tenement apartments as reminders of a world lost but not forgotten."⁴⁹ To be sure, such reminders border on the pathetic, more likely perhaps to diminish memory than to preserve it. But the mnemonic powers of the cinema go beyond those of pictorial reproductions on the wall. If the spurious miracles of second nature succeeded in stirring up memories of the first, they did so not necessarily on the basis of literal correspondences but by way of figurative and unconscious processes. The "sunlight shifting through leaves" that captured Vorse's imagination might not have been lost on the naive spectator entranced by the narrative; on the contrary, the emotional absorption into the latter might have fed on such ephemeral details, images charged with a different past, with memories of loss.

Benjamin described this aspect of filmic reception with the metaphor of the "optical unconscious," insisting on the hidden, figurative dimension of film's "mimetic faculty."⁵⁰ The memory mobilized by the optical unconscious differs from any form of premeditated, discursive remembering or reminiscing; it belongs to the side of Proust's *mémoire involuntaire* or the Surrealists' exercises in "profane illumination" (and thus, by implication, to the realm of psychoanalysis). Generally, Benjamin is better known for placing the cinema on the other side of that distinction, since the cinema epitomized the expansion of the archive of voluntary memory at the expense of involuntary recollection, the destruction of spatio-temporal distance, and hence of the conditions of experience—the disintegration of the "aura." But he was above all concerned with redeeming the possibility of experience in an irrevocably transformed world, seeking it in the track of the very agencies of transformation—technology, fashion, consumer culture—in the accumulated debris of second nature. If the cinema has a place in this project, it is through the back door of the optical unconscious, through the camera's exploration of an "unconsciously permeated space," whether that space pertains to preindustrial nature or the naturalized settings of urban life: "Our taverns and city streets, our offices and furnished rooms, our train stations and factories appeared to have us locked up beyond hope. Then came film and exploded this prison-world with the dynamite of one-tenth seconds, so that now, in the midst of its far-flung ruins and debris, we calmly embark on adventurous travels."[51] Revealing the "natural" appearance of the capitalist everyday as an allegorical landscape, the cinema thus parallels the investigations of the Surrealists or the flaneur who seek in that landscape a mode of experience traditionally reserved for phenomena of an ostensibly more primary nature: "the metamorphosis of the object into a counterpart [*Gegenüber*]." In this process, as Habermas paraphrases Benjamin, "a whole field of surprising correspondences between animate and inanimate nature is opened up, wherein even *things* encounter us in the structures of frail intersubjectivity."[52]

If Benjamin's speculations bear on the question of the cinema's function as a public sphere, they do so in a twofold way. As an aesthetic category, the optical unconscious is more likely to erupt in some films or some genres, and during certain periods of film history rather than others. Thus, it would seem to be more germane to the cinema of attractions, to a mode of exhibition that allows for a more centrifugal, less textually predetermined reception of filmic images. As a category based on the history of human interaction with nature (*Naturgeschichte*), the optical unconscious would have had a heightened significance for groups like the new immigrants who encountered the impact of industrialization, urbanization and commodification in an accelerated, telescoped form—by lending expression to traumatic disjunctions in the social experience of nature.

If the cinema helped immigrants organize their experience on their own terms, then, not only by creating a space for the actualization of involuntary memory, of disjunctive layers of time and subjectivity, it also offered a collective forum for the production of fantasy, the capability of envisioning a different future. More than any entertainment of the period the cinema figured as the site of magical transformation—of things, people, settings, and situations. To transpose Howe's remark, it was "something of a joke" *and* "something of a miracle."[53] As utopian images of "America," fostered by oppression and deprivation in the Old Country, crumbled under the realities of immigrant life, the cinema to some extent absorbed the functions of the utopian imagination, albeit in a diminished, alienated, and depoliticized form. Immigrant testimonies suggest that fantasies of a better life mingled older hopes with more specifically modern dreams, promises of abundance with scenarios of mobility and self-transformation.[54] While advertising was promoting such scenarios with cynical hyperbole, the cinema rehearsed them in a more structural manner—with its peculiar form of perceptual identification, its dispersal of subjectivity across a multiplicity of objects. Kracauer describes the disposition of one who "lets himself be polymorphously projected in a movie theater": "As a fake Chinaman he sits in a fake opium den, turns into a well-trained dog who performs ridiculously clever acts to please a female star, gathers himself into an alpine storm, gets to be circus artist and lion at once."[55] The mobilization of the gaze that transcends physical laws as well as distinctions between subject and object, human and nonhuman nature, promises nothing less than the mobilization of the self, the transformation of seemingly fixed positions of social identity.

This mobilization, however, is promise and delusion in one. The projection of subjectivity onto the world of things, or their reflections, does not automatically open up correspondences, "structures of frail intersubjectivity." For Kracauer, who was both more familiar with and more skeptical vis-à-vis the cinema than Benjamin, this mode of reception entails just as much a sense of de-realization, isolation, and loss: "One forgets oneself gazing, and the big dark hole is animated with the semblance of a life that belongs to no one and consumes everyone." The subject consumed is of course the consumer, who adapts to the object of his or her desire mimetically, by the logic of reification.

We return here to the question raised toward the end of the previous chapter, concerning the intersection of cinema and consumer culture, particularly in view of the tensions, contradictions, and ambiguities in the development of the latter. I have discussed some aspects of this question under the general heading of the industrial-commercial public spheres—their simultaneous recognition and appropriation of hitherto unrepresented discourses of social experience, their initial instability and non-synchronicity. What remains difficult to ascertain is the pace at which these new structures and media of publicity were effective in implementing the ideological and economic tenets of consumer capitalism, or, conversely, the extent to which they were used in ways that enabled and prolonged an autonomous organization of ethnic working-class experience. Lizabeth Cohen, writing on Chicago during the 1920s, argues against the critical historians who assume that mass culture instantaneously "succeeded in integrating American workers into a mainstream, middle-class culture." Instead, she claims, the immigrants' encounter with new commodities and technologies of reproduction took on shapes that resisted that kind of homogenization and actually helped preserve older forms of collective identity, at least for some time. The phonograph, for instance, often accused of plugging the immigrant family into a national network of standardized taste, was put to quite different uses by Chicago workers. "In story after story they related how buying a victrola helped keep Polish or Italian culture alive by allowing people to play foreign-language records, often at ethnic gatherings." Thus, Cohen concludes, "owning a phonograph might bring a worker closer to mainstream culture, but it did not have to. A commodity could just as easily help a person reinforce ethnic or working class culture as lose it."[56]

The analogy between phonograph and cinema carries only so far, considering basic differences between the apparatuses, in particular the listener's greater degree of control over the process of reception (closer in kind to today's consumption of films on videotape). After all, phonographic recording, especially of foreign or ethnically specific music, still presumed the existence of a tradition independent of the product, and thus a community of listeners and potential participants. Yet early cinema depended crucially on familiarity with extratextual sources as well, at least until the final implementation of the classical paradigm. Furthermore, while record buyers might have had a wider choice among products, the emphasis on cinematic diversity persisted throughout the nickelodeon period, notwithstanding the dominance of the narrative film after 1907. As exhibitors reported in the trade press, scenics remained a favorite with audiences, and slapstick comedy, with its antisentimental, antiauthoritarian, and anticonsumerist appeal, survived the protests of gentrifiers and guardians of culture for many years.

Most important, unlike the victrola, the cinema was predicated on collective reception; it mandated reception in a public space. Even films designed to link the cinema to mainstream culture could be received differently depending on environment, audience composition, programming, and mode of exhibition; Vitagraph's *The Life of Moses* (1909–10), for instance, provoked a hardly mainstream response among Russian Jewish audiences.[57] To go further, I believe that even explicitly Christian films, like the Italian import *Quo*

Vadis? (1912), could have been reclaimed by such audiences. The relatively confused, elliptical narrative foregrounds the spectacle of religious persecution, graphic images of people huddling together against the onslaught of absolute and irrational power, making these images available for projective identification and reappropriation into the viewers' own memories.

The question of consumerism and public life, of industrially appropriated experience and the possibility of its reclamation, cannot be approached exclusively in terms of class and ethnic background. So far I have situated the cinema in relation to the historical dynamics of three distinct though overlapping types of public life: the remnants of a bourgeois public sphere (high culture, the Genteel Tradition); the new industrial-commercial public spheres (the modern entertainment market with its new middle-class, upwardly mobile, maximally inclusive clientele); and the ethnically segregated public spheres drawing on older traditions of working-class and peasant culture. The rest of this chapter focuses on a discourse that both overlays and interacts with these different types of organization: the definition of the demarcations between public and private along the lines of gender.

Women's "Passion for the Cinema": The Erosion of the Separate Spheres

The cinema's role in changing the boundaries and possibilities of public life was perhaps most pivotal for women, across—though related to—distinctions of class, racial and ethnic background, marital status, and generation.[58] Women's relations to the public sphere were governed by specific patterns of exclusion and abstraction, and the transformation of these patterns made a major difference in the conditions under which women could articulate and organize their experience. As outlined in the Introduction, the delimitation of public and private in terms of gender and sexuality was a central feature of the bourgeois public sphere in its European and American variants. From the 1820s and 1830s on, public life in the United States was a predominantly masculine arena to which women had access only in a highly controlled and dependent form. Accordingly, the private realm of the family came to be identified as the domain of an idealized femininity, defined by domesticity, motherhood, sexual purity, and moral guardianship. Throughout the nineteenth century the doctrine of separate spheres, the hierarchy of public/male over private/female, not only shaped—and maimed—relations between the sexes, but crucially determined the mappings of social life, of cultural institutions, itineraries of everyday life and leisure activities.[59]

The gender hierarchy of public and private structured the lives of middle-class and working-class women alike, though in different ways. Toward the end of the century, for instance, middle-class forms of leisure increasingly were becoming family-centered, that is, they encouraged women's patronage as long as they were contained within the family. At the same time, popular entertainments maintained strong segregation along gender lines: most institutions of working-class culture, such as ethnic saloons, burlesque shows, or sports events, remained exclusively male affairs; a woman could join only at the risk of her reputation. Certainly there were significant variations among immigrant groups (Germans, for instance, had no problem with women drinking in beer gardens); and many women, especially married ones, attended ethnic theaters, church-sponsored events, or the annual balls, picnics, and entertainments of their husbands' fraternal organizations.[60] By and large, however, the higher the social status of a commercial entertainment form, the more acceptable it became for mixed company; conversely, the ability of an establishment to attract reputable women emerged as the touchstone of middle-class respectability.

Authorized by middle-class observers and reformers, this syllogism was employed by entertainment entrepreneurs eager to attract a more affluent, upwardly mobile, and inclusive clientele. Vaudeville, in so many respects a model for the institution of cinema, is an excellent example of the dialectic of gender and status that was transforming the outlines of the public sphere. Pioneers of vaudeville gentrification, notably Tony Pastor, began to upgrade the reputation of the male-oriented variety shows by introducing "refined" matinees for "ladies" on weekday afternoons. By the 1880s and 1890s, evening shows too were refashioned to meet (middle-class) standards of feminine taste—by efforts to suppress working-class audience behavior, such as the ban on boisterous response, talking, drinking, and smoking, and to eradicate sexual innuendo and bawdy humor from the performance. As a back-up strategy, however, Pastor is reported to have hired prostitutes to dress up as "respectable" women and attend the shows so as to lure patrons "seeking a refined atmosphere." This ploy seems to have worked as well as the others. In the long run, Robert Allen writes, "vaudeville achieved its economic success by bringing women into its audience."[61]

That the appearance of respectability could be purchased, and that it was supplied by women who physically and ideologically figured as the repressed other of an idealized femininity, makes this anecdote symptomatic of the contradictions at work in the transformation of the public sphere. The invocation of middle-class notions of gentility in the effort to legitimize female participation in commercial entertainments testified to the erosion of the very demarcations these notions were founded upon, the gendered segregation of public and private spheres. This erosion was not happening in vaudeville alone. It was initiated, on a much larger scale, by the emergence of a consumer economy and attendant forms of culture and ideology.[62]

The new culture of consumption blurred class and ethnic divisions in an illusive community of abundance; it also undermined bourgeois divisions of public and private, above all the hierarchy of male and female spheres. Crucial to the shift from a production-centered economy to one of mass consumption was the female shopper whose numbers had increased ever since the Civil War. By 1915 "women were doing between 80 and 85 percent of the consumer purchasing in the United States."[63] For middle-class women this meant a liberation from the narrow confines of domestic space, but also, in the long run, the surrender of a traditionally female sphere of influence to the corporately organized empire of mass consumption. For working-class women, especially recent immigrants from Southern and Eastern Europe, consumerist styles and fashions—to the extent they could afford them—promised access to a modern, American world of freedom, romance, and upward mobility. At the same time, it was *their* cheap labor that enabled the mass manufacturing and sale of consumer goods.[64]

Although the rise of consumerism changed women's relationship to the public sphere fundamentally, it would be a mistake to consider consumer culture in itself as "public" in the emphatic sense of the word. It was, and continues to be, a direct function of the capitalist marketplace, of private property relations; and no doubt it aimed to transform social processes of identification and interaction into private acts of acquisition. But because of its industrial-commercial basis, consumer culture introduced a different principle of publicity than that governing traditional institutions, a more direct appeal to the customers' experience, to concrete needs, desires, fantasies. In catering to aspects of female experience that hitherto had been denied any public dimension, the media of consumption offered an intersubjective horizon for the articulation of that experience. Such a horizon was precarious and at best temporary, since the appeal to women as consumers fluctuated between experimental differentiation (to satisfy as many diverse constituencies as possible) and long-term homogenization (predicated on a notion of "woman" as white, heterosexual, and middle-class).

The emerging culture of consumption, centering on advertising and the department store, was flanked by the mushrooming commercial entertainments already mentioned—amusement parks like Coney Island, vaudeville, cabarets, dance halls, and, of course, the cinema. What distinguished these new forms of leisure from the traditions of both high culture and popular amusements, indeed the mark of their modernity, was that they encouraged the mingling of classes and genders. Despite the ideological character of such (self-)displays of equality, the mingling of genders must have had a greater significance for women, as a group whose movements and mode of social existence had been severely restricted by the homosocial arrangements of the traditional public spheres. Moreover, the styles of a heterosocial modernity promoted with the new leisure culture changed the definitions of female identity in relation to the family, superimposing the values of motherhood and domesticity with the appeals of pleasure, glamour, and eroticism. This shift in the social construction of femininity, generally associated with the discourse on the New Woman, exacerbated the rift between the generations, especially between immigrant mothers and their American-born or American-raised daughters. Yet it also loosened the circumscriptions of the domestic maternal role and self-image, not least because the same young working women who sought diversion outside the family and kinship networks tended to take up that role as soon as they married.[65]

More than any other entertainment form, the cinema opened up a space—a social space as well as a perceptual, experiential horizon—in women's lives, whatever their marital status, age, or background. As Kathy Peiss observes in her study of working women and leisure in turn-of-the-century New York, the cinema most strikingly "altered women's participation in the world of public, commercial amusements." With the rise of the nickelodeon, "women's attendance soared; women comprised 40 percent of the working-class movie audience in 1910."[66] Unlike vaudeville, even cheap or "family vaudeville," the movies offered women a more casual participation in the world of entertainments, an experience that could easily be incorporated into a variety of everyday itineraries and, at the same time, a relief from the monotony of housework. Thus, married women would drop into a movie theater on their way home from a shopping trip, a pleasure indulged in just as much by women of the more affluent classes. Schoolgirls filled the theaters during much of the afternoon, before returning to the folds of familial discipline. And young working women would find in the cinema an hour of diversion after work, as well as an opportunity to meet men. As a reporter for the *Chicago Daily Tribune* observed in 1907,

> Around 6 o'clock or just before that hour the character of the audiences in the lower State street shifted again. This time they were composed largely of girls from the big department stores, who came in with their bundles under their arms. . . . They remain . . . as late as 7 o'clock with the excuse that they have no other recreation and that the street cars are uncomfortably crowded at that time of the day. . . . It is certain they

frequently are found talking with men of mature years, whom they could not have met before going to the theaters. [67]

Although such encounters were precisely what the middle-class opponents of the nickelodeons objected to, within the working-class community, moviegoing was considered quite innocuous, certainly in comparison with dance halls and other heterosocial amusements. Especially among recent immigrants, the movements of daughters were highly circumscribed—not only by economic necessity but even more so by the behavioral double standard of the old-world patriarchal family. For young Italian women, as for the daughters of relatively more liberal East-European Jewish families, going to the movies several times a week was often the only unsupervised leisure activity they were permitted and could afford. Though less prestigious than the more expensive and permissive entertainments in the eyes of their peer group, moviegoing allowed even well-guarded immigrant daughters an opening into the emerging subculture of dating and treating. [68]

The cinema was a place women could frequent on their own, as independent customers, where they could experience forms of collectivity different from those centering on the family. Unlike mass-market fiction, which, much as it constituted a social horizon of experience, was still predicated on individual consumption in a private space, the cinema catered to women as an audience, as the subject of collective reception and public interaction. It thus functioned as a particularly female heterotopia, because, in addition to the heterotopic qualities already discussed, it "simultaneously represented, contested and inverted" the gendered demarcations of private and public spheres. The cinema provided for women, as it did for immigrants and recently urbanized working class of all sexes and ages, a space apart and a space in between. It was a site for the imaginative negotiation of the gaps between family, school, and workplace, between traditional standards of sexual behavior and modern dreams of romance and sexual expression, between freedom and anxiety. Bounded by familiar surroundings and culturally accepted, within the working-class community at least, the movie theater opened up an arena in which a new discourse on femininity could be articulated and the norms and codes of sexual conduct could be redefined. [69]

This arena consisted not merely of the theater's physical space and the social environment it assimilated, but crucially involved the phantasmagoric space on the screen, and the multiple and dynamic transactions between these spaces. Again, it is difficult to know how female viewers received and interpreted the films they saw, and although there are contemporary accounts of individual women's viewing habits (like the one by Vorse), it would be premature to generalize on the basis of such accounts.[70] But we can trace some of the ways in which the industry responded to the historically unprecedented formation of women as an audience, both in terms of the logic of supply and demand and in terms of strategies designed to contain the threat this new female audience posed to the patriarchal organization of the public sphere.

The problem confronted by the industry resulted from the overlap of different types of public sphere that we saw operating in the case of *The Corbett-Fitzsimmons Fight*. On the one hand, film production drew heavily on the subject matter, genres, and performance conventions of the popular entertainment tradition, including such male-oriented spectacles as the burlesque and the peep shows; on the other hand, the establishment of the cinema as an institution hinged upon its appeal to an inclusive, heterosocial mass audience. In the eyes of middle-class reformers and advocates of censorship this overlap was at the very core of the nickelodeon problem— in the unruly conjunction of previously restricted sexually suggestive material on the screen and the large number of women in front of the screen, along with the permissive behavior that might be going on during the screening. The problem was compounded by the high proportion of juveniles in motion picture audiences: in a New York survey of 1911, 33 percent of all moviegoers were boys and girls under eighteen (as compared to 19 percent in vaudeville audiences). The writer in the *Chicago Tribune* cited earlier complains about the popularity of *The Unwritten Law* (Lubin, 1907), a reenactment of the notorious Thaw-White murder case (involving seduction and scandal), with the schoolgirl crowd: "A good many grown women got up and went out before the completion of the series. It shocked them. But the girls remained."

Following the model of vaudeville, the gentrifiers of cinema sought to make the shows acceptable to middle-class standards of feminine taste—at the same time as they promoted female patronage as an indicator of middle-class respectability. But the industry's efforts were not merely defensive, aimed at pacifying public opinion. Rather, both exhibitors and producers began to cater to female audiences more aggressively, appealing to women on the basis of particular intertexts and ideological discourses, with particular genres, stars and sentiments. Throughout the 1910s these attempts to respond to and expand an existing market betray an experimental quality and thus register both the upheaval of public and private in terms of gender and sexuality and the generation gap resulting from it. A well-known example of films addressing a new type of female audience, specifically young working women, were the serials, such as *The Hazards of Helen* (Kalem, 1914 on), which featured adventurous, physically active heroines. Drawing on successful columns in women's magazines, fashion journals, and newspapers, the serials located pleasure in images of female competence, courage, and physical movement (often involving triumphant transactions between women and technology, especially trains) that marked a striking distance from Victorian ideals of femininity.[71]

Alongside this more modern, egalitarian discourse the appeal to women on the basis of domestic ideology—sexual purity, passivity, emotional superiority, and moral guardianship—persisted in various guises and blends: in genres like melodrama, which tried to manage the breakdown of the separate spheres; in virginal stars like Lillian Gish and Mary Pickford; and even in the work of women directors like Alice Guy Blaché, Ida May Park, and Lois Weber who used the rhetoric of domesticity to justify their position in a predominantly male industry. The appeal to women viewers in terms of essential feminine virtues also structured films of an ostensibly gender-neutral, political concern, like the films debating the U.S. entry into the war, whether their message was pacifist (as in Ince's *Civilization* and Brenon's *War Brides*) or prointerventionist (as in Blackton's *The Battle Cry of Peace*).[72] Yet, in other genres, such as films dramatizing the fate of the fallen woman, the cult of true womanhood was invoked ideologically only to be challenged by strategies of representation and address: the appeal to the viewer to sympathize with the victims of social circumstance—or even to identify with the morally condemned exercise of female sexual power—necessarily "blurred the distinction between true women and their fallen counterparts."[73]

In the long run, the contradictions between the New Woman and the old, like tensions within the ideology of domesticity itself, were submerged in the consumerist discourse that had enabled the public articulation of competing models of female identity in the first place. No longer grounded in the topography of separate spheres, domesticity was updated for an age of technology and consumption. As Mary Ryan observes with regard to 1920s films, the "mischievous vivacity" of the flapper, the vitality of stars like Clara Bow, Madge Bellamy, or Gloria Swanson, increasingly served to instruct the female viewer "on how to become *correctly* modern, . . . to train the female audience in fashionable femininity."[74] And the accidental transgressions of the homosocial taboo that had troubled the arbiters of early cinema came to inspire the more systematic appropriation of female desire at work in the marketing of stars like Valentino or the films of Cecil B. DeMille. The integration of the female address with the culture of consumption not only seems to have leveled generational differences among various types of address, but also caused the dialectic of domesticity and consumerism that had propelled the transformation of public and private spheres to collapse.

That the cinema came to function as a powerful catalyst for this transformation, that films could effectively determine the way they were received on a mass-cultural scale, hinges upon the paradigmatic shift from early to classical cinema—and the concomitant differentiation of the spectator as a hypothetical term of the film's discourse from the empirical viewer as a member of a plural, social audience. The creation of such a spectator involved the stylistic elaboration of a consistent yet *indirect* mode of address that granted the viewer access to the diegesis from a position of voyeuristic immunity and fetishistic distance. From a feminist perspective, however, the imbrication of the cinematic apparatus with psychic mechanisms of voyeurism and fetishism means yoking the spectator position to traditionally masculine perversions; these epitomize the patriarchal hierarchy of vision that constitutes the man as agent and the woman as prime object and challenge of the gaze.[75] If this scopic economy is inscribed in the *structural* organization of classical cinema, in the spectator's interaction with the film on both conscious and unconscious levels, it must have been operative, in tendency at least, during the transitional period, at the same time that the cinema was assuming a major social function for women across class and ethnic boundaries.

How do we account for this seeming paradox, posed by the intersection of history and theory, of, on the one hand, women's increased significance for the film industry as fans and consumers and, on the other, the systematic imposition, on the textual level, of masculine forms of subjectivity, of a patriarchal choreography of vision? In her study of the 1940s woman's film Mary Ann Doane argues that the paradox of women's simultaneous agency and subjection turns upon the logic of reification, the consumer's mimetic empathy with the commodity. Like Kracauer before her, Doane sees the specific link between consumerism and film spectatorship in a "curiously passive desiring subjectivity," a desire defined by narcissism and a fixation on appearances. More explicitly than Kracauer, she relates this form of subjectivity to the cultural construction of the feminine, traditionally aligned with affects of empathy and over-identification. In its simultaneous appeal to the female consumer and assertion of a patriarchal hierarchy of vision, she concludes, classical cinema reduces female desire to positions of narcissism and masochism, making her the subject of a transaction designed to turn her into a commodity.[76]

This analysis undoubtedly pinpoints a powerful ideological mechanism, but its historical implementation complicates the issue. There has been a tendency in feminist film theory, especially approaches indebted to Lacanian psychoanalysis, to take the imposition of patriarchal structures of vision and desire as an expression of an essential and ostensibly timeless symbolic order (and thus, on the methodological level, as a somewhat predictable and ultimately inevitable conclusion). I consider the codification of such structures a defensive symptom, a reaction against the historical challenge the cinema presented to the gendered hierarchy of private and public spheres. The force of this reaction testifies to the power of the patriarchal tradition, but it also indicates the extent of the crisis unleashed by women's massive ascendance to a new horizon of experience.

The challenge to the gendered hierarchy of the public sphere violated a taboo that predated bourgeois sexual arrangements: the taboo on the active female gaze that pervaded traditions of representation in art, mythology, and everyday life. If modern advertising and the department store had mobilized the female gaze in the service of consumption, the cinema seemed to have institutionalized women's scopophilic consumption as an end in itself, thus posing a commercially fostered threat to the male monopoly of the gaze. The conflict between economic opportunism and patriarchal ideology provoked a profound ambivalence toward the female spectator—as a subjectivity simultaneously solicited and feared, all the more so because of its collective dimensions.

The ambivalence toward the female gaze—as a manifestation of the power clustering around the female consumer—was especially acute in men like Griffith, whose own relationship with the mass market was fairly problematic (even when he seemed to have conquered it). Griffith's obsession with a sense of femininity in crisis is at the heart of *Intolerance*, a film that dramatizes the fate—and fatal power—of unmarried female characters throughout the ages. This crisis of femininity not only precipitates the multiple catastrophes in the diegesis, increasingly so as the film gets closer to the modern era; it also destabilizes the film's textual system, unraveling its self-consciously ingenious architectonic structure. The very deployment of the gaze as the medium of cinematic subjectivity is contaminated with the power of the perverted female look. This hampers the film's effectivity in engaging the spectator—or creating a coherent spectator position at all— at least by the standards of the emerging classical paradigm.

Throughout the transitional period and beyond, the implementation of classical codes was accompanied by allegories rehearsing at once the empowerment and containment of the female gaze, of female desire in general. This dynamic can be observed through a variety of textual figurations, ranging from Porter's Goldilocks through the figure of the Vamp epitomized by the marvelous Theda Bara, from the spinster and prostitute in *Intolerance* through the flapper of the 1920s. The drama played out in the field of cinematic vision echoes the chiasmus effect Jackson Lears discerns in the shifting gender connotations of advertising. If nineteenth-century advertising had attracted the consumer with images of abundance envisioned as feminine and maternal, the spirit that presided over twentieth-century consumption was the male genius of mass production.[77] Similarly, one could argue, the alternative public sphere that began to crystallize around the abundance of female moviegoing was harnessed by the structural masculinization of the spectator position endemic to classical cinema. However, as the cinema sought to align its appeal to women audiences with a prevailing patriarchal order of vision, it both recognized and absorbed discourses of experience that conflicted with the latter, thus reproducing the conditions for the articulation of female subjectivity along with the strategies for its containment.

Most important, the alignment of female spectatorship with a gendered hierarchy of vision was as complex and contradictory a process as the implementation of the classical system in general, neither as instantaneously effective nor ever as complete as film theorists have made it seem. If, in the fissures and detours of this process, the cinema assumed the function of an alternative horizon of experience for a large number of women, it was enabled by the same conditions that were working in favor of working-class and immigrant audiences: the instability of the cinema as an industrial-commercial public sphere, conflicts between short-term economic and long-range ideological interests, and the uneven development of modes of production, representation, and exhibition. Thus, the discrepancy between film experience and theater experience I have elaborated must have played as much a part for women audiences as for other groups, if not more so, given the structural problematic of a textually anchored female address, its incompatibility with the masculine inscription of the gaze.

The industry's catering to the female consumer seems to have focused more unequivocally on "the discursive apparatus surrounding the film than the text itself," as, for instance, fan magazines devoted to "the purportedly female obsession with stars, glamour, gossip and fashionability."[78] While such discourses were designed to enhance the consumption of films on a national scale, they still belonged to the sphere of exhibition—to the side of locally specific, socially, and culturally differentiated audiences and to the side of the "show," of singular and to some extent unpredictable performances. The star system in particular harbored this bifurcation, since it was predicated on the oscillation between filmic and extrafilmic discourses. As we shall see in the case of Valentino, the female address was lodged on two levels—the publicity surrounding the star as well as textual strategies which thematized the contradictions of female spectatorship. Although these two sets of discourses were crucially intertwined, the cult they had spawned took on a momentum of its own, eluding the control of its industrial promoters. Thus, the historical reception of Valentino opened up a public horizon for women's experience, marked by the contradictory dynamic of entrenched sexual and racial hierarchies and the consumerist appropriation of female desire.

Finally, if we accept the hypothesis of feminist film theory that the classical apparatus renders the place of the female spectator a "locus of impossibility,"[79] there is yet another turn to the argument about the cinema as an alternative public sphere. The mismatch between the female spectator and the subject of classical cinema, her notorious over-identification with the image and structural alienation from the symbolic order rehearsed by the narrative, makes way for a mode of reception that is potentially in excess of textually constructed positions of subjectivity. It is no coincidence that, even at this early point in film history, female spectators were depicted as excessive, whether on account of their obstreperous headgear (*Those Awful Hats* [Griffith/Biograph, 1908]) or their unsuitable, hysterical behavior, as in *Rosalie et Léonce à théâtre* (Gaumont, 1910).[80]

Doane sees this peculiarly female mode of reception predicated on the consumerist glance, which "hovers over the surface of the image, isolating details which may be entirely peripheral in relation to the narrative. It is a fixating, obsessive gaze which wanders in and out of the narrative and has a more intimate relation to space—the space of rooms and of bodies—than with the temporal dimension."[81] I share her observation, but I do not think that this type of gaze is entirely rationalized by the subsidiary strategies surrounding the film (the purpose of consumption), nor would I emphasize its diminished sense of time. As I have argued, the cinema allowed for the experience of competing temporalities, especially on the part of people who bore the brunt of modernization. The gaze distracted by the lure of consumption may not keep up with the pace of linear narrative, but it may feed on other registers of time and experience, linked to involuntary memory and associational processes in the spectator's head—the register of the "optical unconscious."

In her 1914 dissertation on motion picture audiences, German sociologist Emilie Altenloh found that women viewers of all classes and ages responded more strongly to the synaesthetic and kinetic aspects of films, and that they were more likely than men to forget the plot or title of a film but vividly remember sentimental situations as well as images of waterfalls, ocean waves, and drifting ice floes. Similarly, Iris Barry defends her own passion for the cinema, asserting in 1926 that "even in the crudest films something is provided for the imagination, and emotion is stirred by the simplest things—moonlight playing in a bare room, the flicker of a hand against a window."[82] And Virginia Woolf, in an essay published the same year, speaks of those rare moments, when, "at the cinema in the midst of its immense dexterity and enormous technical proficiency, the curtain parts and we behold, far off, some unknown and unexpected beauty."[83] The gaze that is captured by such ephemeral images is certainly not of an essentially female, let alone feminine quality, nor are these images untouched by social meaning, even and especially in their distance from a social reality that exerted increasing control over the production of experience. But if this mode of reception was more typical of female audiences, it should be theorized as a historically significant formation of spectatorship.

Just as the imposition of patriarchal structures of vision and narration appears as a response to the unprecedented mobilization of the female gaze, so is female spectatorship inevitably constituted in relation to dominant subject positions, compensating for its structural impossibility with a greater mobility and multiplicity of identifications. Yet the gap confronted by women—or, for that matter, other groups alienated from dominant positions of subjectivity—is neither accidental nor merely personal, nor just another variant of the general dynamic of misrecognition that constitutes the subject in Lacanian theory. It is part of their historical and social experience as women, contingent on sexual preference, class, race, and ethnic background. Whether it can be interpreted as such—and thus be reclaimed by the experiencing subjects—depends upon, or is a measure of, the extent to which the cinema functions as an alternative public sphere. Although this alternative function cannot be measured in any empirical sense, the conditions of its possibility can be reconstructed. At the same time, a tradition of female spectatorship can be traced through concrete historical manifestations—such as fan cults surrounding stars of both sexes, women's clubs engaged in film-cultural activities, or the numerous women playing the piano in movie theaters as well as women writing on film— in short, a variety of configurations, often ambiguous and contradictory, in which women not only experienced the misfit of the female spectator in relation to patriarchal positions of subjectivity but also developed imaginative strategies in response to it.

Babel in Babylon:
D. W. Griffith's Intolerance (1916)

II

Reception, Textual System,
and Self-Definition

. . . .

4

I tried in Part I to situate the question of spectatorship within a broader historical argument. Part II closes the heuristic focus down to the level of a single film: Griffith's *Intolerance*. Methodologically, this means that I proceed by and large from a textual analysis, tracing possible relations between film and viewer through patterns of representation and address. It does not mean, however, that the textually inscribed, hypothetical relations of reception are limited to the formal parameters of spectatorship. Instead I will develop, from the film's textual idiosyncrasies, obsessions, and pressure points, a possible horizon of reception in terms of the issues traversed in Part I: the emergence of the classical paradigm; the notion of film as a new universal language; the cinema's status as a public sphere; the upheaval of traditional demarcations of gender and sexuality. This horizon of reception can be no more and no less than an interpretive construction, a suggestion of constellations in light of which the film assumes a complex historical significance.

To pursue questions of spectatorship and reception with a reading of *Intolerance* may seem somewhat paradoxical, considering that the film has the reputation of having been the "first" major box-office disaster in the history of American cinema. *Intolerance* presents a challenge not least because of its alleged failure, which needs to be reexamined in light of issues already developed in this book. Initially the film did not do badly at all. Released with unprecedented advance publicity, it drew large crowds following its New York opening on September 5, 1916; after the first eleven weeks in Chicago, it had broken the record of *The Birth of a Nation*. With very few exceptions, notably Alexander Woollcott's devastating review in the *New York Times*, the critical response was enthusiastic, though often defensively aware of a conflict between the film's advance in motion picture "art" and its

potential of "popular appeal." Yet after four months' running time, attendance began to drop in every major city, and it became obvious that *Intolerance* could not match the sustained box-office success of films it had been
compared to, such as *Civilization* (Thomas Ince, 1916), *The Dumb Girl of Portici*
(Lois Weber, 1915), or Griffith's own *Birth*.[1]

With its curious pattern of reception—initial success and subsequent
inability to maintain box-office momentum—the film throws into relief
diverging concepts of representation and spectatorship at a historically
crucial juncture, the threshold of Hollywood's classical period. In the long
run, however, the failure of *Intolerance* became one of the standard myths of
American film history; as such it helped legitimize the very tradition whose
norms it had once called into question. Cultivated by Griffith himself and
largely exaggerating the financial and personal consequences of the event,
the myth of failure has enshrined *Intolerance* as a "classic" of film history, as a
monument that marks both a limit and a solitary peak of classical cinema.
The rhetorical elevation, like the publicity surrounding the film's initial
release, resorts to hyperbolic cliché—"the world's largest film, . . . [the]
proof and triumph of American film power" (Seymour Stern)—or, more
often, to oxymoronic constructions, such as "a magnificent failure" (Terry
Ramsaye), "a towering compound of greatness and cheapness" (Jay Leyda),
"a baroque work of confusion and genius" (Jean Mitry).[2] Whatever their
degree of complexity, most attempts to vindicate *Intolerance* as a failed masterpiece tend to isolate the film from its institutional and historical contexts,
or at best reduce these contexts to a few milestones in the evolution of film
language, mostly Griffith's own. Accordingly, the textual difference of *Intolerance* rests on the uniqueness of Griffith's technical and artistic genius.

Revisionist historians have argued in recent years that the "masterpiece
approach" in film history has often served an ideological function for the
hegemony of classical cinema, a function to which *Intolerance* lent itself in
more than one way.[3] In the founding narrative of classical cinema, perpetuated by the standard film histories, the film usually occupies one of two
mutually exclusive places. Philip Rosen sums up one version of this narrative: "The classical cinema has a genius father (Griffith), a first-born (*Birth of
a Nation*) and a magnificent freak (*Intolerance*)."[4] While the "magnificence" of
the film is generally attributed to Griffith's visionary power, its failure is
often discussed in terms of particular "mistakes"—such as the excess of
spectacle over narrative, of theme over character, of sentiment over
motivation—judgments that implicitly validate the norms of the classical
paradigm as timeless, objective, and natural.

Another variant of this story, in a sense closer to Freud's notion of the "family romance," reverses the hierarchy between *Birth* and *Intolerance* and reclaims the later film as the unrecognized child of a nobler lineage, a prodigy who in turn fathers the "true" if still somewhat underground tradition of American cinema. Such clearly was the message of the revival of *Intolerance* during the 1930s, notably by the Museum of Modern Art in 1936. Iris Barry, then curator of the Museum's newly established Film Library, praised the film as "the end and justification of that whole school of American cinematography based on the terse cutting and disjunctive assembly," a heritage that had inspired the Soviet tradition of montage.[5] By 1939 Lewis Jacobs would assert that *Intolerance* had been restored to "its rightful position as the peak in American movie making, the consummation of everything that preceded it and the beginning of profound new developments in the motion picture art."[6] In contrast to later writers who denied—or simply ignored—the difference between *Intolerance* and mainstream American cinema,[7] the critics who helped revive the film explicitly endorsed this difference, claiming it for the tradition of an alternative film culture. Yet during the later 1940s, with the beginning of the Cold War and McCarthyism, the project of an alternative film culture was tacitly absorbed into the discourse of art cinema, or else it remained confined within an experimental subculture. It is no coincidence that during that time *Intolerance* also became a site of political realignment, its reputation sliding from that of a milestone of "social realism" (Jacobs, Agee) to that of a keystone in Seymour Stern's paranoid construction of "American film supremacy."[8]

If the commercial failure of *Intolerance* made the film available for conflicting causes and positions, its status in the masterpiece and art film discourse may in turn be responsible for blocking any serious critical debate on the film. This is not to deny the value of individual interpretations by a variety of scholars and critics, but the film has not provoked the detailed, theoretically inspired readings that have been undertaken over the past decade for the work of director-auteurs like Hitchcock, Ford, or Welles.[9] Nor does it fare better in the discipline of film history, considering the revisionist shift away from a genealogy of masterpieces or first usages to a reconstruction of interdependent stylistic and economic developments that make up the institution of cinema. This shift inevitably—and necessarily—centers on the so-called normal or typical film, the "quietly conformist film." The difference of *Intolerance*, accordingly, can be discussed only in terms of random deviations from the classical paradigm.[10] Eluding the preoccupations of both theory and history, the film's textual idiosyncrasy, its historical moment, and its complex and troubled relationship with the institution for the most part have remained unexplored.

Reading *Intolerance*, therefore, requires a dual focus which maintains a tension between idiosyncrasy and historicity, two terms that should emerge as thoroughly mediated and inseparable. This task involves, among other things, subjecting the film to questions alien to its self-definition, questions ostensibly preempted by the special status asserted for and by the film. How, for instance, does *Intolerance* compare to conventions of narration widely accepted by 1916? How does the film articulate space in narrative terms, and how does it position the viewer in relation to that process? What types of identification does it encourage—or deny—and how are they organized along the lines of gender, class, and nationality? How, in short, does *Intolerance* relate to the horizon of expectation of the average viewer, insofar as such a horizon can be historically reconstructed?[11]

The question of historicity also pertains to the implications of the film's failure for the course of film history, especially its unrealized possibilities. Which modes of narration and address, which types of film-viewer relations, were discarded and relegated to the archaeology of cinema? Like certain aspects of early cinema, *Intolerance* offers "a number of roads not taken," ambiguities eliminated from commercial narrative cinema, which however need not to be seen as "history's dead-end streets."[12] Without succumbing to a teleology in reverse, one cannot avoid reading *Intolerance* from a perspective of the present, along the vanishing lines of a tradition of alternative filmmaking that includes names like Dziga Vertov, Sergei Eisenstein, Jean-Luc Godard, Alexander Kluge and Chantal Akerman. These names (others might be added) stand not just for stylistic alternatives to mainstream film but, more important, for an alternative organization of experience, both through film and in the cinema. They project a different organization of the public sphere.[13]

If *Intolerance* asks to be read in this tradition, it is not because Griffith would have anticipated or shared the political and theoretical underpinnings of later oppositional film practices. The gap that opens up between the conception of a public sphere implied in *Intolerance* and the type of public sphere emerging with the classical paradigm seems to have more to do with a certain anachronism in Griffith's self-image as a narrator, with his particular psychosexual obsessions and his idealistic vision of the cinema in relation to other institutions of culture. At the same time, this anachronism is unthinkable without the contemporaneity of the means and modes of expression, the technology of film and its mass-cultural distribution. This nonsynchronous mixture, which Eisenstein described as a disjunction between Griffith the Victorian and Griffith the modernist, left *Intolerance* stranded between the branches of film history, a gigantic ruin of modernity.[14]

Reading *Intolerance* presents the same difficulties as reading any film—difficulties owing to the specific temporality of cinematic projection and reception, to the constitutive split between moving image and discontinuous discrete frames.[15] Such difficulties are exacerbated if not epitomized by the peculiar impact of *Intolerance*. It is no coincidence that the film has been described, over time, either in metaphors of ruins, quarry, and archaeology, or, often simultaneously, in metaphors of rivers, torrents, a cataract—as flooding the screen and drowning the viewer in an "intense hail of images."[16] To this day, even the most analytic reader of *Intolerance* will find it hard not to feel engulfed in its maelstrom of images, not to get shipwrecked between the film's will to coherence and its sheer diversity. Exhaustion, irritation and revenge may not be the worst motives to fuel the work of textual reclamation—as necessary as the draining of the Zuider Zee—but they should also remind the reader not to lose touch with the experiential undercurrent.

Another, more pragmatic difficulty pertains to the textual basis of this enterprise. The prints of *Intolerance* circulated by the Museum of Modern Art are about 1,670 to 1,870 feet shorter than the version released in 1916 (which was itself reduced from a first cut of eight hours). Griffith not only kept revising the print during the film's first runs, gauging audience response, but worse, he cut up the original negative in 1919 and recycled part of the footage in two separate films, *The Fall of Babylon* and *The Mother and the Law*. Upon a request from England, Griffith reedited *Intolerance* in 1922 from memory, since there had never been a shooting script; it is this version that he later donated to the Museum of Modern Art. The Museum recently presented a reconstructed version of the film, aiming to recreate the film as it premiered in New York in September 1916. Given the instability of the text even prior to its 1919 mutilation, as well as the significant historical impact of the 1922 version, such a reconstruction necessarily privileges one, albeit a relatively less arbitrary moment in the film's history; it cannot—nor does it pretend to—"restore" the work in a supposedly timeless originality.[17]

Since a description of *Intolerance* remains provisional at best, I might as well begin with those aspects of the film that everyone seems to agree upon, bearing in mind that the description of any film presents what Stephen Heath calls "an intolerable necessity": "intolerable because it has to be tolerated against the grain of the film; necessity because it answers to the 'intolerance' of the film itself."[18] *Intolerance* consists of four distinct narratives, all set in different historical periods and parts of the world, interlaced with each other through parallel montage. A modern American narrative traces the fate of a young couple through the vicissitudes of a labor struggle, tenement violence, false charity, and an inhumane legal and penal system. A

French narrative dramatizes the Saint Bartholemew's Day Massacre (A.D. 1572) through the destruction of one Huguenot family, focusing on the daughter and her fiancé on the eve of their wedding. Episodes set in Judea evoke the life and passion of Jesus Christ. And the Fall of Babylon to Cyrus (538 B.C.) is narrated mostly from the point of view of a young girl in love with Belshazzar, himself about to marry a foreign princess. As these plot strands are intercut in an increasingly rapid rhythm, enhanced by accelerated crosscutting within each narrative (except the Judean), the historical episodes culminate in slaughter and catastrophe. Only the modern story ends happily, with the young husband saved from the gallows in the nick of time.

In addition to these narratives, *Intolerance* contains materials that are diegetically unrelated to any single epoch, meaning that they do not belong to any particular story space: a visionary epilogue of about twenty shots presenting images of warfare and oppression that dissolve into images of harmony, bliss, and millennial peace; a number of intertitles that either instruct the viewer as to the organization of the plot or point out analogies between different narratives—for example, "equally intolerant hypocrites of another age" [514][19]; recurring shots that emphasize the theme and furnish transitions between the different narratives (the title-card of the Book of Intolerance, the emblem of the Woman Who Rocks the Cradle); as well as graphically distinct title-cards for each of the three historical narratives.

As film historians of various backgrounds and persuasions have asserted over the decades, the uniqueness of *Intolerance* rests on its combination of parallel and accelerated montage—subcodes of editing which no doubt are crucial to the design of the film. This emphasis has remained unquestioned, even by proponents of supposedly more rigorous methods of textual analysis, notably Christian Metz in *Langage et cinéma* (1971). Metz uses *Intolerance* to illustrate the imbrication of "cinematic" and "non-cinematic codes"—for example, the encounter between parallel montage and Griffith's "humanitarian ideology"—in a singular textual system. [20] Although Metz insists that the "textual system" is always an analytic construct (as opposed to a structure inherent in the film itself), he covertly relies on received opinions of film history, treating them as if they were established facts. David Bordwell argues that Metz fails to historicize the particular subcodes at work in—and worked by—*Intolerance*: "How do we know that this particular conjunction of accelerated montage and parallel montage is a reworking of two subcodes and not itself a single subcode? Even if it is a reworking, how do we know that it is unique to this film? Furthermore, how do we know that the subcodes of accelerated and parallel montage are the salient ones? How do we know that subcodes of lighting, acting, shot-scale, etc. are less significant in the mixture that is the film?"[21]

A lack of historical awareness is not the only problem with Metz's remarks on *Intolerance*. His reading of the film fails even by the standards of immanent textual analysis, assuming for the moment that such analysis is possible or desirable. Parallel and accelerated montage are not merely analytical terms that may—or may not—be useful in describing the idiosyncrasy of *Intolerance*; parallelism (more explicitly than acceleration) is also the film's most manifest intention, the term by which the film *defines itself* as a textual system. Like many traditional film historians, Metz takes this self-definition at face value, assumes it to be the key to the filmic system (a concept previously defined as "an ultimate principle of unification and intelligibility"), and then, not surprisingly, arrives at a pejorative assessment of *Intolerance* as a "primarily univocal," "closed," "simple" film. Untouched by the more radical implications of his own notion of textual displacement, or by his speculations on cinema and writing later in the same book, Metz's reading of *Intolerance* reproduces the familiar confusion of textual process with manifest structure. [22]

Instances of self-definition in *Intolerance*, indeed the whole arsenal of meta-fictional discourse, are just as much part of the text as the seemingly less self-conscious aspects of the narration. In their excessive urge to regulate the latter, they compound—rather than resolve—the difficulties of the film. The prologue titles introduce parallelism as the organizing principle of the film, preparing the viewer for the heterogeneity of the narrative(s): "Our play is made up of four separate stories, laid in different periods of history, each with its own set of characters." Before a textual gap has even opened, the next title assures the viewer of an underlying coherence of theme: "Each story shows how hatred and intolerance, through all the ages, have battled against love and charity." This thematic continuity in turn motivates and justifies the discontinuity caused by the interlacing of the discrete narratives: "Therefore you will find our play turning from one of the four stories to another, as the common theme unfolds in each."

With these instructions, the film defines and acknowledges its double strategy. On the fictional level meaning is supposed to evolve gradually with the development of the individual stories and their interplay across the historical periods. Posited as analogous by parallel editing, the connotations of the fictional material are expected to merge and form another level of narration, a metaphysical level, whose meaning subsumes and transcends the mere contingencies of history. Ostensibly *Intolerance* relies on the self-evidence of its narrative images and their inherent ability to convey an unequivocal, identical meaning. Yet this meaning has been written before the film begins, anchored in a symbolic discourse which ordains the film's construction and which materializes in the metafictional intertitles, the Book of Intolerance, the emblem of the Cradle, and the epilogue.

Thus, the system that is the film's most manifest intention is at the same time the source of a potential crisis. In attempting to join the two levels of narration, *Intolerance* puts itself at the mercy of textual forces that threaten to pull the film in opposite directions. While parallel editing asserts a unity of theme in the overall design of the film, it has a quite different effect in the step-by-step interweaving of the narratives, in the detailed and manifold cross-references between periods. The "gravity"[23] of *Intolerance* undoubtedly results from the latter: from extended variations on thematic motifs such as courtship, erotic triangles, and sexual exchange or the abuse of social and political power; from similarities of situations, characters, and character constellations, even of minute gestures and expressions. These variations suggest an amazing web of possible, often overdetermined, often indeterminate, ambiguous, and contradictory relations, a many-layered palimpsest rather than a system in the Metzian sense. The question, whether "it all coheres" (Ezra Pound) or whether, as Eisenstein argues, the elements of *Intolerance* remain basically uncollatable, is undecidable if not ultimately inadequate, because the relations in question depend upon a term that is both inside and outside the film, both a function of the text and the condition of its intelligibility—the spectator.

By 1916 the spectator was no longer an unknown figure, but a concept that had emerged with the stylistic and narrative conventions of the classical mode. To recall Kristin Thompson's argument, these conventions were the result, not of an organic evolution of techniques and styles, but of a paradigmatic "shift in assumptions about the relation of spectator to film and the relation of a film's form to its style."[24] Norms of unobtrusive and linear narration, of compositional unity and character-centered motivation had been developed to enhance the effect of a self-contained fictional world which the viewer could enter from an ideal vantage point. The reception of a film would thus no longer depend upon the composition of particular audiences, their social identity and cultural background, but could be anticipated and standardized by conventions of narrative and editing. To what extent individual films actually conformed to this model is another matter, and *Intolerance* was probably not the only film that deviated from classical norms. Still, the model had been formulated in manuals and other writings and was being elaborated in film practice through particular strategies of narration.

Given this awareness, the choice of a narrative model based on parallelism harbored a certain anachronism and risked conflicting with the norms that Griffith himself had tested so effectively in *Birth*. Cutting back and forth between independent lines of action meant disrupting the linear flow of the narrative, which called attention to the act of narration and jeopardized the diegetic effect. Where parallel narration was used successfully during the transitional period, as in George Loane Tucker's remarkable feature film *Traffic in Souls* (Universal, 1913), it was subordinated to narrative functions—suspense, ramifications of the plot, the topography of surveillance. *Intolerance*, by contrast, harks back to earlier instances of parallelism—Porter's *The Kleptomaniac* (1905), or Griffith's *The Song of the Shirt* (1908), *A Corner in Wheat* (1909), and *Gold Is Not All* (1910)—in which the parallel construction was geared toward a conceptual point, an argument of a social, political, and aesthetic nature. This preoccupation with message ran counter to the growing tendency of narrative film to organize patterns of linear causality around individual characters and their psychology, allowing ideology to work, all the more insidiously, underground. In refusing to submerge the conceptual in the personal, however, Griffith also renounced strategies of viewer identification that had already proven their success at the box office, strategies centering on the dynamic of character, individual personality, and star.[25]

The feature-length revival of parallelism at a point when the classical paradigm was already more or less in place involved a definite abstention from such strategies—if not a conscious option for an altogether different concept of spectatorship. By 1916 the stakes in this choice were certainly higher than only a few years earlier, a risk of which Griffith was quite aware:

> I have endeavored to make the incidents which I have shown on the screen of such a nature that the audience on viewing the picture conceives and elaborates the story in his [sic] mind. In other words, the greatest value of the picture will be in its suggestive value to the audience, in the manner in which it will force it to create and work out the idea that I am trying to get over. I have made little or no attempt to tell a story, but I have made an attempt to suggest a story, and to my mind, it is a mighty big story. Whether or not it will succeed in its object remains to be seen.[26]

Like some of his critics, Griffith understood that parallelism undermines the diegetic effect, the effect of continuity and presence that ensures the viewer's temporary belief in the truth of the fiction. Instead of relying on the identity and positivity of its images, *Intolerance* invests meaning in the gaps between its diverse fictional materials, requiring the viewer to make the connections. This shift in emphasis, however, invited a return of early modes of spectatorship, readmitting the variability factor of empirical audiences which proponents of the classical paradigm had been striving to minimize and control. [27]

Such regression was not intended. The deviations of *Intolerance* were put forth as an experimental though logical advance in film aesthetics. If classical narrative promoted the impression of doubling a preexisting reality (history "as it really happened," or the world of a novel), Griffith sought to justify his new method by claiming an analogy with the workings of the human mind. Reviewers interested in aesthetic questions quickly elaborated on this analogy, citing it to defend the film against charges of incoherence and violations of dramatic unity. In a follow-up review in *The New York Dramatic Mirror*, Frederick James Smith responded to critics like Woollcott:

> Let us, once for all, consider the argument, advanced by a number of theatrical reviewers, that "Intolerance" is incoherent. These critics, knowing little or nothing of the screen drama, are puzzled by the film spectacle's lack of so-called dramatic technique. Indeed, the screen authorities seem puzzled by its variance with accepted script standards.
>
> Mr. Griffith himself explains this point. "Events are not set forth in their historical sequence, or according to accepted forms of dramatic construction, but *as they might flash across a mind seeking to parallel the life of the different ages.*"[28]

To back up Griffith's claim, Smith invokes the scholarly authority of Hugo Munsterberg who had explored the mental analogy in his *Psychology of the Photoplay*, published a few months prior to the release of the film. With even greater conviction, Vachel Lindsay, praising Munsterberg's study in a February 1917 obituary, proclaims that the late Harvard psychologist "unintentionally wrote the guide-book to the newest photoplay experiment, Intolerance"—which launches Lindsay's attempt to rescue the film from premature oblivion. [29]

The connection between Munsterberg and *Intolerance* appears somewhat strange, considering that *Psychology of the Photoplay* offers a theory of spectatorship that seemed tailored to the classical paradigm. Ennobling the latter with the trappings of a neo-Kantian aesthetics, Munsterberg insisted on compositional unity ("the perfect unity of plot and pictorial appearance") and "complete isolation . . from the practical world" as a prerequisite of a film's artistic success. *Neptune's Daughter* (a 1915 film starring Annette Kellermann which had converted the professor to the movies) might have passed this test, but hardly *Intolerance*, a film that flaunts stylistic diversity and narrative discontinuity: "If the scene changes too often and no movement is carried on without a break, the play may irritate us by its nervous jerking from place to place." Yet Munsterberg's treatise also suggests a diverging tendency—in its emphasis on the affinity of film with the "free play of mental experiences," with processes of memory and imagination. Passages like the following, echoing the familiar celebration of film's suspension from spatio-temporal laws, support Lindsay's observation:

> [The] photoplay can overcome the interval of the future as well as the interval of the past and slip the day twenty years hence between this minute and the next. In short, it can act as our imagination acts. It has the mobility of our ideas which are not controlled by the physical necessity of outer events but by the psychological laws for the association of ideas. . . . Life does not move forward on one single pathway. The whole manifoldness of parallel currents with their endless interconnections is the true substance of our understanding. [30]

If films were actually to put this analogy into practice (which *Intolerance* does to some extent), they would call into question not only the principles of unity and isolation advocated by Munsterberg but his ultimately behavioristic conception of viewer activity, which naturalizes Hollywood's particular constructions of subjectivity and social identity.

In its contradictory implications, Munsterberg's theory marks the historical point from which *Intolerance* could be seen as at once a continuation of and a departure from the classical model. As Munsterberg was one of the first to recognize, the film on the screen always depends on what Kluge calls "the film in the spectator's head." The actual activity required of the viewer and, conversely, the freedom of association granted by an individual film may differ from the classical paradigm only by degree and emphasis. This difference, however, becomes one of quality if a film acknowledges the viewer as a potential presence (rather than a structural absence), as a term that is crucial to the textual process but one that cannot be reduced to a function in a chain of signifiers. An alternative conception of spectatorship thus involves certain blind spots in the film itself, which mobilize, not merely appropriate, the viewer's experience—in its historical specificity, its conscious as well as unconscious layers, and its intersubjective resonance in a particular public sphere. [31]

Intolerance may not have been intended as such an alternative film, but it does invest a remarkable confidence in the viewers' willingness to abandon themselves to associational "manifoldness" and "endless interconnections." At the same time, the film is inevitably caught up in the competition with the classical paradigm and, therefore, overly anxious to compensate the viewer for thwarted expectations of narrative clarity and closure. Hence it resorts to authorial interventions that are not only blatantly didactic and redundant at times; they actually exacerbate the problem by constantly violating the principle of unobtrusive narration. The heterogeneity ensuing from the film's parallel design demands an unusually strong hand to clarify and stabilize the proliferating connotations. This additional layer of narration, however, increases the textual heterogeneity it was meant to regulate and contain. Whether encouraging the viewer's associational and interpretive competence or paralyzing the viewer with its infinite regress of self-definition and abstraction, *Intolerance* renders spectatorship problematic in a number of ways.

"A Radiant Crazy-Quilt": Patterns of Narration and Address

5

The parallel design of *Intolerance* may have been a major stumbling block in the popular reception of the film, but other textual features impede the viewer's access to the film as well—by deviating from conventions which, by 1916, had shaped expectations of viewer orientation, absorption, and identification. [1] These deviations can be traced, within one and the same narrative, on the most detailed level of enunciation, in the articulation of space, vision, and subjectivity, in the assertion of narrative authority. [2] Bracketing to some extent the parallel design, I will focus on a part of the film that is usually considered unproblematic: the Modern narrative.

In an illuminating essay on the emergence of narrative subjectivity, Tom Gunning observes a tension between Griffith and the industry as early as 1908–09: "Griffith's work appears curiously overdetermined, fulfilling certain expectations and aspirations of the film industry of the time, and yet also running into conflict with them—exceeding them." [3] On the one hand, Griffith was instrumental in developing a mode of narration that became the hallmark of classical cinema: the interweaving of multiple strands of action moving toward resolution and closure, a web of thorough motivation centering on the psychology of individual characters, and the concomitant effect of an autonomous fictional world offered to the spectator from an ideal vantage point. On the other hand, Griffith's particular elaboration of these principles often produced an excess of narrational activity, an excess that implicitly acknowledged the viewer as addressee. Because of this, Griffith's style increasingly conflicted with the norm of unobtrusive narration and indirect address advocated from about 1910 on, which was widely accepted by 1915. [4]

The tension observed by Gunning recalls the competition between presentational and representational styles that marked the transition from early to classical cinema. As Griffith was advancing the development of the latter, he supplemented an overall classical mode of narration with interventions that hark back to the early paradigm. This can be seen in *The Birth of a Nation*, specifically in the dual strategy to persuade the viewer of the historical veracity of the events portrayed. At its most "advanced" (by classical standards), the film offers sequences such as the Lincoln assassination sequence, which transforms a predetermined historical event into a masterpiece of suspense prefiguring Hitchcock. It does so by combining omniscient narration (crosscutting between the public space of the theater and the hidden wait of the assassin) with optical point of view (that of Elsie Stoneman, played by Lillian Gish), which lends the reconstruction of a well-known past event the presence of subjective experience and absorbs the viewer into the fiction of witnessing "history in the making." Alongside such classical practices, Griffith resorts to historicist tableaux and didactic intertitles that assert the authenticity of the representation by reference to particular sources, as the footnotes beginning "An historical facsimile of." Such moments of direct address resonate with the voice of the on-stage lecturer and, like the latter, they potentially rupture the very type of identification that sustains the fictional presence effect. [5]

Beyond the tradition of screen entertainments, Griffith seems to have modeled his narratorial voice on literary sources older than the ones that influenced the elaboration of classical codes. To cite another well-known example from *Birth*, a novelistic self-consciousness speaks from the figure of parallelism introduced by the intertitle, "While the women and children weep, a great conqueror marches to the sea." The establishing shot shows a group of anonymous women and children huddling at medium range, then slowly pans right and, with a further opening of the iris mask, reveals Sherman's army in the distance below; the figure is subsequently broken down into an alternation between these two elements. Such epic gestures, dramatizing the fate of private individuals at the margins of great historical events, are no doubt inspired by the nineteenth-century historical novel, notably Sir Walter Scott. In light of the literary and dramatic models favored by the advocates of the classical mode, however, Griffith's recourse to that tradition seems a touch anachronistic. As Kristin Thompson points out, the conventions of omnipresent yet unobtrusive narration have sources in the traditions of the well-made play, the popular romance and especially the late nineteenth century short story which, in standardized versions, lingered into the twentieth century and made their way into manuals for scenario writers. [6] Griffith's concept of narration, by contrast, seems shaped by earlier novelistic traditions, whether echoing Scott or other writers, such

as Dickens and George Eliot, known for strong authorial interventions and
an unmistakable moral voice.

"This invisible but sensed hand" of the nineteenth-century story-teller,
Gunning concludes, reaches "its apogee in Griffith's commercial disaster
Intolerance." Whether linking historically distinct segments or structuring
individual sequences, pronounced narratorial gestures abound throughout
the film, not least in the Modern narrative. Even in the strike sequence,
which is usually lauded for its "realism," the narrator's voice intervenes with a
highly stylized expository title, "The Loom of Fate weaves Death for The
Boy's father." More important, a long shot showing the factory owner,
Jenkins (Sam de Grasse), at his desk, supplies that loom with a name and a
face. Bracketed by fades, this shot could be ascribed—as a mental image—
to the Boy (Robert Harron), who, kneeling next to his dying father, raises
his head in the direction of the factory. At the same time, the insert could be
read as an editorial comment, as an element in a conceptual montage such as
Eisenstein found generally lacking in Griffith's work. This reading definitely
suggests itself when, a little later, the heroine's father has died ("Inability to
meet new conditions . . ."), and the shot of Jenkins at his desk is repeated,
now as the closing shot of the sequence. Although the Boy's presence in the
room is a possible subjective source, which would make the shot a flashback,
it has a more objective status than before. It assumes a critical function by
tracing a parallel of responsibility from the violent death of The Boy's father
to the ostensibly more "natural" death caused by the pressures of industrial
work. [7]

What is remarkable in this case is not just an excess of narratorial intervention but also a disparity of narrational styles: the relatively disguised and
decidedly modern voice of interpretive editing versus a somewhat archaic,
allegorical voice which one associates with Griffith the Victorian moralist. [8]
As I will show in greater detail in Chapter 9, allegory as a figurative mode
plays a major part in the textual and sexual economy of the film. In terms of
narration, the allegorical tendency of *Intolerance* is most obviously bound up
with the title and the conception of the film and thus with the metafictional
apparatus that props up the parallel design. Yet the allegorical discourse is not
limited to this apparatus. Compensating for the more immediate effects of
temporal and spatial discontinuity, it inevitably—and quite intentionally—
spills over into the narrative space of individual episodes.

The most graphic instances of allegorical narration are the recurrent
emblems of the Woman Who Rocks the Cradle and of the Book of Intolerance which first appear following the prologue titles quoted earlier. The
initial close-up of the book shows a leather cover bearing the gilded inscrip-

tion "Intolerance"; in the same shot the book is being opened by an invisible hand. With this device the film asserts its cultural respectability by invoking the Western tradition of the Book, a prime token of authority and continuity, of closure and truth. The shot also prefigures the convention of beginning adaptations with a close-up of the literary original. The text printed on the open page, however, does not commence a narrative; rather, it repeats the reading instructions from the prologue titles. While a certain degree of narrative self-consciousness is not unusual for openings during the mid-teens, the impersonal tone set by the book differs from the more common type of introduction that involves a presentation of the cast and often highlights individual stars. [9]

With the intertitle, superimposed upon the printed pages, "Our first story—out of the cradle of the present," the emblems of Cradle and Book are intertwined as metaphoric sources of narration. Having thus introduced the Modern narrative, the title continues, "In a western city we find certain ambitious ladies banded together for the 'uplift' of humanity," which motivates the presence of the three middle-aged women who occupy the first diegetic shot. These characters will initiate a causal chain of events that all

Figure 5.1

Figure 5.2

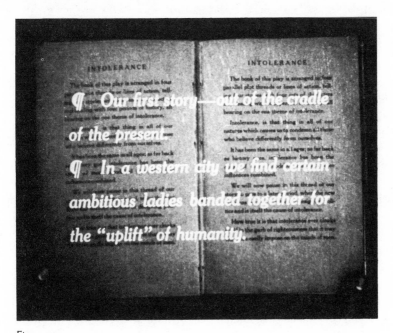

Figure 5.3

but destroys the lives of the Modern hero and heroine. Yet they also echo the three Fates in the background of the Cradle shot and thereby enjoin metafictional and diegetic levels of the narration. Tagged as the "Vestal Virgins of Uplift," they remain personified abstractions throughout the film. Moreover, as we shall see, they are endowed with considerable enunciative power: they authorize structures of looking and precipitate significant narrative events. In that sense they can be said to function as "primitive narrators" (to borrow a term from Judith Mayne), who are staged by an omniscient, ostensibly more classical narration only to be suppressed eventually by its greater authority. [10] Indeed, the suppression of these primitive narrators defines the task of the narration, its formal prerequisite for a happy ending.

A tension between conflicting styles of narration is evident beginning with the film's first sequence. The protagonist of this sequence is Miss Jenkins (Vera Lewis), the "unmarried sister of the autocratic industrial overlord," whose appearance is prompted by the interest of the Uplifters in *"her money."* Herself a casuality of a repressive sexual economy, Miss Jenkins is established as the catalyst through whom metaphysical evil, embodied by the Uplifters, invades the familiar and familial world of the Dear One, the Boy, and their respective fathers—"common" people. Situated on the threshold between allegorical and narrative space, the characterization of the old maid oscillates between psychological motivation and melodramatic caricature.

The sequence involves two ambiguously related spaces: the public space of a lounge opening out into a ballroom (a deep space shot with sidelighting) and the more enclosed space of a library which sight links establish somewhere to the right and in front of the ballroom. The transition from the ballroom to the interior of the library is prompted by Miss Jenkins' leaving one space and entering the other (though there is no match on action). The following shots, however, instantaneously interpret her spatial movement in symbolic terms—as a withdrawal from a social, heterosexual world into the barren seclusion of spinsterhood, a withdrawal that immobilizes the woman in a position of inactive looking. This abstraction of narrative meaning is suggested by a triangular pattern of character looks established as such by almost identical repetition. Each time Miss Jenkins can be seen talking to a young man, a cut interrupts to show a young girl, either in a group or by herself, as she catches sight of the young man. The girl's gaze in turn dictates a shot change which allows the young man to reciprocate and join the younger woman. Only then is Miss Jenkins granted a look of her own, a

Figure 5.4

look enframing the newly formed couple, and a reaction shot in which her smile turns from motherly to bitter. As the second couple has left her, occasioning a last view toward the ballroom, the camera stays behind with her alone in the library.

At this point psychological motivation gives way to allegorical performance: the character's look is now altogether abstracted from any function of articulating a coherent narrative space.[11] Again Miss Jenkins is shown looking, now at a three-quarter range, turning from the direction of the ballroom toward a gilt-framed mirror on the table to her right. This look is answered by a vignetted close-up of the mirror, but not from the spatial position of the character. Instead of a reflection of Miss Jenkins' face, the mirror yields a totally unreadable (not even anamorphic) image. After a cut back to Miss Jenkins' horrified expression, an intertitle offers a stereotypical summary of the entire sequence: "Seeing youth drawn to youth, Miss Jenkins realizes the bitter fact that she is no longer a part of the younger world." Yet the smug third-person comment is not the last word. In the final shot (closing with an iris out), the character raises her hands to the lines around her right eye and turns frame left in a theatrical aside—a pantomimic gesture which decenters an incipient diegetic space and freezes narrative movement in an emblematic figure. [12]

This sequence has important implications for the articulation of cinematic space and the organization of the look. As soon as space is articulated in narrative terms, it is abstracted by excessive allegorical connotations— the world of youth and love versus that of age, singleness, and frustration— connotations that make expectations of spatial verisimilitude appear secondary. Such allegorical overdetermination may account to some extent for the peculiar texture of narrative space throughout *Intolerance*. Griffith was known for a somewhat cavalier attitude toward the emerging continuity system in general, [13] but the film's parallel design, with its assertion of a transhistorical, *temporal* omnipresence, might have further weakened the narratorial concern with *spatial* coherence and closure. If the strike sequence, for instance, with its montage of workers, boss, manager, militia, families, and unemployed, did not succeed in making a political argument in

Figure 5.5

the Eisensteinian sense, the violations of screen direction alone would render the sequence illegible.

Throughout *Intolerance* the shorthand quality of many sequences—at times foreshortened into a single shot—creates a relatively incomplete, porous diegesis, with few overlapping or clearly contiguous spaces. Accordingly, the film displays a large number of unauthorized, unclaimed, spatially ambiguous shots, especially close-ups of objects and faces that assume an autonomous, emblematic quality. Narrative space is stitched together much more loosely than in the typical film of the transitional period, including *Birth*; it is also less dependent, for coherence and intelligibility, on the agency and psychology of individual characters.

By 1916 the mutual anchoring of narrative space and character psychology had become an accepted practice, relying on an ensemble of editing devices such as shot/reverse and point-of-view shots—devices handled with great ease and sophistication in films like *The Bargain* (Ince/Barker/Hart, 1914) or *The Cheat* (Cecil B. DeMille, 1915). Although *Intolerance* does use the glance of characters to provide the viewer with a rudimentary degree of spatial orientation, the film seems to resist the more advanced possibilities of making that glance a relay of viewer identification. Thus, although editing relations are frequently motivated by a character's glance, that is, by sight links, there are very few point-of-view shots. A character will be shown looking and a responding shot will show what the character sees (from which we infer a proximity of the two spaces), but not from his or her spatial position.[14] The camera—and with it the viewer—is rarely allowed to penetrate the scenic space; rather, we are "wedged" into that space at an angle of usually more than 30 and less than 90 degrees. This placement preserves a sense of frontality reminiscent of the primitive use of proscenium space, which was being superseded in the institutionally more advanced films of the period by a classical inscription of the spectator within a virtually unbounded narrative space.

The avoidance of point-of-view shots should certainly not be overrated as a mark of *Intolerance*'s nonclassical style.[15] This avoidance is significant only in conjunction with other salient features of the film, such as the allegorical overdetermination of narrative space, the relative unconcern with continuity, and the impersonal if idiosyncratic voice of the narrator—gestures "of a storyteller unwilling to relinquish the authority of the image to the subjectivity of any one character."[16] Still, a character's scopic agency is an important aspect of character subjectivity (though not the only one), and a film's inscription and distribution of that agency crucially defines the viewer's access to the story and attendant processes of identification. By not granting individual characters a greater measure of enunciatory control the narrator also circumscribes the viewer's fictive gratification of penetrating a private space unseen, unmediated by the public dimension of exhibition. In the particular configurations of *Intolerance,* moreover, the mistrust against character-look is bound up with the peculiar sexual economy of the film. In fact, it betrays a more systematic blockage of scopic, that is, visually articulated, desire.

In the Miss Jenkins sequence the withholding of a point-of-view shot—in spite of the fact that she is clearly the central consciousness of the sequence—has symbolic significance. In the iconography of mirror shots the absence of a reflection has to be read as an emblem of death—which places it in diametrical opposition to the symbolic image of the Rocking Cradle. Having gone, in the span of one sequence, through the allegorical stages of the female life cycle, [17] Miss Jenkins cannot return to the world of the ballroom; she is cut off from a "natural" function of femininity in heterosexual society. Even within her own private space she is denied a coherent image of herself, reduced to a position of looking in on "life" from the outside—a position that parallels that of the spectator.

Equally significant is the opposition established, in the same sequence, between the look of the younger woman and that of the old maid. Although neither of the young women has any function in the subsequent narrative, they are both endowed with unusual enunciative power. It is their look, rather than that of the young men, which initiates the choreography of couple formation. This is remarkable for a number of reasons. For one thing, the patriarchal organization of vision that tends to make male characters the subject and female characters the object of the look had already pervaded the cinema, in conjunction with classical modes of representation and address. The woman who authorizes a look is therefore, in tendency at least, transgressive. [18] It is no coincidence that the exchange of the look in the service of romance occurs between anonymous characters who will not play any part in the story, and, furthermore, that it remains one of the rare unequivocal instances of such an exchange throughout the film.

What is unusual about the articulation of vision in *Intolerance* is the large number of structures of looking attributed to the agency of female characters. In *Birth* the only female character granted narrationally significant looks is Elsie Stoneman. Her status as a virgin and her acquaintance with Lincoln make her a superior historical witness and raise the function of her look above mere erotic interest. Thus, when she discovers John Wilkes Booth *before* he fires the fatal shot—a handsome vignetted portrait shot retroactively attributed to Elsie's point of view (by a round mask suggesting her view through opera glasses)—this look functions primarily as a suspense strategy, playing with the competing epistemological registers of narrative and history. In a merely private, nonhistorical context, Elsie's view of Booth would be considered transgressive, given the classical taboo against the woman who looks—and desires—independent of the male gaze that usually initiates the romantic exchange. In *Intolerance* almost all female characters, across the historical periods, participate in the enunciative relay of the look, but the taboo against a desiring female gaze crucially impairs the power of that vision. The price for the woman's access to structures of looking is a fragmentation and abstraction of the gaze, its dissociation into an innocent but regressive virginity, and a perverse, fatal femininity as epitomized by the Uplifters.

The foremost agent of the innocent look is the "little Dear One" (Mae Marsh), who also provides a major focus of identification on the narrative level. In the course of the film her look traverses a typology of shot patterns that governs the vision of other characters as well, a formal gradation ranging from (extremely rare) point-of-view shots, sight links, and mental images to looks that are denied the power of authorizing a reverse shot. One set of close-ups responding to her look involves simple childish pleasures, such as the shot of a glass of soda she offers to a friend at the mill workers' dance or the shot of the kissing geese that introduces her look in the beginning of the film. But most of these simple pleasures are not as innocent as they appear. The view of the kissing geese, for instance, displaces that of the father, the object of her overly coquettish affections (an excess rationalized by the absence of a mother). Similarly, her preoccupation with "the hopeful geranium" is sidetracked by a look out of the window, motivating a street-level shot of an attractive young woman pursued by men, which initiates the Girl to adult mating rituals ("I'll walk like her and maybe everybody will like me too"). After the imitation of the gait yields results and the father interrupts the Boy's first attempt to kiss his new "chicken," the father, in a violent movement, forces her down on her knees and makes her pray to be forgiven. As if to support a paternal authority shown as it is failing, the narration grants her an unambiguous, spatially contextualized (low angle) point-of-view shot of a statue of Madonna and Child. Yet again, as she reconciles with her ailing father under the eyes of the Madonna, this restoration of innocence is coupled with unmistakably incestuous overtones.

Significantly, there is no exchange of looks to stage the Dear One's romantic encounter with the Boy. On the contrary, though the formation of the couple is codified, legalized in a classical alternation of shots that leads

Figure 5.6

Figure 5.7

to the Boy's proposal and a shy, tender kiss, this alternation takes place between inside and outside the closed apartment door, a threshold which the Dear One had promised "Our Lady" and her father no man would ever cross. Shortly thereafter, when the Boy has been "intolerated away" for a term, we see the Dear One at home, looking up from her child in the cradle, and her wistful expression calls forth a mental image of the Boy in prison. (This shot is echoed later when the same power of evocation is granted to the character called the Friendless One who, being herself the murderer, is haunted by the image of the Boy awaiting execution.) Only near the film's end is there an exchange of looks between the couple in the courtroom sequence ("love's brave encouragement"). Under the eye of the Law, however, these glances are childlike and ineffective.

Restrained from functioning in the articulation of heterosexual desire, unequivocal point-of-view shots are granted only of objects that are "safe"— the Madonna, the child. Yet the child is also the object that causes the opposition of innocent and perverse female look to slide into similarity. As the narrative drifts toward crisis, any active female look seems associated with failure, envy, frustration, destruction, and death. When the Uplifters get a similar point-of-view shot of the baby as its mother, their evil eye precipitates her loss of custody, thus putting her in a position of lack analogous to their own. The Dear One's attempt to catch a glimpse of her child shows her looking up a forbidding wall with the letters "Jenkins Foundation," but the responding shot of the baby, looking frightened while the nurses dance with each other in the background, is supplied by an omniscient narrator. Contaminated by the perversion of femininity, the Girl is shown in the next sequence as she engages in a "new dissipation—watching the happiness of others." Sneaking up to a lit window, she peeps inside and provokes a shot of a family idyll, followed by a medium close-up of an infant who smiles and seems to acknowledge her. (In *The Mother and the Law*, this illicit look is interrupted but nonetheless condoned by the friendly policeman who will later aid the Boy's rescue.) Like Miss Jenkins' relation to the world of the ballroom, the voyeuristic inscription of the bereft mother's look can be read as a metaphor of the activity of the spectator.[19]

As the baby occasions a slippage between an innocent and a perverse female look, it also becomes a locus of uncertainty on the level of the narrative, especially in light of amazing discrepancies between the different versions of the film. In the prints reedited by Griffith in 1922 the fate of the baby remains unresolved, despite the happy ending of the Modern story. In the earlier version, alas, the baby is returned after the Boy's rescue from the gallows.[20] Yet in *The Mother and the Law* we get a moving shot of Mae Marsh staring into a little coffin, a fate foreshadowed by the withholding of a reverse shot of the child the last time the anxious mother is shown looking at it alive. (The only other point-of-view shots in *The Mother and the Law*— besides the initial one of the baby shared by both mother and Uplifters— are likewise emblems of mortality: the Boy's high-angle view of an empty grave and the Girl's desperate stare at the face of a clock during the "death watch" the night before his execution.) These contradictory versions of the baby's fate are not accidental. The rebirth of the couple in the final shots of the Modern narrative, under the parental gaze of the Priest and the Governor's wife, suggests that their own parenthood is dispensable, all the more since their childlike bliss blends into the image of the two toddlers in the apotheosis. While ideologically linked to the idealization of childhood that informs both *Intolerance* and Griffith's social and racial attitudes, the displacement of the baby also ties in with a certain infantilization of the spectator position, with the systematic removal of the gaze from the economy of difference and desire.

If the film presumes to restore the Modern couple by situating them in a presexual realm, it locates the forces of destruction on the other side, in the realm of sexual repression and its monstrous returns. As I suggested earlier, the Uplifters function as "primitive narrators" in the Modern episode, similar to Catherine de Medici (Josephine Crowell) in the French. They first have access to the level of enunciation when, in their effort to obtain the Jenkins' support, they evoke images of vice, introduced by a dialogue intertitle— "There is drinking in…"—followed by a shot of a bar and, after a respective intertitle, a shot of people dancing in a café. Not only do they authorize these images, they are also granted the power to transform written speech into visual presence. This pattern is repeated later, when they report their successes to the head of the foundation, with intertitles like "It is peaceful in the…" and "No more dancing in…," followed by shots of the same spaces as before but now showing the effects of their intervention. The third intertitle—"You yourself were with us when we raided…"—prompts a flashback of a police raid of a brothel. The scene it recalls, however, enacts the Uplifters' loss of narrative authority and thus initiates a reversal in the enunciative power structure.

The flashback of the raid is one of the most curious configurations of spectatorship in all of *Intolerance*, and it is no coincidence that this configuration is occasioned by the problem of prostitution, a key term in the film's obsessive figuration of a femininity in crisis. The sequence stages the interplay of three looks directed at the object: a long shot of police leading the prostitutes out of the brothel into a patrol wagon. Instead of elaborating on the victims of the raid, the camera dwells on the onlookers, a group of Uplifters watching from the balcony, their sadistic and voyeuristic reactions singled out by close-ups. Then it shifts to a medium shot of two well-dressed men, possibly civilian officers, also looking on approvingly. (In the reconstructed version of the film, another scene showing these men seducing young boys links their negative image in sanctioning the raid to the theme of homosexuality—or, rather, exclusion from heterosexuality—and thus to the lesbian subtext of a femininity gone awry.) Finally, there is a cut to a toothless, unshaven old man, a close-up not anchored in the diegesis, which leaves his look ambiguously suspended between the prostitutes and the Uplifters, and even briefly winking at the camera. The power of the Uplifters' evil eye is broken as they themselves become the butt of a misogynist joke, prefaced by the satirical comment, "When women cease to attract men they often turn to reform as a second choice" (like many of the intertitles, this was written by Anita Loos). Thus, although the flashback is formally attributed to these characters, it centers on the disruption and containment of their scopic agency and narratorial power. As the task of intervention is relegated to an anonymous male lower-class spectator figure, the omniscient narrator at once reclaims and disavows possession of the gaze.

While the Uplifters continue to wreak havoc on the narrative level, their enunciative authority is challenged, checked by the omniscient gesture of the next sequence which opens with the title, "But these results they do not report:" (there follows a series of non-narrative shots of bootlegging and illicit prostitution). Without this disempowerment of the primitive narrators the happy ending of the Modern story would not be possible. In the French narrative, by contrast, the enunciative power of Catherine de Medici prevails, resulting in certain and violent death for the fictional protagonists. Medici's authorship is foregrounded not only in the articulation of the look (her evocation of a flashback to the killing of Catholics at Nîmes, designed to inflame the court against the Huguenots) but also in the control she exerts over her weak epileptic son, King Charles IX, which is crucially associated with the activity of writing.

As the King becomes a tool of the perverse, phallic mother by signing the decree for the massacre of the Huguenots, the character of the Mercenary carries out her fatal desire through the medium of the gaze, in the "private," "common" sector of the French narrative. The moment the virginal heroine is introduced to the film, in an emblematic close-up that abstracts her from

Figure 5.8

Figure 5.9

Figure 5.10

Figure 5.11

the diegesis, she is positioned between two competing male looks: the impotent look of her fiancé, Prosper, and that of the Mercenary thematized by an intertitle. Even though the Mercenary is not granted a direct point-of-view shot of Brown Eyes, the close-up of her face is still closer to his angle of vision than Prosper's. Like the look on the part of black men in *Birth*, or that of the character called Evil Eye in *Broken Blossoms* (1919), the Mercenary's desiring gaze stands for an aggressive masculinity which inescapably leads to the destruction of its object. Sure enough, his scopic fixation of Brown Eyes prefigures her later perforation by his sword. Most disturbingly, in the later scene the narration becomes complicit with the Mercenary's gaze by exploiting her distorted face in an extreme close-up and, with the same sadistic appeal, prolongs her fear of death, delaying the fatal thrust by cutting back to the Modern narrative.

In the Modern narrative we find a similar dissociation of male character-look into connotations of impotence and repression, on the one hand, and an aggressive masculinity, on the other—but with different implications and consequences. An interesting instance of a repressed, and repressive, figuration of scopic desire occurs early in the film, when Jenkins drives up to the dance hall to study the "habits" of "his employees." Between the two young women at the entrance and a dime he spots on the pavement, the capitalist typically chooses the dime. The displacement of desire is enacted by his authorizing of an unequivocal point-of-view shot (close-up) of the coin, while refusing to reciprocate the young woman's flirtatious look. Echoing the two young women in the Miss Jenkins sequence yet with a marked difference in class and power relations, this vignette, one might say, comments upon the psychopathology of male identity under industrial capitalism. The displacement and blockage of desire, however, the paralysis of male subjectivity between money and female sexuality (the two later linked in the figure of the prostitute), can also be read as an unwitting premonition of the dilemma of *Intolerance*—its self-defeating disarticulation of the gaze along the lines of sexual difference.

Ultimately the unstable and destabilizing force of the female gaze exceeds and impairs even the power of an aggressive masculinity, represented in the Modern narrative by the "Musketeer of the Slums." His reputation of ruthless masculinity is asserted primarily on the level of casting and of mise-en-scène, as in an unclaimed close-up panning up a phallic statue of a nude embracing a tree trunk (which counterpoints the statue of Madonna and Child in the Dear One's apartment), centerpiece of a pornographic still life that subsequently is located in the corner of the Musketeer's room.

Significantly, he is played by Walter Long, the same actor who, in *Birth*, plays Gus, the black rapist. On the enunciative level, however, his power is minimal. The one time he appears to be authorizing a shot change, looking through the keyhole of the Dear One's apartment, the responding shot is taken from an angle exactly opposite his spatial position. More important, the Musketeer's look is constantly undermined by that of his mistress and eventual murderer, the complex and fascinating character of the Friendless One (Miriam Cooper).

The Friendless One is the focal point of a crisis of femininity which, as I will elaborate later, at once fuels and destabilizes *Intolerance*. Her position in the Modern narrative, both in relation to other characters and in terms of the configuration of the look, is marked by a triangular pattern. She is introduced to the film as a "superfluous" female, yet her singleness is not that of an old maid but, as an intertitle explains, a result of the strike (which is indirectly blamed upon the Uplifters). The brief encounter between the Friendless One and the Boy during their exodus to the city—an exchange of looks though not articulated through editing—has a much more adult quality to it than does the Boy's encounter with his future wife. (In *The Mother and the Law*, his attention toward the Friendless One is motivated by the caption, "His first sweetheart.") The memory of this scene of mutual affection remains a subliminal bond between the Friendless One and the Boy throughout *Intolerance*. When she has become the Musketeer's mistress and the Boy a member of his gang, a three-shot stages another significant exchange of looks between them (again not broken down into individual shots), behind the back—and much to the dismay—of their new employer.

As the intrigue develops, with the Musketeer trying to insinuate himself to the Dear One under the pretext of helping her retrieve the child, the Friendless One becomes the rejected element in two overlapping triangles. More important, her subjectivity becomes the relay for the articulation of narrative events. Focusing on *her* jealousy, bitterness, and hysteria—and making the spectator complicit with her efforts to emasculate her patron—the narration grants her a series of auditory point-of-view shots which lead up to the murder. As she watches the fight between the Boy and the Musketeer from a ledge outside the window (no POV), a flashback to her initial encounter with the Boy both caps and disrupts the classical economy of the murder sequence; it motivates the fatal shots while leaving the murderer's motives thoroughly overdetermined and ambiguous. Were it not for the eventual triumph of her conscience and, consequently, the last-minute rescue of the Boy from the gallows, the Friendless One would have killed not

Figure 5.12

only her oppressor but the unavailable object of her affections as well.

The triangular choreography of desire is invariably linked to fatality, whether it translates into narrative action, as in the case of the Friendless One or the French Musketeer; whether it is allegorically mediated, as in the Miss Jenkins sequence; or even when it is ostensibly sublimated and resolved, as in the Babylonian Mountain Girl's dying view of Belshazzar and the Princess Beloved united in death. By emphasizing this triangularity in patterns of looking, the film puts the viewer in a peculiar bind. On the most rudimentary narrative level, the viewer is asked to identify with the legitimate couple. At the same time, he or she is excluded from that relationship by the very fact of spectatorship and occupies a position structurally analogous to that of the envious third, figured in *Intolerance* as evil eye, old maid, and hysteric. With this configuration of spectatorship, *Intolerance* spells out a basic contradiction of classical cinema, if not cinema *tout court* (as could be inferred from the behavior of Uncle Josh): that the mobilization of voyeuristic mechanisms harbors the risk of latent displeasure, of jealousy feelings potentially arising with the spectator's structural exclusion.

Without the centering frame of a linear narrative, without the centering force of heterosexual desire, the look disintegrates into its perverse facets. *Intolerance* could be said to reflect upon and take to its logical conclusion—albeit unintentionally and at considerable cost—the repressive make-up of classical spectatorship. To be sure, the perverse manifestation of the look is disavowed on the level of the narrative; the evil eye, whether male or female, French or American, is marked as the antagonist, the destroyer of family members and the family as such. But identification with the victims is not, for the most part, sustained by scopic desire. Instead, the viewer is solicited on a more abstract level, asked to identify with the lot of the powerless and unprotected, with the timeless (excepting Babylon) values of courtship, marriage, and motherhood.

The slippage between innocent and perverse variants of the female look (instantiated in different ways by both the Dear One and the Friendless One) cannot but undermine the moralistic oppositions of the narrative. In the end all character subjectivity is tainted with the connotation of perversity. And since even an anachronistic omniscient narrator depends upon some degree of character subjectivity, vision itself is compromised, contaminated with the crisis of femininity. *Intolerance* thus betrays a profound ambivalence toward a crucial ingredient of cinematic fascination, an ambivalence that fragments the position of the spectator and weakens possibilities of access and identification.

All this is not to deny the traditional claim that *Intolerance* contains some of the most moving, most intimate, psychologically most perceptive moments in silent cinema; the close-up of Mae Marsh's fingers in the courtroom scene is often cited. Yet these moments, however "unforgettable," remain moments at best. They elicit sympathy rather than identification in the classical sense, as a process that requires a sustained interplay of seeing and seen, of scopic and narrative registers.[21] The insufficient anchoring of emotional display in a narrative—that is, in its classical version, Oedipal—construction of subjectivity may also account, in part at least, for the excessive sentimentality for which *Intolerance* has been criticized from the time of its release.[22]

At this point we turn to some of the more obvious ways in which *Intolerance* deviates from contemporary strategies of address, in particular the industry's increasing focus on the dynamic of character, individual psychology, and the personality of a star. The star system had been flourishing since 1910, and by 1916 the cultivation of stars was more than an established publicity device. It also provided a major incentive for centering narration on individual characters and their psychology. Lillian Gish, shrewder than most critics, attributes the failure of *Intolerance* to the fact that Griffith resisted the practice of star-billing (as well as demands for star salaries), renouncing thereby the "pulling power" that could have saved the film at the box office.[23] The abstention from the star system ties in with the narrator's refusal to fully individualize his characters, much as he may grant them nuanced psychological traits and moments. As even in later Griffith films, characters are introduced as types—the Dear One, the Musketeer, Brown Eyes, the Mountain Girl. None of them, except for the industrialist and his sister (and of course the historical personages), have proper names.[24] Again we hear the epic narrator, the archaicizing, allegorizing voice that interposes itself between its own creations and the spectator. This reluctance to submerge character construction in the aura of an actor's personality presented a major obstacle in view of the classical relay of character subjectivity and viewer identification.

While the peculiar withholding of character subjectivity is a familar aspect of Griffith's narratorial signature—and a significant aspect of his ambiguous status in film history—*Intolerance* exacerbates the problematic impact of such withholding by the film's overall parallel design. Just as the protagonists of the various periods compete for time and space on the screen, they inevitably divide the viewer's capacities of identification. The discontinuity of the individual narrative impedes any consistent involvement with a particular set of characters (though one could argue that the pleasure of recognition may compensate for the lack of continuity). The sheer proliferation of fates decenters the viewer's emotional focus. This problem was noted in 1916 by Julian Johnson, reviewing *Intolerance* for *Photoplay*: "we wish to follow, undisturbed, the adventures of a single set of characters, or to thrill with a single pair of lovers. Verily, when the game is hearts, two's company, and the lovers of four ages an awful crowd."[25]

If this is indeed the effect, the game is perhaps not hearts. What, then, is it? Why did Griffith forego strategies of spectatorial engagement that were already recognized, conventionalized, and successfully employed, even in his own work? What did he hope to gain by leaving the safe ground of linear narrative, character-relayed subjectivity, and diegetic effect?

Genesis, Causes, Concepts of History

·   ·   ·   ·   ·   ·   ·   ·   ·   ·

6

The belief in progress—in infinite perfectibility, in an infinite moral task—and the idea of eternal recurrence are complementary.
—*Walter Benjamin, Das Passagen-Werk*

I turn but do not extricate myself,
Confused, a past-reading, another, but with darkness yet.
—*Walt Whitman, "The Sleepers"*

The peculiar textual make-up of *Intolerance* is inseparable from the historical moment at which the film was conceived and released. This moment significantly turns on the success and controversy surrounding *The Birth of a Nation*. Although the status of *Birth* as a mythical watershed has rightly been challenged by economic and social historians of the cinema, we should not underrate its impact as a catalyst of institutional change, nor its paradigmatic function for the cultural self-definition of classical cinema. Besides establishing Griffith's reputation as the artistic "genius" of the industry, the film marks a point of no return both in economic terms and in terms of public discourse on the cinema.

That *Intolerance* somehow owes its existence to *Birth* is a familiar story, yet the premises and purposes of that story vary considerably. It usually begins with *The Mother and the Law*, a melodrama with an urban lower-class theme reminiscent of the Biograph period, which Griffith had made while editing and working on the score for *Birth*. Joseph Henabery, who played Lincoln in *Birth* and worked as a one-man research department on *Intolerance*, dismisses the first version of this film (from a distance of five decades) as a "sort of potboiler," "a little, cheap, quickie picture," "a tearjerker"—a judgment not unmotivated by the writer's emphasis on his own role in the eventual improvement of the film. Karl Brown, assistant to cameraman G. W. Bitzer, remembers the film for "its brutally effective excoriation of things as they are," which would grant it a greater affinity with its second version, the Modern narrative of *Intolerance*. Film historian Arthur Lennig, making a case for the *The Mother and the Law* as released separately in 1919, goes so far as to suggest that the original version suffered by being cut down for the "pyrotechnics" of *Intolerance*. Whatever its intrinsic merits, after the monumental success of *Birth* and Griffith's emergence from relative anonymity, such a film could not but appear "too small." Not only would it have failed to cash in on *Birth's* consolidation of the rise of the longer film, particularly the "special" feature, but its release would have undercut Griffith's efforts to endow the cinema with the trappings of middle-class culture. [1]

In addition to the logic of expansion, *Birth* also furnished a cause, linking the controversy over the film's racism with the large-scale threat of censorship legislation impending on both state and federal levels. Griffith himself had joined the industry's lobbying efforts against censorship by publishing, shortly before the release of *Intolerance*, a pamphlet entitled *The Rise and Fall of Free Speech in America*. In January 1917 he was put in charge of a nationwide campaign mounted by the National Association of the Motion Picture Industry. [2] In his pamphlet Griffith demanded for film the same constitutional protection that was granted to "the art of the written word" ("that art to which we owe the Bible and the works of Shakespeare"), warning that a suppression of motion pictures would ultimately lead to a suppression of the press. The pamphlet, whose layout resembles contemporary avant-garde manifestos, locates "the root of all censorship" in the evil of "INTOLERANCE," a word that heads every other page and introduces examples of martyrdom and oppression throughout world history. [3]

Such a construction served at least two functions. First, it deflected attention from the political charges against *Birth* by merging them with the issue of film censorship in particular and the cause of free speech in general, at a time when the latter was becoming an especially acute concern for the radical left. [4] Second, it gave publicity—encoded though not exactly subtly—to the current production of *Intolerance*, while offering a "philosophical" motivation for the economic and institutional ambitions of the new project. Thus the founding myth of *Intolerance* is crucially intertwined with the masking of racist ideology in and surrounding *Birth*, just as the film's attack upon uplifters and "meddlers" conflates contemporary reformers with the tradition of abolitionism denounced in the earlier film. It is no coincidence that later commentators who take Griffith's "ideational" motivation of *Intolerance* at face value also tend to minimize and gloss over his racism—or even, like Seymour Stern, explicitly endorse the film as a counterattack against the liberals who betrayed the cause of White Supremacy in their efforts to suppress *Birth*. [5]

The relationship of *Intolerance* to *Birth* could also be phrased in terms of the precarious position of the cinema within the public sphere. As long as films could be accused of serving special interests—whether commercial, social, or political—they were vulnerable to censorship. The ideological task, then, was to establish the cinema on a level allegedly above the sphere of private interests, a level equivalent to the classical European model of the public sphere. Although in the case of *Birth* the debate over the legitimacy of the medium was hooked onto the legitimation of a particular ideology— White Supremacy—the fact that it was negotiated as a matter of national interest attests to the inroads film had made into the area of public discourse.

Birth pleaded immunity primarily on two counts: its "scientific" accuracy (invoking the authority of photographic representation and scholarly sources) as well as the general value of topics of national history. Since that strategy failed with precisely those people from whom Griffith had expected approval—intellectuals and critics of culture—*Intolerance* pursued other paths to public legitimacy. Taking the industry's bid for middle-class respectability more literally than anyone else, Griffith resorted to textual devices that would lend *Intolerance* the status of a work of art, an enterprise for which poetry, painting, and music were just as paradigmatic as the anachronistic models of narration discussed in Chapter 5. Not surprisingly, the film elicited labels like "an epic poem" or "a film fugue" and comparisons with a Wagnerian *Gesamtkunstwerk*. But Griffith's ambition went beyond the tokens of aesthetic autonomy that had subtended European concepts of culture and of the public sphere. He sought to affiliate the cinema with a particular tradition of American culture, a vision of an organic national culture epitomized in the period's rediscovery of Walt Whitman.[6]

Finally, *Intolerance* was linked to *Birth* by a genealogy of representation, the founding of a universal language of gestures, situations, and sentiments that exceeded the individual film, a narrative idiom capable of rendering the essential moments of universal history. While shooting the Huguenot part of the film, Griffith, to everyone's bewilderment, kept referring to it as *The Mother and the Law*. Brown recalls that the working crew, not being privy to Griffith's master plan, distinguished between the "widely different pictures" by number: *The Mother and the Law* became F-2 (F for feature), the Huguenot episode F-3 and so forth. F-1, however, was reserved for *Birth*. Brown himself observed certain parallels between the "French picture" and *Birth* which made him ponder the question of repetition and originality.

> It was the same story, only in a different period. A lot of important people forever picking on a lot of unimportant people. In *The Clansman* [*Birth*], Joe

Henabery, playing Lincoln, was shot in the back of the head with a derringer pistol. In this one Henabery, playing Admiral Coligny, was stabbed in the front of the throat with a sword. Same story, different period. It seemed odd. Others were copying Griffith all the time, but for Griffith to copy himself seemed to be a little out of keeping with one who had become known as the great originator.[7]

Since Griffith had already "copied himself" in so many Biograph films, the retroactive assertion of *Birth* as point of origin can refer only to the more principled, epic crossing of narrative and history that was to establish him as the mythical father of American cinema.

For much as the defenders of *Birth* claimed historical authenticity, the film would not have had the overwhelming impact it did without the means of "drama," without the emerging conventions of classical narrative. The mediation of narrative and history in *Birth* suggests a configuration that Philip Rosen has aptly associated with Georg Lukács's analysis of the historical novel, in particular the work of Walter Scott.[8] Thus, the film claims to represent historical processes as a meaningful totality, determined by "great motive 'truths' of history" (such as the eternal separation of races). These "motive truths" are staged through the fates of individual characters who live "on the margins of great events" yet are to be taken as representative of historically typical situations. Moreover, the film features protagonists who are caught between conflicting historical forces and who depend, for a resolution of this personal conflict, upon plot structures in which purer personifications of the opposing forces are brought to a cathartic clash. To resume an earlier example, the (re)construction of Lincoln's assassination is authenticated, made "realistic" for the spectator, by the presence of fictional characters; Elsie Stoneman and her brother just "happen" to attend the show. Yet Elsie is also the focus of conflicting loyalties—her allegiance to the cause of abolition (represented by her father) and her love for Ben Cameron (founder of the Klan)—a conflict which, ironically, her liberal Northern upbringing permits her to act out (in contrast to Margaret Cameron, her Southern counterpart). Eventually, the narrator cuts this knot by pitting vicious caricatures of black "renegades" against the heroic knights of the Invisible Empire, leaving the white women only one choice.

Another, somewhat less organic (and more peculiarly American) version of the relationship between history and individual which might have left its mark in Griffith's work is Ralph Waldo Emerson's essay "History" (1841), which he undoubtedly had read. By the time of the Progressive Era, literary approaches to history had been displaced, under the impact of German historicism, by a more professional, scientific ideal of historiography.[9] Yet Emerson's essay had lost little of its cultural power and could be said to anticipate later critiques of the very type of historical empiricism advocated by Griffith's more scholarly contemporaries. In an elaboration of his notorious remark that "there is properly no history, only biography," Emerson elucidates the stake of the individual subject in the representation of history: "All inquiry into antiquity, —all curiosity respecting the pyramids, the excavated cities, Stonehenge, the Ohio Circles, Mexico, Memphis, —is the desire to do away this wild, savage and preposterous There or Then, and introduce in its place the Here and the Now. [It is to banish the *Not me* and supply the *Me*. It is to abolish difference and restore unity.]"[10] This passage registers the imperialist tendency underlying much of the nineteenth-century obsession with history. But it also offers a metaphor of the psychic mechanism at work in the subject's assertion over historical contingency, calling into question the objective order, the closure ostensibly achieved by the historical novel.[11] For Emerson the meaning of history is a matter of reading, a self-deciphering of the subject, since all facts of history that manifest the workings of a manifold spirit are latent in the individual. "This human mind wrote history, and this must read it. The Sphinx must solve her own riddle. If the whole of history is in one man, it is all to be explained from individual experience" ("History," p. 3).

Ambiguous as any American writing, Emerson's essay foreshadows Hollywood's systematic tendency to domesticate historical contradictions and contingencies, to translate them into manifestations of continuity and identity. In the watered-down Emersonianism of classical cinema, the emphasis on the individual is crucially intertwined with a patriarchal discourse on the family, with romance plots that appeal to—and appropriate—the viewer's own investment in primary objects.[12] To return to the example of *Birth*, capitalizing as it did on the still traumatic memories of the Civil War and Reconstruction, the film allowed its viewers to understand a larger historical conflict through the experience, not merely of individual characters but, more important, that of families and family members. Character subjectivity in *Birth* is yoked to being a member of a family. This familial structuring of viewer identification is ultimately the most effective catalyst of the film's racist ideology. Blacks not only have no family (unless, like "the faithful souls," they are members of the extended Southern family), they are also shown to be a fundamental threat to the survival of the family as an institution.[13]

Just as the imbrication of history, narrative, and a particular kind of subjectivity makes *Birth* in a sense a model classical, a model American film, the dissociation of these very elements is largely responsible for making *Intolerance* a "model" failure. Nonetheless, Griffith may have conceived of his new enterprise as a continuation and elaboration of some of the same principles. Thus, if film could bring to life history, "as it really happened," then the representation could be lifted out of the referential context and employed freely for its connotative meanings. If history was merely the incarnation of eternal truths telling "the same story" throughout the ages, then narrative motifs and situations were interchangeable and could be freely intercut at liberty. And if the narrative of history manifests itself in the fates of individuals, and these remain fundamentally the same over time, then it should be possible to engage a contemporary viewer through and into this ostensibly transhistorical subjectivity.

While these assumptions are already problematic in and by themselves (and their interplay precarious even in *Birth*), they also mark the seams at which *Intolerance* is torn apart, as it were, by its own textual ingenuity. The project of the narrativization of history, overdetermined in four—if not five—different ways, disintegrates from both ends simultaneously. The eternal truths of history (such as the theme of Love versus Intolerance) stand out in unmediated abstraction, spawning an allegorical style that fragments the narration even on the level of individual sequences. Conversely, as I have shown, the relay of narrative subjectivity is decentered by the proliferation of characters and impaired by a disarticulation of scopic desire, linked in turn to the film's concern with the crisis of femininity and its threat to the family.

Nonetheless, although *Intolerance* abstains from a classical, character-oriented narrativization of history, it conveys a particular vision of history in its overall design. Indeed, the film offers a *philosophy* of history both as a justification and as an effect of its textual design. Rather than revealing historical truth in the development of a single linear narrative, the film traces the laws of history through its montage of historically distinct narratives, in their very relationship to each other. Eclectic as anything in the film, this metahistorical construction draws on a variety of traditions, including contemporary Progressive, late-nineteenth-century Populist, and earlier American discourses on history.

The major assumption underlying *Intolerance*, the message of its parallel construction, is a concept of history as eternal recurrence. Like its eighteenth-century antecedents, such a concept implies an analogy between the course of civilizations and the human life cycle; accordingly, all civilizations tend to head toward decline and cataclysm.[14] Cyclical and cataclysmic concepts of history had a currency well into Griffith's own time—in cultural criticism, social and political theory, and popular fiction—combining older millennialist notions with more modern fears precipitated by industrialization and the rise of the urban masses. Novels like Ignatius Donnelly's *Caesar's Column* (1891), for instance, or Jack London's *The Iron Heel* (1907) drive their antiutopian plots to a point of total destruction and annihilation. Yet, like *Intolerance*, they are sufficiently imbued with millennialist (or, more precisely, postmillennialist) thought to convert the apocalypse, with a narratively sudden and improbable turn, into visions of a better future.[15]

In terms of the self-definition of *Intolerance* as a textual system, the cyclical concept of history is anchored in the foregone attribution of the individual narratives to timeless metaphysical principles; the course of history is merely a replay, in each period, of the antagonism of Love and Intolerance. At the same time, the cyclical structure of history is articulated, step-by-step, in the repetition of narrative motifs, character traits and constellations, in parallels of social and political structure (the Populist dualism of common people and those in power), in patterns of gender relations and sexual behavior, even in details of gesture and emotional response.

This emphasis on detail, this empathy with the texture of everyday life throughout the ages echoes the poetic sensibility of *Leaves of Grass*, a book that Gish tells us Griffith admired "passionately."[16] More likely than not, he was inspired by Whitman's line, "Ages and ages returning at intervals," assimilating it in the same literalizing spirit to which we owe the emblem of the Rocking Cradle. Aside from many more such one-line images that might have made their way into *Intolerance*, Griffith's narration, throughout the film, shares Whitman's grandiose compassion with just about everything and everyone under the sun ("I am the man, I suffer'd, I was there"), the omnivorous sense of a poetic ego that creates itself as it recreates history: "The past and present wilt—I have fill'd them, emptied them, / And proceed to fill my next fold of the future." At its worst, *Intolerance* lacks the anarchic imagination of its literary patron saint, reducing his vision to an assertion of a timeless human essence, and historical development to differences in costume and setting.[17] The possibility of historical change becomes a matter of rescue races whose outcome is scripted elsewhere.

Running counter to the pattern of eternal sameness and cyclical return, however, is a teleological movement that culminates in the happy ending of the Modern narrative. This teleological concept of history hinges upon a

Christian theology of redemption, rendered explicit in the crosscutting between the Boy's walk to his execution and Christ's ascent to Golgatha—indeed the sacrifice and suffering of all ages are fulfilled in the Boy's rescue from the gallows. In a more secular vein, the teleology of history manifests itself in the progress of technology, the superior means of transportation and communication that make possible the last-minute rescue in the Modern story, as well as the moral perfectibility of the individual, exemplified by the final victory of conscience in the Friendless One. The triumph of Modern technology is no less a triumph of American democracy, especially in light of the particular choice of historical periods. The temporal succession of settings—pagan antiquity, Judeo-Christian period, Renaissance-Protestantism, and the Modern age—corresponds to a geographical movement from the Orient via Mediterranean and Western Europe to the United States—and thus to the millennial prophecy that was mobilized in the nineteenth century by the ideology of Manifest Destiny: "Westward the course of empire takes its way."[18]

Undoubtedly *Intolerance* participates in the discourse of American imperialism of its time.[19] But the film's "ideological project" seems more elusive and more specific than that. The difficulty of reconstructing a singular ideological project (as the editors of *Cahiers du Cinéma* have done in the case of *Young Mr. Lincoln*) may be the result of the film's eclectic vision of history, in particular the tension between cyclical and teleological elements. This tension, however, is more than "a contradiction between the ideological and the textual."[20] It can be traced on both these levels and demonstrates the ways in which textual and ideological strategies interact within a larger rhetorical framework.

Mapping the nineteenth-century myths of modernity, Walter Benjamin has remarked upon the complementary relationship between the doctrine of eternal recurrence and the ideology of progress, identifying them as the irreducible antinomies of mythical thought. Each tendency in its way eclipses the historicity of time which, for Benjamin, meant the reality of catastrophe—"that things 'just go on' *is* the catastrophe." Because catastrophe happens to be a key figure in the textual make-up of *Intolerance* (perhaps less because of Griffith's historical insight than because of the psychosexual dynamic that propels the film), the film could be said to reveal these antinomies for what they are. In such moments of contradiction, myth congeals into allegory (in the Benjaminian sense) and becomes readable, against its manifest ideology, as an emblem of a failed utopian desire, pointing to "the small fissure in the ongoing catastrophe."[21]

To establish the difference of the Modern narrative may well be the major ideological project of *Intolerance*—albeit in a more complex sense than in its predictable conformity with imperialist discourse. Accordingly, the task of the textual system is to maintain a stable distribution of parallel and difference in the process of interweaving the four distinct narratives. The possibility of difference, however, is founded on the trajectory of sameness, of that which enables comparison in the first place. It is on this trajectory that the systematic oppositions begin to slide, that the ideologically posited difference of the Modern narrative is in jeopardy. (The problem is spelled out, illuminating the confusion with unusual clarity, in an advertisement for the film's first run. The ad announces D. W. Griffith's *Intolerance* as "A Sun Play of the Ages," "in which four *paralleled* stories of the world's *progress* unfold before your vision in thrilling sequence." It then lists the historical episodes, ending with "a gripping modern story *contrasted* with these historic periods" [emphasis mine].)

Despite—or, in Benjamin's sense, because of—the assertion of universal progress, the internal movement of each of the historical narratives is toward cataclysm, suggesting a vision of history as an accumulation of catastrophe. As has often been observed, the rhythm of accelerating montage seems to merge the four different spaces into a single movement, creating the impression that the Babylonian chariot is racing with the car and train in Modern America.[22] But this cross-diegetic thrust likewise causes the multiple scenes of devastation and annihilation to contaminate the Modern narrative with their cataclysmic frenzy.[23] In the psychic economy of accelerated parallelism, therefore, the ending of the Modern narrative is determined just as much by the experience of catastrophe (and the perverse pleasures it affords the viewer) as are those of the other three—rather than by the victory of love and life ostensibly inaugurated with the last-minute rescue of the Boy from the gallows. Anticipated by the disturbing shot of a leather dummy dropping through the trap in the sequence of the hangmen's test, as well as by the decentered extreme close-up (after the trial) of Mae Marsh's face, numb with terror, the Boy's execution can no longer be stayed within the motivational framework of a realistic narrative. The rescue can be accomplished—and experienced by the viewer—only as an act of divine mercy, a miracle. This tour de force assimilates the happy ending of the Modern narrative to the posthistorical, apocalyptic images of the epilogue and thus undermines the ideological assertion of linear progress.

The claim to historical difference ultimately may be defeated by the multiple drift toward catastrophe, but its assertion constitutes a large part of the textual work of *Intolerance*. The Modern narrative articulates this claim not merely through its happy ending on the fictional level, its apotheosis of Manifest Destiny; it does so even more forcefully on the level of filmic discourse, by setting into play stylistic differences between the Modern and the three historical narratives.

Film History, Archaeology, Universal Language

.   .   .   .

7

To me, *Intolerance* recalls Mr. Griffith's words: "We have gone beyond Babel, beyond words. We have found a new universal language, a power that can make men brothers and end war forever. Remember that! Remember that when you stand in front of a camera!"
—Lillian Gish, The Movies, Mr. Griffith, and Me

Babylon is the foundation stone, and seems to have been the original inspiration, of this visual Babel.
—*Julian Johnson, in* Photoplay Magazine, *December 1917*

If the Modern, "American" narrative wins out at the expense of the historical, "foreign" narratives, it owes its triumph to a particular kind of technology—of which cars and locomotives are only a metaphor. The happy ending is after all an effect of cinematic narration, more precisely, of a specific mode of narration. According to this logic, the relation between the Modern and the historical narratives, the very choice of periods dramatized, can be read as an allegory of the American cinema during the transitional period. The constellation that would warrant such an allegorical reading is defined, on the one hand, by the American film industry's bid for hegemony on both domestic and foreign markets and, on the other, by Griffith's personal ascendancy over his rivals.

As a number of critics have pointed out, the individual narratives allude—and partly respond—to different types of film then competing for the favors of American audiences. [1] The Huguenot narrative invokes the French productions of Films d'Art, in particular its most successful example, set in the same period, *L'assassinat du Duc de Guise* (1908). With its dramatic ambitions and sumptuous decors, this tradition had a major impact on American productions, from Griffith's Biograph films, *The Fool's Revenge* and *Resurrection* (1909), to Zukor's Famous Players in Famous Plays (beginning with Sarah Bernhardt's appearance in the four-reel *Queen Elizabeth*, 1912). [2]

The Judean narrative resumes the string of Passion Plays mostly imported from France, but also follows in the footsteps of the enormously popular

Kalem release, *From the Manger to the Cross* (1912, directed by Sidney Olcott). Another reference point may have been the Italian spectacle, *Satan* (Luigi Maggi, 1912), in which the Christ story figures as one of four historical episodes in which the devil tests humanity.[3]

The Babylonian narrative has thematic antecedents in a number of early French productions of the Book of Daniel (also Vitagraph, 1913) as well as Gaumont's *The Fall of Babylon* (1910). More acutely, however, it responds to the success of Italian spectacles dramatizing themes from Mediterranean antiquity, such as *Quo Vadis*, *The Last Days of Pompeii*, and, especially, Giovanni Pastrone's *Cabiria* (all released in 1913). Moreover, it continues Griffith's own venture into this genre with his feature-length *Judith of Bethulia* (1913, produced for Biograph but shelved by the studio until 1914).

In the Modern narrative, finally, Griffith displays the trademarks of his Biograph period such as the last-minute rescue race and psychological character delineation, unfolding them in a "realistic" melodrama set in a lower-class urban milieu, of which *The Musketeers of Pig Alley* (1912) is the best-known precursor. Thus, by the logic of competition alone, it is not surprising that the narrative which most distinctly bears Griffith's signature should turn out the only one with a happy ending. Indeed, one could argue that the victory of Love over Intolerance in the Modern story projects the economic triumph—ennobled by the virtues of American democracy—of the American narrative film over its international rivals.

With *Intolerance*, Griffith was not just entering the competition in any one of the categories listed above but redefining the very terms of that competition. Rather than giving a summary of "tendances de l'art cinématographique" of film history to date (as Baudry suggests), *Intolerance* constructs that history in the first place. It converts the relative anarchy of the marketplace into a hierarchy of present over past. Just as the still-competing precursors are neutralized into pastness, reduced to a depository of styles that are passé, this move too involves the transformation of the present into a mythical presence. As Griffith put it elsewhere: "It is the ever-present, realistic, actual now that 'gets' the American public."[4] This effect of presence, a distinctive mark of classical cinema, safeguards the Modern style from becoming passé, thus designating it as the cinema of the future. Finally, by relegating the "foreign styles" to "mere" historicity, the film marks them as merely particular, hence inferior to the universal idiom of American narrative film.

Yet, by staging the ascendancy of the American narrative film through a textual agon of heterogeneous styles, *Intolerance* violates the norms of transparency and linearity characteristic of the emerging classical paradigm. In its foregrounding of discursive variance, the film departs from the concept of representation advanced in defense of *The Birth of a Nation*. If the latter had mobilized a naive concept of referential realism (a claim to transparency again and again belied, on the level of filmic discourse, by moments of narratorial intervention and textual overdetermination), the production of *Intolerance* simultaneously assumed and transcended such a concept. As a metahistorical film, *Intolerance* no longer professes the historicist ambition to show, in Ranke's phrase, "what actually happened" (*wie es eigentlich gewesen*). It is concerned instead with the connotations attached to specific traditions of representation, whether popular or scholarly, thus acknowledging—in order to manipulate— the iconographic conventions associated with the respective historical periods.

Intolerance still makes demonstrative bows toward historical accuracy and authenticity in the manner of *Birth*, with its pedantic intertitles that footnote the source of a representation ("AN HISTORICAL FACSIMILE of" or "after cylinders recently excavated"). As in *Birth*, such titles attempt to anchor the truth of the historical tableau they advertise, not so much in an iconic equivalence with the actual event as in a genealogy of representation that links the image with its ostensible referent—an imprint of meaning guaranteed by tradition. In *Intolerance*, however, this rhetorical gesture is rendered ineffectual by the sheer eclecticism and promiscuity of sources, drowned out in an unprecedented fetishism of costumes, props and decor.[5]

It seems as if Roland Barthes's analysis of realism as an effect of "pastiche," of "copying a (depicted) copy of the real,"[6] had been a cheerfully avowed working principle on the *Intolerance* set. Karl Brown remembers that the research for the Judean narrative, guided by Tissot's illustrated Bible, was determined by the following considerations:

> Griffith cut the knot of bewilderment [presented by conflicting artistic conceptions] with a single decisive stroke. People believe only what they already know. They knew all about how people lived, dressed, and had their being in Biblical times because they had been brought up on Bible pictures, Bible calendars, Biblical magic-lantern shows, Christmas cards, Easter cards, pictures of every incident with which we were concerned. Never mind whether these pictures were accurate or not. Follow them in every detail because that's what the people believe to be true, and what the people believe to be true *is* true—for them—and there's no budging them.[7]

Other decisions were not even motivated or justified by the continuity of an iconographic tradition. Joseph Henabery recalls the question of the stone elephants in the great court of Babylon, attributing them to a personal whim of Griffith:

> Griffith was very keen on those elephants. He wanted one on the top of each of the eight pedestals in Belshazzar's palace. I searched through all my books. "I'm sorry," I said. "I can't find any excuse for elephants. I don't care what Doré or any other Biblical artist has drawn—I can find no reason for putting elephants up there. To begin with, elephants were not native to this country. They may have known about them, but I can't find any references."
>
> Finally, this fellow Wales found someplace a comment about the elephants on the walls of Babylon, and Griffith, delighted, just grabbed it. He very much wanted elephants up there![8]

One could read this anecdote as a parody of an effect in search of an origin, but it problematizes the nature of the effect as much as that of the source. In the film itself the rampant elephants can hardly be said to work as a descriptive detail, producing a realistic effect that would support the authority of the narrative.[9] On the contrary, they stick out like a sore

Figure 7.1

Figure 7.2

thumb—hyperbolic, obscene, monumental. As an emblem of the film's
elephantine ambition, these sculptures altogether unhinge the Babylonian
spectacle from pretensions to historical accuracy and authenticity, revealing
it as the Orientalist phantasmagoria it was to begin with. Moreover, while
exposing the insistence on verifiable research as hypocritical, Henabery
obscures a much more obvious source for Griffith's obsession: he wanted
those elephants, not because they would have been typical of the Babylonian court or its iconography, but because he, like millions of moviegoers,
had seen them on the set of *Cabiria*.[10]

  If *Intolerance* departs from the concept of representation underlying *Birth*, it
is not simply a question, in semiological terms, of Griffith's "working on the
possibilities of the signifiers," momentarily abandoning his usual preoccupation with the signified.[11] The rhetorical complexities of *Intolerance* elude the
distinction between signifier and signified, thus calling into question the
usefulness of the Saussurean concept of the sign. One might describe the
film's representational eclecticism as an unabashed blurring of a conventional "realistic" hierarchy of denotation and connotation, a promiscuous
mobilization of meanings in which the ostensibly first, denotative level is

just one among a whole range of representations and figurations marked by graphic particularity, by a variety of textual and intertextual resonances. [12]

Like the competition between omniscient narrator and primitive narrator figures described in Chapter 5, the subsumption or, better, transumption of the historical genres takes place in the very process of their reinscription, even prior to their subordination by means of parallel montage. Each narrative, in its introductory sequences, establishes its own spatial and temporal parameters, accustoms the viewer to a specific stylistic system. Yet each of the historical narratives also includes, almost from the start, a point of condensation, a tropological moment in which the film comments and reflects upon these parameters, thus calling for a double process of reading.

The Judean narrative, which perhaps should be called a set of episodes, opens with a series of shots in the manner of a travelogue ("Everyday Life in the Holy Land"). A street in Jerusalem, a group of merchants, a camel (a medium close-up moving back from its object), a mother cradling her child, an old man in Arab garb, pigeons at his feet—all aim at the combined effect of authentic locales (as in *From the Manger to the Cross*) and the popular iconography cited by Brown. Contrary to standard descriptions of *Intolerance*, the space of the Judean episodes is more than an outdated tableau space. It oscillates between the individual tableaux it stages (the Marriage of Cana, the Woman Taken in Adultery) and a rudimentary breakdown of the scene—not strictly speaking alternation, though certainly more than mere juxtaposition. [13] The space of the Judean episodes is one of devotion, drawing the viewer into a semicircle of familiar images—hence no need for an illusionist diegesis—while the time of ritual suspends both narrative and historical time.

The temporality of devotional space, its difference from the speed and forward momentum of classical narration, becomes thematic in the first, and only fictional, episode of the Judean set. A sequence of nineteen rather tightly framed, alternating shots shows how the Pharisees (introduced with the same type of backtracking as the camel) interfere with the activities of people in the street—a potter working at his wheel, a toothless old man eating, and a youth carrying a heavy bundle—by forcing them to pause in a kind of freeze-frame effect for the duration of the Pharisees' prayer. This moderately comic vignette has at least two implications. On the thematic level it resumes the social dualism already proposed in the modern narrative; it urges the viewer to side with the "common man," as a representative of a "normal," everyday sense of time. On the level of enunciation, however, even such minimal identification acknowledges, and to some degree encourages, the viewer's impatience with any type of film that deviates from the "normal" pace of classical narrative. With this twofold appeal, the sequence asserts the superiority of the Modern idiom, even within the stylistic system of the type of film it ostensibly—and parasitically—invokes.

The French narrative contains a similar moment of doubling and commenting upon its particular mode of representation. In another variation on the dualistic social theme the opening shots juxtapose a quaint cobblestoned street (again featuring street vendors, this time a girl) with a sumptuous tableau of the court of Charles IX. Following a static long shot, a traveling shot moves in from a total view of the tableau to a medium shot of the king on his throne. Camera movement independent of figure movement had been used in a number of films since *Cabiria* (hence called "Cabiria movement"), to add depth to sets of epic and theatrical dimensions. [14] Paradoxically, in this case it calls attention to the two-dimensional and static quality of the representational space it traverses. The two-dimensionality is further emphasized by the predominance of the decor, especially the tapestry that looms large and central above the heads of the characters (at one point the frame virtually decapitates them) and seems to trope on the immobile pageantry below. As soon as it is stamped with the allusion to Film d'Art, the theatrical space is broken down, invaded by devices that bear Griffith's own signature: a close-up of puppies in the lap of the decadent Monsieur La France, [15] an alternation (using sight links) which introduces the opposing factions and suggests a narrative cause for the fatal intrigue. Finally, in a similar vein, the third to last shot of the sequence shows a page, kneeling (as the closing shot establishes retroactively) at the extreme left of the tableau, holding a book, and yawning furtively but heartily.

Again the viewer is solicited on two levels. On the one hand, the sequence appeals to a voyeuristic delight in Old World pomp and decadence. On the other, we are asked to share the reaction of the yawning page, the spectator at the edge of the tableau, who is not only a representative of the common man at court but also a youth whose boredom projects a different standard of pace and vitality.

The intrusion of Griffith's signature into the historical episodes marks their predominant stylistic features by contrast as other, as un-American, while it asserts the Modern (more classical) style as neutral, functionally subordinate to the narrative and "naturally" responsive to the viewer's own sense of time and standards of subjectivity. In the same move these interventions domesticate the foreignness of the historical episodes, coopt them as merely exotic, and thus prefigure the great melting pot of styles, techniques, subject matter, and decor on which Hollywood was to thrive in the decades to come.

A similar pattern, a similar intertextual tension at the most detailed level of enunciation, can be observed in the Babylonian narrative. Far more obtrusive than in the French narrative, "Cabiria movement" dominates the viewer's relation to the Babylonian space, culminating in Bitzer's legendary traveling shot of Belshazzar's Feast. Again, Griffith has to go one notch beyond the precursor film. In the opening sequences, which show the great gate and walls of Babylon, the effect of sweeping movement results from a combination of irises opening up from frame right or left and slow lateral pans; likewise, the sweep into the great hall combines a forward dolly shot with a vertical movement of the camera (stationed on an elevator which in turn was mounted on parallel tracks).[16] These traveling shots invite the viewer to marvel at the sights displayed, like a visitor to a world's fair or an archaeological site, but never without a cicerone; they draw attention to their own virtuosity as much as they display the monumental dimensions of the set. Thus, the prototypical fetishization of cinematic technique is at the same time a throwback to instances of camera movement in early cinema whose primary function was to demonstrate "the camera's ability to mobilize and explore space."[17] By 1916, however, such pleasures conflicted with the norms of invisible narration, since they entailed "a sense of mechanics," which, as a contemporary commentator noted, "to some may destroy the illusion of the picture."[18]

An illusionist effect of presence may not have been a priority for the Babylonian narrative anyway, certainly less so than for the modern narrative or even the French.[19] On the contrary, the use of independent camera movement, the tableauesque vistas, and the relative paucity of continuity devices work to maintain the viewer's subliminal awareness of a preexisting set—a set such as had never existed before in the history of American cinema—and thus mobilize the discourse of superlatives that surrounded the film's production. That this impression was not altogether unintended is confirmed by the fact that most of the stylistic peculiarities of the Babylonian narrative (along with its deviant sexual economy) were eliminated, by Griffith himself, in *The Fall of Babylon* (1919), in an attempt to salvage part of *Intolerance*.

The lack of diegetic closure can be related to a series of self-reflexive moments articulated within the Babylonian narrative. Like the tapestry at the French court, a bas-relief frieze appears prominently above the heads of the characters in the opening sequence at the great gate of Babylon. On a slightly more abstract scale, this frieze repeats the live procession of people and animals that pass through the gate. Yet it also points beyond this particular sequence to the stone-carved hieroglyphs of the Babylonian title-cards. More than merely doubling the representation, this frieze accentuates the different temporal and figurative layers involved in the process of representation.

A more obvious metaphor of the textual enterprise occurs about a third of the way into the film, when all is as yet well and peaceful in Babylon (except for the jealousy of the priest of Bel), while in the Modern narrative events have already gained a somewhat fatal momentum. An intertitle announces that Belshazzar's father, the senile King Nabonidus, "has a red letter day. He excavates a foundation brick of the temple of Naram-Sin, builded 3200 years before." While the archaeological preoccupation is linked with the loss of patriarchal power—the childish eagerness of Nabonidus as he rushes to show Belshazzar the brick—the vignette also can be read as a comment on the belatedness of narrative action, the reign of spectacle at the expense of narrative. "Incidentally," the next title reads, "he [Nabonidus] remarks that Cyrus the Persian, Babylon's mighty foe, is nearing the city" (Huff, 606–07).

Nabonidus' brick, among other things, becomes a trope of the lack of closure, of a gap in the Babylonian diegesis. Rather than attempt an illusionist re-presentation of the past, the Babylonian space is already figured as an archaeological site, as a space of reconstruction. At the same time, the archaeological orientation is counterbalanced by emphatic references to the future, such as the imminence of the royal wedding and, more important, Belshazzar's three-times stated promise to build a city for the Princess Beloved, "beautiful as the memory of her own city in a foreign land." This promise is visualized in repeated tableau shots showing the couple at a screenlike window in a tower overlooking the city. Thus, the archaeological site is also a potential site of construction, of a vision projected but never fulfilled.

What is this vision and what are its implications for the way Griffith rewrites Babylon, for the ways we read *Intolerance?* These questions require a brief return to the question of the structural relations between the four narratives. In a number of respects the Babylonian narrative claims a special status in the film. While it undeniably exceeds any other in its value as spectacle, it is also the most complex—in terms of intrigue and action—of the historical narratives. It is introduced, as if with a special flourish, only after the narration has reverted again to the Modern period. Following this pattern, the Modern narrative more frequently alternates with the Babylonian than with any other narrative, and it is no coincidence that most of the transitional Cradle shots occur between these two historical antipodes. In typological terms, moreover, the Babylonian narrative is set off as the only non-Christian one; it is therefore in a sense prehistory, exempt from the political, ethical, and sexual norms the film reworks for the Christian era.

That dividing line, however, is a problematic one, considering the reputation of Babylon in the Hebrew Bible and the New Testament which Griffith, raised a Methodist, could not have ignored. The Judeo-Christian tradition, after all, takes sides with Cyrus, welcoming his victory as an end to the Jews' captivity and to the reign of sin, wealth, and idolatry which was to inspire the famous metaphor of Hollywood Babylon. Griffith did rely on other sources, such as books on Assyrio-Babylonian archaeology, Herodotus, and nineteenth-century paintings depicting Babylonian scenes, but the revisionist gesture implied in the Babylonian narrative, especially its positive image of Belshazzar, cannot be explained away. Nor did it go unnoticed. Reviewers were quick to cite it as further proof of film's contribution to a scientific historiography. (A headline in the *San Francisco Chronicle* read: "Stripping Off Belshazzar's Cloak of Infamy—Was He Really a Hero? Now the Newest Research Shows That Modern Moralists Are Wrong When They Attack the Babylonian King as the Symbol of Wickedness, and How He Was, instead, a Gentle, Peaceful and Most Tolerant Monarch, a Brave and Highly Gifted Sovereign Whose ONLY WEAKNESS Was That He BELIEVED LOVE WAS ALWAYS RIGHT.")[20] If science provided a convenient cover, the vision itself was part of a more ambitious enterprise, indebted to the antinomian impulses of American Protestantism.

With its deviant inscriptions of sexual and social difference, the Babylonian narrative can be read, among other things, as a counterimage held up against the encroachment of Puritanism on all spheres of life, projecting an ideal civilization that would overcome divisions between love and sexuality, individual and society, public and private, law and justice, rulers and ruled, beauty and everyday life. The particular elaboration of these themes coincides to a great extent with topoi of reformist and radical discourse during the Progressive Era. Consider, for example, the rhetoric of urban reform and its use of millennialist images such as the City on the Hill or the New Jerusalem; the concept of an "integral society" and concomitant notions of charismatic "leadership" (Walter Lippmann, Herbert Croly); the critique of Puritanism in general and of vice-crusaders like Anthony Comstock in particular, voiced by such intellectuals as H. L. Mencken and Van Wyck Brooks; finally, the vogue of paganism, advocacy of free love, and a Whitmanian cult of the body promoted by the Greenwich Village bohemians.[21]

Surely, Griffith would not have endorsed the political implications of many of these ideas, least of all those concerning the social organization of sexuality. The formation of the couple in the Modern narrative, for instance, reasserts traditional codes of sexual behavior in no uncertain terms. But the film's critique of contemporary moral reform, compounded with an all-around denunciation of an instrumentalist, acquisitive, and repressive mentality, needs and feeds on the alterity of the Babylonian dream, filtered through—and enabled by—the screen of exotic fantasy. It is this utopian surplus of the Babylonian narrative that disturbs the dominant distribution of parallel and contrast among the four narratives, undermining the ideological assertion of progress and teleological fulfillment. Babylon thus becomes the source of a different economy of signification, one that threatens to collapse carefully constructed oppositions and distinctions.

To fathom this antinomian investment in the Babylonian dream, we must turn once more to the trope of archaeology. What layer of Babylonian history or mythology is Nabonidus digging up, and why does he have to find a brick? Obviously the utopian power of the Babylonian narrative owes much to its conflation of various legends and traditions, from the evocation of Babylon as one of the Seven Wonders of the ancient world through the cult of Ishtar to the more ambiguous allusion to the Whore of Babylon, the sybaritic splendor that encompasses both low and high eros (suggested by deep space composition) yet also accounts for Babylon's fall. The most equivocal layer in this palimpsest, however, is a figure most powerful in its absence: the image, archetype, allegory of the Tower of Babel.

Traces of Babel can be detected in unmotivated details like Nabonidus' brick—Genesis 11:3 emphasizes that the Tower was built with brick not stone—which would add the ironic twist that a material which is already a substitution (of an artificial for a natural material) is made to figure as the foundational layer of a civilization whose materials of representation consist largely of plaster of Paris and celluloid.[22] When they are first framed together as antagonists, both Belshazzar and the Priest of Bel, who will betray the city to Cyrus, wear hats shaped like towers; Belshazzar's imitates a completed ziggurat with a pointed tip, the Priest's has the shape of a more primitive tower with a flattened top. Yet the most explicit reference to the Babelistic tradition occurs at the beginning of Act II, when a series of titles inform us that the events portrayed are based on actual sources, "the recently excavated cylinders of Nabonidus and Cyrus." "These cylinders," the next title reads, "describe the greatest treason of all history, by which a civilization of countless ages was destroyed and a universal written language (the cuneiform) was made to become an unknown cypher on the face of the earth."

This title links the trope of archaeology with the discursive activity of the film itself, as an activity of translation, transcription, and reconstruction.

Moreover, it draws an implicit line from the disappearance of the last universal written language (dramatically conflated with the Fall of Babylon) to the vision of film as a new universal language, as it was being advanced by Griffith in defense of his own film practice. The insertion of the universal language theme at this point suggests a reading of the Babylonian narrative as an allegory of the cinema as Griffith perceived it at the time, at a crucial juncture between prehistory and a virtually limitless future. The attack on reform and reformers in the Modern narrative is usually taken as Griffith's response to the threat of censorship, in particular to such liberal intellectuals as Jane Addams, Frederic Howe, Rabbi Wise, and groups like the NAACP who had condemned the racist slant of *The Birth of a Nation*. But a similar case could be made for the Babylonian narrative. Like the priests of Bel who betray Belshazzar, thus causing the destruction of an ideal civilization, the advocates of censorship not only infringe on the freedom of speech but unwittingly jeopardize the possibility for film to become the new universal language "that had been predicted in the Bible."[23]

The invocation of Babel is probably the most overdetermined moment in the *Intolerance* text, opening up an abyss of self-reflexivity. For the Tower of Babel stands not only for the project of a universal language but also for its opposite, the impossibility of such a project, the punitive diversification of tongues. According to popular etymology, "Babel" is derived from the Hebrew word for "confusion" (according to another tradition, it signifies "the father of God," the "city of God"). Babel is thus also an archetypal metaphor of confusion, according to Jacques Derrida, a metaphor of the necessity and impossibility of translation, a metaphor of metaphor. Bearing out the fate of the metaphor, the Babylonian narrative is associated with images of distraction, dissemination, and destruction—images that contaminate the relative stability and clarity of the other narratives and thereby assault the structure of the film as a whole, indeed, the very possibility of its construction. "The 'tower of Babel,'" to quote Derrida, "does not merely figure the irreducible multiplicity of tongues; it exhibits an incompletion, the impossibility of finishing, of totalizing, of saturating, of completing something on the order of edification, architectural construction, system and architectonics. What the multiplicity of idioms actually limits is not only a 'true' translation, a transparent and adequate interexpression, it is also a structural order, a coherence of construct." If *Intolerance* escapes the rigor of its parallel design on any count, it is by embodying, as a text, in its readability, "something like an internal limit to formalization."[24]

To surrender without a fight to the deconstructive power of Babel would blind us to the specific ways in which Griffith rewrites the myth. As Derrida and other commentators have pointed out, Babel is also a scene of contradiction. The metaphor refers, simultaneously and inseparably, to the confusion of tongues and to the project that provoked the divine act of dispersion in the first place, a project that consisted of more than just raising a tower: "And they said, Go to, let us build us a city and a tower, whose top may reach unto heaven; and let us make a name, lest we be scattered abroad upon the face of the whole earth" (Genesis, 11:4). The desire to found a unique genealogy, to constitute an autonomous collective in an identifiable and identifying place (implying a foregoing displacement and disparity), becomes synonymous with the question of language. The project of Babel recasts the Edenic act of naming as a quest for a universal language, a language that would ensure a unity and transparency of signifying and social relations. If God's punishment has stamped this quest as a forbidden repetition, as mimicry and idolatry, it has likewise perpetuated its utopian appeal.

Griffith wanted to make a name for himself as the father of American cinema, but he wanted to do so by making a new name, by founding a new language of images that would recover a prelapsarian transparency and univocity. By emphasizing, in millennialist fashion, the Edenic undercurrent of the myth, he appears more heretical than he might have intended. Buried, enciphered, rewritten in the Babylonian narrative of *Intolerance*, the story of Babel reads more like a parable of God's jealousy than one of human hubris. The Tower is missing from the construction imagery, the envisioned City feminized by association with the Princess (echoing the legendary queens Semiramis and Nitocris, but also Griffith's own *Judith of Bethulia*). Bel has been ousted by Ishtar, the goddess of love. The phallic threat is displaced, literally externalized, onto the Persian assault towers whose demolition is staged as a supreme spectacle. The cause of dispersion, God's intolerance, is attributed to the jealous Priest of Bel. Angry at Belshazzar's enthronement of Ishtar, the Priest of Bel "resolves to re-establish his own god—incidentally himself." Even as it is marked as arbitrary and illegitimate, this substitution spells out a trajectory from Babel to *Intolerance*: the struggle for authority in language.

I grant that such a reading of the Babylonian narrative resorts to somewhat esoteric evidence—though somewhat less esoteric if we consider the popular dissemination of millennialist thought at the time. The linking of *Intolerance* to the defense of cinema as a new universal language opens up perspectives, not only on Griffith's attempt to ground the cinema in the tradition of American culture (an oxymoronic enterprise on several counts) but also, and perhaps most important, on the difficulties and peculiarities of the *Intolerance* text. To take the argument one step further, I suggest that these difficulties to some degree result from the ambition, articulated in the configuration of Babel and Babylon, to put the universal language proposition into textual practice, to demonstrate at once the analogy and superiority of film in relation to verbal language.

This ambition is most explicit in the structural (if not proto-structuralist) conception of the film, the parallel imbrication of the four narratives whose ultimate meaning lies in their relation to each other, their value within a differential system. Since such a system does not preexist as in verbal language, the film has to establish it through and simultaneously with its own textual movement; hence the emphasis on the paradigmatic quality of narrative motifs, constellations, and gestures. Yet the demonstration of paradigmatic patterns also pushes the limits of the linguistic analogy. It disrupts the syntagmatic flow and thereby violates codes of unobtrusive and linear narration that viewers had come to expect by 1916; it thus impedes conventional routes of access and identification.

Many of the "problems" of *Intolerance* could be rephrased in terms of the theoretical issues surrounding the dis/analogy of film and verbal language, especially the contradictory notion of film as a visual Esperanto. As Metz points out in his influential essay, "The Cinema: Language or Language System" (1964), the notion of film as Esperanto compounds a language system that is "totally conventional, specific and organized," more linguistic than ordinary languages, with a medium that appears "universal" precisely because of its "dearth of linguisticity," in particular the ostensible self-evidence of its signs and its lack of a second articulation. [25] With this contradiction in mind, one could return to questions of systematicity in *Intolerance* raised earlier, such as the film's problematic self-definition or the difficulty of maintaining stable relations of parallel and contrast between the narratives, their sliding between opposition and similarity. Given the excessive self-consciousness with which *Intolerance* asserts its systematic character, however, the linguistic model also functions a bit like a red herring, as it is itself part of the problem that it purports to explain. Thus, in the end linguistically derived categories fail to register the peculiar ways in which the film figures and disfigures its own textual activity.

Griffith's advocacy of the universal language myth should not be exempted from a critique of ideology, especially in view of the myth's complicity with the most advanced forces of expansion and monopolization in other types of discourse, such as advertising or apologetic journalism. Yet the attempt to translate that myth into a film as idiosyncratic as *Intolerance* creates a textual density that effectively impedes the myth's ideological availability. If the notion of film as language is always a metaphor, then that of film as a universal language can only be an extended trope, weaving into an ideal conception of film a whole history of metaphysical projects. This means that the self-definition of *Intolerance* in terms of the Babelistic tradition has to be treated as a figure in its own right, a figure that complicates and derails the very system it sets out to perform. Like the tropes of archaeology, of construction and reconstruction, of the translation of materials and empires I have traced so far, the figuration of the universal language myth initiates a self-reflexivity that deflates any claims to unity and transparency asserted in its name. [26]

Hieroglyphics, Figurations of Writing

. . . .

8

As image, the hieroglyphics [of mass culture] are the medium of regression in which producer and consumer collude; as writing, they supply archaic images to modernity.
—*Theodor W. Adorno, "Prologue to Television" (1963)*

If we read *Intolerance* as a reinscription of the universal language myth, we must ask what type of language the film envisions and which model of language history it implies and dramatizes. These questions are of great significance, not only for elucidating the film's peculiar mode of address, its reverberations of early film-spectatorship relations, but also with regard to Griffith's ambitions for the film in relation to the public sphere, as well as his conception of that public sphere and the cinema's place in it.

In the title essay of his book, *Der sichtbare Mensch oder die Kultur des Films* (Visible Man or The Culture of Film, 1924), Béla Balázs too emphasizes the historically unique opportunity film offers to redeem the curse of Babel: "For on the motion picture screens all over the world we currently witness the development of *the first international language*: that of facial expression and physical gestures [die der Mienen und Gebärden]."[1] Leaving aside for a moment the difference between film theory and film practice, what matters here is the difference of traditions claimed in support of the universal language analogy. Balázs, drawing on phenomenology, physiognomy, and a somewhat mystical (and explicitly ethnocentric) anthropology, mounts his argument on the *opposition* between a lost ideal language and a hegemonic written language. Accordingly, Gutenberg's invention marks a second Fall rather than, as in most American instances, an evolutionary stepping-stone toward the invention of cinema. By the same token, intertitles are dismissed as nonessential, external, and irrelevant to the new language of film—an aesthetic position exemplified, the year Balázs' book was published, by Murnau's *The Last Laugh*. The ideal language film promises to restore is a language of immediate expression, projecting a visible integrity of body and soul. Balázs posits the origin of such a primordial language ("humanity's mother tongue") in the spontaneous expressive movement (*Aus-*

drucksbewegung) of the whole body, which includes the movement of lips and tongue. He does not assert the primacy of speech; sound is merely a by-product of this primary language of expression. Still, in conceptualizing film as the utopian other of an "abstract," "literary" culture, he participates in the cinema's suppression of writing and thus in an ideological tendency that culminates, historically, with the transition to sound.[2]

Intolerance (which Balázs saw in 1923 and admired greatly) may reflect a variety of concepts of "film language," including a physiognomic one, but it unequivocally joins a tradition of language history which assumes the primacy of writing. In an article published during the production of *Intolerance*, Griffith (or whoever wrote in his name), in a more evolutionist vein than usual, postulates a genealogy from cavemen drawing to the motion picture, a beginning of language in "carved rude images on stone."[3] To be sure, the "written word" is as soon reduced to a means of expression (for "that wild something evolving in the inner man"), a vehicle for the masterworks of religion and art. Yet in *Intolerance*, a film that flaunts the trope of archaeology, something like these "carved rude images on stone" persists, indeed becomes a mark of its textual idiosyncrasy.

The motif of archaic inscription surfaces, quite literally, in the design of

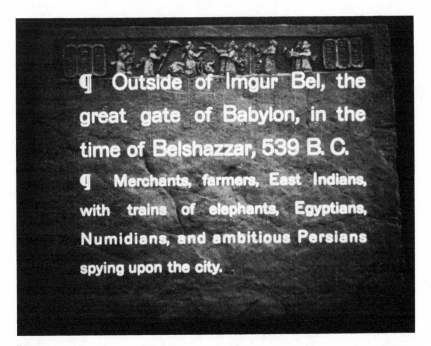

Figure 8.1

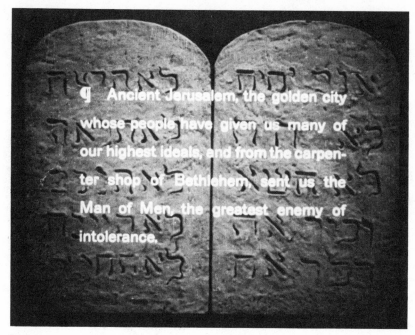

¶ Ancient Jerusalem, the golden city whose people have given us many of our highest ideals, and from the carpenter shop of Bethlehem, sent us the Man of Men, the greatest enemy of intolerance.

Figure 8.2

the title-cards for the Babylonian and Judean narratives, which are distinguished by a background, respectively, of stone-engraved hieroglyphics and Hebrew tablets.[4] Thus, whenever English intertitles are superimposed upon non-Western and nonphonetic script, different systems of graphic notation are made to coexist within one and the same shot. Likewise, the transitions between historically distinct sequences throughout the first half of the film tend to feature a whole series of discrete emblems: the Cradle shot, The Book of Intolerance, a graphically marked title-card, and, finally, a narrative image that opens the particular sequence. In such display of graphic specificity, *Intolerance* preserves a sense of the labor and artifice of inscription which effectively dispels fictions of film as a spontaneous expression or natural presence. The self-conscious mixing of heterogeneous materials throws into relief a dialectical tension between written characters and images, a dialectic that Horkheimer and Adorno discerned as the critical difference of silent film in general, and which collapsed with the advent of sound when writing was "banished from film like a foreign substance."[5]

The lines of *Intolerance*'s self-definition and of textual idiosyncrasy converge in the analogy with a particular type of writing, in the conception of film as a kind of hieroglyphics. As a manifest theme and organizing principle of the film, hieroglyphics are put forth as a model of signification that would reconcile the millennialist claim of universal communication with the necessities of conventionalization and differentiation. As a textual symptom, the figure of the hieroglyph urges a reading of the entire film as a "hieroglyphic text," a concept elaborated in recent film theory primarily within a Derridean framework. The model of hieroglyphic writing seems useful here because of its emphasis on the irreducibly composite character of the hieroglyphic sign (consisting of pictographic, ideogrammatic, and phonetic elements) and its constitutive plurality of meanings. Especially important is the connection made by Derrida—and of course Freud—between hieroglyphic writing and the figurative script of dreams. Both these textual phenomena in their way resist immediate perception and understanding, requiring instead an activity of reading and interpretation.[6]

The validation of hieroglyphics in the name of *écriture* needs to be complicated with a more historical and institutionally specific perspective, suggested by Horkheimer and Adorno's analysis of the ideological mechanisms of mass culture. Proceeding from a historico-philosophical framework diametrically opposed to Derrida's (though ultimately not so different in its

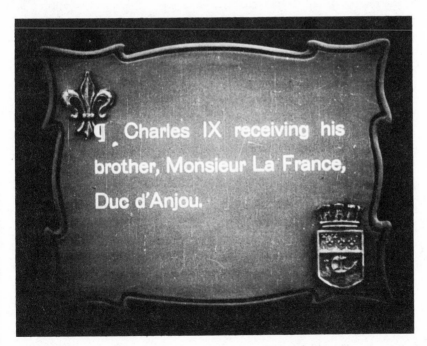

Figure 8.3

implications), Horkheimer and Adorno observe a return of hieroglyphic configurations in the industrial manufacturing of archetypes that spell out orders of social identity—ways of being, smiling, and mating. These modern archetypes consummate the historical transition from image to writing, the reification of mimetic capacities under the universal law of commodity culture. The ideological complicity of mass culture's "priestly hieroglyphics" lies not so much in their reflection of this process of reification as in their masking of it, in their disguising of script as pure image, as humanized presence. The scriptural character of mass-cultural phenomena, on the other hand, is the very condition of their critical readability; only as figurations of writing can these naturalized images be deciphered, and be made to yield their secret historical meaning. Echoing Benjamin's programmatic transformation of myth into allegory, Adorno (in a later essay; see the epigraph to this chapter) resumes the notion of mass-cultural hieroglyphics and elaborates it as a double vision, defined by a dialectic of consumerist regression and archaeology of modernity.[7]

If *Intolerance* provokes such a double vision more than any other American film, it is because in its naive self-consciousness the film displays, promotes, and experiments with the hieroglyphic tendency of mass culture. The image of the hieroglyph surfaces in a constellation of displacement, resulting, as does the Tower of Babel, from a conflation or cannibalization of various layers of tradition. The "universal written language" whose disappearance the narrative joins to the Fall of Babylon is the cuneiform, a system of writing older than, and probably unrelated to, Egyptian hieroglyphics. Yet it resembles the latter in the structural organization of its signs: the cuneiform code plays on both ideographic and phonetic registers, and even the individual graphic form may have a double value along the same line of division.[8] The reference to the cuneiform in the intertitle introducing Act II—as the universal language about to be destroyed—might be read as a token compliance with the self-imposed standard of historical authenticity (if we leave aside, for the moment, the minor detail that the cuneiform actually survived into the first century A.D. though only in the hands of the priests). The script on the Babylonian title-card, however, is not cuneiform, but a design unmistakably imitating a hieroglyphic pictograph, similar in style to Belshazzar's seal.

What are we to make of this apparent inconsistency? For one thing, the cuneiform is a much more abstract type of script, which by the time of the historical period dramatized (538 B.C.) had long since lost any pictographic dimension. It would not have supported the implicit analogy of film as a new universal, ostensibly self-evident language. Moreover, by substituting hieroglyphs for the Babylonian cuneiform, Griffith could affiliate himself with a particular tradition in American culture, a tradition of literary as well as popular significance.

In *American Hieroglyphics* John Irwin traces the symbol of Egyptian hieroglyphics, especially as redefined by Champollion's deciphering of the Rosetta Stone (1822), in the writings of the American Renaissance.[9] Griffith, who was greatly influenced by this group of writers, especially Whitman, Poe, and Emerson, could not have escaped being fascinated by the hieroglyph, its impact on both mystical and literary concepts of representation and interpretation. As Irwin points out, this fascination converged with a long-standing popular undercurrent, ranging from the publication of hieroglyphic Bibles (the latest in 1852) to children's books like *Mother Goose in Hieroglyphics* (1849; reprinted at least until the late 1860s). He makes a case for Whitman's conception of *Leaves of Grass* as a hieroglyphic Bible, a format linking esoteric writing with the popular tradition. Whitman's self-image as a popular, democratic poet is a highly complex issue—as is his purported quest for a language of natural correspondences. Nonetheless one can draw a trajectory, albeit through a sequence of misreadings, from the tradition of popular hieroglyphics through Whitman to Vachel Lindsay, self-appointed guardian of Whitman's legacy in Hollywood.

It is likely that Griffith had read Lindsay's *The Art of the Moving Picture* (1915). As I discussed in Chapter 2, Lindsay elaborates the notion of film as a new American hieroglyphics, paving the way for a democratic culture as envisioned by Whitman. Thus he describes the close-up of a symbolic spiderweb (spider devouring fly, ants destroying spider) in Griffith's *The Avenging Conscience* (1914) as "the first hint of the Poe hieroglyphic."[10] By placing *Intolerance* in the hieroglyphic tradition, Griffith might have hoped to gain access to this particular lineage of American culture, a filiation that would offset the risk he was taking in forgoing the more calculable effects of classical narration. Yet the tradition of American hieroglyphics is anything but monolithic or linear. It seems to blend Champollion's discovery of the composite character of the hieroglyphic sign with an older, epistemologically incompatible notion of hieroglyphics as a medium of mystical correspondence, prefigured by the divine script of nature.[11] Like Lindsay's notion of hieroglyphics, *Intolerance* oscillates between both sides of this epistemological watershed, a schism most manifest in the paradox of the film's excessive textuality and its simultaneous claim to iconic self-evidence.

As far as the reinscription of the universal language myth is concerned, it makes much more sense to read *Intolerance* as a self-styled hieroglyphic text rather than in terms of the linguistic distinction between language and language system. The repetition across historical periods of gestures, narrative motifs, and character behavior suggests a process of differentiation that does not necessarily presume a closed, totalized system. This emphasis on repetition goes beyond the programmatic assertion of history as eternal recurrence; it is evident even within individual narratives, specifically the Modern and the Babylonian. Rather than concealing repetition by variation, as became the norm in classical cinema, *Intolerance* stresses the similarities of particular situations, emotions, and physical expressions more than accidental differences of time, place, and agents.[12] Seriality becomes a pedagogical gesture, both infantilizing and esoteric, engaging the spectator in the position of someone just learning to read, while at the same time stimulating an open-ended activity of cross-referencing and deciphering.

The hieroglyphic analogy illuminates the peculiar organization of space discussed in Chapter 5, the traces of frontality, the frequency of ambiguous if not unclaimed shots, such as the emblematic close-ups of faces and objects.[13] Instead of attributing these deviations from classical standards to a return of theatrical space, the space of *Intolerance* can more precisely be characterized as a *reading space*, as a space of hieroglyphic signification and interpretation. In terms of the film's metafictional economy, the hieroglyphic discourse exceeds and unmakes the confines of the book, literalized in the Book of Intolerance (title-card), whose defeat is dramatized in the happy ending of the Modern narrative. In terms of enunciation and address the spectator's solicitation as a hieroglyphic reader projects a specific organization of the relations of reception, a different type of public sphere.

To circle back to the allegory of Babel in Babylon, the hieroglyphic analogy, with its historical connotations of veiling and deciphering, has particular political implications for Griffith's genealogy of the cinema and its place in American culture. The Fall of Babylon signifies not so much the end of one kind of language and the beginning of another, qualitatively different one, but a catastrophe that occurred within the history of writing (a history encompassing both clay tablets and celluloid), an event that destroyed the public availability of writing. With this construction *Intolerance* reenacts Bishop Warburton's discovery that hieroglyphics were not originally a sacral, esoteric script but a popular medium of preserving knowledge and of civil organization (the radical revision of the prevailing view which had enabled Champollion's discovery). The film affirms Warburton's contention that the deflection of hieroglyphic writing from common usage, its "encryptment," was an event of historical, political significance in that it rendered writing an instrument of power in the hands of a caste of "intellectuals."[14] What first seemed a historical inconsistency in the Babylonian narrative—the conflation of the disappearance of the cuneiform with the Fall of Babylon—more likely constitutes an act of interpretation, suggesting that any type of writing loses its universal potential when it falls into the hands of an intellectual elite. The Fall of Writing would thus be synonymous with the triumph of linguistic arbitrariness (epitomized by the Priest of Bel's nominating himself as God), which destroys not only a communal medium but, by synecdoche, the utopian unity in all spheres of life which Babylon holds up as a counter-image to the other periods.

As an allegory of an impossible unity and transparency, the Babylonian narrative also dramatizes the impossibility of historical continuity. Repairing the ruins of Babel requires an apocalyptic break, such as prefigured or, more precisely, precipitated by the narrative movement of the entire film; the future lies in the unfulfilled promises of prehistory. This metaleptic tendency defines both the genealogy of film within a history of writing and the relationship between cinema and literature in the context of that history. Rather than merely assimilate or reject the institution of literature as a whole, Griffith, for personal and ideological reasons, traces a rift within the institution of literature between an intellectual elite pursuing its own particular, selfish, and arbitrary interests and a marginalized popular tradition, reincarnated in the figure of Whitman. [15] If *Intolerance* is proposing to recover a unity of popular and high art, it does so not by replacing writing with a superior language of visual presence, but by retrieving the common roots of both film and literature in the hieroglyphic tradition.

Beyond the Babylonian allegory, *Intolerance* stages the Fall of Writing through its figurations of competing types of written language—that is, phonetic versus hieroglyphic writing—guided by the effort to dissociate its own textual activity from the curse of Babel. Across the four narratives we find a series of images of phonetic writing, headed by the Book of Intolerance, linked to arbitrariness, violence, and death. The most powerful instance of such figuration—or disfiguration—is the sequence in which Charles IX signs the decree for the massacre of the Huguenots, the document being shown twice in close-up, first during the signing and then bearing the completed signature. Besides translating into destruction for the fictional, personalized characters of the French narrative (the chalk mark on their door), the very act of signing is associated with extreme violence: the king's body, writhing in epileptic contortions, becomes itself a writing tool for the perverse phallic mother, Catherine de Medici, and the effeminate brother, Monsieur LaFrance. It is no coincidence that the perversion of writing is yoked, in the monstrous figure of Catherine, to the most violent figuration of the perverse female gaze.

In the Modern narrative too the source and agents of oppression and death are associated with images of signing (Jenkins' handing his sister a check for her devastating charities); with public inscriptions (the stark, functional letters on the office door and on the cornerstone of The Jenkins Foundation); with documents (not shown in detail) such as the warrant that enables the Uplifters to take away the child or, ironically, the pardon for the Boy, which nearly arrives too late because the executioner ignores the intervention by telephone. Even when written language appears in seemingly more neutral contexts, such as the sign at the entrance of the dance hall ("3rd Annual Dance, given by the Employees of the Allied Manufacturers Association"), it becomes readable only as Jenkins arrives at the scene and casts an ominous shadow on the workers' amusement by rejecting an erotic exchange of looks in favor of a dime on the pavement.

The most curious image of writing in the Modern narrative is a slogan written on a fence in the strike sequence: "The same today as yesterday." In narrative terms this slogan refers to the workers' protest against the wage cut (ordered by Jenkins to finance his sister's charities). But the narrative meaning is not immediately evident, all the more so since the motivation for the

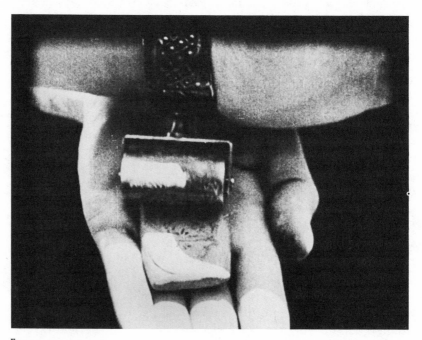

Figure 8.4

strike appears somewhat preposterous (it delegitimizes any strike for higher pay). Rather, the writing assumes an allegorical meaning, one that assimilates itself discursively to the metafictional titles that comment on the film's construction, the parallelism that posits history as an eternal struggle of metaphysical principles: "the same today as yesterday." In this sense the phrase reinscribes the film's conservative stance, despite the acute political analysis of the strike on the level of cinematography and editing. It also reiterates the fatalistic association of writing with death and defeat. [16]

Counterpointing these images of phonetic writing, the Babylonian narrative features a more dignified act of signing: the dispensation of Belshazzar's seal which releases the Mountain Girl from the economy of the marriage market. The close-up of the seal, stamped on a wax tablet by a rolling machine, emphasizes the indexical nature of the process, the unity of gesture, tool, and imprint that ensures the proper name its magic power. The seal, echoed by the design of the Babylonian title-cards, epitomizes the hieroglyphic language of film both in its utopian implications and in terms of Griffith's ambitions of authorship. The ideographic sign projects an alternative model of social relations, a direct and organic relation between ruler and ruled as opposed to the mediated ("meddling") relations typical of modern institutions. The seal grants the Mountain Girl freedom from repressive social conventions, yet it also fixes female desire in an unconsummable erotic hierarchy, to be fulfilled only in death. The Judean narrative resumes this ambiguity with the episode of the Woman Taken in Adultery, which shows Jesus writing Hebrew letters with his finger in the sand (close-up). Defying the Pharisees' tyrannical adherence to the letter of the Law, he saves the woman from being stoned—but not without the familiar injunction to go and sin no more. In both cases the utopia of hieroglyphic communication is bound up with the curious sexual economy of *Intolerance*, its anxious attempt to regulate an otherwise destructive excess of femininity.

At this point, at last, we have to confront the difficulty of distinguishing between hieroglyphics as a figure of the film's self-definition and the process of hieroglyphic figuration that seems peculiar to the film's textual activity. The distinction is a sliding one, not least because the rhetoric of self-definition had to be traced as well, teased out from among the more obvious messages of *Intolerance* in the process of reading. On the one hand, the hieroglyphic analogy does serve as a rallying point of a "strategic reflexivity," a kind of master trope designed to marshall the film's diverging textual elements. [17] On the other, however, since this self-definition ventures onto the slippery ground of writing, it puts itself at the mercy of the same rhetoricity that it set out to contain and stabilize. As a metaphor of the film's textual activity, the hieroglyph joins other figures that simultaneously generate and disfigure the filmic text.

One such figure is the tableau of the Woman Who Rocks the Cradle—in Lindsay's words, "the key hieroglyphic" of the film.[18] But the tableau also presents a hieroglyphic configuration in Adorno and Horkheimer's sense, in that it marks a pivotal disjunction between the claim to iconic self-evidence, transparency, and universality and an irreducible textual heterogeneity, a disjunction that makes it the site and vortex of multiple and irreconcilable meanings. Moreover, the Cradle shot returns us to the peculiar inscription of femininity observed in the organization of the look and the sexual entanglements of narrative authority. Thus, it opens up questions of the psychosexual scenario rehearsed in—and with—*Intolerance* and of the psychic stake of its textual deviations.

Riddles of Maternity

9

If you tasted it, it would first taste bitter,
then briny, then surely burn your tongue.
It is like what we imagine knowledge to be:
dark, salt, clear, moving, utterly free,
drawn from the cold hard mouth
of the world, derived from the rocky breasts
forever, flowing and drawn, and since
our knowledge is historical, flowing, and flown.
            —*Elizabeth Bishop, "At the Fishhouses"*

With the tableau of the Woman Who Rocks the Cradle, freely appropriated
from Whitman, *Intolerance* sets up an image apparently undisturbed by sexual
or textual ambiguity—a universally human, familiar, maternal, almost
matriarchal image. As a counterpoint to the historical proliferation of catastrophe, this image is suspended in space and time: it has no diegetic reference point in any of the four narratives. From a vantage point outside—and
beyond—history, the Cradle shot a priori claims the status of a generative
symbol, anchored in a metaphysical truth which would make the film
cohere, which would lend order and unity to its diverse and diverging
meanings. However, in its obsessive repetition, in its positional and compositional overdetermination, the shot fragments the very discourse whose
coherence and transparency it protests. Thus, it becomes the focal point of
a self-reflexivity that not only unravels the film but also suggests alternative
constellations in which the film can be read.

From the prologue on, the Cradle shot occurs twenty-six times throughout *Intolerance* (in the tinted MOMA print).[1] Providing transitions between
the different narratives, it links diegetically discontinuous segments and
asserts a thematic continuity in lieu of a temporal one. It serves as a copula
along with the title-card of the Book of Intolerance, which does not belong
to any one particular narrative either. During the first half of the film the
Cradle shot appears in conjunction with the title-card of the Book seven

Figure 9.1

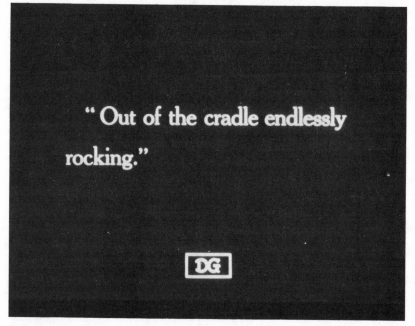

Figure 9.2

Figure 9.3

Figure 9.4

times, usually followed by an intertitle with the graphically distinct back-ground design of each narrative: hieroglyphics for the Babylonian; Hebrew plates for the Judean; the Fleur-de-Lis for the French (see fig. 8.3); neutral for the Modern period, except for the framed DG centered above the bottom line. The Book alone appears as a copula thirteen times, though in one of these it invokes the absent image of the cradle by a superimposition of the verse that allegedly inspired it: "Out of the cradle endlessly rocking." Although both emblems are distributed quite equally throughout most of the film, the Book of Intolerance disappears before the final act of the parallel catastrophes. Its function is transferred to the Cradle shot with the title, "Intolerance burning and slaying," which is superimposed, overwriting and overriding the familiar image. As the parallel editing accelerates, some-times at the frequency of a single shot, transitions between the different narratives often take place without the Cradle shot. The emblem finally returns, framed at a closer range, after the visionary epilogue, as the closing shot of the film.

In its non- or, rather, metadiegetic status, the Book of Intolerance is just as significant and just as problematic as the Cradle shot. Eponymically linked to the film *Intolerance*, it belongs to the numerous strategies through which Griffith sought to affiliate the cinema—and himself—with the Great Tradition of the Book, from the Bible through Shakespeare to Whitman. Hence it is not surprising that, unlike the Cradle shot, the title-card of the Book is rarely mentioned in *Intolerance* criticism. As a shorthand for cultural respectibility, it could be more easily assimilated, since it conventionalizes and domesticates Hollywood's relation with the institution of literature.[2] As the script of a metaphysical Intolerance, however, the Book also presides over the devastating figurations of phonetic writing described in the pre-vious chapter. In that sense it is imperative that the regime of the Book be overcome by the end of the film, that it be superseded by a different kind of writing so the Modern narrative can achieve a happy ending.

Along with the film's use of parallel montage, the Cradle shot has been perceived as an obstacle to the popular reception and commercial success of *Intolerance*. Conversely, critics bent on rehabilitating the film have tried to determine the shot's symbolic meaning and to assert its function for inte-grating the film's heterogeneous narratives. Many writers do not even bother to analyze this allegedly "central symbol," the "common denomina-tor" of the film, simply reproducing it on the level of cliché: "the cradle out of which the whole of mankind has grown" (O'Dell); an image representing "the indefinite continuity of the human race into the uncradled future"

(Stern); or "a symbolic mother-woman . . . representing the eternal evolution of humanity, fulfilling the purpose of the creator," "a figure of peace, of light . . ., of fertility . . ., of ultimate goodness that will eventually triumph" (Mast). And Metz's facile reference to "the 'leitmotif' of a blond and sunny *Maternity*" is hardly more precise or self-aware. Other commentators, like Edward Wagenknecht, raise the problem of the shot's meaning, as a rhetorical question, only to close it off with a single, more correct interpretation: "One gentleman objected that she [the Woman Who Rocks the Cradle] had nothing to do with the story, yet she obviously has everything to do with it, for all the characters are her children." A more scholarly version of this type of argument can be found in Marcel Oms's proposition that the number of the shot's appearances—fourteen times plus once each in prologue and epilogue (in a different print)—is patterned on the Fourteen Stations of the Cross.[3]

Eisenstein must be credited for the most perceptive assessment of the Cradle shot, even though he dismisses it as "unsuccessful." He criticizes the shot for remaining on a literal, representational level, offering *"an isolated picture"* rather than a "montage trope." Failing to convey an abstract historical concept, the shot shows "simply a *life-like* cradle, calling forth derision, surprise or vexation in the spectator." The shot's lack of "fusion" with other textual elements epitomizes the failure of the film's overall design. Reflecting "a thematic and ideological error," the film remains precisely what Griffith advertised, "a drama of comparisons," instead of *"a unified, powerful, generalized image."* Yet what Eisenstein may have objected to is not just the sheer lack of figuration, but a deviation from the type of figuration privileged at this stage in his own theoretical work. Measuring *Intolerance* against a concept of the organic symbol, which he was trying to rescue for a legitimation of modernist practices, he recognizes a basic "incollatability" of its textual elements. Thus, though pejoratively, he assigns the film to the tradition of allegory.[4]

Pierre Baudry, in one of the few theoretically informed readings of the film, resumes Eisenstein's analysis but falls short of the latter's recognition of the shot's irreducible allegorical quality. Although Baudry notes a gap within the shot, between the image of a concrete cradle and whatever meanings are shored against it in the course of the four different narratives, he himself closes that gap in an almost New Critical manner: "In the end, [the Cradle shot] rehearses the incompleteness of its thematic inscription in such a manner that, with each new appearance, its emptiness is filled, progressively, with the meaning and emotion produced by the four episodes." The final, closer shot of the Cradle thus completes the meaning of the whole film, turning it into "a familiar and decipherable figure."[5]

In view of the investment of the Cradle shot with claims to the film's coherence as a whole, the shot must be reconsidered in rhetorical terms, so as to emphasize, rather than reconcile, the discrepancies between the force of the figure and the textual system. Also, against its assertion of a metaphysical timelessness (which critics have extolled as the shot's aesthetic value, its "timeless quality"), the image should be historicized, both in its intertextual layers and in its simultaneous repression and deployment of particular psychosexual forces.

In many ways the Cradle shot could be said to illustrate definitions of allegory in traditional rhetoric, as a literary device that has certain equivalents and overlapping areas in art history. In the narrow sense of the term the shot is made up of "personified abstractions"—the Eternal Mother, the three Fates—the figure Quintilian calls prosopopoeia. These personifications are anchored in a hierarchical, cosmic order in which they represent absolute and, in relation to each other, diametrically opposed values. Thus, the shot becomes the site of a dualistic conflict of rival authorities, which has often been noted as a typical feature of the allegorical mode. Moreover, as a figure in a horizontally unfolding narrative, the Cradle image presumes to give meaning to a larger structure, yet is itself not an organic part of that structure (Eisenstein's complaint); it is discursively isolated from the space surrounding it and removed from the flow of narrative and historical time. Finally, as a spatial, visual figure, properly speaking an emblem, the shot juxtaposes elements plucked from a particular interpretive tradition, or a melange of traditions, which it quotes in a fragmentary and elliptical form and reinterprets in the very act of juxtaposition. Contrary to its aura of self-evidence and self-sufficiency, the meaning of the Cradle shot depends upon the viewer's familiarity with these traditions, upon a willingness to engage in a process of deciphering and reassembling.[6]

The ostentatious and excessive nature of allegorical construction, its urge to invoke and reinterpret tradition, and, above all, its provocation of the reader have moved literary theorists from Northrop Frye to Paul de Man to emphasize a paradigmatic affinity between allegory and the activity of criticism in general. This emphasis has an idiosyncratic precursor in Walter Benjamin, whose concept of allegory evolved from the study of an esoteric literary tradition (the Baroque *Trauerspiel*) into a master trope of modernity, referring at once to a mode of reading and writing (in Baudelaire, in the Surrealists) and to the unintentionally mortifying, fragmenting tendency of the commodity world. Benjamin's notion of the "allegorical gaze," a kind of X-ray directed at the naturalized physiognomy of modern life, is useful here in a strategic sense, as it is mobilized against any attempt to disguise the commodity character of things—whether under a liberal ideology of progress, or the anthropomorphic images of advertising, or a belated cult of the organic symbol. [7] Despite its vast scope, Benjamin's critical enterprise has a precise focus: the slippage between allegory as a symbolic mode implying a stable, hierarchized, and meaningful order of existence and allegory as a cognitive device that registers the historical dissolution of that very order. It is in this slippage that Griffith's Cradle shot demands to be read, even though—and all the more so *because*—it pretends to a symbolic fullness and a timeless meaning.

In the tradition of American cinema allegorical tendencies are associated with primitive modes of narration, often in conjunction with parallelism. These tendencies persist in Griffith's own Biograph films, most notably *A Corner in Wheat* (1909). An earlier and purer instance of primitive allegory can be found in Edwin S. Porter's *The Kleptomaniac* (1905). This film juxtaposes scenes showing a rich woman stealing out of compulsion, with scenes showing a poor woman stealing bread to feed her starving children. The parallel strands of the narrative come together when the two women meet in court and are sentenced according to a double standard. The film closes with a tableau, announced by an intertitle as "Tableaux" [sic], which depicts an allegorical representation of Justice, blindfolded but with one eye uncovered, holding scales on which a loaf of bread weighs lighter than a bag of gold. This tableau (which Charles Musser has traced back to a *New York World* cartoon of 1896)[8] exemplifies the principles of allegorical construction, tipping the scales toward its radical potential. A familiar figure, a female personification, is defamiliarized by an alteration of detail, which turns a critical meaning against a conventional one; the whole configuration is further denaturalized by the deliberately redundant intertitle. Although the meaning in this case is not exactly opaque, the arrangement could be said to prefigure the revival of allegorical modes in the more iconoclastic manifestations of the post-World War I avant-garde—in Dadaist and Surrealist assemblages and collages, in the ready-mades of Marcel Duchamp and Man Ray, in the photo-montages of John Heartfield. [9] Like those works, Porter's tableau disrupts conventional modes of reception and forces the beholder to read and decipher.

The Cradle shot in *Intolerance* does not provoke such a comparison, for it resumes the allegorical tradition in its most conservative aspects. Nonetheless, it flaunts a similar rhetorical structure, a similar gesture of fragmentary quotation and elliptical reinterpretation, not just in the literalizing and forced allusion to Whitman. The emblematic invocation of the cradle belongs to the repertory of a nineteenth-century ideology of domesticity: "the hand that rocks the cradle rules the world." This slogan was quoted in J. Stuart Blackton's *The Battle Cry of Peace* (Vitagraph; released September 1915), a pro-war film which, in Kevin Brownlow's words, "made a special appeal to the women in the audience."[10] The success and controversy accompanying this Vitagraph production might have prompted Griffith to pursue a similar tack, albeit in the name of the pacifist cause. Thus the allegory is recast, revised, and released into the strange textual economy of *Intolerance.*

Contrary to Eisenstein's verdict, the shot enters into a complex relationship with other elements of the film. The difficulty here is to describe those textual links without sliding into a symbolization of the figure. The shot itself displays the dualistic structure noted earlier. Lillian Gish is seated at the cradle in the foreground to the right, etherealized under a cone of light

Figure 9.5

(which varies between straight and oblique at different points in the film). To the left of the frame, three hooded old women huddle in the background, tagged as the mythological Fates by their spinning, measuring, and cutting of yarn. Even such preliminary description, however, depends on prior textual and intertextual knowledge; only the mythological designation of the group allows us to recognize their barely visible activities. (Nor, for that matter, would the cradle be identifiable as that of Whitman's poem, were it not for the quotation preceding the first appearance of the shot.) Moreover, Griffith himself had invoked the emblematic triad in the centerfold of *The Rise and Fall of Free Speech in America,* by depicting a censor, a policeman, and the proverbial Mrs. Grundy busy unwinding, inspecting, and cutting a reel of film—caption: "The Three Fates."

Opposing a sense of fate to an image that, on the most superficial level, signifies hope, the figure of the three Parcae allies itself to the fatal script of the Book of Intolerance, which is syntactically intertwined with the Cradle shot throughout the film. Thus, the dualistic structure of the shot becomes emblematic of the conflicting principles of narration traced in Chapter 5. The shot is polarized not merely by thematically opposed meanings but also by a basic schism in its discursive materials: a translucent, "living," "universally" appealing image versus the ancient and disturbing allegory that associates a fatal femininity with a particular kind of writing, violently troped by Dickens in the knitting Madame Defarge, a "primitive narrator" par excellence. Like *A Tale of two Cities, Intolerance* has its own primitive narrator figures—in the three Vestal Virgins of Uplift and in Catherine de Medici, each of whom in her way weaves a fatal script for the innocent protagonists. In its condensation of narrative conflict (the forces of Love versus the forces of Intolerance) with the struggle for narratorial authority, the Cradle shot could therefore be called an allegory whose programmatic theme is the suppression of allegory.

The composition of the Cradle shot, pitting a figure of three against a figure of one, is echoed throughout the film, primarily in the Modern narrative, where it enjoins emblem and narrative in a process of mutual contamination and disfiguration. The most obvious instance of this compositional pattern, articulated either within one and the same shot or in alternating shots, is the heroine's confrontation with the three Uplifters over the baby in the cradle. (In *The Mother and the Law* this composition is repeated in a stormy courtroom scene in which the young mother is denied custody of her child.) In terms of screen direction these shots repeat the placement of the Fates to the left and the Woman Who Rocks the Cradle to

Figure 9.6

Figure 9.7

Figure 9.8

the right of the frame, graphically underlining the parallel between Uplifters and Fates. In the same manner the Fates are invoked with the triad of the executioners, especially in the sequence of "the hangmen's test." Alternating with shots of the Boy in his cell, this sequence culminates in an insistent close-up of the three knives eager to cut the "cord of life." The act of cutting in turn prompts a cut to a leather dummy as it drops through a trapdoor, metaphorically anticipating the fall of the Boy's body.

On a larger structural level, the three-versus-one figure could be said to telescope the opposition between the three historical narratives, with their well-known fatal outcomes and their pronounced stylistic particularity, and the ostensibly neutral, realistic, and "universal" idiom of the Modern narrative, with its fictional characters and classical suspense strategies. It is this effect of homogeneity, identity, and presence that enables the Modern narrative (an "American" film, a Griffith film) to prevail over the fatal script of History. In that sense the three-versus-one figure is part of the film's overall attempt to dissociate its own textual activity from the work of the Weird Sisters.

In its textual proliferation and overdetermination, however, the figure advances a different kind of self-reflexivity, one that dispels any fiction of presence and transparency, any sense of achievement or resolution. For the

Figure 9.9

Figure 9.10

analogy—and literal coincidence—of the hangmen's cutting with the cinematic code of editing suggests a more far-reaching parallel between the Fates, by definition both weavers and editors, and the narratorial activity of the film itself, specifically its obsessive use of parallel editing. *Intolerance*, like few other American films, exemplifies the truism that linking requires cutting: for every connection between periods, one narrative is necessarily disrupted at the expense of another.

The violence done to the viewer's expectation of linearity is justified not merely in the name of a higher unity of theme and cause but also for the sake of artistic experiment. Thus, the drama of narrative authority is invariably linked to the drama of Griffith's authorship, the scar of his failed literary ambitions. Whatever its assignment on the conscious level of the text, the image of the hangmen's knives could be traced back to another, most singular and unique blade: Griffith's father's sword, which, he told an interviewer in 1916, had first inspired him to become a writer. [11]

The self-reflexive dynamic of the Cradle shot returns us to the textual dilemma observed in the film's "argument" with outdated representational styles. By citing the styles and modes of representation that American narrative film claimed to be superseding, *Intolerance* clashed with classical norms of homogeneity and unobtrusive narration. By staging the triumph of Love over (the) Fate(s) as a contest with the primitive narrators of the Modern period (the Uplifters), the narration itself is fragmented, tainted with the allegorical mode whose defeat it dramatizes. It is not coincidental that the Fates remain present in the final shot (rearranged for the closer framing), ostensibly transformed into Eumenides. Even domesticated, they remind the viewer of the discursive operations that are at once required and denied by the classical effects of presence, fulfillment, and closure.

By a similar logic the Cradle shot undermines its own attempts to structure the excess of femininity that troubles *Intolerance*, to organize it into clearcut oppositions and parallels. The very pattern of three plus one, pitting a fatal femininity against an innocent maternity, allows these oppositions to slide into affinities. For the pattern also governs groupings within the Uplifter camp, between the Vestal Virgins and individual reformers, in one shot a sympathetic motherly type and in another a stern masculine overseer. Even more curious is the repeated variant in which the place of the single figure is occupied by Miss Jenkins, unmarried sister of the industrialist, whom the opening sequence has established as the linchpin between sexual imbalance and social repression. The graphic parallel that thus links the Cradle with Miss Jenkins destabilizes the narrative opposition between life-sustaining maternity and the cliché of the frustrated old maid who turns to self-righteous charities. Finally, the compositional association with the childless woman accentuates the fact that there is no child in the cradle, that fertility is sublimated into symbolic flowers.

In its idealization of motherhood *Intolerance* assimilates major tendencies of the Progressive Era, such as the persistence, if not revival, of nineteenth-century domestic ideology (the maternal function as the basis of women's moral guardianship and hence an argument for their sharing in political representation and power), as well as a new cult of motherhood promoted by liberals, socialists and even some feminists. [12] This new discourse on motherhood responded to the large-scale changes in sexual and gender relations that came to a head with World War I. These included the massive integration of women into the work force and their active role in an emerging consumer economy, the breakdown of traditional family structures, the professionalization and radicalization of the birth-control movement—developments that shifted motherhood from the realm of metaphysical vocation into the contested arena of a social redefinition of female roles. The celebration of the "maternal instinct" as the highest expression of a New Womanhood is therefore inseparable from other sexual issues that exercised the Progressive mind, such as birth control and prostitution. [13]

Mothers rarely figure as protagonists in Griffith's films. The proverbial Griffith heroine combines youth and virginity with a variety of qualities (seldom maternal), depending upon the actress. The ignoring of the mother invariably is linked to the repression of female sexuality. [14] Even in *Intolerance*, except for a few moments when Mae Marsh escapes the persona of the gamine, the representation of motherhood remains on the surface of sentimental stereotypes. Under the sign of the Madonna, motherliness reverts to presexual virginity, a regression that is not reversed by the last-minute restoration of the baby in the Modern narrative. The idealization of motherhood, however, is not without cost. The repressed returns, both on the narrative level and in the very emblem that is supposed to anchor the idealization, an emblem overdetermined by its compositional and intertextual implications.

No reading of the Cradle image can decontaminate it from the association with Miss Jenkins, the barren and poisonous womb, nor from the powerful representations of perverted femininity surrounding it. In the end the idealization of the motherhood fails because the oppositions designed to sustain it are themselves an expression of psychic ambivalence—which, as Angus Fletcher has pointed out, destabilizes allegorical dualism in general. [15] Ironically, this ambivalence has its most effective catalyst in the alleged textual source of the image—Whitman's poem.

In "Out of the Cradle Endlessly Rocking," the first of the Sea-Drift poems, the cradle is linked metaphorically to the nocturnal ocean, itself troped as a mother. The deferred simile occurs at the end of the poem: "(Or like some old crone rocking the cradle, swathed in sweet garments, bending aside,) / The sea whisper'd me." Whitman's mother, however, is anything but sweet and innocent. She is a "fierce old mother," a "savage old mother," and whether in "angry moans" or "hissing melodious," the word she whispers to the awakening poet is the "low and delicious word death, / And again death, death, death, death."[16]

The trope of the maternal ocean provides "the undertone" in the "trio" that releases "the outsetting bard." But the term that the poet inserts between himself and the deadly mother—the mockingbird singing for his dead mate—is equally problematic. Its voice, being that of a "mocking"-bird is not original; it needs the poet as a translator. Its song ends up as nothing more than a variation of the "undertone." In the second of the Sea-Drift poems, "As I Ebb'd With the Ocean of Life," in which the third term—the trope of island and father—is seemingly stronger than in "Out of the Cradle," the association of the maternal with death is yet more pronounced. Even the imputation of motherly feelings to the "fierce old mother" as she "endlessly cries for her castaways" bespeaks an ineradicable ambivalence toward the figure that authorizes the casting away in the first place. This ambivalence dissolves the contours of the speaker's body and disfigures the text with beautiful, morbid images.

> Me and mine, loose windrows, little corpses,
> Froth, snowy white, and bubbles,
> (See, from my dead lips the ooze exuding at last,
> See, the prismatic colors glistening and rolling . . .)

The crucial antithesis here is not one of death and a natural force of life, but a struggle between the negativity of Nature and the negativity of the poet's voice ("Because I have dared to open my mouth to sing at all"), both inextricably intertwined in the process of figuration.

Griffith might have thought he was simply adapting a symbol upon whose continuity and self-evidence he could rely, but he chose lines that are as difficult and self-reflexive as anything in Whitman. Nothing could be further away from a "blond and sunny maternity," or the persistence of love and life—meanings traditionally attributed to Griffith's Cradle shot. Instead, the connotations of the Whitmanian trope pull the cradle in the direction of the very image of a "fierce old mother" it seemed so confidently to oppose: the figure of Catherine de Medici, the hissing serpent, who instigates the massacre of small children by seducing her own.[17] In one of the film's rare point-of-view shots Medici is granted a moment of subjectivity and conscience, when she hears, and then sees, the bell of Saint Germain swinging and ringing in the day of Saint Bartholomew. From this point on, the distance between the rocking of the cradle and the swinging of the bell is in jeopardy, just as the carefully constructed opposition between idealized maternity and perverse female sexuality threatens to collapse, submerging the film in chaos and catastrophe.

The constellation of rocking cradle and swinging knell suggested by the Whitmanian subtext highlights the connotation of mechanical repetition in the Cradle imagery. Certainly the final Cradle shot, with its closer framing and fuller lighting, belongs—and contributes—to the film's efforts toward climax and resolution, consummating as it were the multiplied effects of accelerated editing. But the repetitive motion of the cradle and its occurrence throughout the film traces a countermovement that militates against the classical assertion of linear development and closure, a movement not unlike the repetitive narration of the mythical Parcae: Whether motivated by narrative-historical parallelism or by the project of a hieroglyphic grammar, the persistence of figures of repetition in *Intolerance* is excessive, lacking the variation that masks and naturalizes repetition in classical cinema. This sense of excess is notable in minor details of mise-en-scène—the bell, the autoerotic ball game of Monsieur LaFrance, the shuttle of doves in Babylon—details consciously or unconsciously marked by perversion, impotence, and death.

In Freudian terms, the compulsion to repeat is linked to the death drive, and it is no coincidence that the simultaneous fear of and fascination with repetition, in Griffith as in Whitman, is projected onto women, specifically in the figure of the mother. In a plot summary of a play entitled *The Treadmill*, which Griffith had begun writing at the age of eighteen or nineteen, this configuration of repetition, femininity, and death is spelled out even more clearly. With its anxious counterpatriarchal vision, the cosmic allegory of *The Treadmill* recalls the obsessional script rehearsed in *Intolerance*, including the fetishistic play with numbers, like the three-plus-one pattern:

> It is a story of the beginning of life to the ending of life. It is a play about the earth and the solar system, with the idea of eternal recurrence. . . . It says that the universe is nothing but foredoomed to annihilation, of the essence of dust. . . . It says that not man is God, but woman, the poor mother of the skies, and she has an ugly duckling running around her back yard and she is worried because the great son, Orsus, is streaming through

the skies, streaming fecundity for twice three thousand trillion miles. And
then all the little planets are drinking up the fecundity and each little
planet is revolving and re-revolving through the great heavens. And then
the poor mother wonders and says: "Where is my great son lost in the
depth of eternity?" And then she finds one of the little planets, a trio of
little ducklings, lost, a little duckling—his name was Earth—the ugliest
duckling of them all—Earth, an atom on a tail part of a louse. [18]

This synopsis could easily be read as an Oedipal fantasy: just substitute
the name Griffith for the name Earth—and Father for Orsus. But the focus
of this fantasy is diffuse, if not confused, the narrator overwhelmed by
ambivalence toward the mother. Presiding over a universe of death, she is
denied even her procreative power; instead Orsus, like Whitman, becomes
the source of a terrifying autoerotic fecundity. Still, desire revolves around
the wish to be lost, found, and rescued by this "poor mother of the skies," to
be recognized and chosen by her against odds of cosmic dimensions. In its
megalomania such a scenario reveals repetition as a function of a profound
anxiety, of a built-in anticipation of failure.

The ambivalence and anxiety provoked by the image of the mother
returns us once more to the question of narrative authority, especially the
female narrator figures headed by the emblematic Parcae. For the threat of
women as spinners, weavers, and cutters of yarn would be void, were it not
for new technologies of writing and reproduction, which had drawn women
into the work force in large numbers and granted them some degree of
access to the public sphere—as writers, readers, educators, journalists,
typists, editors, and even directors. The graphic analogy between the triads
of Fates, Uplifters, and hangmen's knives is therefore less archaic than it may
seem. It articulates the rather modern fear that the father's sword, which had
propelled the son's ambition to become a writer, might pass, or might
already have passed, into the wrong hands. Since the sword had failed to
dispatch him on a literary career, this failure is rationalized—as the
inferiority of phonetic writing in relation to the new hieroglyphics of
cinema—and projected onto the feminine.

The entanglement of femininity and writing is so crucial to *Intolerance* that
the ambivalence toward the mother and the anxiety of authorship may be
interchangeable terms. The film actually suggests this connection by can-
nibalizing Whitman's poem in yet another way, by superimposing on the
Cradle shot the title, "Out of the cradle endlessly rocking, Uniter of here
and hereafter." In Whitman's text the second part of the phrase occurs

twenty lines into the poem, "I, chanter of pains and joys, uniter of here and hereafter." The subject who claims to do the uniting, therefore, is not whatever emanates from the cradle, as some mystical generative force, but the figure of the poet who projects his voice into the future. In substituting the Eternal Mother for Whitman's more defiant sense of poetic ego, Griffith may disavow the risks of authorship, but he cannot escape them. Like Whitman, he associates maternal authority—the Fates that unite past and present—with repetition, failure, and death. The proleptic desire that wants to break this cycle, however, that wants to make a difference in the "hereafter," depends upon an equally anxiety-provoking term: the anonymous reader/spectator, both in the present and into an unbounded future.

In their quest for cultural centrality the poet and the director-narrator part ways. For the poet, the relation with the reader can become thematic only as a highly problematic one (as, for instance, in "Crossing Brooklyn Ferry" and "Poets to Come"), considering the dynamics of the poetic tradition and the extent to which fundamental changes in the structure of the public sphere had made writing and reading poetry irrevocably precarious. The cinema, on the other hand, playing a crucial part in those very changes, not only attracted an audience of unprecedented multitudes but, more important, it offered a narrative technology that helped constitute—and reproduce—that audience as a subject of mass-cultural consumption. Scarred by downward mobility and failed dramatic ambitions, Griffith was well aware of the gap between cultural tradition and the marketplace. Thus, he took it upon himself to redeem, single-handedly, the latter in the name of the former.

Griffith's eclectic reading of Whitman unwittingly brings out an allegorical dimension in the poetic text, a disturbing quality often eclipsed in conventional interpretations. The literalized representation of the Cradle image, which disfigures the borrowed figure and makes it a catachresis, confronts us all the more inevitably with the difficulties and discontinuities of the poetic text. Similarly, the professed affiliation of the cinema with the literary tradition only emphasizes the discrepancy between the two institutions, putting into question visions of an integral culture, of a possible continuity of cultural history. If Whitman and Griffith had anything in common, it is a precarious image of their own activity, an ambivalent relationship with the reader or spectator, and a self-defeatingly projective, utopian stance.

Under Whitman's allegorical gaze the film's idealized image of maternity no longer seems opposed to the fatal powers it was deployed to contain and defeat. On the contrary, the Cradle shot becomes the involuntary point of eruption for a repressed female sexuality, epitomizing the crisis of femininity that pervades the whole film. *Intolerance* is literally littered with "wayward" and "neglected girls," "fallen women" and anonymous prostitutes.[19] The closer we get to a contemporary setting, the less redeemable becomes this unmatched, uncovered, ungovernable femininity. It is indistinguishable from the social chaos that presumably precipitated the sexual crisis. It is marked, through structures of vision and narration, as the source of all murderous activity—in figures like Catherine de Medici, the Uplifters, and the Friendless One. The return of the repressed as perverse femininity does not only threaten the continuity of life within the narratives; it unleashes a rhetorical force that crucially destabilizes the film's textual system.

Crisis of Femininity, Fantasies of Rescue

. . . .

10 [Griffith's] originality as a constructor of narrative form is exactly the inverse of Freud's: he lives the scenario, but doesn't want to know its secrets.

—*Nick Browne, "Griffith's Family Discourse" (1981)*

If *Intolerance* could be called the most "modern" of Griffith's films, this is not only because of formal practices that resemble those of literary and artistic modernism but also, in ways attendant upon the film's textual idiosyncrasy, because of its excessive representation of women and femininity, its violent registration of social and sexual change. [1] Among these configurations of violence and femininity, the character of the Friendless One deserves special attention for a number of reasons. As I argued in Chapter 5, her character functions as an enunciatory focus for much of the second part of the film. Oscillating between perpetrator and victim, she is granted a far greater degree of complexity and ambiguity than any other female character in the film. Moreover, she figures as the symptomatic center of a fantasy that complements the Whitmanian scenario implicit in the Cradle shot—a rescue fantasy that links the narrative project of *Intolerance* with the familiar scenario of other Griffith films.

If the Friendless One becomes an important (if unpleasurable) relay of identification for the spectator, she also displays an uncanny affinity with the obsessional symptoms of the *Intolerance* text. As the Modern narrative threatens to take a catastrophic course—the Boy has been sentenced to death for a murder she committed—the Friendless One is made to enact a vernacular version of the compulsion to repeat, the murderer's "irresistable impulse" (intertitle) to return to the site of the unexpiated crime. The repeated assertion of this impulse eventually leads to her confession, thus enabling, in one and the same move, the rescue of the Boy's body and the salvation of the murderer's soul.

Griffith himself could be said to have followed such an "irresistable impulse"—by casting Miriam Cooper as the Friendless One and coupling her with Walter Long as the Musketeer of the Slums. In *The Birth of a Nation*

Long played Gus, the black rapist, while Cooper was the oldest daughter of the Camerons, a melancholy and proud incarnation of Southern woman-hood. As Michael Rogin argues with regard to the sexual and racial econ-omy of *Birth*, the castration of the black male (excised from the final print) both displaces and consummates the repression of female sexuality, in a violent effort to restore a defeated patriarchal power.[2] The love-hate rela-tionship between Musketeer and Friendless One resumes this constellation—but undoes the displacement. Long, introduced as a collec-tor of fetishistic paraphernalia (like the pornographic statue in his study), is once again emasculated, this time without the detour of racist projection. And Cooper's transformation from a Southern virgin into an anonymous urban tramp reconstitutes the object of male anxiety: the sexual woman,

Figure 10.1

fantasized as phallic woman (Cooper in a pantsuit, slapping her lover; Cooper with a gun).

Cooper is not merely resexualized, she is modernized. The role allows her to shatter the Victorian delicacy that Griffith favored in his actresses as well as his lovers. The Friendless One could almost pass for a contemporary of her literary cousins Maggie Johnson, Sister Carrie, or Susan Lenox. Cooper's performance actually points beyond the Progressive conception of the character. Anthony Slide, remarking on "the modernity of her beauty and her eyes," calls her a star of the wrong decade: "she belonged more to the era of Clara Bow and Louise Brooks."[3] If not quite the carefree flapper, Cooper's Friendless One comes closest to the image of the New Woman, the problematic yet undeniably distinct construction of femininity that crystallized significant—and, for men like Griffith, traumatic—changes in women's social, sexual, and economic roles.

Although the Friendless One is not a working woman (she does not support herself by means of wage labor), her fate is motivated by economic exigency as a result of the strike which leaves her stranded, hungry, and lonesome, in the city. She is unmarried, though definitely not a virgin; she is a kept woman, though not exactly a prostitute; she is economically dependent, though not without erotic initiative of her own (her flirt with the Boy). In short, despite her name, the character of the Friendless One eludes the rigid dichotomies of middle-class morality such as they persisted in mainstream reformist discourse throughout the Progressive Era.[4] To be sure, moral judgment is waiting in the wings; it is displaced onto the murder, which is attributed to her neurotic jealousy, or, more precisely, onto her pinning the murder on someone else. At the end of the film her fate remains unresolved, but there is little doubt that she will rejoin her Victorian predecessors whose redemption invariably was tied to suffering and early death.[5]

The multiple ambiguities surrounding the character of the Friendless One evolve on the most obvious level from contradictions in the ideological project of *Intolerance*, especially as pursued by the Modern narrative. To recall the familiar reading: Griffith's attack on uplift and reform was aimed at the liberal critics of *Birth*, whose objections to the film's racism played into the general campaign for censorship. The peculiar sexual—and sexist—turn of his polemics may have a more specific source in Jane Addams and Lillian Wald, prominent NAACP members who joined the protest against *Birth*. Addams, founder of Hull House, leading social reformer and suffragist, must have vexed Griffith in a number of ways, not merely on account of her political dissent. Besides possessing the public authority he longed for, she was unmarried and childless, and, like Wald, had life-long primary relationships with women. The insinuations of lesbianism in Griffith's caricature of the Vestal Virgins of Uplift, not to mention the imputation of sexual frustration as a motive for reform, are unmistakable hints in Addams' direction.[6]

Addams had written a major work on prostitution, *A New Conscience and an Ancient Evil* (1912), a subject that held a strong fascination for Griffith. In this book she stressed the analogy between the fate of blacks under slavery and the plight of the prostitute. This analogy was present in the label "abolitionist" for the dominant Progressive position on prostitution, which aimed to abolish rather than regulate or segregate prostitution, as well as the popular term "white slavery."[7] By ridiculing this "new abolitionism" in *Intolerance*, a film designed to establish its director as above racial prejudice, Griffith implicitly resumed his denunciation of the struggle against slavery in *Birth*. This ideological trajectory is further supported by the parallel between Modern Uplifters and the Priest of Bel, who betrays Babylon to Cyrus. With the exotic display of various tribes ("Ethopians," "Barbarians"), the Persian camp is marked as the locus of both racial difference and brute masculinity, forces unleashed by selfish intellectuals to destroy the Babylonian dream—without a Klan to ride to the rescue.

By including prostitution among the social problems ostensibly exacerbated by the Uplifters' meddling, *Intolerance* both acknowledged and opposed the shift in reformist discourse that had made the prostitute the prime target of Progressive moral reform. As Ruth Rosen elaborates in *The Lost Sisterhood*, "what earlier Victorians had discreetly regarded as a 'necessary evil,' turn-of-the-century Americans came to view as the 'Social Evil,' a moral problem and a national menace."[8] While the nineteenth-century preoccupation with "fallen" women had focused on saving the souls of individual prostitutes (as evidenced in the tradition of the Magdalen homes), the Progressive crusade wanted to abolish prostitution through the agency of the state, primarily on the municipal level but on a national scale. As a result, prostitution was driven underground and criminalized.

Intolerance's concern with prostitution reiterates the Victorian position, with a highly specific link to the Magdalen tradition. Yet, with its ambiguous analysis of the raid on the brothel, the film also echoes contemporary critics of the Progressive vice campaign, though with a misogynist slant.[9] In the context of the popular media, *Intolerance* capitalized on the White Slavery panic of the prewar years—as did a number of films before it, most notably *Traffic in Souls* (Universal, 1913). The public obsession with innocent women being lured into profitable bondage was linked, as historians have pointed out, to other anxieties precipitated by the pressures of industrialization, urbanization, and immigrantion. Whether in its concern for the victim, the newly arrived immigrant girl, or in its vilification of the procurers, allegedly all foreigners, the crusade against organized prostitution often assumed a nativist tone, projecting the problem on an ethnic-racial other. [10]

At the same time, ethnic (though not avowedly racial) difference played a significant part in the fascination with commercially available sex—as Griffith's own memoirs, written in 1938–39, illustrate graphically. Reminiscing on his first exposure to the Lower East Side in 1899, when he was twenty-four years old and poor, Griffith reflects upon the inaptness of the term "melting pot"; it was "more like a *boiling pot.*"

> Here were Italians, Greeks, Poles, Jews, Arabs, Egyptians, all hustling for a living. Emotional, tempestuous, harrowing Rivington Street was perpetually a steaming, bubbling pot of varied human flesh. And the Bowery by night! I would not attempt to describe it; that has been done by experts. But I knew every hot spot there. . . . Gaudy women swung in and out of doors of the various bagnios and bistros. . . . The skin of the Bowery women was of every known hue. After the age-old manner of the siren, they chanted in many languages and accents the one hymn to lust. [11]

Following the conventional prohibition against representing ethnic difference, the Modern narrative of *Intolerance* does not thematize this source of fascination. The suppressed connotations of ethnic otherness, however, persist on the intertextual level, both in Cooper's dark persona and in the film's mobilization of contemporary discourse on prostitution. Perhaps the film's preoccupation with erotic triangles, both Modern and Babylonian, also feeds on these connotations, which would link the troubling figuration of "the other woman" to the cultural repression of the "other" woman. [12]

Another source of fascination—and ambivalence—in the focus on unmarried women must have been the different standards of respectability that governed gender and sexual relations among the urban working class. The simple joys and leisure-time pleasures that *Intolerance* so piously defends against the puritanical reformers—dancing, drinks, a day at Coney Island—were available to most single working women only at the price of sexual favors, as to his chagrin Griffith had discovered when he first came to New York. With the increased commercial organization of leisure activities, a "subculture of treating" had come into being which allowed the working woman to "have a good time," to enjoy male attention and company without being stigmatized as a "fallen woman." [13] *Intolerance* acknowledges these needs most explicitly in the character of the Dear One, who is introduced to the art of attracting men by watching a flamboyant young woman on the street. (The coquettish aspects of the Mae Marsh character are more developed in *The Mother and the Law*, with its systematic repetition of dating scenes.) Yet soon enough her flirtatious urge is channeled, rather violently, into the itinerary prescribed by middle-class morality. The ambivalence attached to working-class sexual culture remains to be acted out, no less violently, by the Friendless One.

The antireform, antipuritan agenda of *Intolerance* was bound to confuse the repressive oppositions that Griffith had been asserting so relentlessly in earlier films. These oppositions were anything but stable to begin with: many of the Biograph films in fact register a traumatic breakdown of boundaries—between domestic and public space, between good and evil, between virgin and prostitute—and the work of the narrative usually consists of reaffirming these boundaries. Staged most forcefully through last-minute rescue races, the ideological project relies crucially on parallel narration, on subcodes of cross-cutting and accelerated editing. Yet, as Rick Altman demonstrates in his reading of *The Lonely Villa* (1909), difference and resemblance easily become sliding terms, particularly in the alternation between male aggressor and paternal rescuer figures. Parallel narration itself sets up the basis for a radical critique of the conservative oppositions it set out to restore. [14] If crosscutting within one and the same diegesis can trigger such processes, the multiple use of parallel editing in *Intolerance*, overriding conventions of diegetic simultaneity and linearity, would be likely to subvert its own binary constructions all the more thoroughly—and perhaps even more self-consciously.

Hence the ambiguities surrounding the character of the Friendless One can also be described as one of the more radical effects of parallel montage. While the narrative construction of the character is circumscribed by the gender economy of the Modern narrative—the familiar stereotypes of old maid, virgin mother, and prostitute—these stereotypes are put into question by transdiegetic references between the Friendless One and various female figures in the other narratives. Much of the first third of the film (Huff, 265–574), which is relatively weak in narrative exposition and development, actually reads like an essay on sexual and gender relations throughout the ages, revolving around the precarious status of the single woman. [15] The historical women characters of course are just as constructed as the Modern ones and respond, as projections, to the same crisis as the latter. But by multiplying perspectives on female identity, the parallel narration poses this identity as discursively constructed and historically changeable.

Figure 10.2

The interplay of these perspectives is palimpsestic, rather than structural, soliciting the spectator's activity without predetermining it in every
detail and direction. Of all the female characters in *Intolerance*, the Friendless
One most thoroughly disturbs the lines of the film's parallel structure, in the
sense of an architectonic, hierarchical construction. She shares certain
attributes and positions with individual historical characters, but those characters in turn have little in common with each other. As a neurotic murderer,
for instance, she resembles Catherine de Medici, the phallic mother; like
the Babylonian Mountain Girl, she is defined as a casualty of the marriage
market and by her precarious position in erotic triangles; like Mary Magdalen, she is granted a sexual nature, albeit under the auspices of economic
exchange, but like the Woman Taken in Adultery she gets a chance to repent
and partake of redemption.[16]

The episode of Mary Magdalen was originally part of the first Judean
sequence, following the prayer vignette (and preceding Jenkins' nonen-
counter with the mill girl). Spurned by the Pharisees, the Magdalen (Olga
Grey) appears "bedizened . . . in a luxurious litter" and surrounded by slaves
who carry her palanquin.[17] This shot must have been cut after the film's first
run; in the reedited versions, the character was conflated with the Woman
Taken in Adultery. (The episode of the latter is the only non-Modern

sequence of *Intolerance* included in *The Mother and the Law,* as a mental vision on the part of a stern older woman who comforts a fallen girl in a Magdalen home.) By invoking the Magdalen tradition, Griffith might have hoped to legitimize the film's interest in prostitution and prostitutes, both Babylonian and Modern—a ruse that did not go unnoticed in contemporary reviews.[18] Yet more important, the figure of the penitent Magdalen provides an interpretive parallel for the fate of the Friendless One and thus elucidates the rescue scenario of the Modern narrative.

The psychosexual complex that is pertinent here is that of a particular type of male object-choice for which Freud uses the semivernacular term *Dirnenliebe,* "love for a prostitute." This precondition for loving—that the woman be like a harlot—and the attendant need of experiencing jealousy are often pursued with such compulsive intensity that the corresponding relationships tend to replace one another frequently and hence to form a long series. In conjunction with this type of object-choice, Freud observes a "most startling" tendency: the urge, on the part of the infatuated man, to "rescue" the woman he loves, to keep her on the path of "virtue." As in other contexts, Freud relates the debasement of the love object to "the mother complex," meaning an unresolved libidinal attachment to the mother which is reactivated at a later stage, with the boy's initiation to sexual knowledge by hearsay (often involving references to prostitutes), and which survives in its fixation on fantasies formed during puberty.[19]

The "rescue-motif" as such has a more archaic history, which Freud traces through the child's wish to return the gift of life to the mother. Rescuing his mother, with a slight twist of meaning, "takes on the significance of giving her a child or making a child for her—needless to say, one like himself." By "wishing to have by his mother a son who is like himself," the son, in the rescue fantasy, "is completely identifying himself with his father. All his instincts, those of tenderness, gratitude, lustfulness, defiance and independence, find satisfaction in the single wish *to be his own father.*"

Both strands of this fantasy are easily detected in Griffith's favorite narrative paradigm: the last-minute rescue plot of victimized womanhood, rehearsed in so many Biograph films and consummated in *Birth*—a psychic drama of threat, hysteria, and penetration enacted through crosscutting and accelerated editing. In addition to the element of danger and the affect of anxiety (which Freud links to the experience of birth), the incestuous subtext of the rescue motif accounts not only for the relative weakness of male protagonists in many of these films, but also for the "jealous" interventions of the director-narrator, ostensibly in support of the hero's efforts to save the untouchable object of desire. In such a reading the identification with a paternal authority that restores itself in the act of rescue indicates less an achieved Oedipal transition than an unresolved erotic fixation on the mother—or, more likely in Griffith's case, his unmarried elder sister, Mattie. By projecting repressed incestuous desire onto a social or racial other and preventing the violation in the nick of time, Griffith's rescue scenario permits the narrator to pursue an "essentially . . . chivalrous project," which ennobles both object and subject of the rescue fantasy.[20] To be hyperbolic: every blithe virgin trapped in domestic space is a proleptic version of a prostitute in need of rescue.

Griffith's rescue scenario, like that described by Freud, has a compulsive quality, a built-in tendency to repeat. The economic pressure of serial production, especially under the conservative production policy of the Biograph Company, provided an incontestable rationale for the compulsive repetition of rescue plots. At the same time, it allowed Griffith to rehearse and refine a narrative idiom that would win him public success, which would eventually make him the phantom father of American cinema. With the overwhelming success of *Birth* the repressive shield that masks repetition as progress, maintained by financial and social insecurity, might have broken down temporarily. Hence *Intolerance* could be said to spell out the unconscious layers of the chivalrous rescue fantasy.

In the rescue scenario of the Modern narrative, the figure of virginal victim and paternal rescuer is inverted, giving way to a constellation of a maternal figure, split into the familiar halves of fallen woman and virgin mother, and an Oedipal son in need of rescue, ultimately from his own incestuous desire. By the logic of the narrative, the (spiritual) rescue of the Friendless One is synonymous with the (physical) rescue of the Boy; indeed her timely conversion makes her at once an object and an instrument of rescue. The logic of parallel editing furthermore suggests that the gender roles in the rescue scenario are reversible, pointing up, in terms of Freud's transformational rhetoric, an earlier layer of the fantasy. Thus the Mountain Girl's race for Belshazzar's life, reciprocating for his having saved her twice before, emphasizes the initiative and active role of the female characters in the Modern period. Making women the rescuers rather than helpless victims besieged in a domestic space (with the exception of the Huguenot Brown Eyes), *Intolerance* resurrects the female prototype represented in earlier Griffith films by Blanche Sweet, especially in her performance as the parricidal heroine of *Judith of Bethulia*.[21] This inversion also confirms the hypothesis as to the subject in need of rescue: the Oedipally entangled son.

It might be argued that, despite such deviations from the familiar Griffith scenario, the telos of the rescue fantasy in *Intolerance* remains the same: the "restoration of the holiness of the American family."[22] Certainly this is the message of the last shot of the Modern narrative, in which the baby is returned to the reconstituted couple. But the happy ending is undermined, and not only by its imbrication with the parallel catastrophes in the historical narratives; it appears tacked on in view of the regressive sexual dynamic observed earlier (the couple's exclusion from scopic desire), in particular the curiously incomplete Oedipal itinerary of the Bobby Harron character.

If we reconsider the first third of the film from the point of view of that character, the Boy, the large segment beginning with his exodus from the city (Huff, 265–574) charts the young man's transition from a dark woman of sexual knowledge, the Friendless One, to the haven of domesticity offered by the Dear One. The conflict enabling that transition, however, is decentered, involving the Dear One's dead father (her promise not to let any man violate the space of the Madonna) as well as the Boy's resolve to break with the Musketeer, which also means severing his lingering ties with the Friendless One. Both of course return with a vengeance, preventing the Boy from acting as a parent—the Musketeer by sending him off to prison before the baby is born, and the Friendless One by setting him up to get killed or castrated (which is visually equated by the emphasis on the hangmen's knives). The real antagonist—Jenkins, the industrial overlord and evil father responsible for the deaths of the couple's actual fathers and the fate of the Friendless One—remains distant, unaccountable, and invulnerable. The Boy is authorized merely to invoke his image (a long shot of Jenkins at his desk, isolated and unattainable) and to react to it in helpless wrath.[23]

At this point we get a glimpse of the perverse bind that both animates and scrambles this itinerary. Positing the son—whom he calls "Boy" throughout the film—as Oedipally defeated in advance, the director-narrator empowers the dark sexual woman to kill the father, charging the Boy with a guilt that all but destroys him. To compound his helplessness, the last-minute rescue is made to depend upon both women: the virginal mother and the incestuous one whose spell he had been trying to escape all along and who (because she is bound to return in some incarnation) can only be dropped from the narrative. Thus, in terms of the unconscious logic of the rescue fantasy, the figure of the mother is beset with an irreducible and fatal ambivalence—the same ambivalence that unravels the emblem of the Cradle and links *Intolerance* with the morbid scenario of *The Treadmill*.

Like the ugly duckling, Earth, the Boy drifts about in the social wilderness, at the mercy of the deadly fecundity and institutionalized violence of American capitalism, represented by the father figures of Jenkins, the Musketeer, the Judge, and the Executioner. As in Griffith's cosmic fantasy, the wish to be rescued revolves around the figure of the mother who, like Whitman's "fierce old mother," has given him life but not immortality, who has displaced a failing patriarchal lineage with an even greater threat of chaos and loss of identity. Since desire seems fixated in this incestuous bind, all erotic relationships in *Intolerance* are doomed to remain unconsummated. In almost Keatsian stylization, death freezes the Babylonian nuptials and, with more explicitly sadistic violence, reaps the fruit of the impending double marriage in sixteenth-century France.

Critics have associated the obsessional and neurotic configurations of Griffith's films with the problematic image of his father, Jake Griffith, whose ignominious decline and posthumous mythification by his son have been read in light of a more general crisis of patriarchy at the end of the nineteenth century. [24] Apposite as these readings may be, the critical emphasis on the father figure often tends to reproduce the exclusion of the mother—or other primary female figures—in the familial scenarios that were to inspire familiar narratives on screen. To the extent that biographical trajectories are capable of illuminating the psychosexual economy of filmic texts, *Intolerance* urges us to reconsider the female part of Griffith's own rescue fantasy and to add his sisters, especially his favorite, Mattie, to the ghoulish presences that trouble his films.

If *Birth* attempts to lay the ghost of his dead father, *Intolerance*, less explicitly but as least as violently, seems to struggle with the conflicting feelings surrounding his dead sister. Mattie Griffith, about seventeen years older than David, was, Griffith told an interviewer at the time he was making *Intolerance*, "a brilliantly cultured woman." Not only did she give him and the other children their basic education, but, unlike their somewhat distant mother, she was the only person who had emotional access to the father. "Mattie found in her father an intellect that met her requirements and a character that she adored; she never married, and would say, either jokingly or seriously, I was never certain which, but suspect the latter, that she never had found a man equal to her father and that none of less quality would ever satisfy her as a husband." Having just moved the fatherless family to Louisville, she died in 1889, at the age of thirty, by popular standards an "old maid." [25]

Griffith's father died when the son was ten, too early for him to come to terms with the father's violence and defeat, let alone his own resentment of both. Mattie died when Griffith was still an adolescent, and left to him a powerful incestuous fantasy, a model of the father-daughter relations he was later to put on the screen—Austin and Elsie Stoneman, Ben Cameron and the Little Sister in *Birth*; the Dear One and her father in *Intolerance*; and, in a more perverse variant, Lucy and Battling Burrows in *Broken Blossoms*. The case of the "missing mother" in so many Griffith films is more likely a case of the dead sister. Whatever Mattie's problem might have been—and the phrasing in the interview suggests that it was at least as much Griffith's as hers—he appropriated her incestuous fantasy as part of his own, doubling the stakes of repression, fixation and guilt. The obsession of these films with father-daughter incest is not merely a vague and general defense against that between mother and son (as Rogin argues); it functions as a fantasy within another fantasy, involving a complex triangle of father, son, and older sister.

Considering *Intolerance's* concern with the fate of the single woman, Mattie's spirit seems to preside over the host of abandoned, unadjusted, excessive women that populate the film, its major source of fascination and anxiety. From that perspective, the vehemence and crudity with which the film exploits the stereotype of the old maid, as well as its nonchalance regarding the figure of the prostitute, can be read as symptoms of one and the same repressed desire, revolving around the dead mother surrogate. These two symptoms are linked, however, not only by an economy of incestuous guilt but also by an urban-industrial economy of exchange that clashed with traditional values of femininity and culture—values Griffith associated with the memory of his dead sister.

Prostitution provided a metaphor in which the mysteries of sexuality and those of the marketplace converged—the commodity form become flesh and blood.[26] A populist anticapitalist by background and conviction, Griffith was sensitive to the inequities of exchange, especially if it involved an object traditionally defined as a value in itself—like chastity, like art. Thus, even in *Judith of Bethulia*, a film set in biblical antiquity, one gets a sense of the scandal involved in the quid pro quo, when Judith, the righteous widow, uses her sexuality to liberate the Jewish town from the Assyrian siege. Revising the Apocrypha, Griffith inserts a moment of private agony before she kills Holofernes, explaining that Judith has fallen in love with her victim. The fiction of erotic reciprocity—in sentiment at least—may be intended to soften the blow against masculine pride; yet it also makes clear that her phallic victory, based on an unholy exchange, requires the sacrifice of her own sexuality.[27]

In *Intolerance* the conjunction of money and femininity becomes thematic early in the film, in a series of marginal figures like Mary Magdalen, the young woman peddler in the streets of sixteenth-century Paris, and the mill worker who tries to solicit Jenkins as a date. By the code of parallelism the Pharisee who rejects the favors of Mary Magdalen has to be read as a variant of the puritanical industrialist who displaces the erotic look onto a dime. This may explain why, contrary to the New Testament, the voluptuous courtesan remains uncensured in the Judean narrative. (It may also explain why the whole sequence eventually was cut.) The revisionist pleasure notwithstanding, the parallel reanchors the figure of the prostitute in the economy of incestuous desire, repression, and guilt that it so demonstratively tries to escape. For Jenkins' money derives its value not only from the expropriation of human labor (as suggested, on a secondarized, narrative level, by the strike sequence) but, on the level of figuration, is bound up with the repression of female sexuality. It is the same money that finances his sister's charities, and the film's first dialogue title—"If we can only interest Miss Jenkins—with *her money*"—establishes it as the missing link between a femininity gone stale and the fatal chain of events in the Modern narrative. [28]

The contamination of money and femininity reveals the spinster and the prostitute as two sides of the same coin, both obstacle and challenge to the circulation of desire. Not having balanced their sexuality with the only legitimate equivalent, a child, they turn into the many-headed gorgon of incestuous guilt and economic threat. In the sinister pact between Jenkins and his sister, money figures as the compensation for the sister's projected sacrifice, her having remained "pure" for her brother's sake. This deadly variant of a sibling relationship, however, presents the flipside of Griffith's own family romance. Mattie's "sacrifice," imagined as the stake of Oedipal rivalry, crucially depended on her capacity of earning money—which the father not only failed to accumulate, but had lost drinking and gambling. Yet in *Intolerance* the only women who work, who support themselves by means of paid labor, are prostitutes. The metaphoric debasement of the woman who makes money—and the concomitant investment of money with sexual guilt—inscribes Mattie even more inescapably in the psychosexual quandary elaborated by Freud.

The emphasis on the cash nexus suggests yet another level of the rescue fantasy, involving Griffith's relation to both industry and audiences, the construction of his public persona. Griffith's fascination with the prostitute was very much part of his belated encounter with modernity, in its economic, social, and cultural manifestations. Given his still recent initiation to the more advanced capitalist society of the East Coast, the display of female flesh that overwhelmed the young actor on the Bowery came to symbolize, along with the troubling appeal of ethnic diversity, the pervasiveness of the marketplace, whether in eros or in art. The passage from his memoirs recently quoted concludes with a rhetorical gesture familiar from his films, a defensive transmuting of traumatic aspects of modernity into a mythologizing and allegorical idiom: "After the age-old manner of the siren, they [the Bowery women] chanted in many languages and accents the one hymn to lust . . . the same against which Ulysses had roped himself to the mast. That was one man who had the right idea. These women sang only to the cash register." The choice of this particular mythological example is no coincidence: the episode of the Sirens in the *Odyssey* marks, in Horkheimer and Adorno's reading, the birth of art in its bourgeois form, as a promise of happiness to be endured only at the price of a social division of labor.[29] Griffith, without the means to indulge in the Siren's song, registers the economic mediation of desire, but he attributes it, in a provincial and universalizing manner, to the women who happen to be the most striking incarnation of this economy, as if it were an expression of female sexuality.

Yet since the Sirens also sing the dirge of his own family romance, prostitution offered itself as a shorthand of his own artistic-erotic impasse. With its more compassionate attitude toward the fallen woman, *Intolerance* suggests an aspect of Griffith's fascination which the philistine reminiscence veils: a secret, if unconscious, affinity with the fate of the prostitute on the part of the artist. As an actor seeking a career on the legitimate stage, Griffith knew what it felt to put oneself body and soul on the cultural marketplace, even if his eventual success as a director restored for a while the belief that he was still his own entrepreneur. A threshold figure like the nineteenth-century poet-*flaneur* (Benjamin's characterization of Baudelaire), Griffith entered the newly created marketplace of the cinema, ostensibly surveying it for its artistic possibilities, though already in search of customers. The image of the prostitute, vendor and commodity in one, encapsulated this historical ambiguity. As a phenomenon of urban society and mass production, the prostitute came to personify the artist's ambivalence toward the urban masses—whom he embraced as consumers but blamed for the alienation which linked their fate to his own. In other words, the metaphorical debasement of the woman who works betrays both fear and desire of the woman who has money to spend—the female consumer.[30]

Figures of sexual exchange in *Intolerance* are thus linked to Griffith's ambivalent relation with a consumer-oriented art, his romance with the Muse who had brought him success but not the undivided acclaim of the cultural arbiters. The way he conceptualized the discrepancy between his, to put it mildly, anachronistic notion of "art" and the standards of mass-cultural entertainment resembles the neurotic split that characterizes the figurations of femininity in his films. "In Griffith's trenchantly binary world," Dudley Andrew observes, "art was . . . associated with the quiet, the uplifting, the moral, the delicate and (certainly for him) the feminine." The cinema, as an art form that thrived on intimate commerce with the urban masses, promising happiness to everyone but faithful to no one, could only be troped as a prostitute.[31]

In return for her having enabled him to resurrect the father's sword, Griffith felt called upon to redeem the cinematic Muse, to secure her a place among—or even above—the traditional, more respectable arts. This chivalrous project of grandiose ambition made him enact, for his public persona, a version of the rescue fantasy just outlined. In that scenario *Intolerance* would figure as a gift to the dead sister, repaying the debt of his emotional life, his education, his cultural values—by "purifying" the power that had liberated him into creativity. In a mixture of naïveté and hubris, Griffith seems to be testing the "virtue" of the market he himself had conquered so aggressively with *Birth*, risking the capital, in both a literal and a metaphorical sense, he had attached to his name. *Intolerance's* abstention from classical strategies of viewer absorption and identification—in particular its nonlinear narration and curious fragmentation of the look—might be considered part of such a test. Its reward would be a new hieroglyphics that would establish the cinema as the model and centerpiece of an integral American culture. Whatever the rationale, the deviations of *Intolerance* raised the stakes of the rescue project to a self-defeating dimension—not unlike the parallel deployment of danger, anxiety, and catastrophe within the film itself.

Yet the cards were stacked against Griffith; the odds, to resume a figure discussed earlier, were precisely three to one. The father's sword, transformed into a "flashing vision" with *Birth*, returns in *Intolerance* with a double edge. While asserting itself as a strong narratorial voice, a unique artistic signature that makes everything cohere, that mythical sword is also reincarnated in the three hangmen's knives. Thus, as an image of narration, it is related to the obsessive cutting that haunts the entire film. Experimenting with a type of editing that he knew to be in excess of emerging continuity conventions, Griffith cut himself off from the spectator-consumer of classical cinema; transferring his sexual guilt to the realm of art, he also turned the father's sword against himself and performed something like a metaphorical self-castration.

The failure of *Intolerance* would be less glorious, and Griffith's rescue effort a gloomy exercise, were it not for another prostitute saved from the philistines: the magnificent Whore of Babylon. If the narratives set in the Christian era represent the nexus of money and femininity as one of impos-

sible desire, repression, and guilt, the Babylonian narrative tries to overcome this economy, by releasing it into a bacchanalia of fetishism. The very
juncture of female bodies and money signals a fetishistic impulse throughout
the film, a need to come to terms with an excess of lack, an attempt to trope
one kind of lack with another. But this impulse is not strong enough to dispel
the threat of castration that propels the Modern hero's Oedipal itinerary to a
precarious closure. (The fetishistic option in the Modern narrative is further
discredited by being projected onto the childless or nonmotherly women
who disavow their femininity, defined as lack, compensating for it with such
monstrous results. From that perspective, the child, linchpin of the Oedipal
logic of the Modern narrative, would ironically revert to the fetishistic logic
it opposes.)

As Rogin contends, Babylon is the domain of the Great Mother, Ishtar. [32]
As the pagan personification of Griffith's matriarchal mythology, however,
Ishtar ordains a cosmos in which actual familial roles are negligible. There
are no children in Babylon, and hence no mothers, whether virtuous or
vicious. There are no fathers to kill: Belshazzar rules for the senile
Nabonidus and spends his time promoting the cult of Ishtar at the expense
of the father god, Bel-Marduk, regulator of the universe and master of
chaos. The city appears as a polymorphously perverse enclave, in which
difference of any kind—whether sexual, racial, social, or linguistic—is
either blurred, absorbed, or disavowed. The hieroglyphic utopia of visual
communication corresponds to the illusion of imaginary plenitude. Difference, like the threat of castration, resides outside the walls, in the camp of
Cyrus who, if anyone in *Intolerance*, embodies the phallus. Babylon is oblivious even to the possibility of an imminent assault. The warning is relayed
by the powerless father, amateur archaeologist, like a message from a forgotten age. In the belatedness of Nabonidus' gesture, the metaphor of
archaeology comes full circle, resuming Freud's troping of psychic non-
synchronicity in terms of the layers of Rome (see Chapter 6, note 11). It is
this fissure in the ego that describes Babylon's relation to the other
narratives.

The deviant sexual topology of Babylon is suggested on a more or less
conscious level—conscious insofar as it is systematically eliminated from
The Fall of Babylon—just as images of fetishistic displacement are presented
with a wink of adolescent lewdness. The Mountain Girl (Constance Talmadge), a living example of what Freud describes as a fixation of the phallic
stage, is shown milking a goat in semi-close up and looking up dreamily,
presumably thinking of her beloved Belshazzar—a shot that recalls a similar
one of Lillian Gish caressing the bedpost in *Birth*.[33] While the bawdy joke

Figure *10.3*

makes the goat's udder substitute for a specific penis, another instance of displacement recognizes it as a function of lack, not incidentally with reference to a sword. The first Babylonian sequence introduces Belshazzar's "mighty man of valor," a character patterned on a muscular giant in *Cabiria*, as a "two-sword man." But the subsequent close-up shows—and accentuates with a diagonal mask—a single sword as it is being sheathed. What is the object of this sleight-of-hand, and what is being disavowed by demonstrating the very process of disavowal?

A sequence crucial to an understanding of the Babylonian perversity and its function within the film is that of the marriage market (Huff, 282–341). Based on a passage from Herodotus and a fin-de-siècle painting inspired by that passage—Edwin Long's *The Babylonian Marriage Market*—this sequence translates the problem of the surplus woman into an elaborate allegory, the most explicit confrontation of money and femininity in the whole film. [34] An intertitle explains the way the market works: "Money paid for beautiful women given to homely ones, as dowers, so that all may have husbands and be happy." Here again is a modern issue projected back into a (more or less) mythic past, for the term "marriage market" had been used by contemporary critics of American marriage to denounce the materialistic

Figure 10.4

degradation of love and courtship.[35] Griffith turns the term inside out, by advertising the Babylonian institution as one way of handling the threat attached to the uprooted single woman. The proposal, however, is somewhat disingenuous, considering that the market illustrates a principle of exchange that is not capitalist but compensatory. It depends upon a paternalistic system to protect the woman who does not command a value on the free market, the same authority that cares for the beauties who adorn the bottom of the tableau ("women corresponding to our street outcasts, for life, the wards of Church and State").

The marriage market is introduced only to be overruled—on behalf of the Mountain Girl, who functions as the focus of narrative activity and character-relayed identification for the Babylonian period. The heroine does not find a buyer, not even with a dowry added into the bargain; she lacks value even as a symbol of lack. The scandal of her display on the auction block foreshortens the distance between viewer and exotic tableau and, stamping the institution as barbarian, solicits a "modern" response that happens to coincide with a chivalrous one. The prince appears in time to rescue her, by suspending the law of the market, but he simultaneously suspends the question of her sexual identity. The answer is as ambiguous as the object in question. Obviously dissenting from the judgment of the customers, the narration protests her desirability as a woman, both with vignetted close-ups that transfigure her face as she gazes upon Belshazzar and by crosscutting to the Rhapsode who is pining away for her in Nineveh. But these narratorial gestures are themselves fetishistic operations, in particular the close-up which abstracts her from the scene of lack and inequity, framing her face as a perfect object.

With this peculiar rescue action, Belshazzar grants her the freedom to marry or not, to identify herself as a woman or to remain in that bisexual realm of which he, Belshazzar, is the foremost representative. What is more, the narrator becomes complicit with the Mountain Girl's self-image as a phallic girl, even authorizing her to hold up a standard of manly behavior, to the Rhapsode as to all of Babylon. Hence she alone knows the enemy and is alert to the danger of a second assault. The real scandal of her appearance on the auction block is that she did not belong there in the first place, because she is fantasized—and allowed to fantasize herself—as a woman with a penis (the missing penis which is more likely the object of displacement in the milking of the goat). Why then does she not provoke the same horror as her counterparts in the French and American narratives?

For one thing, the threat is defused by the comic touch allowed the character, especially with Talmadge's slapstick performance. As a genre, comedy tends to encourage—as well as absorb—sexual deviation, deriving many of its effects from the reversal of traditional gender roles. More important, the phallic antics of the Mountain Girl are kept under control by a fetishistic operation on a much larger scale, coextensive with the Babylonian enterprise. Her containment, after all, is achieved at the expense of hundreds of depersonalized female bodies offered up for display, whether nude or in exotic costumes, whether fragmented by close-ups or serialized in long or extreme long shots. Griffith himself, rather than his persona as narrator, is the master of this spectacle, a role reminiscent of that of the conjurer in early films, most notably Méliès, whose manipulation of the female image reflects upon the psychosexual economy of cinematic representation. [36]

This "primitive" fetishism most clearly distinguishes the style of the Babylonian narrative from the rest of *Intolerance.* Thus we return once more to the difference of the Babylonian dream, to the question of its antinomian impulse. While the fetishistic gaze focuses on the female body as its prime object, it casts its spell on just about everything in and about Babylon: architecture, decor, statues, chariots, war machinery, elephants and other exotic animals, costumes and surreal headgear, masses of bodies, male and female, dead and alive; the gigantic dimensions of the set as well as the camera work that mobilizes them. The excess of lack that troubles the narratives set in the Christian era is released, under the condition of irreality, into a surplus of visual pleasure, a celebration of abundance, a squandering of production values. At the same time the very juxtaposition of the Babylonian and the other narratives can be described in terms of a fetishistic split—between the disavowal of lack and its simultaneous recognition ("I know perfectly well . . . but all the same")—the coexistence of two incompatible attitudes which Freud, especially in his later texts, found characteristic of fetishism.[37]

Here the psychoanalytic framework, which is self-consciously reductive needs to be opened up to include another kind of fetishism, in which psychosexual and economic, historical, and social forces converge—the cult of the commodity, the ideology of consumerism. Preceding the systematic interlocking of cinema and consumerism that became the rule during the 1920s, Griffith's Babylonian extravaganza recalls a more archaic stage of consumer fetishism, exemplified by the tradition of the World Expositions that flourished during the middle and late nineteenth century (for example, London, Crystal Palace, 1851; Paris, 1867; Chicago, 1893; Paris, 1900; Buffalo, 1901; St. Louis, 1904). These expositions, to paraphrase Benjamin, organized the worship of the commodity on a public and international scale, glorifying the exchange value of its exhibits at the expense of their use value, even of their immediate commercial availability. Visitors entered this phantasmagoria for the purpose of distraction, rehearsing modes of collective reception that were to become the domain of the entertainment industry, which in turn appropriated this distracted receptivity by raising its consumers to the level of the commodity.[38]

Griffith, on a research tour of prisons for *The Mother and the Law*, visited the San Francisco Exposition of 1915. According to Karl Brown, he was especially impressed with the major attraction of the show, the Tower of Jewels, which he asked Bitzer to photograph. The exposition no doubt spurred Griffith's ambitions for the Babylonian set—in terms of sheer size, grandiosity, and feasibility—far beyond the scope of any film, including *Cabiria*. It also encouraged him to take advantage of the vogue of Orientalism, which, having swept the European expositions, had begun to invade American consumer culture in many branches, shapes, and designs. Ideologically complicit as they were, Orientalist clichés of luxury and languor, of ornamental abstraction and glamorous surfaces, of ritualistic eroticism and stylized androgyny, offered instant fuel for a fetishistic flight, material already inscribed with disavowal (of lack in both sexual and economic senses) and the simultaneous investment of the visual with phantasmagoric value.[39]

The Babylonian narrative betrays an aesthetics of exposition in more than its Orientalist and gigantic features. It celebrates the power of the means of technological and artistic production by converting unprecedented profits (from *Birth*) into a surplus of spectacle. To pursue the analogy, the Babylonian fantasy is low in narrative-use value, when compared to the endless ramifications of the Modern plot. Accordingly, it is deficient in heterosexual desire, generational conflict, and the reproduction of the family. In the diffuse erotic atmosphere of the court every gesture remains foreplay, displayed for the sake of consumption rather than consummation. One cannot help feeling that even if Babylon were not to fall, these lovers, like those on Keats's Urn, would never know satisfaction.

Accordingly, the aesthetics of exposition determines the way in which the Babylonian narrative addresses the viewer, setting it apart from both the Modern narrative and, even more so, from the voyeuristic organization of spectatorship that was becoming the norm of classical narrative cinema. The viewer is guided through the Babylonian sights as through a site of archaeological activity. That metaphor has to be situated within the larger framework of consumer culture in which all social activities and interactions were increasingly predicated on scopic and specular relations. What distinguishes this rather archaic courting of the consumer from later, more refined strategies is that it does not mask its intentions by disguising the commodity in human and narrative form. Like the early "cinema of attractions," Griffith's Whore of Babylon is shamelessly exhibitionist, soliciting the viewer's scopophilia in a most explicit manner. Rather than tying visual pleasure to a narratively motivated and diegetically invisible vantage point (the one-sided voyeurism of classical cinema), the Babylonian sequences seek a direct erotic rapport with the audience, addressing them as a public, collective and intersubjective body.

Similarly, the quality of fetishistic displacement varies from its more classical manifestations. It is important to recall that Griffith adamantly resisted the star system—and actually lost a number of actors to rival directors and studios.[40] Whatever his reasons—and vanity was not the least of them—the absence of any individual star, in particular any single female star, made his films refrain from a rather common route of cinematic fetishism that focused on the female body and the power of the gaze that controls her image. Although some instances of this tendency can be found in *Intolerance*, the more significant object of fetishistic displacement is ultimately the body of the film itself. If *Intolerance* was advertising anything, it was not a life-style to be copied or aspired to, not a way to smile, dress, and secure an upwardly mobile marriage. The only commodity the film can be said to glorify was Griffith as director, his artistic genius, his mastery of styles and spectacle, his vision of the cinema.

The phantasmagoric images that transfigure the industrial marketplace, as Benjamin insists, deserve attention for more than their basically ideological function. They radiate with an ambiguity that makes them promise and delusion in one. Griffith's Babylonian pageant is shot through with a utopian pathos which prevents it from sliding into camp—unlike later Orientalist spectaculars such as *The Thief of Bagdad* (Douglas Fairbanks, 1924) or Valentino's *Sheik* films. The invocation of Babel and the hieroglyphic tradition, the image of an integral civilization and a model welfare state, an aesthetics of abundance and polymorphous eroticism—these aspects of Babylon may suspend it in a mythical otherness, but they also hold up a mirror (admittedly a perverse one) to the deficiencies of contemporary American life, to any society that uses the threat of castration to perpetuate a system of economic, social, and cultural deprivation.[41] More specifically, Babylon projects the concrete utopia of a cinema that would develop, uninhibited by studio accountants and moral arbiters, into a publicly available medium for the articulation and organization of experience.

At the same time Griffith, even in his confused megalomania, knew necessity too well not to mistrust his own idealizations. So, the Babylonian myth eventually congeals into allegory, displaying the timeless ruins of impossible desire. Much as Griffith yields to the fetishistic temptation, especially if it concerns, as it were, prehistory, he—or rather, the film—recognizes the affinity of fetishism with death, its surrender to the "sex appeal of the inorganic."[42] Prophetic of many films to come out of Hollywood in future decades, Babylon shows up the other side of consumer aesthetics, the source as well as the cost of distraction: alienation, fragmentation, fixation on the detail, on momentary effect, the cult of novelty and endless repetition. Precipitating the fall of what is doomed anyway, the regime of narrative returns with a sadistic vengeance.[43] The viewer is swept along with the hordes of Cyrus—shots that blend with equally sadistic images from other ages, like the close-up of the foot on the gas pedal or that of Brown Eyes before her perforation by the Mercenary's sword.

Spectatorship in *Intolerance* seems to disintegrate into the fetishistic and scopophilic pleasures of Babylon on the one hand and the failed, self-censoring, and destructive voyeurism of the French and Modern narratives on the other. Or, to invoke the Emersonian law of compensation, the price of the Babylonian indulgence is the ambivalence toward scopic desire in the

Modern period, as it erupts in the slippage between innocent and perverse female look. The very term of spectatorship, as a unified and unifying process by which the viewer becomes the subject inscribed in a film, is put into question by the textual peculiarities of *Intolerance:* its multiplication of positions of identification and fragmentation of vision and character subjectivity; the direct address implied in its narratorial and metafictional interventions; its decentered articulation of space and nonlinear temporality; its hieroglyphic heterogeneity and palimpsestic condensation of meanings and connections that are neither subordinate nor indispensable to an understanding of the various narratives. These deviations from the classical model both overdetermine the position of the spectator and leave it relatively indeterminate. Thus the film mobilizes a greater variety of readings, contingent upon historically and culturally specific audiences and their experience. The failure of *Intolerance* may have resulted not so much from Griffith's miscognition of the kind of spectator that evolved with the norms of classical cinema, as from a much nobler infatuation with the viewer as a collective body, investing confidence in their imagination, curiosity, and interpretive capabilities. Whether or not Griffith was aware of it, his self-image as chivalrous rescuer made him forgo the wisdom of the trade press and risk a leap into the open space of the public sphere.

This risk converges with another, discussed earlier: *Intolerance's* obsession with a femininity in crisis and its destabilizing figurations. Allowing the incestuous subtext of the rescue fantasy so close to the surface, Griffith put his narrative project at the mercy of the sexual-textual Fates it was designed to appease and contain. The proliferation of "primitive" narrator figures, the feminization of the gaze and the vicissitudes of the emblem of the Rocking Cradle are only the more gender-specific aspects of the precarious inscription of spectatorship, the partial return of an empirically diverse form of address. Much as this juncture may have to do with Griffith's own family romance, it is also related to a particular historical development, a particular moment in the dynamics of the American public sphere.

As elaborated in Chapter 3, the cinema came to function as a catalyst for the transformation of public life, in particular the erosion of the separate spheres and the gender hierarchy of public and private. During the transitional period the industry responded to the unprecedented and growing share of women in motion picture audiences both defensively, by ensuring a standard of middle-class respectability, and, more aggressively, by catering to female viewers with particular genres, stars, and modes of representation and address. Strategies of female address were imported from other branches of consumer culture, such as women's magazines with their serialized romances, fashion features, and advice columns. Yet given the more public quality of cinematic reception, as well as the different psychosexual mechanisms operating in cinematic representation, the address to a female viewer potentially conflicted not only with the masculinist organization of the public sphere but, more specifically, with the emerging classical paradigm and its gendered economy of vision.

Intolerance is marked by the violence of this transformation and by the contradictions it unleashed, particularly between the market's cultivating of the female consumer and patriarchal structures of vision and subjectivity— contradictions which in the long run were absorbed by the discourse of consumption. The integration of women as consumers involved the assimilation of woman as image and the simultaneous suppression of her authorship, her authority as narrator. Griffith's curious and confused antipatriarchal yearnings illuminate this link between an idealized femininity and the suppression of a particular kind of writing, a link that sustains the ideology of classical cinema. Figurations of writing and of femininity combine in *Intolerance* to shatter the apparent unity, transparency, and accessibility of the cinematic image, and with it the hope for an unproblematic cultural centrality. As a commercial failure, already obsolescent as it was being made, *Intolerance* displays an allegorical surface that makes these figurations readable, recognizable in a way which more linear films, such as *Birth*, or most classical narratives, do their best to conceal.

The Return of Babylon:
Valentino and Female Spectatorship

·   ·   ·   ·   ·   ·   ·   ·   ·   ·   ·   ·   ·

III

Male Star, Female Fans

11

One is Rodolph Valentino—he of the penciled eyebrows and the patent leather hair; the symmetrical chin and nose and cheek; the deep, hypnotic, subtle and alluring eye. . . .

The other is Will Rogers, Ugly Will. With the eyebrows nature gave him; Will of the rough, ill-fitting clothes, and deep-lined face, and frank eyes in which you read no musings of hidden romance. Cowpuncher Will—who probably never spent so much as a dollar on a manicure in his life, and thinks of a beauty parlor as a place for women only.

—*"Does Beauty Pay? Take a Look at These Two, Then Answer,"*
Cleveland Press (*16 May 1922*)

Nothing illustrates the sweeping ascendancy of the classical paradigm more strikingly than Griffith's full-scale mutilation of *Intolerance* in 1919 and the release of linearized chunks of the film as *The Mother and the Law* and *The Fall of Babylon*. And yet, although the classical system undoubtedly defeated alternative options on the level of film style, American cinema during the decade that followed displayed significant features that cannot be grasped in terms of the classical model alone. The persistence of exhibition practices that privileged theater experience over film experience in tendency conflicted with the monopolistic interests of production and distribution companies, the effort to control and precalculate the reception of films through particular textual strategies. The conception of the show as performance, the continued importance of nonfilmic activities, and neighborhood orientation of the smaller theaters gave local acts of reception a certain margin of unpredictability and autonomy. This made the cinema an institution with relatively more diversity than later, more standardized modes of exhibition would allow. It is therefore very likely that a considerable tension remained, even *after* the final implementation of the classical codes, between the textually constructed spectator-subject of classical cinema and empirical audiences that were defined by particular and multiple social affiliations and capable of sharing culturally and historically specific readings. This tension calls into question not only the assumption of an immediate, unproblematic efficacy of classical codes but also the centrality of such an assumption in current models of film history and attendant notions of the cinema as an institution.[1]

A similar challenge to the classical paradigm, both as an industrial norm and as a historiographic construct, came from the star system. The star phenomenon not only eludes the formalist focus on narrative (principles of thorough motivation, clarity, unity, and closure), but also complicates the psychoanalytic-semiological preoccupation with the illusionist mechanisms of the classical apparatus and the unconscious workings of classical modes of enunciation. Because the star is defined by his or her existence outside of individual films, by the publicity that surrounds his or her professional and "private" personality, the star's presence in a particular film blurs the boundary between diegesis and discourse, between an address relying on the identification with fictional characters and an activation of the viewer's familiarity with the star on the basis of production and publicity intertexts. Ideally the levels of discourse and diegesis are designed to interlock and reinforce each other. The casting of a star binds the viewer all the more firmly into the fictional world of the film by drawing on more sustained structures of identification, mobilizing long-term psychic investments in particular ego ideals and primary object substitutes. At the same time the reincarnation of the star with each new film reconfirms, inflects, and keeps alive his or her publicity existence.[2]

However, as Richard deCordova points out, the star system also encourages a specific mode of reception, undermining the disposition that allegedly constitutes classical spectatorship:

> It is important to recognize that star discourse has historically involved regimes of pleasure and modes of address that are not coextensive with (and at times are relatively distinct from) those which follow from the codes of vision in the classical cinema. . . . The star system involves an orientation of attention that moves the spectator away (however momentarily) from the orientation of attention toward vision and narrative that, from Munsterberg to Mulvey, has defined spectatorship.[3]

By lending a focus to the film's narrative and scopic regime, the presence of a star actually undercuts that regime's apparent primacy, unity, and closure. By activating a discourse external to the diegesis, the star's presence enhances a centrifugal tendency in the viewer's relation to the filmic text and thus runs counter to the general objective of concentrating meaning in the film as product and commodity. The star performance weakens the diegetic spell in

Who's Married to Whom, etc., etc.   By R. L. Goldberg

Figure 11.1

favor of a string of spectacular moments that display the "essence" of the star (and which are often circulated separately in the form of publicity stills and trailers). In such moments of display the star system seems to tap a persistent undercurrent of the "cinema of attractions."

Like the exhibitor's cinema, the star system is a prime instance of an industrial-commercial public sphere, characterized by a similar voracity, opportunism, and volatility. The fascination with the star began during the nickelodeon period, when audiences started to show interest in particular actors, even though individual production companies, notably Biograph, persisted in anonymous casting. Soon the star system was regularized and exploited by all studios—as a strategy of product individuation and standardization, a nationally and internationally effective marketing device.[4] The promotional activities surrounding the star—fan magazines and clubs, interviews, contests, public appearances—were designed, cynically speaking, to mobilize grassroots support, but these activities were fully orchestrated from above. The very arbitrariness of the cinematic marketplace, the element of chance in the "discovery" of a star, became part of that promotional discourse, essential to the myth that the star was a creation of his or her loving public.

Still, the dynamics of the star cult as an industrial-commercial public sphere also entailed a certain amount of real unpredictability and instability and thus harbored potentially alternative formations. One source of instability was the star him/herself who, especially in the decade following World War I, wielded an economic power that could oppose the studio hierarchy. The actions of Chaplin, Pickford, and Fairbanks that led to the formation of United Artists are well-known. In addition, the moral conduct and sexual behavior of individual stars became an issue during the early 1920s, evidenced by the unholy alliance of discourses of industrial self-regulation and journalistic scandalmongering that destroyed the career of Fatty Arbuckle and cast a shadow on Valentino as well.[5] Another, more pervasive source of instability was the programmatic mobilization of audience participation as a *collective activity*, which, even though it was organized from above, conflicted in tendency with the isolated and relatively passive disposition required of the classical spectator. As the Valentino cult demonstrated, it could elude the control of studio publicity and gain a momentum of its own. As a commodity whose value turned on his or her ability to touch an experiential nerve in people's lives, the star came to function as a linchpin between immediate market interests and long-term ideological structures, and often embodied the contradictions that erupted in the tension between the two.

These contradictions were especially virulent in the area of gender and sexuality, considering the cinema's pivotal role in transforming and regulating women's access to the public sphere. As I argued in Chapter 3, the industry's catering to—and thriving on—female audiences precipitated the erosion of the hierarchic segregation of public and private. It also undermined a long-standing patriarchal economy of vision that began to assert itself all the more forcefully in the formal organization of the emerging classical paradigm. The paradox between women's increased importance as consumers and the simultaneous imposition of masculine forms of vision and subjectivity was exacerbated by the proliferation of stars, especially if they were male.

Although I have touched upon these questions in earlier chapters, the focus on a male star warrants more detailed discussion of the issues involved, elaborated over the past decade and a half in feminist and psychoanalytically oriented debates on representation and spectatorship. These debates invariably return to Laura Mulvey's essay on "Visual Pleasure and Narrative Cinema" (1975), which first spelled out the implications of Lacanian-Althusserian models of spectatorship for a critique of patriarchal cinema. Whatever its limitations and blind spots, the significance of Mulvey's argument lies in her pinpointing the mechanisms by which the classical Hollywood film perpetuates sexual imbalance in the very conventions through which it engages its viewer as subject—its modes of organizing vision and structuring narratives, its particular types of pleasure. Drawing on psychic proclivities of voyeurism, fetishism, and narcissism, Mulvey argues, these conventions depend upon—and reproduce—the conventional polarity of the male as the agent of the look and the image of woman as object of both spectacle and narrative. In aligning spectatorial pleasure with a hierarchical system of sexual difference, classical American cinema inevitably entails what Mulvey calls "a 'masculinization' of the spectator position, regardless of the actual sex (or possible deviance) of any real live movie-goer."[6]

Besides being a somewhat monolithic notion of both the classical cinema and the male subject—as well as a provocatively manichean stance on visual pleasure—Mulvey's argument has been criticized for the difficulty of conceptualizing a female spectator other than in terms of an absence.[7] In the decade since her essay was published, however, feminist critics have attempted to rescue female spectatorship from its "locus of impossibility," particularly in areas elided by the focus on women's systematic exclusion. The question of female spectatorship has been posed, for the most part, from two perspectives, involving the distinction between the spectator as a hypothetical term of address of the film's discourse and the spectator as a subject of empirical processes of reception. One line of investigation is concerned with overtly male-addressed films, for instance in classical genres such as the Western or the gangster film, and the pleasure and kinds of identification that women viewers (including feminist critics) too experience in the reception of these films. The other perspective is on the body of films, within the Hollywood tradition, explicitly addressed to female audiences and marketed as such, like the "woman's film" of the 1940s and other variants of melodrama centering on female protagonists and their world.

With regard to the reception of male-addressed films, Mulvey, reconsidering her earlier argument, suggests that the female viewer may enjoy "the freedom of action and control over the diegetic world that identification with the male hero provides" by taking recourse to the repressed residues of her own phallic phase. This type of identification requires her, as it were, to put on transvestite clothes; consequently, Mulvey contends, it confirms the dominant sexual polarity of vision by exchanging the terms of opposition for those of similarity. Like the character Pearl in Mulvey's reading of *Duel in the Sun,* the female spectator ends up caught in a conflict "between the deep blue sea of passive femininity and the devil of regressive masculinity."[8]

Mulvey's analysis of spectatorial cross-dressing ultimately upholds the notion of patriarchal cinema as a system of binary opposites. But it also demonstrates the necessity to complicate such terms. The female viewer of "masculine" genres does not fit the mold of the spectator-subject anticipated by these films; she cannot assume this mold as unproblematically as the male viewer is supposed to. At the same time, narcissistic identification with female characters is of marginal interest at best, especially in films which disperse spectacle over landscape and action scenes rather than focusing visual pleasure on the image of the female body. But, as I emphasized earlier, the "misfit" between the female viewer and the spectator-subject of classical cinema does not make her reception merely accidental, arbitrary or personal. Rather, the oscillation and instability that Mulvey and others have observed in female spectatorship constitutes a collectively significant deviation, a deviation that has its historical basis in the viewers' experience as women, as a social group differentiated in terms of class, race, ethnicity, and sexual preference. If this collective deviation was articulated and simultaneously appropriated by the discourse of consumption, the agencies of consumer culture also offered women a public horizon in which the social construction(s) of female subjectivity, as inscribed and negotiated in the textual configurations of the films, could be recognized and reflected upon, in which commercially appropriated experience could be interpreted and reclaimed.

The figure of the transvestite suggests that female spectatorship involves dimensions of self-reflexivity and role-playing, rather than simply an opposition of active and passive. The perceptual performance of sexual mobility anticipates, on a playful, fictional level, the possibility of social arrangements not founded upon a hierarchically fixed sexual identity.[9] However, as Mary Ann Doane objects, sexual mobility is itself "a distinguishing feature of femininity in its cultural construction." Hence, spectatorial transvestism, like transvestism in general, "would be fully recuperable."[10] Would be, perhaps; but I do not think that this objection exhausts the possibilities of the transvestite as concept and metaphor. Sexual mobility, while acceptable in adolescent females, is still considered incompatible with adult standards of femininity. If such mobility is a by-product of women's reception of male-addressed films, it opens up a different register of temporality, allowing for the articulation of nonsynchronous psychic developments. Phallic identification, though officially—in the present tense of the film text, as propelled by the linear flow of the narrative—aligned with positions of masculine agency and control, depends for the female viewer on processes of memory and fantasy (on both conscious and unconscious levels) and thus may reactivate repressed layers of her own psychic history and socialization. [11]

What about films that provide spectatorial positions specifically addressed to a female viewer? In her study on the 1940s "woman's film," Doane shows how the structural instability of the female spectator position in mainstream cinema surfaces as a textual instability in this particular genre: "because the woman's film insistently and sometimes obsessively attempts to trace the contours of female subjectivity and desire within the traditional forms and conventions of Hollywood narrative—forms which cannot sustain such an exploration—certain contradictions within patriarchal ideology become more apparent."[12] The ideological crisis precipitated by the female address, Doane argues, is in turn contained by scenarios of masochism which work to distance and deeroticize the woman's gaze, thus restricting the space of a female reading.

By contrast, critics such as Linda Williams and Tania Modleski emphasize the multiplicity of identificatory positions in female-addressed mainstream films (or, in Modleski's case, TV soap opera), a textual multiplicity which they relate to the problematic constitution of female identity under patriarchy, from patterns of psychic development to a gender-specific division of labor.[13] This difference in emphasis in part may result from the choice of films—maternal melodrama, for instance, as opposed to woman's films that overlap the gothic or horror genre—but it also seems bound up with the conception of spectatorship in general, with the relation between textually constructed positions of gendered subjectivity and historically available possibilities of reception, and with the role of the critical reader in constructing and mediating both of these terms.

The significance of these questions for feminist theory and criticism has been spelled out with exemplary clarity in the debate initiated by E. Ann Kaplan and Linda Williams on *Stella Dallas* (King Vidor, 1937).[14] To what extent, for instance, does the organization of the look (point-of-view editing from a male, upper middle-class perspective) dominate or preempt other relays of identification and options of interpretation? Does the ending of the film unify the variety of conflicting subject positions mapped out before and so, as Kaplan argues, close off the contradictions in terms of a patriarchal discourse on motherhood, asking the spectator to accept desexualization, sacrifice, and powerlessness? Or do we, as Williams suggests, grant some degree of alterity to the preceding 108 minutes? Are processes of identification necessarily synchronous with the temporal structures of classical narrative, and to what extent is closure effective? How do films construct what we remember of them, and how does this memory change over time in relation to the immediate effects of identification? And what is at stake in the critical effort to reclaim a space for alternative female readings or, conversely, to see that space as always already coopted?[15]

A related yet different set of questions is posed by female-addressed Hollywood films that focus spectatorial pleasure on the figure of a male hero-performer—and a star, at that. If a man is made to occupy the place of erotic object, how does this affect the organization of vision? If the desiring look is aligned with the position of a female viewer, does this open up a space for female subjectivity and, by the same token, an alternative conception of visual pleasure?

As with regard to spectatorial transvestism, Doane cautions against premature enthusiasm for such films, arguing that they are merely an instance of role reversal, which allows women the appropriation of the gaze only to confirm its patriarchal inscription: "The male striptease, the gigolo—both inevitably signify the mechanism of reversal itself, constituting themselves as aberrations whose acknowledgment simply reinforces the dominant system of aligning sexual difference with a subject/object dichotomy. And an essential attribute of that dominant system is the matching of male subjectivity with the agency of the look."[16] The figure of the male as erotic object undeniably sets into play fetishistic and voyeuristic mechanisms, accompanied—most strikingly in the case of Valentino—by a feminization of the actor's persona. These mechanisms, however, cannot be naturalized as easily as they are in the representation of a female body. They are foregrounded as aspects of a theatricality that encompasses both performer and viewer, and which may mean something different depending on the viewer's gender and sexual orientation. The reversal thus constitutes a *textual* difference which has to be considered case by case and cannot be reduced, a priori, to its symbolic content within a phallic economy of signification. It seems more promising, tentatively, to approach the textual difference of a male erotic object as a figure of overdetermination, an unstable composite figure that connotes "the simultaneous presence of two positionalities of desire" (Teresa de Lauretis) and thus calls into question the very idea of polarity rather than simply reversing its terms. [17]

If the either/or of sexual difference seems inadequate to an understanding of the textual significance of such composite figures, this inadequacy also indicates the need to complement the methods of psychoanalytically grounded textual analysis with more historically and culturally specific approaches. Thus, Valentino's position in a gendered economy of vision is complicated by a number of other, partially overlapping discourses, such as the fascination with and suppression of ethnic and racial otherness; the perceived crisis of masculinity; the star system and the traditions of the matinee idol—and the impersonator—in popular theatrical entertainments; and the junction between consumerism and the transformation of the public sphere. Therefore, reconstructing a possible horizon of reception for Valentino involves juggling different levels of material and bringing them to bear upon each other in a kind of methodological both/and of textual analysis and historiographic speculation. This means tracing the contradictions of female spectatorship both inside and outside the films: on the one hand, through textual configurations that betray a tension between dominant and subdominant positions of reading, often marked by a dissociation of narrative into spectacle and scenario; and, on the other, through the public discourse surrounding Valentino—reviews, interviews, studio publicity, articles in fan magazines and the general press, popular biographies—sources that at once document, manipulate, and constitute his reception. [18]

This does not mean treating the films as texts and the publicity discourse as a seemingly given, stable, and accessible context. On the contrary, when we consider the diversity of materials, interests, and ideological mechanisms operating in that discourse, both levels emerge only through an effort of reading. This effort takes its cue from symptomatic moments in the filmic texts and from points of friction between the Valentino figure, the cinematic institution, and dominant cultural norms and codes. For both the films and the publicity discourse, my readings are shaped by a particular cognitive interest—as well as of course by hermeneutic vicissitudes that elude the critic's awareness. This cognitive interest translates into a methodological perspective that attempts to be both critical and redemptive, in the Benjaminian sense: to delineate the contours of a female subjectivity, with all its contradictions and complicity, in the institution of cinema and the text of film history. [19]

Thus, I will read Valentino as a figure and function of female spectatorship, illuminating its precarious status as both cult of consumption and manifestation of an alternative public sphere. If we want to maintain this dual vision, we cannot ignore the fact that Valentino provoked an almost hyperbolic display of patriarchal ideology in the media of capitalist culture.

But this should not deter us from tracing, in the textual configurations of his films and in the cult surrounding him, "a specifically female social subjectivity whose political and psychological dimensions far outstrip the economic, consumerist function."[20] The intent is to show these discourses as interrelated and contestatory, part of the unstable dynamic of a historically variable—and changeable—public sphere.

Sexual Ambiguity, Erotic Ethnicity: Stigmata of a Career

It is a commonplace of Hollywood mythology that Valentino's career was founded—and foundered—upon his persona as a Latin Lover. The publicity governing this meteoric career until Valentino's premature death in 1926 and his legendary afterlife revolves around two fatally intertwined issues: his ethnic otherness and the question of his masculinity. In both aspects the perceived deviations from dominant standards of social and sexual identity that troubled and perhaps destroyed his career were the very qualities that made him an object of unprecedented fascination. But the dual scandal of his ethnicity and ambiguous sexuality was a function of the overruling, enabling stigma of Valentino's career: his enormous popularity with women. As Hollywood manufactured the Valentino legend, promoting the fusion of real life and screen persona that makes a star, his female admirers became part of that legend. Never before was the discourse on fan behavior so strongly marked by the terms of gender and sexuality, and never again was spectatorship so explicitly linked to the discourse on female desire.

This configuration merely brought to a head developments I have already discussed, such as the cinema's massive solicitation of the female consumer and women's increased presence in the public sphere. As Gaylyn Studlar asserts, "Valentino was not an anomaly in his construction as a 'matinee idol' for women, nor was his emergence as a star the first evidence of the power of female desire in determining Hollywood's production of pleasure."[21] Certainly he followed in the footsteps of such heartthrobs as Maurice Costello, Francis X. Bushman, or Lou Tellegen, who had provoked similar manifestations of female fandom. During his brief career he had formidable competition in Richard Barthelmess, Thomas Meighan, and, above all, Wallace Reid, John Gilbert, and John Barrymore. Male stars who were marketed as ethnically other, before Valentino, included Antonio Moreno, and, concurrently, Ramon Novarro or Ivor Novello. If Valentino commands a special status, it is not only because of the excessive dimensions of his female reception, its collective theatricality, and its persistence as memory; it is also because he seems to have combined the projections of ethnic and sexual otherness in such a manner that the defensive strategies mobilized around each one of these terms actually fed into the threat of the other.

When Valentino entered the movies in 1917—at first in bit parts and, then beginning in 1918, as a leading seducer-villain in several minor productions—the injunction against casting actors with distinct ethnic, not to mention racial, features in leading roles was as firmly in place as ever. Even a star like the Japanese actor Sessue Hayakawa could succeed only in the part of a villain. The social discourse that maintained this injunction was the nativist movement that had gained momentum in the 1890s and culminated in the 1920s in response to the massive influx of "new" immigrants from southern and eastern Europe—Italians and Jews—the very groups that populated the nickelodeons and entered the industry as exhibitors, distributors, producers, and actors. After World War I, as the failure of concepts of instantaneous "Americanization" became obvious, the discourse on the new immigrants increasingly assumed a racist tone, as differences of class and nationality were submerged into a biological discourse on race. Riding the nationalist wave in the wake of Roosevelt imperialism, "the guardians of white supremacy [began] to discharge their feelings on the new foreign group."[22]

As Griffith's case so graphically illustrates, racial and ethnic stereotypes are inseparable from inscriptions of gender and sexuality, especially female sexuality. The injunction against casting an ethnically distinct actor in a leading role meant, for a large number of films, the role of a romantic lover. With the nativist turn of the discourse on immigrants, older notions of assimilation through intermarriage were superseded by standards of racial purity predicated on the taboo against miscenegation. Like the latter taboo, however, the nativist crusade against interethnic romance was already a displacement, a defense against the threat of female sexuality. The projection of the ethnic and racially male other as sexually potent, uncontrollable, and predatory no doubt reflected anxieties related to the ongoing crisis of WASP masculinity. The source of these anxieties, however, was more likely the New Woman, with her alleged economic independence, liberalized life-style, and new public presence (as voter and consumer), which seemed to advance the articulation of female desire, of erotic initiative and choice.[23]

But as with the taboo on miscegenation, the injunction against interethnic sex betrayed a fascination with it. From the primitivist iconography of nineteenth-century advertising and trade cards, through melodramatic scenarios of suffering and submission to Orientalist fantasies in popular

fiction, images of ethnic and racial otherness were evoked only to be disavowed, transfigured into an exotic spectacle for the purpose of—primarily
female—consumption. Considering such gainfully deployed ambivalence,
Studlar is right in describing Valentino's "apparent subversion of cultural
norms" as "part of a wider web of popular discourses that linked the exotic to
the erotic in forging a contradictory sexual spectacle of male ethnic otherness within a xenophobic and nativist culture."[24] But establishing a discursive tradition does not necessarily mute the contradictions unleashed in the
particular manifestation. If nothing else, Valentino's success pointed up the
double standard that tacitly condoned relations between white men and
ethnically or racially other women (relations which, in the latter case, had
been the ideologically denied historical basis for miscegenation). Moreover, the reception of Valentino indicates that a discourse successfully tolerated or incited in the print medium may have encountered quite a different
set of problems when transferred to the screen, given the specific effects of
cinematic representation and identification as well as the collective, public
dimensions of exhibition.

When Valentino was "discovered," his ethnic otherness did not become
an issue right away, nor was his reception immediately polarized in terms of
sexual difference. Playing the part of the redeemed rake in Rex Ingram's *The
Four Horsemen of the Apocalypse* (Metro, 6 March 1921), Valentino was
acclaimed as "the continental hero, the polished foreigner, the modern Don
Juan," a sensation in familiar roles: "another of the Latin type of male stars
. . . another champion screen love maker."[25] Reviewers who praised his
acting also remarked upon his skill as a dancer, yet without the sneer or
embarrassment that soon would be attached to this aspect of Valentino's
past.

If *The Four Horsemen* propelled him to instant fame, it was only four films
later, with *The Sheik* (Famous Players-Lasky, 30 October 1921), that Valentino acquired his specific aura of notoriety. The stage was set by the novel on
which the film was based, E. M. Hull's *The Sheik* (1919), a prime example of a
colonialist fantasy ostensibly speaking of—and to—female desire. Written
by a middle-aged Englishwoman, this soft-core best-seller projects its
ambivalent fantasies of independence and rape on the exotic-aristocratic
male other, who combines a barbarian masculinity with romantic passion.
Although the film was advertised as a macho spectacle ("when an Arab sees a
woman he wants, he takes her"), this emphasis was actually toned down in
the adaptation, prompting a reviewer to assert that "the Sheik has been
denatured for the movies."[26] Irrevocably, however, the film established
Valentino's ethnicity as a term of discourse, interlocking controversial and

promotional, destructive and defensive functions. While *The Four Horsemen* had motivated his darker features by the Latin-American setting of a popular novel by a Spanish writer, Vicente Blasco-Ibáñez, the production of *The Sheik* deployed them strategically, as a spectacle of exotic eroticism. While the former film rationalized Valentino's difference to circumvent Hollywood's code of casting, the latter stressed it as a source of his appeal. To be sure, the fascination was disavowed on the fictional level (as in the novel), by having the wild Arab turn out to be the son of an English nobleman and a Spanish lady. But this melodramatic formula, rehearsed in a persistent pattern of dual identity in many of Valentino's films, ironically enabled the creation of an ethnically distinctive star.

As *The Sheik* exploited Valentino's ethnic otherness, the film's deliberate lack of "realistic" constraints also gave carte blanche to xenophobic and racist slurs and insinuations of a color continuum between the "olive-skinned idol" and descendants of African Americans, one Valentino was well aware of. These slurs were provoked by the unprecedented dimensions of Valentino's reception by women, whether actual or mythical, which seemed to exacerbate and sanction the threat of his ethnic-racial otherness. Thus, the most overt attacks on Valentino's deviation from Caucasian-American standards of male beauty discount his success by attributing it to the peculiar bias of female audiences, to a specifically female myopic vision. One such attack, entitled "A Song of Hate" and claimed by a demonstratively male writer, is headed by two profile drawings of Valentino facing each other. On the left, a racist caricature gives him a leery look, protruding teeth and lips, as well as an earring; its caption: "as the men see him." On the right is a portrait with smiling, moderately handsome, and ethnically nonspecific features; the caption: "as the women see him."[27] The racist inflection of the nativist prejudice also marks the indictment of a well-known woman journalist, Adela Rogers St. Johns: "Valentino, with his small eyes, his flat nose and large mouth, fails to measure up to the standard of male beauty usually accepted in this country." By a logic similar to that of the cartoon just described, St. Johns frames this presumably neutral observation with a remark discounting the judgment of Valentino's female fans, as she contrasts the "intensity and madness of the 'Valentino craze'" with "the amazing steadfast and loyal quality of the love and affection given Wally Reid."[28]

On the whole, however, the discourse on Valentino's otherness was a defensive one, which often perpetuated the insult in more or less subtle ways (for instance, by mimicking his accent) and kept the issue before the public.[29] One strategy of dissociating Valentino's foreignness from an ethnicity tainted with racial difference—and working-class origins—was to depict

A Song of Hate

By Dick Dorgan

As the men see him   *As the women see him*

I hate Valentino! All men hate Valentino. I hate his oriental optics; I hate his classic nose; I hate his Roman face; I hate his smile; I hate his glistening teeth; I hate his patent leather hair; I hate his Svengali glare; I hate him because he dances too well; I hate him because he's a slicker; I hate him because he's the great lover of the screen; I hate him because he's an embezzler of hearts; I hate him because he's too apt in the art of osculation; I hate him because he's leading man for Gloria Swanson; I hate him because he's too good looking.

Ever since he came galloping in with the "Four Horsemen" he has been the cause of more home cooked battle royals than they can print in the papers. The women are all dizzy over him. The men have formed a secret order (of which I am running for president and chief executioner as you may notice) to loathe, hate and despise him for obvious reasons.

What! Me jealous?—Oh, no—I just Hate Him.

Figure 11.2

him as a European aristocrat, at least in appearance, manners, and taste: "His charm is distinctly Continental . . . He has the European man's appreciation of music, of painting, of literature."[30] Another strategy, somewhat incongruent with the former, was to emphasize his immigrant experience, to hail him as a living proof of the American Dream, a picaresque version of Horatio Alger. At several points in his career, as in numerous obituaries, his life story was introduced by titles such as "An Immigrant Boy Who Became the Idol of America" or "The Romances of Rodolph Valentino,

Sheik of the Desert Sands: Immigrant, Cafe Bus Boy, Dishwasher and Tangoer Became Famous Overnight."[31]

Both strategies, besides potentially undermining each other, played into the other major stigma of Valentino's career: the question of his masculinity. By supposedly all-American standards of ruggedness and authenticity, European manners, taste, and high culture were traditionally charged with connotations of effeminacy. To make matters worse, Valentino personified the Italian man's stereotypical penchant for fashion, by flaunting his spats, ties, custom-made suits and furs, his flamboyant suspenders and notorious slave bracelet. Thus, he inevitably succumbed to the gender economy of fashion, which, with the "Great Masculine Renunciation" of the eighteenth century, had made sumptuous dress (once a mark of aristocratic status) the domain of women, channeling masculine exhibitionism into professional display behavior, scopophilia, or identification with woman-as-spectacle.[32] Valentino's demonstrative undoing of this historical suppression on the level of publicity tallies with similar effects in his films, their persistent emphasis on costumes, disguises, and display.

As for the Immigrant Boy Who Made Good, accounts of Valentino's early days invariably bring up his profession as a dancer. While this aspect of his career forever resonates with the rhythm of the tango, a notoriously macho ritual of sexual power and submission, the fact that Valentino practiced this ritual for hire classed him as a "gigolo," a "lounge lizard," a "tango pirate." Deployed as much against his female customers as against the dancer himself, the popular cliché of the tango pirate carried the connotation of sexual ambiguity, referring to a "sensuous, willfully aggressive male [who] was also effeminate, will-less, and dependent on women for money."[33] The insinuation that Valentino had "lived off women" as a dancer, moreover, became emblematic of his career as an actor whose stardom depended on millions of female fans.

Like his ethnic otherness, Valentino's sexual identity had not yet been called into question with his first major success, even though *The Four Horsemen* presented him with backlighting and soft-style cinematography, textual devices usually reserved for female stars. Again it was *The Sheik* that locked him into a discursive economy that haunted him for the remainder of his career—by dividing viewers and reviewers along the lines of gender and sexual orientation. With the film's overwhelming success at the box office, reviewers began to note its special draw with female audiences—for whom the sheer appearance of "Rudy" on the screen was "just grand"—and at the same time asserted a growing rejection of the star on the part of "real" men. A cartoon in the fan magazine *Classic* depicts an audience watching *The Sheik,* the women's eyes glued to the screen while their male companions lean back in disdain; the caption: "The Nordic sneered at Valentino while his women-folk thrilled to this jungle python of a lover."[34]

The phallic metaphor of the exotic serpent is not coincidental. Although Valentino in a preemptive strike launched an interview campaign with anti-feminist and misogynist apothegms ("all women like a little cave-man stuff"), his success as exotic-erotic spectacle effectively emasculated him, by assigning him to the fetishistic logic he tried so hard to overcome.[35] This tendency, epitomized by *The Young Rajah* (Famous Players-Lasky, 12 November 1922), persisted in most of his films, primarily costume dramas with exotic settings. More than just an effect of the gendered economy of vision, of his being in the position of object of spectacle, the feminization of Valentino's persona functioned as a defense, as a strategy to domesticate the threat of his ethnic-racial otherness.[36]

In the publicity discourse Valentino's feminization involved a complex dynamic of reception, reaction, and defense. On the most general level it was a result of his sexual objectification, his occupying a position that patriarchal tradition usually reserved for the woman. But Valentino was not simply a sexual object, nor was he, as Studlar claims, "never considered to be anything *more* than a sexual object."[37] He was, significantly, a cult object, the center of a collective ritual. This ritual had its institutional framework in the star system, above all in the organized activities of fandom such as popularity contests, write-in campaigns, and the circulation of photographs, autographs, and star paraphernalia. But from the start the Valentino cult seemed to exceed that framework, assuming a public momentum of its own. Its most excessive manifestations were the riots launched by allegedly all-female fans trying to get at their star, beginning in Philadelphia and Boston (December 1922 and January 1923), blazing through London and Paris, and culminating in the infamous funeral riots in New York (August 1926).

To be sure, these excesses became part of the publicity discourse, and in the long run their threat was absorbed into myth. It is unclear from the newspaper reports to what extent women actually predominated in such public demonstrations; photographs and newsreel footage show at least as many men in the crowds.[38] But the point of the publicity—and the source of male anxiety—seems to have been that these events appeared to have been staged by women, to the exclusion of men, more precisely, that the Valentino cult gave public expression to a force specific to relations *among* women. The article accompanying the *Classic* cartoon mentioned earlier elaborates on the consequences of the gender division pictured in the cartoon: "So the Nordic sneered. And his girl giggled—and the next time went to see Valentino alone, or with Mabel, her girl friend. And in the subtle way that is inexplainable, the admiration for Valentino as an actor was transferred to a personal interest among women."[39]

Contrary to one strand of publicity (and promotional activities such as beauty contests in which Valentino functioned as judge), which held out the "secret" hope for each and every fan that she might be the one and only to be discovered by his gaze, the cult seems to have furnished an occasion for collective expression among women—for conversation, intimacy, and joint ventures—a catalyst for the articulation of common experience, fantasies, and discontents.[40] The violence both attributed to the cult and inscribed in the masculinist attacks on Valentino suggests that he might have figured as a synecdoche for a female subculture as strong as, though ideologically quite distinct from, the nineteenth-century cult of domesticity.

That Valentino was nothing more than a puppet in the hands of a band of maenads was also insinuated by the gossip devoted to his personal and professional life. Beginning with his discovery by June Mathis, the screenwriter who got him cast in *The Four Horsemen*, Valentino was perceived as a creation of, for, and by women. His relationships with women—the plural matters here—became notorious in the year following *The Sheik*, specifically with the bigamy charges brought against him for remarrying before the divorce from his first wife, Jean Acker, was legal. His second marriage contributed to the feminization of his public persona in more than one way. Natacha Rambova, a trained ballet dancer and fashion designer and the stepdaughter of cosmetics tycoon Richard Hudnut, left no doubt in the eyes of the press as to who was wearing the pants in the Valentino household—or rather, who was cooking the pasta and who was tending to the business of Art. But Rambova did more than endow Valentino with the reputation of a henpecked husband, jeopardizing his career by inciting him to quarrels with directors and litigation against the studios.[41] She also came to represent his association with deviant forms of sexuality, by her much publicized gift to him of a platinum "slave bracelet" and, above all, her affiliation with Alla Nazimova, the famous lesbian actress and spiritualist. Confronted with the stereotypical question of whether a star's wife felt jealous watching her husband make love to another woman on screen, she answered with a well-placed double entendre: "'A woman,' says Natacha Rambova, smiling her heavy-lidded, scarlet-lipped smile, 'knows more about what other women want.'"[42] Finally, the ambiguous message of Valentino's special relationship with women was compounded by rumors that he was unable to satisfy any one of them.[43]

The endless speculations about the nature of Valentino's "sex appeal" (measured in "scientific experiments" such as attaching graphs to the pulse of female viewers watching a kissing scene) by and large reproduced clichés of mastery and virility, from his hypnotic eyes to his entire body. But many of these speculations registered an awareness that his appeal eluded the heterosexual polarity of male and female, hinting in the direction of sexual ambiguity, incest, and perversion. The very invocation of romantic passion produced such sexually (and ethnically) overdetermined metaphors as "the male orchid," "a Theda Bara in trousers," "the male Helen of Troy—the masculine counterpart of Sappho, Lais, Phryne, and Aspasia."[44] Female fans ostensibly interviewed or writing letters about their admiration for the exotic star tended to mention either certain elements of his appearance (his legs, his movements, his smile) or his special combination of traditionally male and female qualities (strength and grace, will power and courtesy). But there was another strand of speculation:

> Why do girls love Rodolf so? The reason why—(they do not know!) Some of them may THINK they do . . . HOWEVER, for none of these reasons has he set the feminine heart palpitating and the feminine pulse registering above normal. Not at all. The cold, hard truth of the secret of his charm is that Rodolf Valentino appeals to the Maternal Instinct of EVERYWO-MAN . . . What a woman really wants to do for Rodolf is to bandage his wounds; comfort him; stroke that well-brushed hair; spank him; proudly show him off.[45]

This kind of mothering is not exactly a model of nineteenth-century maternal self-sacrifice; if anybody here suffers, it is the incestuous son. Indeed until his death and beyond, Valentino was haunted by a masochistic aura that constituted a major aspect of the fascination inscribed in his films, rehearsed in particular scenarios of identification.

The masculinist attacks on Valentino turned the complexity of his appeal into the stigma of effeminacy, a mere defect in a male symbolic universe. As could be seen in the nativist-racist slurs, the opposition of male and female was overlaid with an equally rigid opposition of American and un-American, which in turn was coupled with binary terms such as natural versus artificial, authentic self versus mask (note the comparison with Will Rogers in the epigraph to this chapter). This campaign reached its peak with the infamous Pink Powder Puff attack, an editorial in the *Chicago Tribune*, July 18, 1926, just five weeks before Valentino's death:

> Is this degeneration into effeminacy a cognate reaction with pacifism to the virilities and realities of the war? Are pink powder and parlor pinks in any way related? . . .

Do women like the type of "man" who pats pink powder on his face in a public washroom and arranges his coiffure in a public elevator? . . . What has become of the old "cave man" line?

It is a strange social phenomenon and one that is running its course not only here in America but in Europe as well. Chicago may have its powder puffs; London has its dancing men and Paris its gigolos. Down with Decatur; up with Elinor Glyn. Hollywood is the national school of masculinity. Rudy, the beautiful gardener's boy, is the prototype of the American male. Hell's bells. Oh, Sugar.

Valentino, with a unique talent for confirming his enemies' worst allegations, felt called upon to defend his virility by a response invoking his Italian ancestry and honor.[46]

It would be a mistake to overrate the masculinist attacks on Valentino or merely take them at face value. To a certain extent they were part of the ritual. If not exactly self-ironic, the paragons of American virility were aware of performing a rhetorical role, playing straight man as it were to the women's follies. Thus, the "Song of Hate" mentioned earlier concludes with the writer's announcement: "The men have formed a secret order (of which I am running for president and chief executioner as you may notice) to loathe, hate and despise him for obvious reasons. What! Me jealous?—Oh, no—I just Hate Him."[47] We should not forget that this rhetoric only presumed to speak for all men. It thus obscured Valentino's popularity with a large number of men, gay and straight—a dimension that Kenneth Anger, among others, has tried to restore to the history of Valentino's reception.[48]

Like the nativist-racist slurs, the masculinist attacks on Valentino were far outnumbered by the defensive and explanatory discourse they seemed to engender. One explanation for men's hostility was, obviously, jealousy (evidenced by the surmise that they secretly tried to imitate him). As one of America's "most eminent psychologists" was announced to expound in an upcoming issue of *Motion Picture Magazine,* Valentino had become the "Phantom Rival in every virtuous domestic establishment," "the standard by which every wife measures her husband" and hence "a terrible indictment of the American husband."[49] (That the article advertised actually turns the last phrase into "a terrific indictment of the American businessman" suggests a slightly more interesting line of investigation.) Valentino irked the American male, another writer advanced, because he upset the compensatory balance between supposedly manly physical and emotional awkwardness and socially rewarded achievements in the marketplace. "What good was it that he could sell more automobiles in a day than the rest of the sales force put together? What mattered it that his lapel glittered with the recognized symbol of the Nobility of North America?"[50] Such observations stop short of making a causal connection between the standard of masculinity enforced by American capitalism and the sexual, erotic, emotional deficiencies of American men—a connection spelled out more clearly in the problematic heroes of late-nineteenth-century novels (such as those by Norris and Dreiser), who embody what "happens to masculinity in America when the male's successful pursuit of his role in accordance with the business ethic drains him of his virility."[51]

If Valentino triggered the fears of American men over the meaning of "manliness," the stigma of feminization he incurred may not have been only a defensive mechanism of projection (the externalization of a part of oneself that threatens to destabilize the ego). The peculiar configuration of Valentino's relationship with women—the homosocial dimensions of the cult as well as the star's affiliation with lesbians—suggests that the male hostility registered a profound bafflement regarding the other sex, a historical legacy of the distance, the alienation between men and women inflicted by the nineteenth-century doctrine of separate spheres. The war cry of Valentino's effeminacy may have betrayed an awareness that he might understand something they did not—or, perhaps even a more deep-seated fear, reminiscent of *Intolerance*, that women did not need men at all.

The publicity defending Valentino against such attacks, including his own self-defeating efforts, resorted to three distinct strategies, each of which backfired, either by compounding the sexual confusion attributed to him or by drawing attention to his ethnic difference. One line of defense, familiar from other stars' attempts to escape the sexual objectification of the matinee idol, emphasized Valentino's status as an artist. In addition to innumerable reviews and reports protesting the Great Lover's acting skills, Valentino himself endorsed the cause of Art versus Industry in a syndicated polemic against the studio system, aligning himself with the prestigious names of Fairbanks, Pickford, Chaplin, and Griffith.[52] He also published a book of poems (*Day Dreams*, 1923) and posed as a connoisseur of literature, music, art, and antiques. But besides the general connotation of Art as feminine and feminizing, Valentino's artistic ambitions soon became synonymous with the rule of Natacha, her constant interference with his affairs, which gave him the reputation of a henpecked husband. Moreover, his altercations with the studios, in the name of Art, were perceived as hypocritical and unprofessional, a failure to adapt to American ways. A cartoon with an article by the editor of *Photoplay*, James R. Quirk, shows a throng of moviegoers—donning an even mixture of male and female hats—flocking to a theater with posters of Ramon Novarro and Tony Moreno, his two most successful competitors in the genre of Latin Lover. On the right, Valentino and Rambova are depicted on a pedestal, spouting slogans, respectively, of "I'm for Art" and "Down with the Producers!" in a cobblestone square populated by a single hobo. [53]

A more aggressive line of defense was Valentino's participation in the cult of physical fitness, with scores of publicity stills showing him working out in seminudity or boxing, fencing, or lifting weights. Articles featuring him as an athlete appeared in such magazines as *Muscle Builder* and *Physical Culture* ("Presenting Rodolph Valentino in a New Light, Revealing Him as the Big Husky and All Around Athlete That He Is"); the *Daily Mirror* ran a series of ostensible fitness lessons under the rubric of "Valentino's Bulging Muscles" or "Valentino's Beauty Secrets." Such articles furnished a pretext for photographs, many of which cut off his body above the waist (thereby concealing the fact that he *is* wearing shorts) or surround him with phallic symbols such as sports equipment, dogs, horses, and cars. The captions often read like an inventory of Valentino's physical assets ("down underneath his shoulder blades he has a particularly strong pair of muscles. They are very hard but also very flexible") and underscore a deeroticizing tendency in the images. [54] Invariably, however, such assertions of Valentino's masculinity played into

Figure 11.3

Figure 11.4

the phallic logic in the name of which his masculinity had been contested:
his entire body assumed the function of a phallic fetish, symbol of the
missing penis. As with the display of his body in films (such as the dressing
scenes in *Blood and Sand* and *Monsieur Beaucaire*), the physical culture pinups of
Valentino merely confirmed the masculinist projection of him as "castrated."
So, the more he protested his virility, the more he assumed the role of a male
impersonator, brilliant counterpart to the female "female" impersonators of
the American screen such as Mae West or the vamps of his own films.

Physical culture magazines at that time also functioned as an important
relay for gay male eroticism. Valentino's "masculine protest" encouraged this
association by yet another strategy of defense, by asserting his preference
for the company of men (and male accoutrements such as cars, dogs, and
horses) as well as his success with male audiences. "I want to be a cowboy—
not a lounging he-vamp," an article quotes him as saying, "Boys seek manhood! Girls seek genuine womanhood." The promotion of Valentino as a
"man's man" continued into reports of his dying moments with "only men" at
his bedside: "Did he miss the women in his last hour? Or was he glad that he

was alone with his own kind? . . . He was a he-man dying in the presence of his he-man friends."[55] Such publicity produced the most vitriolic responses from the masculinist camp, charging hypocrisy and spiced with insinuations of homosexuality. An account of a press conference staged by Valentino's agents revels in the following summary: "The story was told of the swarm of men, sodden in the rain, waiting hours to glimpse for a moment the hero of 'The Eagle' on the day that the picture opened. Apparently, it was a purely masculine aggregation as far as the publicity experts were concerned." Then, as Valentino was walking down Broadway, "it was the men, mind you, the men who followed for blocks, ogling, pushing, innate masculinity magnetizing males."[56] Valentino ran up against the double standards of a persistently homosocial yet homophobic culture; the more he insisted on being "one of them," the less he succeeded on their terms.

In the discursive spiral interlocking strategies of promotion, suppression, and defense, Valentino's career became a battleground for conflicts between the forces of consumerism and ideologically entrenched discourses of ethnicity and sexuality—forces that were actually in the process of incorporating each other. In the measure that his success was built on embodying the contradictions unleashed in that process, he became its most prominent casualty. The public violence he provoked, whether in the form of vicious attacks or passionate demonstrations of enthrallment and defense, made his person increasingly irrelevant. To use a cliché, he became a floating signifier for temporarily antagonistic discourses—a fate epitomized in the fake photographs showing him in heaven and other curious manifestations of his afterlife.[57]

Yet he did em*body* these contradictions, giving them a material expression in the guise of a unique subjectivity, without which the star system would not function. In that sense Valentino seemed to live out the vicissitudes of social change as they affected peoples' lives—affected them differently depending on gender and sexual orientation, on class, race, ethnicity, and generation. Thus, as a kind of living supplement, he did make a difference for the public articulation and negotiation of these vicissitudes. As his body became the site of struggles over the meaning of masculinity, he not only set into play the mechanisms of the phallic double bind, but also rendered visible an alternative delineation of gender identity and gender relations. As some reviewers and many more female (as well as male) viewers seem to have intuited, his fascination devolved upon qualities that made him not less of a man but a different kind of man. He came to personify an alternative form of male identity at a time when "beauty" and "force" were still considered an irreconcilable dichotomy, and "male beauty" an oxymoron tolerated at best in socially marginal characters and professions, in artists, fashion workers, intellectuals, and bohemians.[58]

A more important factor of both fascination and threat was that Valentino called into question the very idea of a stable sexual identity. Beckoning with the promise of sexual—and ethnic-racial—mobility, the Valentino figure appealed to those who most keenly felt the need, yet also the anxiety, of such mobility, who themselves were caught between the hopes fanned by the phantasmagoria of consumption and an awareness of the impossibility of realizing them within existing social and sexual structures.

Patterns of Vision,
Scenarios of Identification

12

At first glance Valentino's films seem to rehearse the classical choreography of the look almost to the point of parody, offering point-of-view constructions that affirm the cultural hierarchy of gender in the visual field. From *The Four Horsemen* to his death, Valentino starred in fourteen films, produced by different studios and under different directors. [1] Illustrating the significance of the star as *auteur* as much as the economic viability of vehicles, each of these films reiterates a familiar pattern in staging the exchange of looks between Valentino and the female characters. Whenever Valentino lays eyes on a woman first, we can be sure that she will turn out to be the woman of his dreams, the legitimate partner in the romantic relationship. Whenever a woman initiates the look, she is invariably marked as a vamp, to be condemned and defeated in the course of the narrative.

In the opening sequence of *The Eagle* (United Artists, 1925; based on Pushkin's novella *Dubrovsky*), the Czarina (Louise Dresser) is about to inspect her favorite regiment, "the handsomest in all Russia," when a runaway carriage nearby prompts the hero into a Fairbanks-like rescue. The first shot of Valentino shows him from the rear, looking through a pocket-sized telescope. The first time we see his face, it is framed, medium close-up, by the window of the coach, directing a curious gaze inside. The reverse shot completing the point of view, however, is illegible, hiding the object under a bundle of fur; only his repeated look makes the image readable, distinguishes the female figure from the setting, literally produces her for the spectator. As the young woman (Vilma Banky) returns the glance, she enters the romantic pact, acknowledging the power of his look(s). Her negative counterpart is the Czarina, a stout, elderly woman who is shown catching sight of Valentino independent of his look, which momentarily transfigures her face in desire. While she is masculinized by a military outfit and at the

Figure 12.1

Figure 12.2

same time ridiculed for her lack of masculine physical skills, desire on her part is most crucially discredited through its association with political power. As she continues her inspection of Valentino's body in the privacy of the imperial suite, encircling and immobilizing him (no point-of-view shot), the expression of horror in his eyes pinpoints the scandal of the situation, the reversal of gender positions in the visual field, unilaterally enforced by the monarch. As soon as Valentino understands the sexual implications of his position, he determines to restore the traditional (im)balance, risking death as a deserter, yet regaining the mastery of the look.

A similar pattern can be observed in *Blood and Sand* (Famous Players-Lasky, 1922): Doña Sol (Nita Naldi), the President's niece, is shown admiring the victorious torero through opera glasses, prior to his looking at her; syntactically, this marks her as a vamp. His future wife, Carmen (Lila Lee), on the other hand, is singled out by the camera within his point of view, similar to the coach sequence in *The Eagle*. A close-up of his face signals the awakening desire, alternating with an undecipherable long shot of a crowd. The repetition of the desiring look, provoking a dissolve that extricates her from the crowd, resolves the picture puzzle for the spectator and, by the same logic of vision, establishes her as the legitimate companion (further sanctioned by the inclusion of his mother in the point-of-view construction that follows).

Figure 12.3

Figure 12.4

Thus, the legitimate female figure is deprived of the initiative of the erotic look, relegated to the position of scopic object within the diegesis. In relation to the spectator, however, she shares this position of scopic object with Valentino.

Valentino's appeal depends to a large degree on the manner in which he combines masculine control of the look with the feminine quality of "to-be-looked-at-ness," to use Laura Mulvey's rather awkward term. When he falls in love—usually at first sight—the close-up of his face surpasses that of the female character in its value as spectacle. In a narcissistic doubling, the subject of the look constitutes itself as object, graphically illustrating Freud's formulation of the autoerotic dilemma: "Too bad that I cannot kiss myself."[2] Moreover, in their radiant pictorial quality, such shots temporarily arrest the metonymic drive of the narrative, similar in effect to the visual presence of the woman, which, as Mulvey observes, tends "to freeze the flow of action in moments of erotic contemplation."[3] In Valentino's case, however, erotic contemplation governs an active as well as a passive mode, making spectator and character the subject of a double game of vision.

To the extent that Valentino occupies the position of primary object of spectacle, he incurs a systematic feminization of his persona. But as with the publicity discourse, his feminization on the level of filmic enunciation

Figure 12.5

involves more complex processes than mere sexual objectification. Comple-
menting the specular evocation of feminine narcissism, the mise-en-scène of
many of his films makes him enact an exhibitionism, which, with the "Great
Masculine Renunciation" of fashion in the eighteenth century, became culturally assigned to women.[4] Although the narration tries to motivate this
exhibitionism by casting Valentino as a performer (torero, dancer) or by

Figure 12.6

situating him in a historically or exotically removed setting, the connotation of femininity persists in the choice of costumes, such as flared coats and headdress reminiscent of a bridal wardrobe, as well as a general emphasis on dressing and disguises. *Monsieur Beaucaire*, a 1924 Paramount costume drama based on the Booth Tarkington novel, combines the effect and its disavowal in a delightfully self-reflective manner. Valentino, playing the Duke of Chartres alias Monsieur Beaucaire, is introduced on stage playing the lute in

Figure 12.7

an attempt to entertain the jaded King, Louis XV. The courtly mise-en-
scène ostensibly legitimizes the desiring female gaze, contained in the
alternation of relatively close shots of Valentino and the female members of
the audience within the film. Unfailingly, however, this sequence enacts the
paradox of female spectatorship. As one woman is shown *not* focusing her
eyes upon him in rapture, he stops midway in indignation and a title redun-

Figure 12.8

dantly explains: "the shock of his life: a woman not looking at him." Sure enough, this refers to the leading romantic lady.[5] The partial reversal of the gender economy of vision is prepared by the film's opening shot, a close-up of hands doing needlepoint. As the camera pulls back, the hands are revealed to be the King's. In the effeminate universe of the French court, Valentino asserts his masculinity only by comparison, staging it as a difference that ultimately fails to make a difference.

Before considering the possibilities of identification implied in this peculiar choreography of vision, I wish to recapitulate some thoughts on female visual pleasure and its fate under the patriarchal taboo. Particularly interesting are certain aspects of scopophilia that Freud analyzes through its development in infantile sexuality, a period in which the child is still far from having a stable sense of gender identity. Stimulated in the process of mutual gazing between mother and child, the female scopic drive is constituted with a bisexual as well as an autoerotic component. Although these components subsequently succumb to cultural hierarchies of looking that tend to fixate the woman in a passive, narcissistic-exhibitionist role, a basic ambivalence in the structure of vision as a component drive remains. As Freud argues in "Instincts and Their Vicissitudes" (1915), the passive component of a drive represents a reversal of the active drive into its opposite, redirecting itself to the subject. Such contradictory constitution of libidinal components may account for the coexistence, in their later fixations as perversions,

Figure 12.9

of diametrically opposed drives within one and the same person, even if one tendency usually predominates. Thus a voyeur is always to some degree an exhibitionist and vice versa, just as the sadist shares the pleasures of masochism.[6]

The notion of ambivalence is crucial to a theory of female spectatorship, precisely because the cinema, while enforcing patriarchal hierarchies in its organization of the look, also offers women an institutional opportunity to violate the taboo on female scopophilia. The success of a figure like Valentino, himself overdetermined as both object and subject of the look, urges us to insist upon the ambivalent constitution of scopic pleasure, the potential reversibility and reciprocity of roles. Moreover, as one among a number of the more archaic partial drives whose integration is always and at best precarious, scopophilia needs to be distinguished, conceptually, from its return in the adult perversion of voyeurism, culturally assigned to men and predicated on the one-sided regime of the keyhole and the threat of castration. Although scopophilia as a component drive does not exist outside the norms of genitality, collapsing it a priori into an Oedipal teleology restricts the possibility of conceptualizing the female spectator (or, for that matter, the male spectator as well) in other than binary, ahistorical terms; it thus tends to reproduce a phallic economy on the level of critique.[7]

The potential dissociation of sexual and survival instincts, which is implicit in Freud's notion of "anaclisis" and which he discusses with reference to the scopic drive in his analysis of cases of psychogenic disturbance of vision, is equally pertinent to an alternative conception of visual pleasure. The eye serves both a practical function for the individual's orientation in the external world and the function of an erotogenic zone. If the latter refuses to accept its subservient role in forepleasure and takes over, the balance between sexual and survival instincts is threatened. To this the ego may react by repressing the dangerous component drive. The psychogenic disturbance of vision in turn represents the revenge of the repressed instinct, retrospectively interpreted by the individual as the voice of punishment which seems to be saying: "Because you sought to misuse your organ of sight for evil sensual pleasure, it is fitting that you should not see anything at all any more."[8]

While the psychogenic disturbance of vision, in the framework of psychoanalytic theory, clearly functions as a metaphor of castration,[9] the potentially antithetical relation of sexual and survival instincts could also be taken to describe the cultural and historical differentiation of male and female forms of vision. Although the neurotic dissociation may occur in patients of both sexes, the balance effected in so-called normal vision seems more typical of the psychic disposition by means of which the male subject controls the practical world as well as the sexual field. Suffice it here to allude to the historical construction of monocular vision in Western art since the Renaissance, the instrumental standards imposed upon looking in technical and scientific observation and other disciplines, areas of cultural activity from which for centuries women were barred. On the flipside of this coin we find a variety of social codes enforcing the taboo on female scopophilia, ranging from make-up fashions like belladonna through the once popular injunction, parodied by Dorothy Parker, not to "make passes at girls who wear glasses."

The construction of femininity within patriarchal society, however, contains the promise of being incomplete. Women's exclusion from mastery of the visual field may have diminished the pressure of the ego instincts toward the component drives, which are probably insufficiently subordinated to begin with. Thus the potential dissociation of the scopic drive from its function for survival may not be that threatening to the female subject, may not necessarily provoke the force of repression that Freud holds responsible for certain cases of psychogenic blindness. If such generalization is permissible, women might be more likely to indulge, without immediately repressing, in a sensuality of vision that contrasts with the goal-oriented discipline of the one-eyed masculine look. Christa Karpenstein speaks in this context of "an unrestrained scopic drive, a swerving and sliding gaze which disregards the meanings and messages of signs and images that socially determine the subject, a gaze that defies the limitations and fixations of the merely visible."[10]

If I seem to belabor this notion of an undomesticated gaze as a historical aspect of female subjectivity, I certainly do not intend to propose yet another variant of essentialism. To the extent that sexual difference is culturally constructed to begin with, the subversive qualities of a female gaze may just as well be shared by a male character. This is precisely what I want to suggest for the case of Valentino, contrary to the official legend, which never ceased to assert the power of his look in terms of aggressive mastery. The studios and fan magazines persistently advertised his hypnotic gaze, and the state of bliss in store for the woman who would be discovered by it, in the measure that he himself was becoming an erotic commodity at the mercy of the gaze of millions.[11]

On the level of filmic enunciation, the feminine connotation of Valentino's "to-be-looked-at-ness" destabilizes his own glance in its very origin, makes him vulnerable to temptations that jeopardize the sovereignty of the male subject. When Valentino's eyes get riveted on the woman of his choice, he seems to become paralyzed rather than aggressive or menacing, behaving like the rabbit rather than the snake. Struck by the beauty of Carmen, in *Blood and Sand*, his activity seems blocked, suspended; it devolves upon Carmen, who throws him a flower, to get the narrative back into gear. Later in the film, at the height of his career as a torero, Valentino raises his eyes to the President's box, an individual centered under the benevolent eye of the State, when his gaze is sidetracked, literally decentered, by the sight of Doña Sol in the box to the right. The power of Valentino's gaze depends upon its weakness—enhanced by the fact that he was actually nearsighted and cross-eyed—upon its oscillating between active and passive, between object and ego libido. The erotic appeal of the Valentinian gaze, staged as a look within the look, is one of reciprocity and ambivalence rather than mastery and objectification.

The peculiar organization of the Valentinian gaze corresponds, on the level of narrative, to conflicts between the pleasure and the reality principle. Whenever the hero's amorous interests collide with the standards of male social identity—career, family, paternal authority, or a vow of revenge— the spectator can hope that passion will triumph over pragmatism to the point of self-destruction.[12] As the generating vortex of such narratives, the Valentinian gaze far exceeds its formal functions of providing diegetic coherence and continuity; it assumes an almost figural independence. Thus the films advance an identification with the gaze itself, not with source or object but with the gaze as erotic medium, which promises to transport the spectator out of the world of means and ends into the realm of passion.

The discussion of gendered patterns of vision opens into the larger question of identification, as the matrix structuring the viewer's access to the film, the process that organizes subjectivity in visual and narrative terms. Most productively, feminist film theorists have insisted on the centrality of sexual difference, questioning the assumption of a single or neutral spectator position constructed in hierarchically ordered, linear processes of identification. Initially, Mulvey reduced cinematic identification to a basically active relationship with a protagonist of the same sex, that is, male; but she subsequently modified this notion with regard to the female viewer, who may not only cross but also be divided by gender lines (which in turn deflects identification from the fictive telos of a stable identity). The difficulty of conceptualizing a female spectator has led feminists to recast the problem of identification in terms of instability, mobility, multiplicity, and, I would add, temporality. Likewise, a number of critics are trying to complicate the role of sexual difference in identification with the differences of class and race, with cultural and historical specificity. This might make it possible to rethink the concept of subjectivity implied, beyond the commonplace that subjects are constructed by and within ideology. The question of the subject of identification is also, and not least, a question as to which part of the spectator is engaged and how, which layers of conscious or unconscious memory and phantasy are activated, and how we, as viewers and critics, choose to interpret this experience. [13]

It seems useful at this point to invoke Mary Ann Doane's distinction of at least three instances of identification that operate in the viewing process: identification *with* the representation of a person (character, star); identification (recognition) *of* particular objects, persons or action *as* such (stars, narrative images); identification with the "look," with oneself as the condition of perception, which Metz, in analogy with Lacan's concept of the mirror phase, has termed "primary."[14] These psychical mechanisms and their effects can be traced through the various levels of enunciation that structure cinematic identification, interlacing textual units such as shot, sequence, strategies of narrative and mise-en-scène. [15] The first form of identification discussed by Doane, identification with the integral person filmed (Metz's "secondary" mode of identification), engages the female viewer transsexually insofar as it extends to the Valentino character as subject. Thus it raises the problem of spectatorial cross-dressing—unless we consider other possibilities of transsexual identification beside the transvestite one. The alternative option for the woman spectator, passive-narcissistic identification with the female star as erotic object, seems to have been advertised primarily by the publicity discourse; it appears rather more problematic in view of the specular organization of the films. [16]

If we can isolate an instance of "primary" identification at all—which is dubious on theoretical grounds—Valentino's films challenge the assumption of perceptual mastery implied in such a concept both on account of the star system and because of the peculiar organization of the gaze. The star not only promotes a dissociation of scopic and narrative registers but also complicates the imaginary self-identity of the viewing subject with an exhibitionist and collective dimension. The fascination with the star, "the observed of all observers" (Pratt), entails both a projection of the fan into the figure of the star as the object of admiration and an awareness that this projection is shared by others who contemplate that same figure. [17] The Valentino films undermine the notion of a unified position of scopic mastery by foregrounding the reciprocity and ambivalence of the gaze as an erotic medium, a gaze that fascinates precisely because it transcends the socially imposed subject-object hierarchy of sexual difference.

Moreover, the contradictions of the female address are located in the very space where the registers of the look and those of narrative and mise-en-scène intersect. In offering the woman spectator a position structurally analogous to that of the vamp within the diegesis (looking at Valentino independent of his scopic initiative) identification with the desiring gaze is both granted and incriminated, or, one might say, granted on condition of its illegitimacy. This may be why the vamp figures in Valentino films (with the exception of *Blood and Sand*) are never totally condemned, inasmuch as they acknowledge a subliminal complicity between Valentino and the actively desiring female gaze. In *The Eagle*, for instance, the Czarina is redeemed by her general's ruse of letting Valentino escape execution under an assumed identity. The closing shot shows Valentino and the Czarina waving each other a never-ending farewell, much to the concern of their respective legitimate partners.

Dressing Up Rudy

The least equivocal instance of identification operating in the Valentino films is that which feeds on recognition, the memory-spectacle rehearsed with each appearance of the overvalued erotic object, the star. [18] The pleasure of recognition involved in the identification of and with a star is dramatized in many Valentino films through the recurring narrative pattern mentioned earlier, in connection with the simultaneous fascination with and disavowal of his ethnic-racial otherness. Often the Valentino character combines two sides of a melodramatic dualism, such as dark versus light or tempting versus legitimate, which he acts out in a series of disguises and anonymous identities, often involving a class differential as well. In *The Sheik* (1921), the barbaric son of the desert turns out to be of British descent; in *Moran of the Lady Letty* (1922), the San Francisco dandy proves himself a hearty sailor and authentic lover; the Duke of Chartres in exile becomes Monsieur Beaucaire; and the Black Eagle pursues courtship instead of revenge under the assumed identity of Monsieur LeBlanc. [19] The spectator-fan recognizes her star in all his masks and disguises—unlike the female protagonist whose trial of love consists of "knowing" him regardless of narrative misfortune or social status.

Like most star vehicles, Valentino films have notoriously weak narratives, and would probably fail to engage any viewer were it not for their hero's charisma; indeed they flaunt a certain dissociation of meaning and pleasure, of diegetic logic and spectacular style. Many of the films are adapted from well-known popular novels, preferably costume dramas. As a reviewer remarked of *A Sainted Devil* (Famous Players-Lasky, 1924): "To be sure it has a plot, but it may be more accurately described as Mr. Valentino entirely surrounded by women and a wardrobe."[20] Though the films convey some delight in action, in the sense of activity, physical movement, and gesture, there is very little suspense, very little of the game of concealing and revealing, of the dialectic of desire, knowledge, and power that has led theorists like Barthes, Bellour, Heath, and de Lauretis to define all narrative as predicated on Oedipus. Identification in terms of narrative movement is apt to fall short of the plot in its totality; closure tends to reside in smaller units, cutting across visual and narrative registers, defined by the succession of masks, disguises, milieus, and scenarios.

The emphasis on costumes and disguises, on rituals of dressing and undressing, undermines the voyeuristic structure of spectatorship, in that it implicitly acknowledges the spectator as part of the scenario. In their unabashed theatrical display, Valentino's films revert to an early "cinema of attractions," above all erotic films in which the performer casts a knowing glance at the camera. This is emblematic in the famous dressing scene in *Monsieur Beaucaire*, during which Valentino punctuates the exercise in procrastination with occasional asides in the direction of the camera. Such rituals of mutual recognition between star and fan, in conjunction with the viewer's epistemological superiority over the female protagonist, encourage identification via a fantasy in which the spectator herself authorizes the masquerade. The publication, as late as 1979, of a Valentino paper-doll book testifies to the persistence of this fantasy in popular iconography. If there is any prototype for such a fantasy—and this is merely autobiographical speculation—it might be the penchant of prepubescent girls to dress up a younger brother as a little sister.[21]

An important aspect of this masquerade is its functioning as a shared, public ritual. In this regard, Doane's catalogue of instances of identification needs to be expanded by a fourth instance, suggested by Freud in *Group Psychology and Analysis of the Ego* (1921). Freud discerns a type of "partial identification" in the perception of an analogy on the part of the ego with others, "a common quality shared with some other person who is not the object of the sexual instinct." In the measure that this common quality gains force, "the more successful may this partial identification become, and it may thus represent the beginning of a new tie."[22] This kind of a collective transference no doubt played a major part in the Valentino cult, as a particular manifestation of a female subculture. In the films, the collective dimension of the star's appeal is accentuated in precisely those moments of direct display which inscribe the viewer as a member of a public body rather than an isolated peeping tom.

A Star Is Being Beaten

The dramatic-erotic fashion show is not the only type of scenario to organize identification in the Valentino films. Spectatorial pleasure is imbricated pervasively with self-consciously sadomasochistic rituals.[23] It may still be within the parameters of the vamp cliché when Doña Sol, holding onto the torero by the muscles of his arms, expresses her desire, according to the intertitle, one day to be beaten by these strong hands—and nearly bites off his thumb in the following shot. Here the sadomasochistic proclivity underlines the general perversity of a woman who dares to appropriate the privilege of the first look.

More interesting sadomasochistic role-playing takes place in the context of the legitimate, romantic relationship. In *The Eagle* Mascha, the young woman from the first sequence, turns out to be the daughter of the odious landowner against whom Valentino, in his persona as The Black Eagle, has pledged revenge on his father's deathbed. At one point his men have kidnapped her, proudly presenting the catch to their leader. As he dismounts from his horse and steps toward her with a whip ready to lash out, the genre seems to slide into pornography: the masks, the whip, phallic hats—

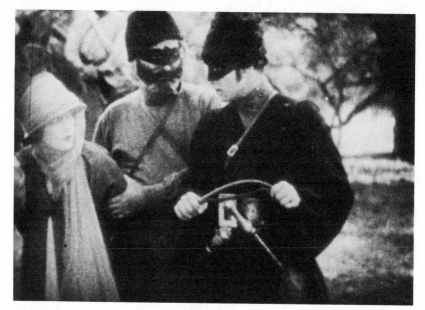

Figure 12.10

Figure 12.11

insignia of anonymous lust, traces of the search for nonidentity in eros.[24] That Valentino actually directs the whip against his own men is the alibi the narrative provides for a kinky shot, the *défilement* into propriety; yet it does not diminish the subliminal effect. Valentino recognizes Mascha as his earlier romantic discovery and, protected by his unilateral anonymity, continues the game in a more or less playful manner. As she rejects his horse and proudly embarks on her journey on foot, he follows her, mounted on the high horse—a constellation the camera exploits in straight-on back-tracking shots. When she finally is forced down by the obligatory fainting spell, Valentino reverses the spatial hierarchy by installing her on the horse, thus making her an involuntary accomplice in the dominance-submission game. This game is accomplished within the legitimate relationship only by means of the mask, which temporarily suspends the mutuality of the romantic gaze in Valentino's favor.

The emphasis on the sadistic aspects of the Valentino persona echoes the publicity pitch for *The Sheik*, the marketing of the star as a "he-man," a "menace," reiterated, as late as 1977 by one of his biographers: "Women were to find in *The Sheik* a symbol of the omnipotent male who could dominate them as the men in their own lives could not."[25] And when in that film the son of the desert forces blue-eyed Lady Diana on his horse, ostensibly for her own pleasure ("lie still you little fool"), millions of women's hearts were said to have quivered at the prospect of being humiliated by the imperious barbarian. However, as I pointed out in the preceding chapter, *The Sheik* initiated the much publicized rejection of Valentino by male moviegoers. Not only the stigma of effeminacy but, equally threatening, a masochistic reputation began to develop in the discourse on his "private" life, especially his associations with lesbians. The masochistic elements in the Valentino persona were enforced more systematically by the sadistic placing of the spectator in the films. There are few Valentino films that do not display a whip, in whatever marginal function, and most of them feature seemingly insignificant subplots in which the spectator is offered a position that entails enjoying the tortures inflicted on Valentino or others. To be sure, the sadistic spicing of cinematic pleasure was quite common in pre-Code films, and displays of the eroticized male body were often motivated and condoned by melodramatic scenes of suffering—but not with such enduring effects on the sexual persona of the actor.[26]

The oscillation of the Valentino persona between sadistic and masochistic positions is another expression of the ambivalence that governs the specular organization of the films. A sadist, Freud asserts in "Three Essays on the Theory of Sexuality," "is always at the same time a masochist, although in one case the active and in another case the passive aspect of the perversion may be more pronounced and may represent the predominant sexual activity."[27] But the question of the origin and economy of masochism haunted Freud over decades and led him to revise his views at least once.[28] Among post-Freudian attempts to theorize masochism, that of Gilles Deleuze has recently been put forward as an alternative model of spectatorship. Deleuze challenges the conceptual linkage of masochism with sadism and the Oedipal regime; he proposes instead a distinct origin and aesthetics of masochism located in the relationship with the "oral mother." Although the revisionist impulse to emphasize pregenital sexuality in spectatorship can only be welcomed, Deleuze's model seems somewhat limited by the parameters of his literary source—the writings of Leopold von Sacher-Masoch—and thus to an elaboration of the masochistic scenario within a basically male fantasy.[29] Therefore, I wish to return to Freud's essay "A Child Is Being Beaten" (1919), not only for its focus on female instances of sadomasochistic fantasy but also because it elucidates a particular aspect of the Valentino figure as phantasmic object.[30]

The formula, "a child is being beaten," which, regardless of any actual corporal punishment, may dominate masturbation fantasies of the latency period, is remarkable in that it stereotypically reiterates the mere description of the event, while subject, object, and the role of the person fantasizing remain indeterminate. On the basis of jealousy aroused by the Oedipal constellation, Freud proceeds to reconstruct three different phases with explicit reference to female adolescents: "My father is beating the child that I hate" (presumably a younger sibling), therefore, "he loves only me"; "I am being beaten—and therefore loved—by my father" (the regressive substitute for the incestuous relationship); "a child is being beaten." The second, sexually most threatening phase succumbs to repression, but the first is reduced to its merely descriptive part and thus results in the third, in which the father is usually replaced by a more distant male authority figure. Thus the fantasy is sadistic only in its form—but grants masochistic gratification by way of identification with the anonymous children who are being beaten. This series of transformations reduces the sexual participation of the girl to the status of spectator, desexualizing the content and bearer of the fantasy (which, Freud remarks, is not the case in male variants of the beating fantasy). Just as important in the present context, however, is the observation that in both male and female versions of the sadomasochistic fantasy the children who are being beaten usually are male. In the girl's case Freud explains this with reference to the "masculinity complex"—the penchant to imagine herself as male—which allows her to be represented, in her daydreams, by these anonymous whipping boys.[31]

The deepest, most effective layer of the Valentino persona is that of the whipping boy—in which he resembles so many other heroes of popular fiction devoured by adolescent girls (one of the examples Freud cites is *Uncle Tom's Cabin*). Freud's analysis of the sadomasochistic fantasy suggests that we distinguish between the sadistic appeal articulated in point-of-view structures, on the one hand, and the masochistic pleasure in the identification with the object, on the other. Transsexual identification, instead of being confined to simple cross-dressing, relies as much on the feminine qualities of the male protagonist as on residual ambiguity in the female spectator. This simultaneous identification is enabled by an interactional structure, a scenario whose libidinal force, protected by a series of repressive-rhetorical transformations, can be traced back to the nursery. (Given the amount of detail that Freud devotes to reconstructing the various stages of this scenario, it is indeed curious—and here one might concur with Deleuze—how briefly he dismisses the role of the mother, especially in view of the emphasis on sibling rivalry.)

Unlike the one-sided masochistic identification with a female protagonist encouraged by the "woman's film," female identification in Valentino films could be constructed to entail the full range of transformations proposed by Freud. As Valentino slips into and out of the part of the whipping boy, intermittently relegating the woman to the position of both victim and perpetrator, he may succeed in recuperating the middle phase of the female fantasy from repression ("I am being beaten—and therefore loved—by my father") and thus in resexualizing it. This possibility is suggested by the unmistakable incestuous aura surrounding the Valentino persona. The appeal here, however, is less that of a relationship between father and daughter than between brother and sister, turning on the desire of both for the inaccessible mother.[32]

The interchangeability of sadistic and masochistic positions within the diegesis potentially undercuts the a priori masochism ascribed by current film theory to the female spectator of classical cinema. In making sadomasochistic rituals an explicit component of the erotic relationship, Valentino's films subvert the socially imposed dominance-submission hierarchy of gender roles, dissolving subject-object dichotomies into erotic reciprocity. The vulnerability Valentino displays in his films, the traces of feminine masochism in his persona, may partly account for the threat he posed to dominant standards of masculinity. The sublimation of masochistic inclinations, after all, is the token of the male subject's sexual mastery and control of pleasure.

Sadomasochistic role-playing most strikingly intersects with the choreography of vision in *The Son of the Sheik* (United Artists, 1926), Valentino's last and probably most perverse film. Because of a misunderstanding that propels the narrative, Yasmin (Vilma Banky) represents a combination of both female types, vamp and romantic companion. Although it is clear to the spectator, Ahmed/Valentino's misunderstanding—that Yasmin lured him into a trap, thus causing him to be captured and whipped by her father's gang—has been carefully planted early on in the film by means of an editing device. The film's first close-up shows the face of Yasmin, lost in erotic yearning, which dissolves into a matching close-up of Valentino. A somewhat mismatched cut reveals him in turn looking at her legs as she dances for a crowd. A dissolve back to Yasmin's face eventually confirms the status of the sequence as a flashback that stages the usual discovery of the woman through Valentino's look. Her objectification is compounded by the demeaning situation, the fragmentation of Yasmin's body as well as the emphasis on money in the deployment of the romantic gaze. The potential misreading of the flashback as a point-of-view shot on the part of the woman falsely implicates Yasmin as a transgressor, thus supporting her double inscription as victim later on in the film, as both scopic and masochistic object. Herself ignorant of her lover's misunderstanding, Yasmin is kidnapped by him and imprisoned in his tent. His revenge, which consists in refusing her the mutuality of the erotic look, culminates in a veritable one-eyed stare with which he transfixes her to the point of rape. Valentino's unilateral violation of the romantic pact supposedly is vindicated by the powerful image of him crucified, humiliated, and whipped earlier in the film. This image of Valentino as victim, however, erroneously ascribed to Yasmin's authorship and not even witnessed by her, is designed primarily for the benefit of the spectator. No doubt there remains an asymmetry in the sadomasochistic role reversal on the diegetic level: a female character can assume an active part only at the price of being marked as a vamp; sadistic pleasure is specularized, reserved for the woman in front of the screen.

The multiple ambiguities articulated on the enunciatory level of *The Son of the Sheik* contrast with the more flatly patriarchal discourse of the narrative, not to mention the simple-minded sexist and racist title prose. As if to conceal—and thus inofficially to acknowledge and exploit—this gap between narrative and visual pleasure, the Oedipal scenario is overinscribed to the point of parody. Valentino's private love-revenge affair is resisted strongly by his father, who bends an iron rod with his bare hands in order to demonstrate paternal power. Valentino, a chip of the old block, responds by straightening it out again. Only when his understanding mother, Lady Diana (Agnes Ayres), invokes a flashback of her own kidnapping in *The Sheik* does the father recognize and accept his successor. They reconcile in the course of yet another kidnapping scene, this time rescuing Yasmin from her

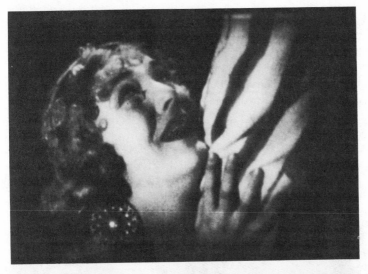

Figure 12.12

father's gang. Father and son shake hands amid tumultuous swashbuckling, temporarily losing sight of the woman, the object of their efforts.

Beneath this Oedipal pretext the film contains a connotative wealth of deviations, which radiate, in a dialectic of repression and excess, from the Valentino character to all levels of mise-en-scène and cinematography.[33] Exotic costumes, oriental decor, and desert landscape provoke a sensuality of vision that undermines interest in the development of the narrative. Extreme long shots show Valentino riding through a sea of sand shaped like breasts and buttocks. He prefers the folds of his tent to the parental palace, and in the allegorical moonlit ruin he experiences the pitfalls of adult sexuality, the threat of castration. Though concealing dangerous abysses, the eroticized landscape becomes a playground of polymorphous desire, in which the signs of virility—sables, pistols, and cigarettes—remain phallic toys at best. The screen itself becomes a maternal body, inviting the component drives to revolt against their subordination. These textured surfaces do not project a realistic space that the hero, traversing it, would be obligated

Figure 12.13

Figure 12.14

to subject. Rather, they construct an oneiric stage that cannot be bothered with perspective and verisimilitude. With a degree of irreality of which the silent screen was yet capable, Valentino's last film admits to the reality of a fantasy that assimilates the Oedipal scenario for its own purposes. Not only does it force the father to identify with the phallic caprices of his youth; it even subverts the Oedipal script in its casting. Valentino himself plays the role of the father in whose mirror image the son achieves a presumably adult male identity that, barely masked, reveals itself as both narcissistic and incestuous.

The appeal of the Valentino fantasy is regressive, beckoning the female spectator (to revise Mulvey) beyond the devil of phallic identification into the deep blue sea of polymorphous perversity. Such an appeal cannot but provoke the connotation of monstrosity, which the films displace onto figures like the vamp or the sadomasochistic dwarf in *The Son of the Sheik*, a vicious caricature of Orientalism. The threat posed by Valentino's complicity with the woman who looks, like the affinity of monster and woman in Linda Williams' reading of the horror film, is not a threat merely of sexual difference but of a different *kind* of sexuality, different from the norm of heterosexual, genital sexuality. [34] While going along with narrative conventions that assert the latter (such as the figure of couple formation), the Valentino films allow spectators to repeat and acknowledge the more archaic component drives, reminders of the precarious constructedness of sexual identity. In locating pleasure in the tension—if not excess—of partial libido in relation to genitality, they project a realm of the erotic that deviates from the socially cultivated ideal of a "healthy sex life."[35]

To claim a subversive function for polymorphous perversity as such is highly problematic, Foucault asserts, given the degree to which disparate sexualities themselves have been appropriated by a discourse binding pleasure and power. [36] It is therefore all the more important to reconsider the historical moment at which Valentino enters that discourse, marking its conjunction with other discourses, in particular those of social mobility and ethnic-racial otherness. In a liberal gesture, Alexander Walker ponders the paradox of the Valentino craze—that it took place alongside the progressive liberation of American women from traditional roles: "It was a perverse way of celebrating your sex's emancipation."[37] Perverse, yes, but not so paradoxical. As revisionist historians have argued, the New Woman was usually not as emancipated as her image suggested, and her access to consumer culture often entailed an underpaid job, loneliness, and social insecurity or, in the case of married women, the multiple burdens of wage labor, housework, and child-rearing. [38] Although the period's demonstrative obsession with sexual reform may well confirm Foucault's argument on sexuality as discourse at large, the issues mobilized by the Valentino cult must have had different implications for women than for men, for men and women of different sexual orientations and different ethnic and racial backgrounds, or for single working women as opposed to, say, upper-middle-class wives— implications varying with respective positions and interests within a relatively unstable and contested public sphere.

However complicit and recuperable in the long run, the Valentino films articulated the possibility of female desire outside of motherhood and family, absolving it from Victorian double standards. Instead they presented a morality of passion, an ideal of erotic reciprocity.[39] Yet, unlike the feminine reaction to sexual liberation as personified by Madame Elinor Glyn (the Edwardian novelist who invented the "It" girl), Valentino did not render the erotic a matter of social etiquette, to be rehearsed by the aspiring female subject.[40] In focusing pleasure on a male protagonist of ambiguous and deviant identity, he appealed to those who most strongly felt the effects— freedom as well as frustration—of transition and liminality, the precariousness of a social mobility predicated on consumerist ideology. Not only did Valentino inaugurate an explicitly sexual discourse on male beauty, but he also undercut standards of instrumental rationality that were culturally associated with masculine behavior. His resistance to expectations of everyday pragmatism, his swerving from the matter-of-fact and reasonable, may account for his subterranean popularity with male moviegoers, gay or straight. In apparent conflict with Hollywood's racist standards of casting and representation, Valentino's films acknowledged his ethnic otherness, in whatever exotic and fetishistic form, and choreographed it as part of his erotic persona. This eroticization of ethnic otherness undoubtedly participates in a long-standing discourse that interweaves racial and sexual difference in a spiral of threat, fascination, and disavowal. It also marks for the institution of cinema a historical shift—if not, considering the violence of the nativist response to Valentino, an accidental leap or lapse—that enforced a transvaluation of the racist taboo and its partial recognition.

Let me return to the public dimensions of the Valentino cult, its function as a horizon for changes in gender roles and the social construction of sexuality. While the massive impact of his appeal illustrated the power of the female consumer as did no other single phenomenon before or after, the social forms it assumed are not exhaustively described by its consumerist and ideological functions. Roland Barthes speaks of the cult of the Valentinian face as "truly feminine Bacchanalia which all over the world were dedicated to the memory of a collectively revealed beauty."[41] No doubt such Dionysian rites were contaminated by the mechanisms of the mass media: the voyeuristic and fetishistic aspects of the Valentino excesses cannot be explained away. How could millions of women have indulged in such specifically male perversions? Barthes may ascribe the cult of Valentino to the aura of his face—"visage" versus "figure"—but, for Valentino and his female admirers it was no less a cult of his body. This body, as we saw in the publicity discourse and the films, could not avoid fetishization; in its entirety, it assumed the function of a phallic substitute. That the commodity marketed as an idol of virility should prove its success as a symbol of the missing penis, however, presents a unique instance of subversive irony. Valentino's miraculous career as a male impersonator illuminates the basic discrepancy between the penis and its symbolic representation, the phallus, thus revealing the male subject's position within the symbolic order as based upon a misreading of anatomy. If women's fascination with Valentino, on whatever level of consciousness, expressed a recognition of that discrepancy, their massive and collective identification with this peculiar fetish also asserted the claim to share in the reputation and representation of phallic power.

What is more important, even as it confirmed the mechanisms of a phallic economy of representation in some aspects, the Valentino cult derailed their effectiveness by appropriating them into a female subculture, a collective horizon of gender-specific experience. Enabled by the temporary friction between consumerism and patriarchal ideology, the Valentino syndrome displayed contradictions that were only partially absorbed into dominant discursive practices. These suggest an alternative organization of erotic relations as well as relations of cinematic representation and reception. In the interaction with female audiences the fetishization of Valentino's body assumed forms of theatricality that subverted the mechanisms of separation intrinsic to cinematic voyeurism and fetishism. His female fans assailed the barriers that classical cinema was engaged in reaffirming, taking the star system more literally than the institution might have intended. Once women had found a fetish of their own, they were not content with merely gazing at it; they strove to touch it. Moreover, they expected Valentino to reciprocate their devotion. He was mailed intimate garments and requested to kiss and return them (which he did).

The cult of Valentino's body extended, finally, to his corpse and led to the notorious necrophilic excesses. Valentino's last will specified that his body be exhibited to his fans. This provoked a fetishistic run for buttons from his suit or at least candles and flowers from the funeral home. But the collective mise-en-scène of fainting spells, hysterical grief, and, to be accurate, a few suicides, cannot be reduced to a spectacle of mass-cultural manipulation. It may be read as a kind of rebellion, a desperate protest against the passivit▾ and one-sidedness with which patriarchal cinema supports the subordinate position of women in the gender hierarchy. In such a reading, even the commercially distorted manifestation of female desire might articulate a utopian claim: that the hollow promises of screen happiness be released into the mutuality of erotic practice.

Notes

Index

Notes

Introduction: Cinema Spectatorship and Public Life

1. I am much indebted to Charles Musser for drawing my attention to *The Corbett-Fitzsimmons Fight* and its reception. His analysis of the event appears in *The Emergence of Cinema: The American Screen to 1907* (New York: Scribner's, Macmillan, 1990), ch. 7. Also see Dan Streible, "In the Non-Classical Mode: Boxing Films from 1894 to 1915," paper delivered at the Society for Cinema Studies convention, Iowa City, April 1989.

2. Annette Kuhn distinguishes between "spectator" and "social audience" in, "Women's Genres: Melodrama, Soap Opera and Theory," *Screen* 25.1 (January-February 1984): 18–28; rpt. in Christine Gledhill, *Home Is Where the Heart Is: Studies in Melodrama and the Woman's Film* (London: British Film Institute, 1987), pp. 339–49.

3. For an example of the latter, see Richard Bolton, "The Modern Spectator and the Postmodern Participant," *Photo Communique* (Summer 1986): 34–45. My rough distinction between classical and postclassical forms of spectatorship omits significant deviations from the classical model already prior to the age of video, in particular as they crystallized around cult films such as *The Rocky Horror Picture Show*. See J. Hoberman and Jonathan Rosenbaum, *Midnight Movies* (New York: Harper & Row, 1983); Timothy Corrigan, "Film and the Culture of Cult," *Wide Angle* 8.3–4 (1986): 91–113.

4. Harriet E. Margolis, *The Cinema Ideal: An Introduction to Psychoanalytic Studies of the Film Spectator* (New York and London: Garland, 1988), p. xiv.

5. Mary Ann Doane, *The Desire to Desire: The Woman's Film of the 1940s* (Bloomington: Indiana University Press, 1987), p. 34. For examples of this approach, see Jean-Louis Baudry, "Ideological Effects of the Basic Cinematographic Apparatus," *Film Quarterly* 28.2 (Winter 1974–75): 39–47, and "The Apparatus," *Camera Obscura* 1 (Fall 1976): 97–126, both rpt. in Theresa Hak Kyung Cha, ed., *Apparatus* (New York: Tanam Press, 1980); Christian Metz, *The Imaginary Signifier: Psychoanalysis and the Cinema* (Bloomington: Indiana University Press, 1982); Teresa de Lauretis and Stephen Heath, eds., *The Cinematic Apparatus* (London: Macmillan, 1980); Philip Rosen, ed., *Narrative, Apparatus, Ideology* (New York: Columbia University Press, 1986), part III. See also Margolis, *Cinema Ideal*, ch. 2.

6. Raymond Bellour, *L'analyse du Film* (Paris: Albatros, 1980); Janet Bergstrom, "Alternation, Segmentation, Hypnosis: Interview with Raymond Bellour," *Camera Obscura* 3–4 (1979): 71–103, 133–34; Stephen Heath, "Film and System: Terms of Analysis," Part I, *Screen* 16.1 (Spring 1975): 7–77, and Part II, *Screen* 16.2 (Summer 1975): 91–113; Stephen Heath, *Questions of Cinema* (Bloomington: Indiana University Press, 1981). Also see David Bordwell, *Narration in the Fiction Film* (Madison: University of Wisconsin Press, 1985), pp. 21–26.

7. See, for instance, Heath, *Questions of Cinema*, pp. 52ff., 62, passim; Teresa de Lauretis, *Alice Doesn't: Feminism, Semiotics, Cinema* (Bloomington: Indiana University Press, 1984), pp. 137ff.

8. On feminist approaches to spectatorship, see Part III of this book. For examples of feminist theory branching out into film history, see Doane, *Desire to Desire*, and Patrice Petro, *Joyless Streets: Women and Melodramatic Representation in Weimar Germany* (Princeton: Princeton University Press, 1989).

9. Robert Allen and Douglas Gomery, *Film History: Theory and Practice* (New York: Alfred A. Knopf, 1985), p. 156. The problem perceived by Allen and Gomery is not only historiographic, but applies also to the field of sociological reception studies which I bracket in this study. For an introduction to the latter, see Leo A. Handel, *Hollywood Looks at Its Audience: A Report on Film Audience Research* (Urbana: University of Illinois Press, 1950); Bruce A. Austin, *The Film Audience: An International Bibliography of Research* (Metuchen, N.J.: Scarecrow Press, 1983); Austin, "Researching the Film Audience: Purposes, Procedures, and Problems," *Journal of the Film and Video Association* 35.3 (Summer 1983): 34–43; Austin, *Immediate Seating: A Look at Movie Audiences* (Belmont, Calif.: Wadsworth, 1989).

10. Bordwell, *Narration in the Fiction Film*; David Bordwell, Janet Staiger, and Kristin Thompson, *The Classical Hollywood Cinema: Film Style and Mode of Production to 1960* (New York: Columbia University Press, 1985).

11. Bordwell, *Narration in the Fiction Film*, pp. 30, 310.

12. See Richard Allen, review of *The Classical Hollywood Cinema*, *Framework* 29 (Autumn 1985): 90.

13. In cinema studies, Judith Mayne, in *Private Novels, Public Films* (Athens: University of Georgia Press, 1988), mobilizes the public-private distinction for areas that partly overlap with my book; the concept of the public sphere underlying Mayne's book, however, varies considerably from the framework I propose.

14. Jürgen Habermas, *Strukturwandel der Öffentlichkeit: Untersuchungen zu einer Kategorie der bürgerlichen Gesellschaft* (Darmstadt and Neuwied: Hermann Luchterhand Verlag, 1962); *The Structural Transformation of the Public Sphere: An Inquiry into a Category of Bourgeois Society*, trans. Thomas Burger, with the assistance of Frederick Lawrence (Cambridge, Mass.: MIT Press, 1989). For English-language discussions of this study see Peter Uwe Hohendahl, *The Institution of Criticism* (Ithaca: Cornell University Press, 1982), ch. 7; Theodore Mills Norton, "The Public Sphere: A Workshop," *New Political Science* 11 (Spring 1983): 75–84; Joan B. Landes, *Women and the Public*

Sphere in the Age of the French Revolution (Ithaca: Cornell University Press, 1988), pp. 5ff., passim. Also see Jürgen Habermas, "The Public Sphere: An Encyclopedia Article" (1964), *New German Critique* 3 (Fall 1974): 49–55.

15. Nancy Fraser, "What's Critical About Critical Theory? The Case of Habermas and Gender," *New German Critique* 35 (Spring–Summer 1985): 112.

16. Habermas, *Structural Transformation*, p. 29.

17. Ibid., pp. 36, 160–61; see also Hohendahl, *Institution of Criticism*, p. 246.

18. Richard Sennett, *The Fall of Public Man: On the Social Psychology of Capitalism* (1974; New York: Vintage, 1978), p. 32. A similar notion of the "public" already appears in Hannah Arendt, "The Public and the Private Realm," in *The Human Condition* (Chicago: University of Chicago Press, 1958). Arendt stresses the necessity of the public as a "common world" in which individuality is reflected from a multiplicity of different perspectives: "Being seen and being heard by others derive their significance from the fact that everybody sees and hears from a different perspective" (p. 57). See also Habermas, *Knowledge and Human Interest* (1968), tr. Jeremy Shapiro (Boston: MIT Press, 1971).

19. Landes, *Women and the Public Sphere*, p. 3. For a sociological, more normative discussion of the same point, see Jean Bethke Elshtain, *Public Man, Private Woman* (Princeton: Princeton University Press, 1981).

20. Habermas, *Structural Transformation*, p. 56; on women's role in the public sphere, see also pp. 32–33, 47–48 and throughout Habermas' discussion of the patriarchal family.

21. Landes, *Women and the Public Sphere*, p. 7. Also see Viktoria Schmidt-Linsenhoff, ed., *Sklavin oder Bürgerin? Französische Revolution und Neue Weiblichkeit 1760–1830* (Frankfurt: Historisches Museum and Jonas Verlag, 1989).

22. Habermas, *Structural Transformation*, p. 161.

23. Theodor W. Adorno, "Culture Industry Reconsidered" (1963), *New German Critique* 6 (Fall 1975): 12–19; 13. Also see Max Horkheimer and Theodor W. Adorno, *Dialectic of Enlightenment* (1947), trans. John Cumming (New York: Seabury, 1972), pp. 186–87.

24. Oskar Negt and Alexander Kluge, *Öffentlichkeit und Erfahrung: Zur Organisationsanalyse von bürgerlicher und proletarischer Öffentlichkeit* (Frankfurt am Main: Suhrkamp, 1972); trans. forthcoming, University of Minnesota Press. For a summarizing review, see Eberhard Knödler-Bunte, "The Proletarian Public Sphere and Political Organization," *New German Critique* 4 (Winter 1975): 51–75.

25. Habermas, *Structural Transformation*, p. 8, Negt and Kluge, *Öffentlichkeit und Erfahrung*, p. 8.

26. Negt and Kluge, ch. 1; on "public spheres of production," *Öffentlichkeit und Erfahrung*, pp. 12, 35ff., 225–48, esp. ch. 5, "Lebenszusammenhang als Produktionsgegenstand des Medienverbunds."

27. In substance Negt and Kluge's notion of a proletarian public sphere converges with English and American directions in radical history, the tradition of history from

the bottom up (E. P. Thompson, Herbert Gutman). Their emphasis on the non-linearity and nonsynchronicity of historical processes is indebted to the philosophy of history of Ernst Bloch and Walter Benjamin.

28. On Benjamin's theory of experience, see Marleen Stoessel, *Aura, das vergessene Menschliche: Zu Sprache und Erfahrung bei Walter Benjamin* (Munich: Hanser, 1983). On the implications of this concept for film theory, see Miriam Hansen, "Benjamin, Cinema and Experience: 'The Blue Flower in the Land of Technology,'" *New German Critique* 40 (Winter 1987): 179–224.

29. For a feminist critique of *Public Sphere and Experience*, see Heide Schlüpmann, "Femininity as Productive Force: Kluge and Critical Theory," *New German Critique* 49 (Winter 1989).

30. For Kluge's rapprochement with Habermas in his revaluation of the "classical" public sphere, see "Die Macht der Bewußtseinsindustrie und das Schicksal unserer Öffentlichkeit," in Klaus von Bismarck et al., *Industrialisierung des Bewußtseins: Eine kritische Auseinandersetzung mit den "neuen Medien"* (Munich and Zurich: Piper, 1985), pp. 72–73.; *Bestandsaufnahme: Utopie Film* (Frankfurt: Zweitausendeins, 1983), pp. 49f. Kluge's shift toward this position is already noticeable in Klaus Eder and Alexander Kluge, *Ulmer Dramaturgien: Reibungsverluste* (Munich: Hanser, 1980), pp. 57–61; excerpts trans. in *New German Critique* 24–25 (Fall–Winter 1981–82): 211–14.

31. Kluge, "Macht," p. 72.

32. The trope of the "film in the spectator's head" is pervasive in Kluge's writings and motivates the montage aesthetics of his film practice. See, for instance, *Bestandsaufnahme*, pp. 101, 45ff., or *Die Patriotin* (Frankfurt: Zweitausendeins, 1979), pp. 294–95; trans. in *New German Critique* 24–25 (Fall–Winter 1981–82): 209. Also see Miriam Hansen, "Alexander Kluge, Cinema and the Public Sphere: The Construction Site of Counter History," *Discourse* 6 (1983): 53–74. In his reading of Benjamin, Kluge again follows Habermas—and Benjamin scholars such as Marleen Stoessel—who caution against a literal reading of Benjamin's celebration of the decline of the aura in the Artwork Essay; see Jürgen Habermas, "Consciousness-Raising or Redemptive Criticism" (1972), *New German Critique* 17 (Spring 1979): 30–59; Hansen, "Benjamin," pp. 191ff., 212ff.

33. Kluge, *Bestandsaufnahme*, pp. 94–95.

34. Walter Lippmann, *The Phantom Public* (New York: Harcourt, Brace, 1925), and *Public Opinion* (New York: Macmillan, 1922). Also see John Dewey, *The Public and Its Problems* (New York: Henry Holt, 1927).

35. Edward de Grazia and Roger K. Newman, *Banned Films: Movies, Censors and the First Amendment* (New York and London: Bowker, 1982), pp. 5.

36. Kenneth Anger, *Hollywood Babylon* (Paris: J.-J. Pauvert, 1959; rev. ed., San Francisco: Straight Arrow Books, 1975).

1. *A Cinema in Search of a Spectator: Film-Viewer Relations before Hollywood.*

1. Kristin Thompson, "The Formulation of the Classical Style, 1909–28," Part 3 of David Bordwell, Janet Staiger, and Kristin Thompson, *The Classical Hollywood Cinema: Film Style and Mode of Production to 1960* (New York: Columbia University Press, 1985); Charles Musser, "The Nickelodeon Era Begins: Establishing the Framework for Hollywood's Mode of Representation," *Framework* 22–23 (Autumn 1983): 4–11; Eileen Bowser, *The Transformation of Cinema, 1908–1915,* forthcoming (New York: Scribner's, Macmillan), and "Toward Narrative, 1907: *The Mill Girl,*" in John L. Fell, ed., *Film Before Griffith* (Berkeley: University of California Press, 1983), pp. 330–38; Barry Salt, *Film Style and Technology: History and Analysis* (London: Starword, 1983) ch. 8, and "The Early Development of Film Form," in Fell, ed., *Film Before Griffith,* pp. 284–98; Paolo Cherchi Usai, ed., *Vitagraph Co. of America: Il cinema prima di Hollywood* (Pordenone: Studio Tesi, 1987), and an earlier version of Jon Gartenberg's contribution, "Vitagraph before Griffith: Forging Ahead in the Nickelodeon Era," *Studies in Visual Communication* 10.4 (Fall 1984): 7–23.

2. Thompson, *Classical Hollywood Cinema,* p. 157.

3. The emphasis on early cinema's paradigmatic difference is indebted to the work of filmmaker and film theorist Noël Burch, especially his influential essay, "Porter, or Ambivalence," *Screen* 19.4 (Winter 1978–79): 91–105. Burch's speculations have been elaborated and modified by film historians such as Tom Gunning, André Gaudreault, and Charles Musser. On the connotations of the term "primitive," see Thompson, *Classical Hollywood Cinema,* p. 158; Gunning, "'Primitive' Cinema—A Frame-up? or The Trick's on Us," *Cinema Journal* 28.2 (Winter 1989): 3–12. As a belated modernist, Burch uses the term "primitive" (with a capital "P") throughout with polemical intention, inasmuch as he claims early cinema for a potentially oppositional tradition against the (later) "Institutional Mode of Representation" ("IMR"), that is, the classical continuity system. See, for instance, "Primitivism and the Avant-Gardes: A Dialectical Approach," in Philip Rosen, ed., *Narrative, Apparatus, Ideology* (New York: Columbia University Press, 1986), pp. 483–506; esp. 486ff.

4. Tom Gunning, "The Cinema of Attraction[s]," *Wide Angle* 8.3–4 (1986): 63–70.

5. This kind of inverse teleology is among the criticisms leveled against Burch by Kristin Thompson and David Bordwell, "Linearity, Materialism and the Study of Early American Cinema," *Wide Angle* 5.3 (1983): 4–15. For a sample of approaches to the classical mode of spectatorship, see *Narrative, Apparatus, Ideology,* especially articles by Raymond Bellour, Nick Browne, Laura Mulvey, Jean-Louis Baudry, Mary Ann Doane, Teresa de Lauretis, and Stephen Heath.

6. A. Nicholas Vardac, *Stage to Screen: Theatrical Method from Garrick to Griffith* (New York and London: Benjamin Blom, 1968); Charles Musser, "Toward A History of Screen Practice," *Quarterly Review of Film Studies* 9.1 (Winter 1984): 58–69. Also see John L. Fell, *Film and the Narrative Tradition* (1974; Berkeley: University of California

Press, 1986), chs. 4, 6, 7.

7. Charles Musser, "The Early Cinema of Edwin S. Porter," *Cinema Journal* 19. 1 (Fall 1979): 1–38; 20; Stephen Heath, *Questions of Cinema* (Bloomington: Indiana University Press, 1981), pp. 4–5; Judith Mayne, "The Limits of Spectacle," *Wide Angle* 6. 3 (1984): 4–15; 6–7, and "Uncovering the Female Body," in Jay Leyda and Charles Musser, eds., *Before Hollywood: Turn-of-the-Century Film from American Archives* (New York: American Federation of the Arts, 1986), pp. 65–66; Lynne Kirby, "Male Hysteria and Early Cinema," *Camera Obscura* 17 (1988): 113–31.

8. Mayne, "Limits," p. 7.

9. Thompson, *Classical Hollywood Cinema*, pp. 196, 174; Gunning, "The Non-Continuous Style of Early Film (1900–1906)," in Roger Holman, comp., *Cinema 1900/1906: An Analytical Study* (Brussels: Fédération Internationale des Archives du Film, 1982), I, 219–29; Gunning, "'Primitive' Cinema"; Burch, "Primitivism," pp. 486ff. Also see this chapter at Note 27.

10. Alan Williams, *The Republic of Images: A General History of French Filmmaking from Its Beginnings to the New Wave*, forthcoming (Cambridge, Mass.: Harvard University Press), chs. 1, 2; the term *"bricolage"* is derived from Claude Levi-Strauss.

11. Robert C. Toll, *On with The Show: The First Century of Show Business in America* (New York: Oxford University Press, 1976); Musser, "Toward a History of Screen Practice."

12. On the relation of film and vaudeville, see Robert C. Allen, *Vaudeville and Film, 1895–1915: A Study in Media Interaction* (New York: Arno Press, 1980), chs. 3, 4. On the variety format, see Brooks McNamara, "The Scenography of Popular Entertainment," *The Drama Review* 18. 1 (March 1974): 16–24. On the introduction of the feature film, see Bowser, *Transformation*, ch. 12.

13. Siegfried Kracauer, "Cult of Distraction: On Berlin's Picture Palaces" (1926), trans. Thomas Y. Levin, *New German Critique* 40 (Winter 1987): 91–96; Walter Benjamin, "The Work of Art in the Age of Mechanical Reproduction" (1935–36) and "On Some Motifs in Baudelaire" (1939), *Illuminations*, trans. Harry Zohn (New York: Schocken, 1969).

14. Michael M. Davis, *The Exploitation of Pleasure* (New York: Russell Sage Foundation, 1911), p. 33.

15. Walter Benjamin, "Paris—the Capital of the Nineteenth Century," *Charles Baudelaire: A Lyric Poet in the Era of High Capitalism*, trans. Harry Zohn (London: Verso, 1983); John Kasson, *Amusing the Million: Coney Island at the Turn of the Century* (New York: Hill & Wang, 1978).

16. Given that only a small fraction of prints survives, our notion of the range of early film must rely to some extent on catalog descriptions, copyright registrations, and reviews; see Charles Musser, ed., *Thomas A. Edison Papers: Motion Picture Catalogues by American Producers and Distributors, 1894–1908: A Microfilm Edition* (Frederick Md.: University Publications of America, 1985); Kemp R. Niver, *Motion Pictures from The Library of Congress Paper Print Collection: 1894–1912* (Berkeley: University of California Press, 1967), and *Biograph Bulletins, 1896–1908* (Los Angeles: Locare Research Group,

1971). The most comprehensive annotated filmography of fiction films between 1900 and 1906, coordinated by André Gaudreault, is Holman, *Cinema 1900–1906*, vol. II; vol. I contains the proceedings of the Brighton Symposium (1978) as well as supplementary papers; see Eileen Bowser, "Preparation for Brighton—the American Contribution," I, 3–29, and "The Brighton Project: An Introduction," *Quarterly Review of Film Studies* 4 (Fall 1979): 509–38. Also see the program of selected early films curated by Leyda and Musser, accompanied by a catalog containing scholarly essays, a filmography, and a bibiography, *Before Hollywood*. For further bibliographic references, see Fell, *Film Before Griffith*.

17. See, for instance, "Moving Pictures ad Nauseam," *The American Review of Reviews* 38.6 (December 1908): 744–45, quoting from C. H. Claudy, *Photo-Era* (October 1908); Walter P. Eaton, "The Canned Drama," *American Magazine* 68.5 (September 1909): 495. For the slippage between documentary and fictional modes, see David Levy, "Re-Constituted Newsreels, Re-Enactments and the American Narrative Film," in Holman, *Cinema 1900/1906*, I, 243–58.

18. Sigmund Lubin, *Complete Catalogue, Lubin's Films* (January 1903): 54; *Edison Catalogue* (September 1902): 122, quoted by Musser, "The Early Cinema of Edwin S. Porter," p. 22.

19. Robert Allen, "Contra the Chaser Theory," *Wide Angle* 3.1 (1979): 4–11; 7; *Vaudeville and Film*, pp. 142–43; Charles Musser, "La American Vitagraph, 1897–1901," and "Vitagraph, 1901–1905," in *Vitagraph Co. of America*, pp. 29–86, 87–102; English version forthcoming (Washington, D.C.: Smithsonian Institute Press).

20. Benjamin, *Illuminations*, p. 231.

21. *The Phonoscope* (August–September 1897): 6, quoted by Charles Musser, "The Travel Genre in 1903–04: Moving Toward Fictional Narrative," *Iris* 2.1 (1984): 47–59; 53–54. For a similar review, see *New York Mail and Express*, Sept. 25, 1897, quoted in Niver, *Biograph Bulletins*, p. 28; Allen, *Vaudeville and Film*, p. 131. On camera movement in early film, see Jon Gartenberg, "Camera Movement in Edison and Biograph Films 1900–1906," *Cinema 1900/1906*, I, 169–80; Tom Gunning, "An Unseen Energy Swallows Space: The Space in Early Film and Its Relation to American Avant-Garde Film," in Fell, *Film Before Griffith*, pp. 355–66; 361ff. A film-à-clef for primitive orality is *The Big Swallow* (Williamson, GB 1901) in which the camera disappears into an approaching man's open mouth.

22. Raymond Fielding, "Hale's Tours: Ultrarealism in the Pre-1910 Motion Picture," in Fell, *Film Before Griffith*, pp. 116–130; Burch, "Primitivism," p. 491. On the historical, perceptual, and erotic conjuncture of train and cinema, see Lynne Kirby, "Romances of the Rail in Early Cinema," paper delivered at the Society for Cinema Studies convention, Montreal 1987. Also see Mary Ann Doane, ". . . When the Direction of the Force Acting on the Body Is Changed: The Moving Image," *Wide Angle* 7.1–2 (1985): 42–57.

23. Gunning, "Cinema of Attraction[s]," p. 66.

24. Ben Brewster, "A Scene at the 'Movies': The Development of Narrative Perspective in Early Cinema," *Screen* 23.2 (July–August 1982): 4–15; 7. Also see

Tom Gunning, "What I Saw from the Rear Window of the Hôtel des Folies-Dramatiques, Or the Story Point-of-View Films Told," in André Gaudreault, ed., *Ce que je vois de mon ciné* . . . (Paris: Meridiens Klincksieck, 1988), pp. 33–43.

25. Thompson, *Classical Hollywood Cinema*, p. 199.

26. I am much indebted to Gunning's essay, "The Cinema of Attraction[s]," although I wish to deemphasize somewhat the opposition between narrative and non-narrative film that sustains his argument.

27. Gunning, "'Primitive' Cinema," pp. 5ff.

28. On *The Kleptomaniac*, see Charles Musser, "Before the Nickelodeon: Edwin S. Porter and the Edison Manufacturing Company," Ph.D. dissertation (New York University, 1986), pp. 382–387. On the primitive tableau in general, see note 9, as well as Heath, *Questions of Cinema*, pp. 26–27, 39–40. On the aesthetics of the *tableau vivant* in the tradition of stage melodrama, see Vardac, *Stage to Screen*, and Peter Brooks, *The Melodramatic Imagination* (New Haven: Yale University Press, 1976), pp. 48, 61ff.

29. Jean Mitry, "Le montage dans les films de Méliès," in Madeleine Maltete-Méliès, ed., *Méliès et la naissance du spectacle cinématographique* (Paris: Klincksieck, 1984), p. 151, quoted in Gunning, "'Primitive' Cinema," p. 9.

30. Thompson, *Classical Hollywood Cinema*, p. 214.

31. The reverse of this effect are films in which the camera is placed in the path of a moving object, as in *How It Feels to Be Run Over* (Cecil Hepworth, 1900), a film that demonstrates the spectator's inevitable identification with the viewpoint of the camera to the point of mock annihiliation. Burch defines this type of identification as "the linchpin of the Institutional Mode" ("Primitivism," p. 491), failing to distinguish, as Gunning points out, classical viewer identification with a *narrating* camera from early cinema's playful exploration and display of the apparatus ("'Primitive' Cinema," p. 9).

32. Christian Metz, *The Imaginary Signifier*, trans. Celia Britton et al. (Bloomington: Indiana University Press, 1982), pp. 43–45, 61–66, 93–96; 64. Metz's emphasis on the reciprocity of theatrical voyeurism points in the direction of Freud's notion of "ambivalence" (see note 44 and my discussion of Valentino in Chapter 12). His emphasis on the "civic" dimension of theatrical voyeurism converges with Richard Sennett's emphatic notion of the public as epitomized by the relations of reception in eighteenth-century theater, *The Fall of Public Man: On the Social Psychology of Capitalism* (New York: Vintage, 1978), esp. chs. 2–4, 6.

33. Gunning, "Cinema of Attractions," p. 64.

34. Vardac, *Stage to Screen*; McNamara, "Scenography of Popular Entertainment"; Lawrence Levine, *Highbrow Lowbrow: The Emergence of Cultural Hierarchy in America* (Cambridge, Mass.: Harvard University Press, 1988).

35. Noël Burch explores the tentative and ambiguous nature of the boundaries of cinematic space in "Narrative/Diegesis—Thresholds, Limits," *Screen* 23.2 (July–August 1982): 16–33; "Porter, or Ambivalence" and "How We Got into Pictures,"

Afterimage 8/9 (Winter 1980/81): 22–39. On *The Burlesque Suicide,* see Gunning, "Unseen Energy," pp. 359–61.

36. Frank Woods ["The Spectator"], *New York Dramatic Mirror* 63 (April 9, 1910): 19; hereafter cited as *NYDM.*

37. Marc Vernet, "The Look at the Camera," *Cinema Journal* 28.2 (Winter 1989): 48–63; 49, 55.

38. Jane Feuer, *The Hollywood Musical* (Bloomington: Indiana University Press, 1982), ch. 1; Rick Altman, *The American Film Musical* (Bloomington: Indiana University Press, 1987), pp. 272ff., and passim.

39. See Chapters 11 and 12.

40. Metz, *Imaginary Signifier,* p. 94. On the association of the look at the camera with erotic recognition—and death—see Peter Lehman, "Looking at Ivy Looking at Us Looking at Her: The Camera and the Garter," *Wide Angle* 5.3 (1983): 59–63.

41. See Mary Ann Doane, "Film and the Masquerade: Theorising the Female Spectator," *Screen* 23.3–4 (September–October 1982): 74–87; and "Masquerade Reconsidered: Further Thoughts on the Female Spectator," *Discourse* 11.1 (Fall–Winter 1988–89): 42–54.

42. Also see Judith Mayne, "Uncovering the Female Body," in Musser and Leyda, *Before Hollywood,* pp. 63–67; as well as Linda Williams, "Film Body: An Implantation of Perversions," rpt. in *Narrative, Apparatus, Ideology,* pp. 507–34.

43. For a more extensive reading of this film, see Mayne, "Uncovering."

44. Sigmund Freud, "Instincts and Their Vicissitudes," *Standard Edition,* 14: 128ff.; "Three Essays on the Theory of Sexuality," *SE,* 7: 156ff., 199f.

45. Gunning, "What I Saw from the Rear Window," pp. 37–38.

46. Judith Mayne, "The Woman at the Keyhole: Women's Cinema and Feminist Criticism," rpt. in Mary Ann Doane, Patricia Mellencamp and Linda Williams eds., *Re-Vision: Essays in Feminist Film Criticism,* The American Film Institute Monograph Series (Frederick, Md.: University Publications of America, 1984), III, 49–66; 54f. Mayne suggests that the role of the peeping wife might actually be played by a female impersonator.

47. Gunning, "What I Saw from the Rear Window," p. 38.

48. Anne Friedberg, "'A Properly Adjusted Window': Vision and Sanity in D. W. Griffith's 1908–09 Biograph Films," in Thomas Elsaesser and Adam Barker, eds., *Early Cinema: Space, Frame, Narrative* (London: British Film Institute, 1990); Tom Gunning, "From the Opium Den to the Theatre of Morality: Moral Discourse and the Film Process in Early American Cinema," *Art & Text* (Melbourne) 30 (September–November 1988): 30–41.

49. Musser, "Toward a History of Screen Practice"; "The Eden Musée in 1898: The Exhibitor as Creator," *Film and History* (December 1981): 73–83; "Early Cinema of Porter," p. 5; and his forthcoming book, *High-Class Moving Pictures: Lyman Howe and the Travelling Exhibitor.*

50. On the legal maneuvers behind Edison's partial sales policy, see David Levy,

"Edison Sales Policy and the Continuous Action Film, 1904–1906," in Fell, ed., *Film Before Griffith*, pp. 207–222.

51.   The most controversial among these extrafilmic activities is the institution of the lecturer. For Noël Burch the lecturer is emblematic of a nonlinear mode of representation; see his discussion of the role of the *benshi* in Japanese film history (which he calls a "'storehouse' of what were universally the Primitive modes of filmic representation") in *To the Distant Observer: Form and Meaning in Japanese Cinema* (Berkeley: University of California Press, 1979), pp. 75–85, 95–97. Bordwell and Thompson dismiss Burch's emphasis on the lecturer as speculative, arguing "that music was a far more common accompaniment for films" ("Linearity," p. 9). For a more detailed discussion of the lecturer, see Chapter 3, following Note 8.

52.   Norman King, "The Sound of Silents," *Screen* 25.3 (May–June 1984): 2–15; 15. Also see Claudia Gorbman, *Unheard Melodies: Narrative Film Music* (Bloomington: Indiana University Press, 1987), ch. 2; and Richard Koszarski, "Going to the Movies," *An Evening's Entertainment: The Silent Feature Picture, 1915–1928* (New York: Scribner's, Macmillan, 1990).

53.   Burch, "Porter," p. 104; "Primitivism," p. 489.

54.   Rollin Lynde Hartt, *The People at Play* (Boston and New York: Houghton Mifflin, 1909), pp. 126–27. Also see Joseph Medill Patterson, "The Nickelodeons: The Poor Man's Elementary Course in the Drama," *Saturday Evening Post* 180 (Nov. 23, 1907), rpt. in George Pratt, ed., *Spellbound in Darkness* (Greenwich, Conn.: New York Graphic Society, 1973), pp. 46–52; 50; Walter M. Fitch, "The Motion Picture Story Considered as a New Literary Form," *Moving Picture World* 6.7 (Feb. 19, 1910): "the thing essential is the story; the methods of production and reproduction do not interest the spectator. He goes to see, to feel, to sympathize" (p. 248).

55.   In a critique of Robert Allen, Charles Musser points out the methodological insufficiency of statistics that rely only on the number of copyrighted titles, considering that as early 1904 significantly more prints were sold of fictional films than of actualities: "Another Look at the 'Chaser Theory'" (with a response by Allen and a counterreply by Musser), *Studies in Visual Communication* 10.4 (Fall 1984): 24–52; 39–40. For Allen's argument, see "Film History: The Narrow Discourse," *The 1977 Film Studies Annual: Part Two* (Pleasantville, N.Y.: Redgrave, 1977), pp. 9–17, and *Vaudeville and Film*, pp. 181, 212.

56.   See especially Janet Staiger, "The Hollywood Mode of Production to 1930," Part 3 of: Bordwell, Staiger, Thompson, *Classical Hollywood Cinema*.

57.   Musser, "The Nickelodeon Era Begins," p. 4. Also see Thompson, *Classical Hollywood Cinema*, pp. 161–63, 181, 196.

58.   The temporal overlap or repeated action edit can be found in a number of films between 1903 and 1905, notably in Porter's *Life of an American Fireman* (Edison, 1903), but also in films from other companies, such as Biograph's *Next!* (1903) and *The Firebug* (1905). Significantly, *Life of an American Fireman* was reedited in the 1940s (Museum of Modern Art) according to continuity rules, that is, deleting the overlap in favor of a complete spatio-temporal match. See Musser, "Early Cinema of Porter,"

26–35; André Gaudreault, "Detours in Film Narrative: The Development of Cross-Cutting," *Cinema Journal* 19.1 (Fall 1979): 39–59; "Temporality and Narrativity in Early Cinema, 1895–1908," in Fell, *Film Before Griffith*, pp. 311–29; Burch, "Porter," pp. 102–104; Gunning, "Non-Continuous Style," pp. 223–24.

59. Rick Altman, "Dickens, Griffith and Film Theory Today," *South Atlantic Quarterly* 88.2 (Spring 1989): 321–59. For numerous examples of theatrical adaptations of novels, see Vardac, *Stage to Screen*.

60. Burch, "Primitivism," p. 488. It is no coincidence that Burch's comment on *Uncle Tom's Cabin*, "Porter," pp. 96–97, reads like an *avant-la-lettre* illustration of Brecht's concept of epic theater. For a critique of Burch on *Uncle Tom's Cabin*, see Janet Staiger, "Rethinking 'Primitive' Cinema: Intertextuality, the Middle-Class Audience, and Reception Studies," paper delivered at the Society of Cinema Studies convention, New Orleans 1986. For other film versions, see William L. Slout, "*Uncle Tom's Cabin* in American Film History," *Journal of Popular Film* 2.2 (Spring 1973): 137–51.

61. These films achieved a certain notoriety because of the copyright case Biograph brought against Edison and the arguments Porter mobilized in the defense of his version—arguments that hinged largely on the distribution of the film as separate "photographs"; see Levy, "Edison Sales Policy."

62. Bowser, "Preparation for Brighton," p. 13. Also see Donald Crafton, "Pie and Chase: Gag, Spectacle and Narrative in Slapstick Comedy," in Eileen Bowser, ed., *The Slapstick Symposium*, May 2–3, 1985, Museum of Modern Art, New York (Brussels: Fédération Internationale des Archives du Film, 1988), pp. 49–60.

63. The fact that the Edison version could be purchased either complete or in nine separate reels underscores the relative autonomy of the erotically titillating sights (Gunning, "Cinema of Attractions," p. 68). The Biograph *Bulletin* advertising the film leaves no doubt about this sort of fascination: "At one time down a steep embankment where several of the girls slip and 'bump the bumps.' The professor in the orchestra plays a solo on the bass drum when this happens" (no. 4, June 1904, quoted by Levy, "Edison Sales Policy," p. 209). On the popularity of impersonators (of both sexes) in American vaudeville during the first decades of this century, see Toll, *On with The Show*, ch. 9: "Only Skin Deep—The Impersonator."

64. Musser, "Early Cinema of Porter," pp. 16–19; Levy, "Re-Constituted Newsreels," pp. 251–52.

65. Musser, "Travel Genre," p. 57. Charles Musser elaborates on the variable reception of *The Great Train Robbery* depending on the situation of exhibition, specifically the alternative of a vaudeville context or an independent outlet like Hale's Tours; the latter probably would have stressed the film's generic affiliation with the travelogue, while the former was more likely to emphasize the violent crime story (pp. 55–57). An even more extreme case of heterogeneity in the intersection of different genres is *Cohen's Fire Sale* (Porter/Edison, 1907), a film torn between a comic chase, trick effects, New York local color, and anti-Semitic cliché.

66. The trope of the "film in the spectator's head" is crucial to both Kluge's film

practice and his writings of the cinema as a public sphere; for excerpts in translation, see Kluge, "On Film and the Public Sphere," *New German Critique* 24–25 (Fall–Winter 1980–81): 206–20. Also see Introduction at note 32.

67. Musser, "Early Cinema of Edwin Porter," p. 6; on *The "Teddy" Bears* in "The Nickelodeon Era Begins," p. 5. On Roosevelt as media President, see Daniel Aaron, "Theodore Roosevelt as Cultural Artifact," *Raritan* 9.3 (Winter 1990): 109–26.

68. *MPW*, July 21, 1917; quoted in Donald Crafton, *Before Mickey: The Animated Film, 1898–1928* (Cambridge, Mass.: MIT Press, 1982), p. 142; I am grateful to Donald Crafton for alerting me to this reference. An earlier source for the film's exhibition context with toys was brought to my attention by Charles Musser, "Teddy Bear Souvenir Reception at Bijou," *The Lewiston Evening Journal* (May 29, 1907): 2; the article announces a Friday afternoon showing "only to women," promising "every lady attending" a small stuffed bear.

69. *English Fairy Tales*, coll. Joseph Jacobs (1898; rpt. New York: Dover, 1967), 93–98, 241–42; Bruno Bettelheim, *The Uses of Enchantment: The Meaning and Importance of Fairy Tales* (New York: Random House, 1977), pp. 215–24.

70. Simi, *Variety* (March 9, 1907): 8, quoted in Musser, "The Nickelodeon Era Begins," p. 5.

71. The review of the film in *MPW* (March 16, 1907): 31, spends much time describing the details of Goldilocks' escape and her rescue by the "great hunter Teddy"—as if the film had finally provided the closure that the story had lacked.

72. Bettelheim, *Uses of Enchantment*, p. 218.

73. Donna Haraway, "Teddy Bear Patriarchy: Taxidermy in the Garden of Eden, New York City, 1908–1936," *Social Text* 11 (Winter 1984–85): 20–64. Roosevelt himself adamantly affirms the scientific imperative to confront animals as "other" in his essay "Nature-Fakers" (September 1907), a polemic against tall-tales that anthropomorphize animals; *The Works of Theodore Roosevelt*, Memorial Edition (New York: Scribner's, 1924), VI, 433–442.

74. Mary Carbine, "The Finest Outside the Loop: Motion Picture Exhibition in Chicago's Black Metropolis, 1909–1928," paper delivered at the Society for Cinema Studies conference, Iowa City, April 1989. Also see Berndt Ostendorf, "Minstrelsy: Imitation, Parody and Travesty in Black-White Interaction Rituals 1830–1920," *Black Literature in White America* (Brighton, Sussex: Harvester, and Totowa N.J.: Barnes & Noble, 1982), pp. 65–94.

75. Musser, "The Nickelodeon Era Begins," p. 5.

76. Levy, "Re-Constituted Newsreels," p. 256.

77. Thompson, *Classical Hollywood Cinema*, p. 217. Also see Brooks McNamara, "Scene Design and the Early Film," *Before Hollywood*, pp. 51–56; 55; Gunning, "Non-Continuous Style," pp. 225–26.

78. John L. Fell, "Motive, Mischief and Melodrama: The State of Film Narrative in 1907," *Film Before Griffith*, pp. 272–83; 280.

79. Musser, "Travel Genre," pp. 50–52. In a more melodramatic vein, *Romance of a Jewess* (Griffith/Biograph, 1908) uses painted drops for a domestic milieu burdened

with un-American marital customs, but breaks their spell, as it were, by sending the dying heroine's child through an unstaged street scene on the Lower East Side, the arena of the melting pot.

80. For contemporary examples of special effects photography see Vitagraph's *A Mid-Winter Night's Dream, or Little Joe's Luck* (1906) or *Princess Nicotine; or, The Smoke Fairy* (1909). Although the use of puppet animation in *The "Teddy" Bears* employed the latest techniques, the type of spectatorial pleasure they convey was already being marginalized by the growing emphasis on narrative realism in the overall output and, to the extent that it survived in individual films, became increasingly subordinated to "ethical and social didacticism" (Russell Merritt, "Dream Visions in Pre-Hollywood Film," in Musser and Leyda, *Before Hollywood*, p. 71).

81. In his catalogue of "the lust of the eyes" Saint Augustine links *curiositas* with a "desire for knowledge for its own sake, ending in the perversions of magic and science," which Tom Gunning in turn links to the type of fascination tapped by the "cinema of attractions." "An Aesthetic of Astonishment: Early Film and the (In)credulous Spectator," *Art & Text* (Fall 1989): 31–45. On the simultaneous recognition and disempowerment of the female gaze in early cinema, see Lucy Fisher, "The Lady Vanishes: Women, Magic and the Movies," rpt. in Fell, *Film Before Griffith*, pp. 339–54.

82. Michael Chanan, *The Dream That Kicks: The Prehistory and Early Years of Cinema in Britain* (London: Routledge & Kegan Paul, 1980), p. 290; Burch, "How We Got Into Pictures," p. 34–35.

83. Brewster, "Scene at the 'Movies,'" p. 12; also see Burch, "Narrative/Diegesis," p. 21.

84. John L. Fell, "Cellulose Nitrate Roots: Popular Entertainments and the Birth of Film Narrative," *Before Hollywood*, pp. 39–44. Comic strips, Fell remarks, provided early filmmakers with "a treasure-trove of proletarian images rendered comfortable" (p. 42).

85. Lewis Jacobs, *The Rise of the American Film: A Critical History* (1939; New York: Teachers College Press, 1968), pp. 20–21. This observation implicitly subverts a key assumption in Jacobs' influential study, that of a correspondence between the social environment represented in early films and the working-class, often immigrant, background of early audiences. It is not coincidental that a number of these films have the tramp envision dreams of a better life, giving the viewers a chance to identify with a particular social memory (or remembered desire) and, at the same time, to feel assured that *their* dreams were becoming reality; compare *The Tramp's Dream* (Lubin, 1899) and *The Tramp's Dream* (Edison, 1901). On the tramp as a vaudeville figure, see Douglas Gilbert, *American Vaudeville: Its Life and Times* (New York, London: Whittlesey, 1940), pp. 269ff. Also see Charles Musser, "Work, Ideology and Chaplin's Tramp," *Radical History Review* 41 (Spring 1988): 37–66; 44ff.

86. Albert F. McLean, Jr., *American Vaudeville as Ritual* (Lexington: University of Kentucky Press, 1965), pp. 41ff., 82; Robert William Snyder, "The Voice of the

City: Vaudeville and the Formation of Mass Culture in New York Neighborhoods, 1880–1930," Ph.D. diss., New York University, 1986. Allen, *Vaudeville and Film*, reduces the ideological dynamic of upward mobility to economic status, that is, simply middle-class.

2. Early Audiences: Myths and Models

1. See, for example, Russell Merritt, "Nickelodeon Theaters, 1905–1914: Building an Audience for the Movies," in Tino Balio, ed., *The American Film Industry* (Madison: University of Wisconsin Press, 1976), pp. 59–79; Robert C. Allen, "Motion Picture Exhibition in Manhattan, 1906–1912: Beyond the Nickelodeon," in John Fell, ed., *Film Before Griffith* (Berkeley: University of California Press, 1983), pp. 162–175; Robert C. Allen and Douglas Gomery, *Film History* (New York: Knopf, 1985), pp. 202–07; Douglas Gomery, "Saxe Amusement Enterprises: The Movies Come to Milwaukee," *Milwaukee History* 2.2 (Spring 1979): 18–28, and "Movie Audiences, Urban Geography, and the History of American Film," *The Velvet Light Trap* 19 (1982): 23–29; Kristin Thompson and David Bordwell, "Linearity, Materialism and the Study of Early American Cinema," *Wide Angle* 5.3 (1983): 4–15; Janet Staiger, "Rethinking 'Primitive' Cinema: Intertextuality, the Middle-Class Audience, and Reception Studies," paper delivered at the Society for Cinema Studies convention, New Orleans, April 1986. For a critique of the revisionists, especially the underlying tendency to diminish the significance of working-class audiences, see Eileen Bowser, *The Transformation of Cinema: 1908–1915* (New York: Scribner's, Macmillan, 1990), ch. 1; Charles Musser, *The Emergence of Cinema: The American Screen to 1907* (New York: Scribner's, Macmillan, 1990), ch. 13; and Robert Sklar, "*Oh! Althusser!*: Historiography and the Rise of Cinema Studies," *Radical History Review* 41 (Spring 1988): 11–35; 22–24; Sklar defends his earlier discussion of the nickelodeon in *Movie-Made America: A Cultural History of American Movies* (New York: Random House, 1975), pp. 14ff.

2. John F. Kasson, *Amusing the Million: Coney Island at the Turn of the Century* (New York: Hill & Wang, 1978); Lewis A. Erenberg, *Steppin' Out: New York Nightlife and the Transformation of American Culture, 1890–1930* (Chicago: University of Chicago Press, 1981); Robert William Snyder, "The Voice of the City: Vaudeville and the Formation of Mass Culture in New York Neighborhoods, 1880–1930," Ph.D. diss., New York University, 1986; Albert F. McLean, Jr., *American Vaudeville as Ritual* (Lexington: University of Kentucky Press, 1965); Alan Havig, "The Commercial Amusement Audience in Early 20th Century American Cities," *Journal of American Culture* (Spring 1982): 1–19. Also see Garth S. Jowett, "The First Motion Picture Audiences," in John Fell, *Film Before Griffith*, pp. 196–206.

3. Roy Rosenzweig, *Eight Hours for What We Will: Workers and Leisure in an Industrial City, 1870–1920* (Cambridge and New York: Cambridge University Press, 1983), pp. 195–98. For a thorough account of the nickelodeon phenomenon, see Musser, *The Emergence of Cinema*, ch. 13, "Nickels Count: The Rise of Storefront Theaters"; and Bowser, *Transformation*, ch. 1.

4. Exhibition patterns vary locally and regionally—theater locations were by no means restricted to working-class neighborhoods—but to what extent these variations can be taken to indicate the social composition of early audiences remains controversial. For revisionist positions on this issue, see Merritt, "Nickelodeon Theaters"; Allen, "Motion Picture Exhibition," pp. 166ff.; Allen and Gomery, *Film History,* pp. 202–07; Gomery, "Saxe Amusement Enterprises," and "Movie Audiences."

5. Rosenzweig, *Eight Hours,* pp. 219–20; McLean, *American Vaudevilles,* pp. 30–31. On female spectators, see Kathy Peiss, *Cheap Amusements: Working Women and Leisure in Turn-of-the-Century New York* (Philadelphia: Temple University Press, 1986), ch. 6; Elizabeth Ewen, "City Lights: Immigrant Women and the Rise of the Movies," *Signs* 5.3 Supplement (1980): S45–65; and Chapter 3 of this book. The inclusiveness of the nickelodeon as a new public sphere did not extend to race. Urban blacks not only were excluded from control over production and representation; they also were barred from integration on the level of reception—more so in fact in the ethnic, working-class nickelodeons than in the upwardly mobile downtown theaters. See Lizabeth Cohen, "Encountering Mass Culture at the Grassroots: The Experience of Chicago Workers in the 1920s," *American Quarterly* 41.1 (March 1989): 6–33. Also see Thomas Cripps, *Slow Fade to Black: The Negro in American Film, 1900–1942* (New York: Oxford University Press, 1977), pp. 9ff. Occasionally the trade press responded to "problems" faced by exhibitors in the South (how to maintain the "color line" in the "small store shows" and, at the same time, not to lose black patronage), for example, *New York Dramatic Mirror* [*NYDM*] 61 (March 27, 1909): 13; 61 (May 15, 1909): 15. Also see *Moving Picture World* [*MPW*] 7.8 (August 20, 1910), which prints a cartoon (signed by H. F. Hoffman, an exhibitor with strong views on the need to recuperate "the most desirable class") showing a mixed audience of middle-class blacks having a good time and middle-class whites obviously resenting just that; the caption: "There's a reason" (p. 403). The occasion for this cartoon was the first major interracial championship fight of July 4, 1910, in which Jack Johnson beat "The Great White Hope," Jim Jeffries.

6. Allen, "Motion Picture Exhibition in Manhattan, 1906–1912"; Allen and Gomery, *Film History,* pp. 204–05; Merritt, "Nickelodeon Theaters," p. 60. Roberta Pearson, "Cultivated Folks and the Better Classes: Class Conflict and Representation in Early American Film," *Journal of Popular Film and Television* 15.3 (Fall 1987): 120–28; Bowser, *Transformation,* chs. 7, 8 and 12.

7. John Collier, "Cheap Amusements," *Charities and the Commons* 20 (April 1908): 73–78; 74. For an extensive documentation of the reformers' response, see Lary L. May, *Screening out the Past: The Birth of Mass Culture and the Motion Picture Industry* (New York: Oxford University Press, 1980), chs. 2, 3; also Garth Jowett, *Film: The Democratic Art* (Boston: Little, Brown, 1976), chs. 4, 5. Also see Havig, "Commercial Amusement Audience," for a comprehensive listing of recreation surveys.

8. Daniel Czitrom, "The Redemption of Leisure: The National Board of Censorship and the Rise of Motion Pictures in New York City, 1900–1920," *Studies in Visual Communication* 10.4 (Fall 1984): 2–6.

9. Kristin Thompson, "The Formulation of the Classical Style, 1909–28," Part 3 of David Bordwell, Janet Staiger, and Kristin Thompson, *The Classical Hollywood Cinema: Film Style and Mode of Production to 1960* (New York: Columbia University Press, 1985), p. 160.

10. Roberta E. Pearson and William Uricchio, "Literary Masterpieces, Biblical Blockbusters and Historical Epics: Intertextuality in the Vitagraph Quality Films," in Charles Musser and Paolo Cherchi Usai, eds., *American Vitagraph*, forthcoming (Washington, D.C.: Smithsonian Institute Press).

11. "'Spectator's' Comments," *NYDM* 62 (Nov. 27, 1909): 13. Also see Myron Osborn Lounsbury, *The Origins of American Film Criticism* (New York: Arno, 1973).

12. Tom Gunning, "Weaving a Narrative: Style and Economic Background in Griffith's Biograph Films," *Quarterly Review of Film Studies* 6.1 (Winter 1981): 11–25; and "D. W. Griffith and the Narrator-System: Narrative Structure and Industry Organization in Biographs Films, 1908–1909," Ph.D. diss., New York University, 1986; also see Pearson, "Cultivated Folks."

13. *Focus on D. W. Griffith*, ed. Harry M. Geduld (Englewood Cliffs, N.J.: Prentice Hall, 1971), p. 57; Zukor, according to his biographer, Will Irwin, *The House That Shadows Built* (1928), p. 151, quoted in Sklar, *Movie-Made America*, p. 46.

14. Jane Addams, *The Spirit of Youth and City Streets* (New York: Macmillan, 1909), pp. 75–103; 86. As early as 1909 a writer in *The Moving Picture World* notes that moving picture audiences have come to "constitute an interesting study in themselves"; "The Variety of Moving Picture Audiences," *MPW* 5.13 (Sept. 25, 1909): 406.

15. Barton W. Currie, "The Nickel Madness," *Harper's Weekly* (August 24, 1907): 1246–47; 1246. For similar accounts, see Joseph Medill Patterson, "The Nickelodeons: The Poor Man's Elementary Course in the Drama," *Saturday Evening Post* 180 (Nov. 23, 1907), repr. in George C. Pratt, ed., *Spellbound in Darkness* (Greenwich, Conn.: New York Graphic Society, 1973), pp. 46–52; anon., "Where They Play Shakespeare for Five Cents," *Theater Magazine* 8.92 (October 1908): 264–65, xi–xii; Collier, "Cheap Amusements"; Lewis E. Palmer, "The World in Motion," *Survey* 22 (1909): 355–65; 356; Rollin L. Hartt, *The People at Play* (Boston: Houghton Mifflin, 1909), ch. 4; Mary Heaton Vorse, "Some Picture Show Audiences," *The Outlook* 98 (June 24, 1911): 441–47. Also see Walter Pritchard Eaton, "Class-Consciousness and the 'Movies,'" *Atlantic Monthly* 115.1 (January 1915): 49–56.

16. Michael Davis, *The Exploitation of Pleasure* (New York: Russell Sage Foundation, 1911), pp. 10–33; 24. Also see Collier, "Cheap Amusements," p. 75, on "the simple and impressionable folk that the nickelodeons reach and vitally impress every day." The fascination of intellectuals with Ghetto life—with the "exotic ethnic"—has a long and ambiguous tradition (exemplified in the writer Hutchins Hapgood) in which even a Greenwich Village radical like Mary Heaton Vorse participates; see Leslie Fishbein, *Rebels in Bohemia: The Radicals of the Masses, 1911–1917* (Chapel Hill: University of North Carolina Press, 1982), pp. 167ff.

17. Patterson, "The Nickelodeons"; Lucy France Pierce, "Nickelodeon," *The*

World To-day (Oct. 15, 1908): 1052–57, repr. in Gerald Mast, ed., *Movies in Our Midst* (Chicago: University of Chicago Press, 1982), pp. 51–56; Jane Elliott Snow, "The Workingman's Theater," *MPW* 6.14 (April 9, 1910): 547, and "The Workingman's College," *MPW* 7.9 (August 27, 1910): 458; Carl Holliday, "Motion Picture Teacher," *The World's Work* 26 (May 1913): 39–49. For a rather cynical parody of this kind of rhetoric, see: "Moving Picture Is An Uplifter: How It Reaches the Multitudes," *Palladium* (New Haven, Conn.), rpt. in *MPW* 6.21 (May 28, 1910): 887.

18. W. Stephen Bush, "The Added Attraction: I," *MPW* 10.7 (Nov. 18, 1911): 533–34; 533; Rosenzweig, *Eight Hours*, p. 208.

19. W. Stephen Bush, "Facing An Audience," *MPW* 9.10 (Sept. 16, 1911): 774; Bush, himself a lecturer, was part of a movement to revive that practice as a strategy of gentrification.

20. Lux Graphicus, "On the Screen," *MPW* 5.10 (Sept. 4, 1909): 312; I am grateful to Eileen Bowser for drawing my attention to this description. Also see Bush, "Added Attraction."

21. Louis Reeves Harrison, "Over Their Heads," *MPW* 10.6 (Nov. 11, 1911): 449; "The Highbrow," *MPW* 9.10 (Sept. 16, 1911): 775; "Mr. Lowbrow," *MPW* 10.1 (Oct. 7, 1911): 21. Also see Bush, "Facing an Audience," p. 774.

22. Harrison, "Over Their Heads," p. 449. For a more sophisticated version of the popular expertise argument, see "A Democratic Art," *The Nation* 97 (Aug. 28, 1913): 193.

23. Frank Woods, "'Spectator's' Comments," *NYDM* 63 (Jan. 29, 1910): 16. For a (later) example of the "always happy ending" campaign, see Epes Winthrop Sargent, "Technique of the Photoplay: Chapter VII," *MPW* 9.8 (Sept. 2, 1911): 613, subheading: "Happy Endings Preferred": "The photoplay theater is a place of entertainment and should not be made the home of gloom."

24. Leo A. Handel, *Hollywood Looks at Its Audience: A Report of Film Audience Research* (Chicago: University of Illinois Press, 1950; rpt. New York: Arno Press, 1976); Bruce A. Austin, *The Film Audience: An International Bibliography of Research with Annotations and an Essay* (Metuchen, N.J.: Scarecrow Press, 1983), and *Immediate Seating: A Look at Movie Audiences* (Belmont, Calif.: Wadsworth, 1989). The notion of "consumer-oriented art" and concomitant directions in empirical reception studies have been most forcefully criticized by Theodor W. Adorno in his "Theses on the Sociology of Art" (1967), *Working Papers in Cultural Studies* 2 (Spring 1972): 121–28, and "Transparencies on Film" (1966), *New German Critique* 24–25 (Fall–Winter 1981–82): 199–205; 204–05.

25. Benjamin B. Hampton, *A History of Movies* (New York: Covici Friede, 1931; repr. Dover, 1970), p. 46.

26. On Jacobs' intellectual and political biography see Myron Lounsbury, "'The Gathered Light': History, Criticism and *The Rise of the American Film*," *Quarterly Review of Film Studies* (Winter 1980): 49–85.

27. Lewis Jacobs, *The Rise of the American Film* (New York: Teachers College Press, 1939), p. 12.

28. Judith Mayne, "Immigrants and Spectators," *Wide Angle* 5.2 (1982): 33; rpt. with revisions in Mayne, *Private Novels, Public Films* (Athens: University of Georgia Press, 1988), p. 73.

29. Jacobs, *Rise of the American Film*, pp. 67, 17, 137, 415, 156; also 48. For a similar argument, see Garth Jowett, *Film: The Democratic Art* (Boston: Little, Brown, 1976), pp. 62–65. More recent social historians of early cinema such as Rosenzweig (*Eight Hours*, p. 199) and Peiss (*Cheap Amusements*, p. 154) explicitly refrain from establishing correpondences between film content and audience composition.

30. A case for the significance of Jewish producers in shaping the institution has been made by a number of scholars, including Sklar, *Movie-Made America*, pp. 40ff., and, in a more popular vein, Lary L. May and Elaine Tyler May, "Why Jewish Movie Moguls: An Exploration in American Culture," *American Jewish History* 72 (September 1982): 6–25; Lester D. Friedman, "Celluloid Assimilation: Jews in American Silent Movies," *Journal of Popular Film and Television* 15.3 (Fall 1987): 129–36 ("the media revolution that was to result from the combination of Jews and films" [p. 130]); and, most recently, Neal Gabler, *An Empire of Their Own: How the Jews Invented Hollywood* (New York: Crown, 1988).

31. H. F. Hoffman, "What People Want," *MPW* (July 9, 1910): 77–78, an invective against "punk melodrama." Also see Pearson, "Cultivated Folks."

32. The Festival di Cinema Muto in Pordenone, Italy, Fall 1987, was devoted to a comprehensive screening of Vitagraph films; see the critical anthology published on that occasion, Paolo Cherchi Usai, ed., *Vitagraph Co. of America: Il cinema prima di Hollywood* (Pordenone: Edizioni Studio Tesi, 1987), and the original version of Jon Gartenberg's contribution to that anthology, "Vitagraph before Griffith: Forging Ahead in the Nickelodeon Era," *Studies in Visual Communication* 10.4 (Fall 1984): 7–23. On the paucity of films fitting Jacobs' category, see Merritt, "Nickelodeon Theaters," pp. 65, 72.

33. See contributions by Eileen Bowser, Barry Salt, and Anthony Slide in *Vitagraph Co. of America.*

34. Patricia Erens, *The Jew in American Cinema* (Bloomington: Indiana University Press, 1984), pp. 42–57.

35. Eileen Bowser, ed., *Biograph Bulletins, 1908–1912* (New York: Octagon Books, 1973).

36. *Biograph Bulletin* (March 28, 1908): "The portrayal of charity is the theme of the Biograph's story, which dissipates the calumnies launched at the Hebrew race." Also see Louis Reeves Harrison's review of *The Heart of a Jewess* (Universal, 1913): "It is a pleasure to see Jewish people play Hebrew roles of comedy and sympathy, especially after so many sickening caricatures have affronted vaudeville audiences for years." *MPW* (July 19, 1913): 300. This observation may be colored by the campaign against cheap vaudeville; it should be noted that vaudeville programs had actually been softening ethnic stereotypes already for some time so as not to alienate the large share of second- or third-generation immigrants in their

upwardly mobile audience (McLean, *American Vaudeville,* p. 23). Also see Paul Antonie Distler, "The Rise and Fall of the Racial Comics in American Vaudeville," Ph.D. diss., Tulane University, 1963, ch. 8: "The Demise of the Racial Comics." Snyder, "Voice of the City," discusses vaudeville's ethnic stereotyping as an ambivalent effect of a "synthetic ethnicity" (p. 180) that uses prevailing clichés as interchangeable masks. Also see Werner Sollors, *Beyond Ethnicity: Consent and Descent in American Culture* (New York: Oxford University Press, 1986).

37. Erens, *Jew in American Cinema,* pp. 29–42; 32. The major producers of Jewish film comedy were Biograph, Lubin, Keystone, and, surprisingly, Vitagraph.

38. *Biograph Bulletins* (Oct. 23, 1908), p. 30. Intertitles the film might have had are missing because between 1908 and 1910 the Biograph Company did not include intertitles in the copyright deposit.

39. Thomas Cripps, "The Movie Jew as an Image of Assimilationism, 1903–1927," *Journal of Popular Film* 4.3 (1975): 190–207; 196. For a similar classification of *Romance,* see Friedman, "Celluloid Assimilation," p. 134.

40. Sollors, *Beyond Ethnicity,* pp. 110ff. Also see Elizabeth Ewen, *Immigrant Women in the Land of Dollars: Life and Culture on the Lower East Side, 1890–1925* (New York: Monthly Review Press, 1985), pp. 44ff. and ch. 13.

41. Erens, *Jew in American Cinema,* pp. 48–49.

42. Raymond Williams, *Culture and Society 1780–1950* (New York: Columbia University Press, 1958), I, ch. 5; Catherine Gallagher, *The Industrial Reformation of English Fiction: Social Discourse and Narrative Form, 1832–1867* (Chicago: University of Chicago Press, 1985); Raymond Grew, "Picturing the People: Images of the Lower Orders in Nineteenth-Century French Art," in Robert I. Rotberg and Theodore K. Rabb, eds., *Art and History: Images and Their Meaning* (Cambridge and New York: Cambridge University Press, 1988), pp. 203–31.

43. Russell Merritt, "The Impact of D. W. Griffith's Motion Pictures from 1908 to 1914 on Contemporary American Culture," Ph.D. diss., Harvard 1970, p. 160.

44. Robert M. Henderson, *D. W. Griffith: His Life and Work* (New York: Oxford University Press, 1972), p. 117; Richard Schickel, *D. W. Griffith: An American Life* (New York: Simon & Schuster, 1985), pp. 179–80. Also see Siegfried Kracauer, *Theory of Film: The Redemption of Physical Reality* (New York: Oxford University Press, 1960), p. 63. James Monaco, *How to Read A Film* (New York: Oxford University Press, 1981), p. 238, prints the well-known still showing Gish walking past the Jewish street vendor; caption: "Famous for its documentary image of New York. . ."

45. Sally Stein, "Making Connections with the Camera: Photography and Social Mobility in the Career of Jacob Riis," *Afterimage* 10.10 (May 1983): 9–16. Schickel, for instance, notes: "[*Musketeers*] is like a series of Jacob Riis photographs come to life" (p. 180).

46. A Ghetto film made the same year, *Blood of the Poor* (Champion, 1912), which uncharacteristically does not have a happy ending, leaving the poor heroine wronged and destitute, was criticized by *The Moving Picture World:* "Subjects of this

character are calculated to arouse class prejudices unless treated in the most delicate manner and it is open to question if good can result from accentuating the social differences of the people" (Erens, *Jew in American Cinema*, p. 50).

47. Roland Barthes, "The Realistic Effect," trans. Gerald Mead, *Film Reader* 3 (February 1978): 131–35; also see Barthes's analysis of the slippage between denotation and connotation in photography in *Mythologies* (New York: Hill and Wang, 1972), pp. 109ff., and in "The Photographic Message," in *Image, Music, Text*, trans. Stephen Heath (New York: Hill & Wang, 1977), pp. 15–31. For an early, if uncritical, recognition of the "realistic effect," see Frederick J. Haskin, "The Popular Nickelodeon," *MPW* 2 (Jan. 18, 1908): "When real pedestrians or disinterested parties of any sort sometimes cross the line of the camera at the critical minute, so much the better for the picture—it gives a greater reality."

48. Charles Musser, "Work, Ideology and Chaplin's Tramp," *Radical History Review* 41 (Spring 1988): 37–66. Chaplin's impressive reception among European intellectuals—from the French Surrealists through Béla Balázs, Siegfried Kracauer, Rudolf Arnheim, Bertolt Brecht, Kurt Tucholsky, Walter Benjamin, and Theodor W. Adorno to Henri Lefébvre and others—was by and large more attuned to his political and social significance than comments by his American defenders, especially in the wake of the McCarthy era; see Wilfried Wiegand, ed., *Über Chaplin* (Zurich: Diogenes, 1978), and Klaus Kreimeier, ed., *Zeitgenosse Chaplin* (Berlin: Oberbaumverlag, 1978).

49. This metaphor is explored in greater detail in Miriam Hansen, "Universal Language and Democratic Culture: Myths of Origin in Early American Cinema," in Dieter Meindl and Friedrich W. Horlacher, eds. *Myth and Enlightenment in American Literature: In Honor of Hans-Joachim Lang*, Erlanger Forschungen, series A, vol. 38 (Erlangen: University of Erlangen-Nürnberg, 1985): 321–51.

50. As Horkheimer and Adorno have argued in *Dialectic of Enlightenment* (1947), trans. John Cumming (New York: Seabury, 1972), the concept of universality harbors totalitarian tendencies in the very realization of its emancipatory intentions.

51. Allan Sekula, "The Traffic in Photographs," *Photography Against the Grain* (Halifax: Nova Scotia College of Art and Design, 1984) p. 77–101, traces the universal language myth in photography from the beginnings through Oliver Wendell Holmes's essay on "The Stereoscope and the Stereograph" (1859) to *The Family of Man* (first exhibited in 1955).

52. Currie, "Nickel Madness." This topos is pervasive not only in sources of the transitional period but in popular discourse on silent film to this day; see, for instance, part 1 of the thirteen-part series on Hollywood, directed by Kevin Brownlow and David Gill, broadcast by PBS in February 1987.

53. W. H. Jackson, "The Moving Picture 'World,'" *MPW* 6.22 (June 4, 1910): 931; Herbert Jump, *The Religious Possibilities of the Motion Picture* (n.p., [1911]), p. 23; also John Collier, "What to Do: The Church and the Motion Picture," *The Gospel of the Kingdom* 3.2 ([New York] February 1911): 26. Also see Rosenzweig, *Eight*

Hours, pp. 205ff. on crucial differences in responses to the cinema among various Christian denominations.

54. Lillian Gish, *Dorothy and Lillian Gish* (New York: Scribner's, 1973), p. 60. Griffith, "Innovations and Expectations," in Harry M. Geduld, ed., *Focus on D. W. Griffith* (Englewood Cliffs, N.J.: Prentice Hall, 1971), p. 56: "A picture is a universal symbol, and a *picture that moves* is a universal language. Moving pictures, someone suggests, 'might have saved the situation when the Tower of Babel was built.'" The phrase, to "repair the ruins of Babel," is from John Wilkins' *Essay Towards a Real Character and a Philosophical Language* (1668); see Hans Aarsleff, *From Locke to Saussure: Essays on the Study of Language and Intellectual History* (Minneapolis: University of Minnesota Press, 1982), p. 260. Also see Chapters 7 and 8.

55. Lindsay, *The Art of the Moving Picture*, 2nd ed. (New York: Liveright, 1922; repr. 1970), pp. 21–22.; also pp. 145, 78, 205, and ch. 13. Also see John Irwin, *American Hieroglyphics: The Symbol of the Egyptian Hieroglyphics in the American Renaissance* (New Haven: Yale University Press, 1980).

56. See Universal advertisements in *The Moving Picture World* from 1912 through 1915, as well as a reprint, without source or date, in William K. Everson, *American Silent Film* (New York: Oxford University Press, 1978), p. 25. On the "inspiration" for the company's name, see John Drinkwater, *The Life and Adventures of Carl Laemmle* (New York: Putnam, 1931), pp. 168–69.

57. "In the Interpreter's House," *The American Magazine* 76 (July 1913): 105. This speech is introduced with the flippant remark: "And he had to have one last fling," suggesting a parodistic awareness of the discrepancy between business and uplift.

58. An excellent example of the universal language metaphor in apologetic discourse is Edward Van Zile, *The Marvel—The Movie: A Glance at Its Reckless Past, Its Promising Present, and Its Significant Future*, with a preface by Will Hays (New York and London: G. P. Putnam's Sons, 1923). Also see Terry Ramsaye, *A Million and One Nights: A History of the Motion Picture through 1925* (New York: Simon & Schuster, 1926; 1986), for whom the movies' popularity with immigrants prefigured universal marketability and worldwide monopoly: "It was a natural consequence that this art, expressed in the simple, primitive and universal language of the pictures, should find its first burst of large development in the populous centers filled with polyglot populations" (pp. 430f.).

59. "Internationalism and the Picture," *MPW* 7.12 (Sept. 17, 1910): 621. Also see Woods, "'Spectator's' Comments," *NYDM* 63 (Jan. 22, 1910): 17; 67 (April 3, 1912): 24; 67 (June 26, 1912): 20.

60. W.C.S., "What is an American Subject?" *MPW* 6.6 (Feb. 12, 1910): 206. *All on Account of the Milk* was the first film directed by Frank Powell. Ironically this all-American film is advertised in the *Biograph Bulletin* (Jan. 13, 1910) as a "Biograph Comedy of a Modern 'Hero and Leander'" (p. 159).

61. Tom Gunning, "Building an Ending: Vitagraph Films and the Cinema of Narrative Integration," published in Italian in Usai, *Vitagraph Co. of America*; Thompson, *Classical Hollywood Cinema*, p. 163; "Narration in Three Early-Teens Vita-

graph Films," *Vitagraph Co. of America*; Bowser, "Toward Narrative, 1907: *The Mill Girl*," in Fell, *Film Before Griffith*, pp. 331, 338.

62. Noël Burch, "How We Got into Pictures," *Afterimage* 8/9 (Winter 1980–81): 22–39; Thompson, *Classical Hollywood Cinema*, pt. 3, and "Narration in Three Early-Teens Vitagraph Films"; Bowser, *Transformation*, chs. 4, 6.

63. Barthes, "The Great Family of Man," *Mythologies*, pp. 100–102.

64. Walter M. Fitch, "The Motion Picture Story Considered as a New Literary Form," *MPW* 6.7 (Feb. 19, 1910): 248.

65. Nick Browne, "The Spectator-in-the-Text: The Rhetoric of *Stagecoach*," rpt. in Philip Rosen, ed., *Narrative, Apparatus, Ideology: A Film Theory Reader* (New York: Columbia University Press, 1986), pp. 102–19; 110–11. Also see David Bordwell, *Narration in the Fiction Film* (Madison: University of Wisconsin Press, 1985), chs. 1, 7, and passim.

66. See texts by Jean-Louis Comolli, Jean-Louis Baudry, and Stephen Heath in *Narrative, Apparatus, Ideology*. On the problematic status of this comparison, see Noel Carroll, "Address to the Heathen," *October* 23 (1982): 89–163; Bordwell, *Narration*, pp. 4–12, 25–26, ch. 7; Harriet Margolis, *The Cinema Ideal* (New York: Garland, 1988), pp. 28–35.

67. Staiger, *Classical Hollywood Cinema*, p. 98–100.

68. Frank Woods, "'Spectator's' Comments," *NYDM* 63 (21 May 1910): 19. On Woods in general, see Lounsbury, *Origins*, pp. 12–38.

69. Frank Woods, *NYDM* 63 (April 10, 1910): 23; 63 (June 25, 1910); also 63 (May 7, 1910): 18, and 68 (August 7, 1912): 24.

70. Noël Burch, "Narrative/Diegesis—Thresholds, Limits," *Screen* 23.2 (July–August 1982): 16–34.

71. Frank Woods, *NYDM* 63 (14 May 1910): 18.

72. Hugo Munsterberg, *The Photoplay: A Psychological Study* (New York: D. Appleton, 1916; rpt. New York: Dover, 1970), pp. 33, 35–36. There are amazing affinities between Munsterberg's study and the work of Christian Metz, especially "The Fiction Film and Its Spectator," part 3 of *The Imaginary Signifier: Psychoanalysis and the Cinema* (Bloomington: Indiana University Press, 1982), but there are also fundamental historical and ideological differences between the two. Munsterberg, after all, was interested in the applicability of his observations for capitalist-industrial goals of rationalization; one of his earlier books, *Psychotechnics*, became a classic of modern advertising.

73. Munsterberg, *Photoplay*, p. 82. See Donald Laurence Fredericksen, *The Aesthetic of Isolation in Film Theory: Hugo Munsterberg* (New York: Arno Press, 1977).

74. Metz, *Imaginary Signifier*, ch. 3; Burch, "Narrative/Diegesis."

75. Burch sees in this shift an aspect of the cinema's emancipation from popular theatrical entertainments which "implicated the audience as a *group*" (my emphasis), whereas the narrating gaze of the camera addresses *each* spectator individually from—and as—a *single* point in space ("How We Got into Pictures," p. 33; "Narrative/Diegesis," p. 22).

76. Jeanne Allen, "The Film Viewer as Consumer," *Quarterly Review of Film Studies* 5.4 (Fall 1980): 481–499; 482. Also see Rachel Bowlby, *Just Looking: Consumer Culture in Dreiser, Gissing and Zola* (New York, London: Methuen, 1985), ch. 1; for further references, see Lynn Spigel and Denise Mann, "Women and Consumer Culture: A Selective Bibliography," *Quarterly Review of Film and Video* 11.1 (1989): 85–105.

77. William Leach, "Transformations in a Culture of Consumption: Women and Department Stores, 1890–1925," *Journal of American History* 71.2 (September 1984): 319–42; 326. For a slightly different assessment of shop window aesthetics, see Stuart Culver, "What Manikins Want: *The Wonderful Wizard of Oz* and *The Art of Decorating Dry Goods Windows*," *Representations* 21 (Winter 1988): 97–116. On the affinity between shop window and movie screen, see Jane Gaines, "The Queen Christina Tie-Ups: Convergence of Show Window and Screen," *Quarterly Review of Film and Video* 11.1 (1989): 35–60; Mary Ann Doane, *The Desire to Desire: The Woman's Film of the 1940s* (Bloomington: Indiana University Press, 1987), p. 24; and Charles Eckert, "The Carole Lombard in Macy's Window," *Quarterly Review of Film Studies* 3.1 (Winter 1978): 1–21. Also see Anne Friedberg, "Flaneur du Mall: Cinema and the Postmodern Condition," paper presented at the Columbia Seminar on Cinema and Interdisciplinary Interpretation, October 1988.

78. Stuart Ewen, *Captains of Consciousness: Advertising and the Social Roots of the Consumer Culture* (New York: McGraw-Hill, 1976), p. 43.

79. Allen, "Film Viewer as Consumer," p. 487. On the promise of "self-transformation" in advertising, see T. J. Jackson Lears, "From Salvation to Self-Realization: Advertising and the Therapeutic Roots of the Consumer Culture, 1880–1930," in T. J. Jackson Lears and Richard Wightman Fox, eds., *The Culture of Consumption* (New York: Pantheon, 1983), pp. 1–38.

80. Friedberg, "Flaneur du Mall"; T. J. Jackson Lears, *The Wand of Increase: American Advertising and American Culture From the Beginnings of a National Market to the Consolidation of Corporate Power, 1820s–1940s*, chapter synopsis presented at the Center for the Critical Analysis of Contemporary Culture, Rutgers University, December 1988.

81. Also see Charles Musser, "The Nickelodeon Era Begins: Establishing the Framework for Hollywood's Mode of Representation," *Framework* 22–23 (Autumn 1983): 4–11; and Musser's debate with Robert Allen, "Another Look at the 'Chaser Theory,'" *Studies in Visual Communication* 10.4 (Fall 1984): 24–52. The concept of "generative mechanisms" is discussed in Allen and Gomery, *Film History*, pp. 15ff.

82. Noël Burch, "Primitivism and the Avant-Gardes: A Dialectical Approach," in *Narrative, Apparatus, Ideology*, p. 489.

83. Pearson and Uricchio, "Literary Masterpieces"; Bowser, *Transformation*, ch. 12.

84. Thompson and Bordwell, "Linearity, Materialism," and Staiger, "Rethinking 'Primitive' Cinema."

85. Davis, *Exploitation of Pleasure*, p. 30. Also see Gunning, "D. W. Griffith," p. 367.

3. *Chameleon and Catalyst: The Cinema as an Alternative Public Sphere*

1. See Chapter 1; Robert William Snyder, "The Voice of the City: Vaudeville and the Formation of Mass Culture in New York Neighborhoods, 1880–1930," Ph.D. diss., New York University, 1986; and Albert F. McLean, Jr., *American Vaudeville as Ritual* (Lexington: University of Kentucky Press, 1965).

2. Roy Rosenzweig, *Eight Hours for What We Will: Workers and Leisure in an Industrial City, 1870–1920* (Cambridge and New York: Cambridge University Press, 1983); Elizabeth Ewen, *Immigrant Women in the Land of Dollars: Life and Culture on the Lower East Side, 1890–1925* (New York: Monthly Review Press, 1985); Kathy Peiss, *Cheap Amusements: Working Women and Leisure in Turn-of-the Century New York* (Philadelphia: Temple University Press, 1986). Also see Lizabeth Cohen, "Encountering Mass Culture at the Grassroots: The Experience of Chicago Workers in the 1920s," *American Quarterly* 41.1 (March 1989): 6–33. Robert Sklar discusses the challenge of the new social history in his essay, "Oh! Althusser!: Historiography and the Rise of Cinema Studies," *Radical History Review* 41 (1988): 10–35. Also see Judith Mayne, *Private Novels, Public Films* (Athens: University of Georgia Press, 1988), ch. 3, "The Two Spheres of Early Cinema."

Only marginal in these studies, and neglected here as well, is the perspective of children and youth which, although often claimed by social workers, reformers, and advocates of censorship, has not been the subject of the kind of historical analysis devoted to the formations of class, gender, race, and ethnicity in which they partake.

3. Oskar Negt and Alexander Kluge, *Öffentlichkeit und Erfahrung: Zur Organisationsanalyse von bürgerlicher und proletarischer Öffentlichkeit* (Frankfurt a.M.: Suhrkamp, 1972). The term "nonsynchronous" was first used in a specific sense, that is, toward an explanation of German fascism, by Ernst Bloch in a chapter of *Erbschaft dieser Zeit* (1935), "Nonsynchronism and the Obligation to Its Dialectics," trans. Mark Ritter, *New German Critique* 11 (Spring 1977): 22–38, but the notion of uneven developments in social relations and cultural organization has a wider currency in Marxist thought, from Marx himself (*Grundrisse*, p. 26) through Walter Benjamin and Raymond Williams.

4. Charles Musser, "The Nickelodeon Era Begins: Establishing the Framework for Hollywood's Mode of Representation," *Framework* 22–23 (Autumn 1983): 4.

5. Janet Staiger, Part 2 of David Bordwell, Janet Staiger, and Kristin Thompson, *The Classical Hollywood Cinema: Film Style and Mode of Production to 1960* (New York: Columbia University Press, 1985).

6. Lawrence Levine, *Highbrow Lowbrow: The Emergence of Cultural Hierarchy in America* (Cambridge, Mass.: Harvard University Press, 1988), p. 195; Richard Sennett, *The Fall of Public Man* (New York: Random House, 1978), p. 206.

7. Snyder, "Voice of the City," pp. 48–51; Rosenzweig, *Eight Hours*, pp. 199–201. On audience behavior in the ethnic theater, cf. John Corbin, "How the Other Half Laughs," *Harper's New Monthly Magazine* (December 1898), rpt. in Neil Harris,

ed., *The Land of Contrasts 1880–1901* (New York: Braziller, 1970), pp. 160–79; on Yiddish theater in particular, see Irving Howe, *The World of Our Fathers: The Journey of the East European Jews to America and the Life They Found and Made* (New York: Simon & Schuster, 1976), pp. 460ff., 484, 494.

8. Although not as controversial as vaudeville acts, slide shows were seen as either conducive to gentrification (especially travelogues) or a plebeian legacy to be reformed (as in the case of song slides); see, for instance, *New York Dramatic Mirror* 61 (Aug. 14, 1909): 15; *NYDM* 63 (Jan. 1, 1910): 16; 63 (Feb. 5, 1910): 16; *Moving Picture World* 4.3 (Jan. 16, 1909) 70; *MPW* 5.18 (Oct. 30, 1909): 597. On the competing status of nonfilmic activities, see W. Stephen Bush, "The Added Attraction (I)," *MPW* 10.7 (Nov. 18, 1911): 533–34.

9. Quoted by Tom Gunning, *D. W. Griffith and the Origin of American Narrative Film* (Urbana: University of Illinois Press, 1991), ch. 6. For the association of the lecturer with genres that were increasingly marginalized, see Van C. Lee, "The Value of a Lecture," *MPW* 2.8 (February 1908): 93–94; H. F. Hoffman, "What People Want," *MPW* 7.2 (July 9, 1910): 77; "Where They Perform Shakespeare for Five Cents," *Theatre Magazine* 8.92 (October 1908): 264–65, xi.

10. Gunning, *D. W. Griffith,* ch. 4.

11. W. Stephen Bush, "The Human Voice as a Factor in the Moving Picture Show," *MPW* 4.4 (Jan. 23, 1909): 86 (emphasis added).

12. Noël Burch, "Primitivism and the Avant-Gardes: A Dialectical Approach," in Philip Rosen, ed., *Narrative, Apparatus, Ideology* (New York: Columbia University Press, 1986), pp. 488–89; and his discussion of the role of the *benshi* in Japanese film history in *To the Distant Observer: Form and Meaning in Japanese Cinema* (Berkeley: University of California Press, 1979), pp. 75–85, 95–97. Also see Joseph L. Anderson, "Spoken Silents in the Japanese Cinema, Essay on the Necessity of Katsuben," *Journal of Film and Video* 40.1 (Winter 1988): 13–33. A similar paradox of greater realism and supplemental fragmentation can be found in the more expensive—and less common—practice of having actors supply dialogue from behind the screen.

13. "Survivors of a Vanishing Race in the Movie World," *The New York Times Magazine* (Jan. 18, 1920): 4.

14. Ralph Cassady, "Monopoly in Motion Picture Production and Distribution, 1908–1915," *South California Law Review* (Summer 1959); Rosenzweig, *Eight Hours,* pp. 199, 204, 216; Cohen, "Encountering Mass Culture," p. 14.

15. Richard Koszarski, "Going to the Movies," *An Evening's Entertainment: The Age of the Silent Feature Picture, 1915–1928* (New York: Scribner's, Macmillan, 1990); draft presented at the Columbia Seminar on Cinema and Interdisciplinary Interpretation, December 1986 (emphasis added).

16. Charles Eckert, "The Carole Lombard in Macy's Window," *Quarterly Review of Film Studies* 3.1 (Winter 1978): 1–21; Jeanne Allen, "The Film Viewer as Consumer," *Quarterly Review of Film Studies* 5.4 (Fall 1980): 481–501; Jane Gaines, "The Queen Christina Tie-Ups: Convergence of Show Window and Screen," *Quarterly*

Review of Film and Video 11.1 (1989): 35–30. For further references, see Lynn Spigel and Denise Mann, "Women and Consumer Culture: A Selective Bibliography," ibid., pp. 85–105.

17. Douglas Gomery, "Toward a History of Film Exhibition: The Case of the Picture Palace," *Film: Historical-Theoretical Speculations*, pt. 2 (Pleasantville, N.Y.: Redgrave, 1977), p. 19; Robert Allen and Douglas Gomery, *Film History: Theory and Practice* (New York: Knopf, 1985), pp. 199–201; Koszarski, "Going to the Movies." Also see Siegfried Kracauer, "Cult of Distraction: On Berlin's Picture Palaces" (1926), trans. Thomas Y. Levin, *New German Critique* 40 (Winter 1987): 91–96.

18. Gomery, "History of Film Exhibition," p. 18; Koszarski, "Going to the Movies." Also see Douglas Gomery, "U.S. Film Exhibition: The Formation of a Big Business," in Tino Balio, ed., *The American Film Industry*, rev. ed. (Madison: University of Wisconsin Press, 1985), pp. 218–28.

19. Rosenzweig, *Eight Hours*, pp. 212–13; Cohen, "Encountering Mass Culture," p. 16; Mary Carbine, "The Finest Outside the Loop: Motion Picture Exhibition in Chicago's Black Metropolis, 1909–1928," paper delivered at the SCS conference, Iowa City, April 1989.

20. Inevitably, as with many other aspects of early film history, New York City, particularly the Lower East Side, figures as a privileged site of interpretation. Not only was it the port through which the largest number of immigrants arrived, it was also a city that was highly self-conscious about its ongoing history, producing an extraordinary wealth of sources (Peiss, *Cheap Amusements*, p. 9). Likewise, by focusing on turn-of-the-century New York, studies of immigrant culture tend to center on two major ethnic constituencies: Southern Italians and Jews from Eastern Europe. Of these two, East-European Jews have commanded a somewhat special status in relation to the cinema, because (a) Jewish immigration was primarily a family movement, with almost twice the proportion of female immigrants (43 percent for 1899–1910) and a much lower repatriation rate than the Italian group (22 percent); and (b) a proportionally larger number of Jews went into the entertainment business and represented a vocal force among the exhibitors (Ewen, *Immigrant Women*, pp. 51ff.; Thomas Kessner, *The Golden Door: Italian and Jewish Immigrant Mobility in New York City* [New York: Oxford University Press, 1977], p. 31).

Recent studies in both social and film history (such as Rosenzweig on Worcester, Merritt on Boston, or Gomery on Milwaukee; see Chapter 2, note 3) have cautioned us persuasively against generalizing from the New York situation. By the same token, the injunction against positing that situation as *typical* should not prevent us from suggesting *significant* patterns and sets of problems shared by New York and other cities with large immigrant populations such as Chicago, Philadelphia, or Baltimore.

21. Herbert Gutman, *Work, Culture and Society in Industrializing America* (New York: Vintage, 1977), p. 22. Also see Howe, *World of Our Fathers*, p. 115. As Howe points out, for a number of East-European Jews, urbanization and proletarianization had already begun in the old country (p. 21).

22. Harry Braverman, *Labor and Monopoly Capital: The Degradation of Work in the Twentieth Century* (New York: Monthly Review Press, 1974).

23. Ewen, *Immigrant Women*, pp. 60ff.; Howe, *World of Our Fathers*, pp. 69–118.

24. Gutman, *Work, Culture and Society*, p. 41.

25. Rosenzweig, *Eight Hours*; Ewen, *Immigrant Women*, pp. 14ff., and p. 271 for further references to the new immigrant history.

26. Howe, *World of Our Fathers*, p. 169.

27. Rosenzweig, *Eight Hours*, pp. 223–24. The distinction between "oppositional" and "alternative" is discussed by Raymond Williams, "Base and Superstructure in Marxist Cultural Theory," *New Left Review* 82 (December 1973): 11.

28. Howe, *World of Our Fathers*, p. 213; Ewen, *Immigrant Women*, p. 216.

29. Peiss, *Cheap Amusements*, p. 149.

30. Mary Heaton Vorse, "Some Picture Show Audiences," *The Outlook* 98 (June 24, 1911): 446. The dependency of the mode of reception on theater location might explain the discrepancy in contemporary descriptions of audience behavior as either remarkably sociable and interactive or totally autistic, passive, and mechanical; for instances of the former, see Lewis E. Palmer, "The World in Motion," *Survey* 22 (June 5, 1909): 356, or Michael M. Davis, *The Exploitation of Pleasure* (New York: Russell Sage Foundation, 1911), p. 24; for a graphic example of the latter, see Olivia Howard Dunbar, "The Lure of the Films," *Harper's Weekly* 57 (Jan. 18, 1913): 20, 22. Also see Levine, *Highbrow Lowbrow*, pp. 197–98.

31. Peiss, *Cheap Amusements*, ch. 4; Ewen, *Immigrant Women*, pp. 209–210; Howe, *World of Our Fathers*, pp. 208ff.

32. Sennett, *Fall of Public Man*, pp. 52, 48, 49; 87.

33. Vorse, "Some Picture Show Audiences," pp. 442–44.

34. For an example of this pervasive tendency, see Peter Wollen, "Godard and Counter Cinema: *Vent d'Est*," *Readings and Writings* (London: Verso, 1982), pp. 79–91. Patrice Petro elaborates an alternative to the male-modernist privileging of categories of distance and detachment in what she calls, with recourse to Heidegger, a "contemplative aesthetics" in her *Joyless Streets: Women and Melodramatic Representation in Weimar Germany* (Princeton: Princeton University Press, 1989), pp. 76–77, and passim. For a critique of 1970s film theory along similar lines, see D. N. Rodowick, *The Crisis of Political Modernism* (Urbana: University of Illinois Press, 1988).

35. Lauren Rabinovitz, "The Air of Respectability: Hale's Tours at Riverview Amusement Park in 1907," paper delivered at the SCS conference, Iowa City, April 1989.

36. Michel Foucault, "Of Other Spaces," *Diacritics* 16.1 (Spring 1986): 22–27; 24, 23–24, 25.

37. Stephen Kern, *The Culture of Time and Space 1880–1918* (Cambridge, Mass.: Harvard University Press, 1983); Walter Benjamin, "The Work of Art in the Age of Mechanical Reproduction" (1935–36) and "On Some Motifs in Baudelaire" (1939), trans. Harry Zohn, *Illuminations* (New York: Schocken, 1969); Wolfgang

Schivelbusch, *The Railway Journey: Trains and Travel in the 19th Century,* trans. Anselm Hollo (New York: Urizen, 1979).

38. Howe, *World of Our Fathers,* pp. 69–77, 96ff.; Ewen, *Immigrant Women,* chs. 4, 7.

39. *Jewish Daily Forward* (July 28, 1914), quoted in Howe, *World of Our Fathers,* p. 213.

40. Mary Ann Doane, "'When the Direction of the Force Acting on the Body Is Changed': The Moving Image," *Wide Angle* 7. 1–2 (1985): 44. Alexander Kluge, "Die Macht der Bewußtseinsindustrie und das Schicksal unserer Öffentlichkeit," in Klaus von Bismarck et al., *Industrialisierung des Bewußtseins* (Munich: Piper, 1985), p. 105. The historical significance—and imminent loss—of the cinema as a site of different temporalities is a topic of Kluge's 1985 film, *The Present's Assault on the Rest of Time* (*Der Angriff der Gegenwart auf den Rest der Zeit,* shown at the New York film festival under the title *The Blind Director*); screenplay and commentary (Frankfurt: Syndikat, 1985), excerpts trans. in *New German Critique* 49 (Winter 1989). For a more systematic focus on questions of cinema and temporality, see Gilles Deleuze, *L'image temps: Cinéma 2* (Paris: Editions de Minuit, 1985).

41. Foucault, "Of Other Spaces," p. 26; Tom Gunning elaborates on the connection between early cinema and the aesthetics of the fairground in his path-breaking essay, "The Cinema of Attraction[s]: Early Film, Its Spectator and the Avant-Garde," *Wide Angle* 8. 3, 4 (1986): 63–70.

42. See Kracauer's essays of the 1920s and early 1930s, collected in *Das Ornament der Masse* (Frankfurt: Suhrkamp, 1963) and *Straßen in Berlin und anderswo* (Frankfurt: Suhrkamp, 1964); on the arcade in particular, "Abschied von der Lindenpassage" (1930), rpt. in both volumes, trans. in Johann Friedrich Geist, *Arcades: The History of a Building Type* (Cambridge, Mass.: MIT Press, 1983), pp. 158–60; Benjamin, *Das Passagen-Werk,* ed. Rolf Tiedemann (Frankfurt: Suhrkamp, 1983) as well as earlier writings such as "A Berlin Chronicle," *Reflections,* trans. Edmund Jephcott (New York: Harcourt Brace Jovanovich, 1978).

43. Kracauer, "Die Photographie" (1927), *Ornament der Masse,* pp. 37ff.

44. Benjamin, "Work of Art," "On Some Motifs," "The Storyteller," and other essays in *Illuminations;* also see Jürgen Habermas, "Consciousness-Raising or Redemptive Criticism" (1972), *New German Critique* 17 (Spring 1979): 30–59; Susan Buck-Morss, "Benjamin's Passagen-Werk: Redeeming Mass Culture for the Revolution," *New German Critique* 29 (Spring-Summer 1983): 211–40; and Miriam Hansen, "Benjamin, Cinema and Experience: 'The Blue Flower in the Land of Technology,'" *New German Critique* 40 (Winter 1987): 179–224.

45. William I. Thomas, with Robert E. Park and Herbert A. Miller, *Old World Traits Transplanted* (1921), repr. with a new introduction by Donald R. Young (Montclair N.J.: Patterson Smith, 1971), pp. 281–82.

46. Rosenzweig, *Eight Hours,* pp. 201, 217.

47. Max Horkheimer and Theodor W. Adorno, *Dialectic of Enlightenment* (1947), trans. John Cumming (New York: Seabury, 1969), p. 139.

48. "Where They Perform Shakespeare for Five Cents," *Theatre Magazine* 8.92 (October 1908): 265.

49. Ewen, *Immigrant Women*, p. 61.; Howe, *World of Our Fathers*, pp. 71–72, 214–15.

50. "Work of Art," sec. xiii; "On the Mimetic Faculty," first version (1935), trans. Knut Tarnowski, *New German Critique* 17 (Spring 1979): 65–69. The attribution of psychic, physiognomic, and even psychoanalytic faculties to film is a topos of 1920s film theory, notably in Jean Epstein and Béla Balázs; also see Theodor W. Adorno's later comparison of film with "the images of the interior monologue." "Transparencies on Film" (1966), *New German Critique* 24–25 (Fall–Winter 1981–82): 199–205.

51. *Illuminations*, p. 236, translation modified.

52. Habermas, "Consciousness-Raising or Redemptive Criticism," pp. 45–46.

53. Howe, *World of Our Fathers*, p. 165.

54. Ewen, *Immigrant Women*, pp. 66–67. Also see T. J. Jackson Lears, "From Salvation to Self-Realization: Advertising and the Therapeutic Roots of the Consumer Culture, 1880–1930," in Richard Wightman Fox and T. J. Jackson Lears, eds., *The Culture of Consumption* (New York: Pantheon), pp. 1–38.

55. Kracauer, "Langeweile" ("Boredom") (1924), *Ornament der Masse*, p. 322.

56. Cohen, "Encountering Mass Culture," pp. 7, 9.

57. As late as two years after the film's release a trade journal reports that during screenings in a Minneapolis theater "the very appearance of Moses on the canvas is the signal for wild applause that often continues for several minutes" (*Motography* 6.6 [December 1911]: 8). Quoted and discussed by William Uricchio and Roberta E. Pearson, *Invisible Viewers, Inaudible Voices: Intertextuality and Conditions of Reception in the Early Cinema*, forthcoming (Princeton University Press).

58. The term, "passion for the cinema" ("*Kinosucht*") in my subheading is used by a woman interviewed by Emilie Altenloh for her 1914 dissertation on (German) cinema as a social institution, *Zur Soziologie des Kino: Die Kino-Unternehmung und die sozialen Schichten*, Ph.D. diss. Heidelberg (Leipzig: Spamersche Buchdruckerei, 1914). Also see Miriam Hansen, "Early Silent Cinema: Whose Public Sphere?" *New German Critique* 29 (Spring-Summer 1983): 176ff., and Petro, *Joyless Streets*, pp. 3–4, 18–20.

59. Barbara Welter, "The Cult of True Womanhood," *American Quarterly* 18 (Summer 1966): 151–74; Nancy F. Cott, *The Bonds of Womanhood: "Woman's Sphere" in New England, 1780–1835* (New Haven: Yale University Press, 1977); Linda Kerber, "Separate Spheres, Female Worlds, Woman's Place: The Rhetoric of Women's History," *Journal of American History* 75 (June 1988): 9–39.

60. Peiss, *Cheap Amusements*, p. 26–30, 140–41.

61. Robert C. Allen, *Vaudeville and Film 1895–1915: A Study in Media Interaction* (New York: Arno Press, 1980), p. 30; Snyder, "Voice of the City," p. 41. Pastor's ploy is described in Albert E. Smith, *Two Reels and a Crank* (Garden City, N.Y.: Doubleday, 1952), p. 46.

62. Although consumerism effectively destroyed the social topography of the separate spheres, its relation with domestic ideology is a dialectical one. As Ann Douglas argues with regard to the sentimentalist tradition in women's fiction, the cult of domesticity might have constituted a proto-consumer mentality to begin with; see *The Feminization of American Culture* (New York: Alfred Knopf, 1977). Douglas' argument seems confirmed for later decades by the facile adaptation of corresponding ideals of femininity into the Hollywood repertoire.

63. William Leach, "Transformations in a Culture of Consumption: Women and Department Stores, 1890–1925," *Journal of American History* 71.2 (September 1984): 333. For further references, see Spigel and Mann, "Women and Consumer Culture."

64. Ewen, *Immigrant Women*, pp. 23ff., 64ff.

65. James McGovern analyzes the break with Victorian notions of female domesticity as a simultaneous shift toward greater sexual permissiveness and desexualization, suggesting that the price of an increased equality was a "diminished femininity"; "The American Woman's Pre-World War I Freedom in Manners and Morals," *Journal of American History* 55.2 (September 1968): 314–333. On the heterosocial appeal of the new commercial entertainments, see John F. Kasson, *Amusing the Million: Coney Island at the Turn of the Century* (New York: Hill & Wang, 1978), pp. 42–43, 94; Lewis A. Erenberg, *Steppin' Out: New York Nightlife and the Transformation of American Culture, 1890–1930* (Chicago: University of Chicago Press, 1981), ch. 3.

66. Peiss, *Cheap Amusements*, p. 148. For a more detailed breakdown by age, gender, and occupation and in relation to other entertainment forms, see Davis, *Exploitation of Pleasure*, pp. 30ff.

67. "Nickel Theaters Crime Breeders," *The Chicago Daily Tribune* (April 13, 1907): 3. I am indebted to Lauren Rabinowitz for this reference.

68. Ewen, *Immigrant Women*, p. 212. On different standards of respectability among working-class women, see Kathy Peiss, "'Charity Girls' and City Pleasures: Historical Notes on Working-Class Sexuality," in Ann Snitow et al., eds., *Powers of Desire* (New York: Monthly Review Press, 1983), pp. 74–87.

69. Peiss, *Cheap Amusements*, pp. 152ff.

70. To my knowledge, there are no empirical studies singling out women's viewing habits and preferences comparable to Altenloh's 1914 dissertation (see note 58)—at least not until the Payne Fund studies undertaken between 1929 and 1932—and even if there were, the social science methods of interrogation used tend to limit the value of such studies for reconstructing a historical horizon of reception.

71. On early serials, see Ben Singer, "The Perils of Empowerment: Agency, Vengeance and Violation in the Serial-Queen Melodrama," longer version of a paper delivered at the SCS conference, Iowa City, April 1989.

72. Sumiko Higashi, *Virgins, Vamps, and Flappers: The American Silent Movie Heroine* (Montreal: Eden Press Women's Publications, 1978); Alice Guy Blaché, "Woman's Place in Photoplay Production," *MPW* (July 11, 1914), rpt. in Karyn Kay and Gerald

Peary, eds., *Women and the Cinema* (New York: Dutton, 1977), pp. 337–40. On the World War I films, see Kevin Brownlow, *The War, the West, and the Wilderness* (New York: Knopf, 1979), pp. 33, 76, 145–46.

73. Leslie Fishbein, "The Fallen Woman as Victim in Early American Film: Soma Versus Psyche," *Film & History* 17.3 (September 1987): 51; also see "The Harlot's Progress in American Fiction and Film, 1900–1930," *Women's Studies* 16 (1988).

74. Mary P. Ryan, "The Projection of a New Womanhood: The Movie Moderns in the 1920's," in Jean E. Friedman and William G. Shade, eds., *Our American Sisters: Women in American Life and Thought* (Boston: Allyn and Bacon, 1976), pp. 370–71.

75. See Chapter 1 at note 39 and Part III of this book.

76. Mary Ann Doane, *The Desire to Desire: The Woman's Film of the 1940s* (Bloomington: Indiana University Press, 1987), pp. 32–33 and passim. On Kracauer and female spectatorship, see Heide Schlüpmann, "Kinosucht," *Frauen und Film* 33 (October 1982): 45–52, as well as contributions by Schlüpmann, Patrice Petro, and Sabine Hake in *New German Critique* 40 (Winter 1987).

77. Jackson Lears, "The Engendering of Abundance," Lecture, Yale University, March 1989.

78. Doane, *Desire*, p. 26.

79. Mary Ann Doane, "Misrecognition and Identity," *Ciné-Tracts* 3.3 (Fall 1980): 29.

80. In the French comedy two women provoke the wrath of the male viewers seated in front of them by first talking and then getting wrapped up in the (theatrical) presentation to the point of a cascade of tears. The film is reproduced—though misdated—in Noël Burch's film, *Correction Please, or How We Got into Pictures* (1979).

81. Doane, *Desire*, p. 31.

82. Altenloh, *Soziologie des Kino*, pp. 79, 88, 94; Iris Barry, *Let's Go To the Movies* (New York: Payson & Clarke, 1926), p. ix.

83. Virginia Woolf, "The Movies and Reality," *New Republic* 47 (Aug. 4, 1926): 310. Woolf's contemporary and friend Dorothy Richardson goes so far as to align the epiphantic quality of silent film with an essentially female quality, when she asserts that the coming of sound brought film closer to its "masculine destiny" ("The Film Gone Male," *Close-Up* [March 1932]). As Anne Friedberg concludes in her introduction to the reprint of Richardson's essay, "for the film to have 'gone male' there had to be *a film once female*" (*Framework* 20 [1982]: 6–8).

4. Textual System and Self-Definition

1. The most extensive collection of material relating to the initial reception of *Intolerance* can be found in the D. W. Griffith Papers, microfilm edition, which consists largely of the papers held by the Museum of Modern Art. Some of the more important reviews are reprinted in George C. Pratt, ed., *Spellbound in Darkness*, rev. ed. (Greenwich, Conn.: New York Graphic Society, 1973), pp. 210–27. For a revaluation of the "double myth" of the financial extremes of the enterprise, both

unimaginable expense and irreparable ruin, see Richard Schickel, *D. W. Griffith: An American Life* (New York: Simon & Schuster, 1985), pp. 325–26, 336–39. Schickel argues convincingly that, contrary to personal and popular mythology, *Intolerance* did not mark an irrevocable turning point in Griffith's career. Griffith's own account can be found in James Hart, ed., *The Man Who Invented Hollywood: The Autobiography of D. W. Griffith* (Louisville, Ky.: Touchstone, 1972), pp. 96–97. Kevin Brownlow, *The War, the West, and the Wilderness* (New York: Knopf, 1979), p. 70, questions a further facet of the myth of *Intolerance's* failure: namely that the public rejected it, on the eve of the American entry into World War I, for its pacifist message (Lewis Jacobs, *The Rise of the American Film* [New York: Teacher College Press, 1939; 1968], pp. 200–01); Brownlow counters this theory by citing the enormous success of Brenon's *War Brides* (1916) and other anti-interventionist films as late as spring 1917. Also see William M. Drew, *D. W. Griffith's* Intolerance: *Its Genesis and Its Vision* (Jefferson, N.C.: McFarland, 1986), pp. 115–26.

2. Seymour Stern, "D. W. Griffith's INTOLERANCE: A Sun Play of the Ages" (1974), in P. Adams Sitney, ed., *The Essential Cinema*, (New York: Anthology Film Archives and New York University Press, 1975), I, 7; Terry Ramsaye, *A Million and One Nights* (1926; New York: Simon and Schuster, 1964), p. 759; Jay Leyda, "The Art and Death of D. W. Griffith" (1949), rpt. in Harry M. Geduld, ed., *Focus on D. W. Griffith* (Englewood Cliffs, N.J.: Prentice Hall, 1971), p. 165; Jean Mitry, *Histoire du cinéma* (Paris: Editions universitaires, 1969), II, 171.

3. Robert C. Allen and Douglas Gomery, *Film History: Theory and Practice* (New York: Knopf, 1985), ch. 4, esp. pp. 67–76; Allen, "Film History: The Narrow Discourse," *Film: Historical-Theoretical Speculations* (Pleasantville, N.Y.: Redgrave, 1977), pp. 91–97; Janet Staiger, "The Politics of Film Canons," *Cinema Journal* 24.3 (Spring 1985): 4–23, and her exchange with Dudley Andrew and Gerald Mast, *Cinema Journal* 25.1 (Fall 1985): 55–64. Alternative approaches to and theoretical problems of cinema history are discussed in a special issue of *Iris*, ed. D. N. Rodowick, *Iris* 2.2 (1984), and Philip Rosen and Patricia Mellencamp, eds., *Cinema Histories, Cinema Practices*, American Film Institute Monograph Series, vol. 4 (Frederick, Md.: University Publications of America, 1984).

4. Philip Rosen, "Securing the Historical: Historiography and the Classical Cinema," in Rosen and Mellencamp, *Cinema Histories, Cinema Practices*, p. 22.

5. Iris Barry, *D. W. Griffith, American Film Master* (New York: Museum of Modern Art, 1940), p. 24: "The sociological implications of the modern episode seem, perhaps, more pointed now than they did in 1916." In a similar vein, see Richard Watts, Jr., "D. W. Griffith: Social Crusader" (1936), in Lewis Jacobs, ed., *The Emergence of Film Art* (New York: Hopkinson and Blake, 1969), pp. 80–84; and James Agee's obituary in *The Nation*, September 4, 1948, rpt. in *Agee on Film* (New York: McDowell Obolensky, 1958), I, 315.

6. Jacobs, *Rise of the American Film*, p. 201.

7. Kevin Brownlow, *The Parade's Gone By . . .* (Berkeley: University of California Press, 1968), p. 28; Paul O'Dell, *Griffith and the Rise of Hollywood* (New York: A. S. Barnes; London: A. Zwemmer, 1970), pp. 38–39.

8. Stern, "INTOLERANCE," p. 8. Stern's rhetoric is remarkable for the ways in which it undermines itself: "*The Birth of a Nation* was the first, *Intolerance* the second, proof and power of American film power. . . . Together, these two Griffith master-pieces . . . stand at the gateway of cinematic art like the Colossi of Memnon at the Necropolis of Thebes" (p. 7). Also see Stern, "The Cold War against David Wark Griffith," *Films in Review* 7.2 (February 1956): 49–59.

9. Among the more elaborate comments on *Intolerance*, see Arthur Lennig, *The Silent Voice: A Text* (Troy, N.Y., 1969); Marcel Oms, "Essai de lecture thématique de INTOLERANCE," *Les Cahiers de la Cinémathèque* 6 (Spring 1972): 28–36; Pierre Baudry, "Les aventures de l'Idée (sur 'Intolerance')," part 1, *Cahiers du Cinéma* 240 (July–August 1972): 51–59, pt. 2, *CdC* 241 (September–October 1972): 31–45; as well as a number of contributions to an international colloquium edited by Jean Mottet, *D. W. Griffith* (Paris: Editions L'Harmattan, 1984), in particular Dominique Chateau, "Intolérance: une encyclopédie du cinéma," pp. 259–272, and Pierre Sorlin, "L'énonciation de l'histoire," pp. 298–317; and, most recently, Michael Rogin, "The Great Mother Domesticated: Sexual Difference and Sexual Indifference in D. W. Griffith's *Intolerance*," *Critical Inquiry* 15.3 (Spring 1989): 510–55.

10. David Bordwell, Janet Staiger, and Kristin Thompson, *The Classical Hollywood Cinema: Film Style and Mode of Production to 1960* (New York: Columbia University Press, 1985), pp. xiii–xv, 3–11; 10. In this momentous study *Intolerance* is men-tioned, for instance, in conjunction with the development of research departments, narrative parallelism, and camera movement. On the relation between a "historical poetics of cinema" (Bordwell) and critical readings of individual films, see Larry Crawford, "Textual Analysis," and David Bordwell, "Textual Analysis Revisited," *Enclitic* 7.1 (Spring 1983): 87–95.

11. That horizon of expectation is of course not limited to the institution of cinema, but a historical analysis of *Intolerance* will necessarily begin with comparing the film's mode of address to that emerging from other films of the period—the difficulty being that this transitional period is just beginning to receive the kind of analytical and historiographic attention that has been devoted to the pre-1907 period. In addition to Bordwell, Staiger, and Thompson, *Classical Hollywood Cinema*, see Paolo Cherchi Usai and Lorenzo Codelli, eds., *Sulla via di Hollywood / The Path to Hollywood, 1911–1920* (Pordenone: Biblioteca dell'Immagine, 1988), which includes critical and historiographic essays as well as notes on the films shown at the 1988 Festival of Silent Film at Pordenone, Italy; the retrospective was motivated by the publication of *The American Film Institute Catalog of Motion Pictures Produced in the United States: Feature Films, 1911–1920*, ed. Patricia King Hanson and Alan Gevinson (Berkeley: University of California Press, 1988).

12. Tom Gunning, "An Unseen Energy Swallows Space: The Space in Early Film and Its Relation to American Avant-Garde Film," in John L. Fell, ed., *Film Before Griffith* (Berkeley: University of California Press, 1983), p. 366; also see Tom Gun-ning, "The Cinema of Attraction[s]: Early Film, Its Spectator and the Avant-Garde," *Wide Angle* 8.3/4 (1986): 63–70.

13. See Introduction between notes 26 and 33.

14. Sergei Eisenstein, "Dickens, Griffith, and the Film Today" (1944), *Film Form*, ed. and trans. Jay Leyda (New York: Harcourt Brace Jovanovich, 1949), pp. 195–255, 198. On the concept of "nonsynchronism," see Chapter 3, note 3. In its particular historicity and temporality ("too early, too late"), *Intolerance* shares something of the utopian obsolescence that Walter Benjamin observed in the phenomena of early modernity and consumer culture; see his unfinished study of the Paris Arcades, *Das Passagen-Werk*, 2 vols. (Frankfurt am Main: Suhrkamp, 1983). Arthur Lennig, calling attention to the affinity of *Intolerance* with modernist texts like *The Waste Land* and *The Cantos*, already remarks on the film's nonsynchronous status: "Griffith had the unhappy lot of being either ahead of his times or behind them, but never, it seems, with them" (*The Silent Voice*, p. 67).

15. Raymond Bellour, "The Unattainable Text," *Screen* 16.3 (Autumn 1975): 19–28; Thierry Kuntzel, "Le Défilement: A View in Close-Up," *Camera Obscura* 2 (1977): 51–65.

16. Barry, *D. W. Griffith*, p. 26; also see Richard Griffith and Iris Barry, in *Film Notes* (New York: Museum of Modern Art, 1969), p. 23. Barry ends her commentary on a more panegyrical tone, suggesting that in the final sequences "history itself seems to pour like a cataract across the screen." Griffith encouraged the fluvial analogy, perhaps invoking the four rivers of Eden (Genesis 2.10): "the stories begin like four currents looked at from a hilltop. At first the four currents flow apart, slowly and quietly. But as they flow, they grow nearer and nearer together, and faster and faster, until in the end, in the last act, they mingle in one mighty river of expressed emotion" (Program Notes, 1916–17).

17. For a history of print variants, see Eileen Bowser, Introduction to Theodore Huff, *Intolerance: Shot-by-Shot Analysis* (New York: Museum of Modern Art, 1966). Unfortunately, the reconstructed version of *Intolerance* was not available to me before the completion of this book. I am grateful to Peter Williamson, the historian in charge of the reconstruction, for valuable information on the project, especially for showing me still frames from the June 1916 copyright deposit (Library of Congress). In addition to the copyright slides, the reconstruction relies upon a surviving though shortened print dated 1917; a copy of the original score by Joseph Carl Breil cued for performance with the film; as well as contemporary reviews and other documents. This reading started out with the tinted print distributed by the Museum, but I have noted print variants whenever they seemed relevant to the argument.

18. Stephen Heath, "Film and System: Terms of Analysis, Part I," *Screen* 16.1 (Spring 1975): 12.

19. Numbers in brackets refer to Theodore Huff's shot-by-shot analysis (see note 17), which is a useful guide to the standard prints, though not always reliable in its transcription of individual shots and intertitles.

20. Christian Metz, *Language and Cinema*, trans. Donna Jean Umiker-Sebeok (The Hague: Mouton, 1974), pp. 77–78, 107–12.

21. David Bordwell, "Textual Analysis, Etc.," *Enclitic* 5:2/6:1 (1982): 125–36; 127.

22. Metz, *Language and Cinema*, pp. 95, 112, 119. In his later work, *The Imaginary Signifier: Psychoanalysis and the Cinema* (Bloomington: Indiana University Press, 1982), p. 29, Metz himself calls his remarks on *Intolerance* "inadequate," revising his earlier notion of the textual system as a singular structure in favor of terms like "structuration," "movement," "activity," "plurality" of readings. Stephen Heath has explicated Metz's "textual system" in a number of essays, refining and occasionally undermining it; see especially *Questions of Cinema* (Bloomington: Indiana University Press, 1981), ch. 5.

23. The term "gravity" is used (with similar intentions as in the present reading of *Intolerance*) in Dudley Andrew's formidable essay, "The Gravity of 'Sunrise,'" *Quarterly Review of Film Studies* 2.3 (August 1977): 356–87. Also see Dudley Andrew, *Film in the Aura of Art* (Princeton: Princeton University Press, 1984), which contains a slightly revised version of this essay.

24. Thompson, *Classical Hollywood Cinema*, p. 158.

25. Ibid., pp. 176, 177ff. also see Chapter 5, following note 22.

26. D. W. Griffith, "A Vital Theme Is Necessary for a Classic Picture," *Motion Picture News* (September 16, 1916), MOMA, Griffith File.

27. The fact that the paradigmatic shift was so recent and barely completed (hence the return of early modes a palpable threat of regression), may explain the dogmatic response on the part of some reviewers, such as Alexander Woollcott, *New York Times* (Sept. 10, 1916); *The Dramatist* (October 1916), or the terse judgment of the reviewer for *New York Vogue* (Dec. 1, 1916): "'Intolerance' . . . is not a work of art, because the narrative is meaningless and incoherent." George Soule, "After the Play," *The New Republic* 8.100 (Sept. 30, 1916): 225, criticizes the film very much for its affinity with what Tom Gunning has dubbed the "Cinema of Attractions" (see note 12): "the illusion is not played for honestly; one is astounded at the tricks, the expense, the machinery of production, more often than one is absorbed in their result. One might enjoy a quarter of it, stretched out to the full time. But as it is, one prefers Messrs. Barnum and Bailey."

28. Frederick James Smith, *New York Dramatic Mirror* 76 (Sept. 23, 1916): 19. Griffith's statement appeared in the program notes for the film's New York opening, quoted in the *New York Times* (Sept. 2, 1916). The analogy proposed by Griffith inspired strikingly different interpretations. In his review in the *Moving Picture World* (Sept. 23, 1916)—subheaded: "True to Mental Processes"—Lynde Denig evoked the scene of a scholarly conversation as the prototype ("He used the screen as a reflection of an extraordinarily quick and cultivated mind"). Prior to the film's opening, though certainly more to the point, the *Tribune* reviewer (Sept. 3, 1916) glossed the mental analogy as "visions that could flash across the mind while contemplating a crisis in one's personal affairs."

29. Vachel Lindsay, "Photoplay Progress," *The New Republic* 10.120 (February 17, 1917): 76–77. Lindsay probably responded to Soule's witty but condescending review of *Intolerance* in the same journal (see note 27).

30. Hugo Munsterberg, *The Photoplay: A Psychological Study* (New York: D. Appleton, 1916; rpt. Dover, 1970), quotations on pp. 81, 82, 45, 41, and 44.

In his introduction to the reprint, Richard Griffith states that Munsterberg did not see *Intolerance* (which is curious, since he died, rather unexpectedly, in December and the film had been shown in Boston earlier that fall), "but if he had it is safe to say that it would have bowled him over" (vi)—indeed, and perhaps in more than one way.

31. See Chapter 1, at note 66, and the Introduction to this book. Kluge's notion of the "film in the spectator's head" in a number of ways echoes the concept of "inner speech" as discussed in the 1930s by Eikhenbaum, Vygotsky, Eisenstein, Voloshinov, and the Bakhtin group; see essays by Stephen Heath and Paul Willemen in Stephen Heath and Patricia Mellencamp, eds., *Cinema and Language,* American Film Institute Monograph Series (Frederick, Md.: University Publications of America, 1983), I, 1–17, 141–67.

5. A "Radiant Crazy-Quilt": Patterns of Narration and Address

1. A "radiant crazy-quilt" are words used by Julian Johnson, with reference to *Intolerance,* in a review of *Joan the Woman* (Cecil B. DeMille, 1916), "The Shadow Stage," *Photoplay Magazine* 11.4 (March 1917), rpt. in Pratt, *Spellbound in Darkness,* p. 240.

2. In this chapter I am indebted methodologically to the work of Raymond Bellour, Thierry Kuntzel, and Stephen Heath, although I do not necessarily share all of their theoretical premises, especially those underpinning the concept of "enunciation." See Bellour, *L'analyse du film* (Paris: Albatros, 1980); Janet Bergstrom, "Alternation, Segmentation, Hypnosis: Interview with Raymond Bellour," *Camera Obscura* 3–4 (1979), 71–103, 133–34; Kuntzel, "The Film-Work," *Enclitic* 2.1 (Spring 1978): 38–61; "The Film-Work, 2," *Camera Obscura* 5 (Spring 1980): 6–69; Heath, "Film and System: Terms of Analysis," Part I, *Screen* 16.1 (Spring 1975): 7–77; Part II, *Screen* 16.2 (Summer 1975): 91–113; *Questions of Cinema* (Bloomington: Indiana University Press, 1981), esp. ch. 2, "Narrative Space" (1976). Also see David Bordwell, *Narration in the Fiction Film* (Madison: University of Wisconsin Press, 1985), pp. 21–26.

3. Tom Gunning, "Weaving a Narrative: Style and Economic Background in Griffith's Biograph Films," *Quarterly Review of Film Studies* 6.1 (Winter 1981): 11–25; 12. Jacques Aumont makes a similar case in "L'écriture Griffith-Biograph," in Jean Mottet, ed., *D. W. Griffith: Colloque International,* (Paris: L'Harmattan, 1984), pp. 233–47, an essay which qualifies Aumont's earlier claims for Griffith's alterity in "Griffith, le cadre, la figure," in Raymond Bellour, ed., *Le cinéma américain* (Paris: Flammarion, 1980), I, 51–67.

4. See Chapter 2, following note 65; David Bordwell, Janet Staiger, Kristin Thompson, *The Classical Hollywood Cinema: Film Style and Mode of Production to 1960* (New York: Columbia University Press, 1985), pp. 172, 214–15.

5. The distinction between these two strategies in *Birth* by and large turns on the binary opposition between "story" (*histoire*) and "discourse" (*discours*), which Christian Metz derives from Emile Benveniste's concept of enunciation in *The Imaginary*

Signifier: Psychoanalysis and the Cinema (Bloomington: Indiana University Press, 1982), pp. 89–98. Metz mobilizes this opposition primarily with regard to the cinematic apparatus—classical cinema's systematic suppression of "discourse" in favor of "story"—rather than the analysis of particular filmic texts. In that sense the story-discourse distinction is useful only insofar as it describes the *formal* parameters of narration, the extent to which the spectator is or is not acknowledged as a hypothetical point of the film's address. As a critical concept, however, it has a rather limited scope (not least because of its linguistic premises), especially for a reading concerned with the historical and rhetorical specificity of particular modes of narration and address. On "overt" and "covert" narration in *Birth*, see Bordwell, Staiger, and Thompson, *Classical Hollywood Cinema*, p. 80.

6. See Bordwell, Staiger, and Thompson, *Classical Hollywood Cinema*, pp. 163–73. For a critique of a historiographic privileging of literary models that ostensibly ordained the norm of classical linearity, see Rick Altman, "Dickens, Griffith, and Film Theory Today," *South Atlantic Quarterly* 88.2 (Spring 1989): 321–60. Also see John Fell, *Film and the Narrative Tradition* (1974; Berkeley and Los Angeles: University of California Press, 1986); and Judith Mayne, "Mediation, the Novelistic, and Film Narrative," in S. M. Conger and J. R. Welsch, eds., *Narrative Strategies* (Macomb: Western Illinois University Press, 1980).

7. In *The Mother and the Law* (1919) the shot of Jenkins at his desk is not repeated after the second death. Instead it is used as a prologue shot, introduced by an intertitle that links the theme of social intolerance with a denunciation of the defeated German Kaiser. This would testify to the emblematic—and, as I will elaborate in Chapter 8, "hieroglyphic"—quality of the shot.

8. This disparity of narratorial voices is again linked to the nonsynchronous quality Eisenstein observed in Griffith, which he found prefigured in the curious mixture of modern and small-town elements in contemporary American life, especially in urban New York. See Sergei Eisenstein, "Dickens, Griffith, and the Film Today" (1944), *Film Form*, ed. and trans. Jay Leyda (New York: Harcourt Brace Jovanovich, 1949), pp. 196–98.

9. For instances of a theatrical cast prologue, see Thomas Ince's *The Bargain* (directed by Reginald Barker, 1914), Cecil B. DeMille's *The Man on the Box* (1914) and *The Cheat* (1915). *The Italian* (Ince/Barker, 1915) opens with a shot of the star, George Beban, reading a novel of which he imagines himself as the hero in the film that follows. (I am grateful to Kristin Thompson for pointing out some versions of narrational openings during the transitional period.) Even if prologue shots of leather-bound books did not occur in any films prior to *Intolerance*, the parasitic juncture of literary tradition and cinema was definitely established by 1916. Janet Staiger reports that as early as 1914 "book publishers were promoting leather-bound, numbered, limited edition copies of the motion picture edition of a novel, with tipped-in stills from the films" (*Classical Hollywood Cinema*, p. 99). Also see David Bordwell, *The Films of Carl-Theodor Dreyer* (Berkeley: University of California Press, 1981), pp. 34–35. More on the Book of Intolerance below, Chapter 9.

10. Judith Mayne, "The Primitive Narrator," lecture presented at the Yale Conference on Film Theory, March 1985.

11. Edward Branigan, *Point of View in the Cinema: A Theory of Narration and Subjectivity in Classical Film* (Berlin, New York: Mouton, 1984), p. 100: "The classical film represents space as if telescoped within its characters." Also see Heath, *Questions of Cinema*, p. 44.

12. This shot also involves a notable change in acting style, foreshadowing the conflict of acting styles (among the various actors as well as in one and the same performer) throughout the film. Vera Lewis' self-dramatizing gesture represents a return to an earlier, pantomimic or telegraphic acting style that had been superseded, from about 1912 on, by what was then perceived to be a more naturalistic approach (*Classical Hollywood Cinema*, pp. 191–92). See Roberta Pearson, "Cultivated Folks and the Better Classes: Class Conflict and Representation in Early American Film," *Journal of Popular Film and Television* 15.3 (Fall 1987): 120–28, and her Ph.D. dissertation, "The Modesty of Nature: Performance Style in the Griffith Biographs," New York University, 1987.

13. Kevin Brownlow, *The Parade's Gone By. . .* (Berkeley: University of California Press, 1968), p. 282.

14. A more common term for "sight link" is "eyeline match"; see Branigan, *Point of View*, p. 110. However, as Tom Gunning has pointed out, the difference of this type of editing relation from point of view is precisely that "the eyelines do *not* match" ("What I Saw from the Rear Window of the Hotel des Folies-Dramatiques, Or The Story Point-of-View Films Told," in André Gaudreault, ed., *Ce que je vois de mon ciné* [Paris: Méridiens Klincksieck, 1988], pp. 33–43; 42). For occurrences of sight links and point-of-view shots prior to 1917, see Thompson, *Classical Hollywood Cinema*, 207–08.

15. Point-of-view shots are generally rare in Griffith's films, but there are usually a few significant ones, even in his Biograph films (as early as *The Redman and the Child*, 1908), and definitely in *Birth*. That the abstention from optical point of view is systematic to *Intolerance* is further suggested by a comparison with *The Mother and the Law* and *The Fall of Babylon* (1919), especially the latter where the addition of point-of-view editing helps advance a more conventional romantic conception of the leading female character. In film theory the point-of-view figure (combined with reverse-field editing) assumed the function of a master trope of classical cinema in conjunction with the Lacanian concept of "*suture*"; see Jean-Pierre Oudart, "Cinema and Suture" (1969), trans. *Screen* 18.4 (Winter 1977–78): 35–47, and, for a somewhat simplified version of Oudart's argument, Daniel Dayan, "The Tutor Code of Classical Cinema" (1974), rpt. in Bill Nichols, ed., *Movies and Methods* (Berkeley: University of California Press, 1976), I, 438–51. This position has been contested, on both theoretical and historical grounds, by a number of critics, for example, William Rothman, "Against 'The System of the Suture,'" ibid. 451–59; Barry Salt, "Film Style and Technology in the Forties," *Film Quarterly* 31.1 (Fall 1977): 46–57;

Nick Browne, "The Spectator-in-the Text: The Rhetoric of *Stagecoach*" (1975), rpt. as ch. 1 of *The Rhetoric of Filmic Narration* (Ann Arbor: UMI Research Press, 1982); Heath, *Questions of Cinema*, pp. 92–98; Bordwell, *Narration in the Fiction Film*, pp. 110–13. Also see the section on point of view in *Film Reader* 4 (1979), especially William Simon's article on early Griffith films, "An Approach to Point of View," pp. 145–51.

16. Gunning, "Weaving a Narrative," p. 23.

17. I am indebted to Richard Allen for this observation.

18. This is a key topos in feminist film theory since the mid-1970s, beginning with Laura Mulvey's influential essay, "Visual Pleasure and Narrative Cinema," *Screen* 16.3 (Autumn 1975). For a more detailed discussion of the gender economy of vision, see Chapters 1 and 12. A number of films of the transitional period actually endow female heroines with the agency of the look—for example, *Suspense* (Lois Weber, 1913), *The Golden Trail* and *The Cup of Life* (both Ince, 1915)—but this look is either linked to a transgressive life style (*The Cup of Life*) or to situations of threat and danger, rarely to the articulation of desire.

19. This configuration of a look originating from lack corresponds to the pattern of the "poor" looking in on the "rich," which Ben Brewster discerns in the development of narrative perspective and viewer positioning from the transitional period on: "A Scene at the Movies,'" *Screen* 23.2 (July–August 1982): 4–15; 12. Also see Chapter 1, before note 83.

20. Copyright deposit, June 1916, and renewal of copyright January 8, 1917; also in the shortened 1917 print. Arthur Lennig, *The Silent Voice: A Text* (Troy, N.Y.: Arthur Lennig, 1969), p. 62, cites a poem written by one of Griffith's admirers in October or November 1916, which recounts the story of *Intolerance*, expressing satisfaction about the restoration of the child. On the "Infant Phenomenon" in Griffith's earlier work, see Russell Merritt, "The Impact of D. W. Griffith's Motion Pictures from 1908 to 1914 on Contemporary American Culture," Ph.D. diss., Harvard University, 1970, pp. 200–05.

21. Teresa de Lauretis. *Alice Doesn't: Feminism, Semiotics, Cinema* (Bloomington: Indiana University Press, 1984), ch. 5; Mary Ann Doane, "Misrecognition and Identity," *Ciné-Tracts* 3.3 (Fall 1980): 25–32; Stephen Heath, "Film and System: Terms of Analysis, Part II," *Screen* 16.2 (Summer 1975): 91–113; 100ff.

22. From George Soule, *New Republic* 8.100 (Sept. 30, 1916): 225, through Marcel Martin, "Un réformateur sentimental," *Ecran* 12 (1973).

23. Lillian Gish, with Ann Pinchot, *The Movies, Mr. Griffith, and Me* (Englewood Cliffs, N.J.: Prentice Hall, 1969), pp. 181–82; also see Chapter 10, at note 40. On the star system and the mechanisms of identification it encourages, see Richard Dyer, *Stars* (London: British Film Institute, 1979).

24. On Griffith's associations with the name "Jenkins" (one of the pseudonyms he used for depositing money in various banks), see Lennig, *The Silent Voice*, p. 55. The refusal of psychological individuality (as a basis of classical viewer identification) and the emphasis on types can be related to the modernist revival of "epic" modes in

the theater, notably by Brecht, who also opposed the star system, though for more consciously political reasons.

25. Julian Johnson, *Photoplay Magazine* 10.7 (December 1916): 81.

6. *Genesis, Causes, Concepts of History*

1. Joseph Henabery, interview in Kevin Brownlow, *The Parade's Gone By. . .* (Berkeley: University of California Press, 1968), pp. 50, 51; Karl Brown, *Adventures with D. W. Griffith* (London: Secker & Warburg, 1973), p. 125 (but see also p. 114: "It was an awful come-down"); Arthur Lennig, *The Silent Voice: A Text* (Troy, N.Y.: Lenning 1969), p. 56; Lillian Gish, with Ann Pinchot, *The Movies, Mr. Griffith, and Me* (Englewood Cliffs, N.J.: Prentice Hall, 1969), p. 166: "Mr. Griffith was in the awkward position of having to surpass himself. Yet he could not afford to discard *The Mother and the Law.*" On the rise of the longer film and the special feature, see Janet Staiger in David Bordwell, Janet Staiger, and Kristin Thompson, *The Classical Hollywood Cinema: Film Style and Mode of Production to 1960* (New York: Columbia University Press, 1985), pp. 132–34; Eileen Bowser, *The Transformation of Cinema: 1908–1915* (New York: Scribner's, Macmillan, 1990), ch. 12; and Alan Gevinson, "The Birth of the American Feature Film," in Paolo Cherchi Usai and Lorenzo Codelli, eds., *Sulla via di Hollywood* (Pordenone: Biblioteca dell'Immagine, 1988), pp. 132–155.

2. *Moving Picture World* (Jan. 27, 1917).

3. D. W. Griffith, *The Rise and Fall of Free Speech in America* (Los Angeles, 1916). The most curious example refers to Czarist Russia: "Pictures and reading matter are rigorously censored in Russia—do they want us to adopt that system?" Three years later, in the prologue to *The Mother and the Law,* Griffith would denounce intolerance as the "cause of the Russian revolution."

4. With the outbreak of the European war and the success of the Russian revolution, the focus of censorship shifted from moral to political issues, from the banning of Dreiser's *The Genius* in 1915 to the *Masses* trials of 1918; see Daniel Aaron, *Writers on the Left* (1961; New York: Oxford University Press, 1977), pp. 41–45. Fear of censorship, for instance, caused white radicals not to support black protests against *Birth;* see Leslie Fishbein, *Rebels in Bohemia: The Radicals of The Masses, 1911–1917* (Chapel Hill: University of North Carolina Press, 1982), p. 166. Floyd Dell, reviewing *Intolerance* in *The Masses,* November 1916, points out a certain irony "in the idea of the producer of that hate-breeding film-play, 'The Birth of a Nation,' telling us to be tolerant," but also warns against precipitating "a trail of film censorships . . . which it will take twenty-five years to abolish!"

5. Seymour Stern, "D. W. Griffith's INTOLERANCE: A Sun Play of the Ages," in P. Adams Sitney, ed., vol. I, *The Essential Cinema,* (New York: Anthology Film Archives and New York University Press, 1975): "The white race is the minority race on the planet Earth. Hence an attempt to suppress a work like *The Birth of a Nation,* treating as it does of the race war in one part of the white world, struck its creator as an intolerable outrage and a treacherous act of intolerance, as by an

enemy. He tried to strike back via the screen. That was the reason *Intolerance* was made" (p. 54). Terry Ramsaye, *A Million and One Nights* (1926; New York: Simon & Schuster, 1964): "The United States had to fight the Civil War and the negro question all over again while the world was coming apart next door. The bitterness of the battle gave Griffith the text for his next great screen effort *Intolerance*, a tremendous endeavor to expose the absurdities of public opinion down the aisles of history" (p. 644; also see p. 756). More restrained, but no less apologetic is Schickel's account, *D. W. Griffith: An American Life* (New York: Simon & Schuster, 1984), p. 310.

6. See Chapter 8. The discourse of film as "high art" was to have a similar function of masking racist ideology in the production, marketing, and programming of *Broken Blossoms*; see Vance Kepley, "Griffith's *Broken Blossoms* and the Problem of Historical Specificity," *Quarterly Review of Film Studies* 3.1 (Winter 1978): 37–47; 43–44.

7. Brown, *Adventures*, p. 130.

8. Philip Rosen, "Securing the Historical: Historiography and the Classical Cinema," in Patricia Mellencamp and P. Rosen, eds., *Cinema Histories, Cinema Practices*, American Film Institute Monograph Series, vol. 4 (Frederick, Md.: University Publications of America, 1984), pp. 23, 26; Georg Lukács, *The Historical Novel* (1947; 1955), trans. Hannah and Stanley Mitchell (Boston: Beacon, 1963). Also see James Chandler, "The Historical Novel Goes to Hollywood: Scott, Griffith, and Epic Film Today," in Gene Ruoff, ed., *Romanticism and Modern Culture* (New Brunswick, N.J.: Rutgers University Press, 1990).

9. Richard Hofstadter, *The Progressive Historians: Turner, Beard, Parrington* (New York: Knopf, 1969).

10. The last sentence, which is in the first version of the essay "History" (1841), was omitted from the 1847 version which serves as copy text for the critical edition, *The Collected Works of Ralph Waldo Emerson, II, Essays: First Series*, ed. Joseph Slater et al. (Cambridge, Mass.: Harvard University Press, 1979), p. 7; variant, p. 268.

11. Emerson's troping of history and subjectivity resonates in Freud's comparison of the nonsynchronous make-up of the ego with the archaeological layers of Rome (to which I will return in conjunction with the peculiar sexual and representational economy of Griffith's Babylon), although Freud actually elaborates this comparison as a *disanalogy*, contrasting the demolitions and replacements that characterize the archaeological make-up of a city with the psychic preservation of earlier layers of experience; Sigmund Freud, *Civilization and Its Discontents* (1930), *Standard Edition*, 21: 69–73.

12. The familial structuring of identification varies from genre to genre, taking on a greater or lesser importance and different shapes in, say, domestic melodrama, the Western, or the musical. Also see Sandy Flitterman, "That 'Once-Upon-a-Time. . .' of Childish Dreams," *Ciné-Tracts* 13 (Spring 1981): 14–26; Heath, "Contexts," *Edinburgh Magazine* 2 (1977): 37–43; Kluge, "The Fundamental Interest of the Feature [Fiction] Film," trans. in *Wide Angle* 3.4 (1980): 28.

13. Pierre Sorlin, *The Film in History: Restaging the Past* (Totowa, N.J.: Barnes & Noble, 1980), pp. 101–05, argues that *Birth* knows in fact only one, the Southern "stem" family, which assimilates the remnants of the incomplete Northern family. I believe, however, that the different, and more explicitly, incestuous economy of the Northern family is an important dimension in Griffith's psychosexual *écriture*, especially in light of his own family romance (see Chapter 10).

14. Stow Persons, "The Cyclical Theory of History in Eighteenth Century America," *American Quarterly* 6.2 (1954). Among Griffith's contemporaries, exponents of the "repeat in history" notably include writers like Brooks Adams, *The Law of Civilization and Decay* (1896), and Ezra Pound, influenced by the latter; turning this concept of history into a textual design, *Intolerance* could be called a primitive precursor of Pound's *Cantos*. On parallelist conceptions of history in Hollywood films, see Gilles Deleuze, *Cinema 1: The Movement-Image*, trans. Hugh Tomlinson and Barbara Habberjam (Minneapolis: University of Minnesota Press, 1986), pp. 148–49.

15. Martin Christadler and Miriam Hansen, "D. W. Griffiths *Intolerance* (1916): Zum Verhältnis von Film and Geschichte in der Progressive Era," *Amerikastudien/American Studies* 21.1 (1976): 36. On the pervasiveness on cataclysmic concepts of history between 1880 and 1916, see F. C. Jaher, *Doubters and Dissenters* (Glencoe, Ill.: Free Press, 1964). On versions of millennialism during the period under consideration, see Timothy P. Weber, *Living in the Shadow of the Second Coming: American Premillennialism, 1875–1925* (New York: Oxford University Press, 1979), and Jean B. Quandt, "Religion and Social Thought: The Secularization of Postmillennialism," *American Quarterly* 25.4 (October 1973): 390–409.

16. Gish, *The Movies*, p. 47: "In later years I often heard him say that he would rather have written one page of *Leaves of Grass* than to have made all the movies for which he received world acclaim." The quotations from *Leaves of Grass* that follow are from *Complete Poetry and Selected Prose by Walt Whitman*, ed. James E. Miller, Jr. (Boston: Houghton Mifflin, 1959), pp. 80, 51, 68.

17. Such ahistorical use of history prefigures a tendency Max Horkheimer and Theodor W. Adorno observed in the later products of the "culture industry": "History is expelled from the plots [*Fabeln*] of cultural commodities, even and especially when they peddle historical subject matter. Like the individual, history itself becomes a costume, a disguise for the frozen modernity of monopoly and state capitalism." "Das Schema der Massenkultur" (1942), draft sequel to the chapter on the Culture Industry in *Dialectic of Enlightenment*, first published in Theodor W. Adorno, *Gesammelte Schriften* 3 (Frankfurt am Main: Suhrkamp, 1981): 299–335; 315.

18. The line is from the poem by Bishop George Berkeley, "Verses on the Prospect of Planting Arts and Learning in America"; see Ernest Lee Tuveson, *Redeemer Nation: The Idea of America's Millennial Role* (Chicago: University of Chicago Press, 1968), ch. 4, "When Did Destiny Become Manifest?"

19. For example, Marcel Martin, "Un réformateur sentimental," *Ecran* 12 (1973): 32, 34.

20. Pierre Baudry, "Les aventures de l'Idée (sur 'Intolerance')," part 1, *Cahiers du*

Cinéma 240 (July–August 1972): 53. Baudry's contention seems implicitly directed against the simple structural correspondence of ideology and parallel editing which both Metz and Eisenstein assert in their readings of *Intolerance*. The concept of an "ideological project" as both articulated and undermined by the textual work of a film was elaborated in the pages of *Cahiers du Cinéma* in the wake of May 1968; for an example, see the editors' famous reading of John Ford's *Young Mr. Lincoln*, which provoked much commentary and debate (rpt. in Nichols, ed., *Movies and Methods*, I; 492–529).

21. Walter Benjamin, *Passagen-Werk* (Frankfurt am Main: Suhrkamp, 1983), I, D 10a, 5; "Central Park," trans. Lloyd Spencer and Mark Harrington, *New German Critique* 34 (Winter 1985): 50. Also see Walter Benjamin, "Theses on the Philosophy of History," in *Illuminations* (New York: Schocken, 1969), and "Theologico-Political Fragment," in *Reflections* (New York: Harcourt Brace Jovanovich, 1978).

22. The effect of the diegetically distinct narratives that interpenetrate and converge into one diegesis, whose temporal and spatial parameters are world history, was parodied by Buster Keaton in *The Three Ages* (1923). It has been commented upon frequently, beginning with Frank S. Nugent's review of the film's revival, *New York Times* (March 8, 1936) up to Deleuze, *Cinema 1*, p. 31. Also see Siegfried Kracauer, *Theory of Film* (New York: Oxford University Press, 1960), who sees the narrative-ideological project of *Intolerance* subverted by the "physical" effects of the "Griffith chase": "It drowns ideological suspense in physical excitement" (p. 228).

23. Even an apologist like Seymour Stern acknowledges, perhaps unwittingly, the textual force by which the ideologically posited difference of the Modern narrative collapses, when he suggests another subtitle for the film "A Tale of Four Cities—All Fallen" ("D. W. Griffith's INTOLERANCE").

7. Film History, Archaeology, Universal Language

1. See Pierre Baudry, "Les aventures de l'Idée, 2," *Cahiers du Cinéma* 241 (September–October 1972): 32–36, and Dominique Chateau, "Intolérance: Une encyclopédie du cinéma," in Jean Mottet, ed., *D. W. Griffith* (Paris: L'Harmattan, 1984), esp. pp. 269–72.

2. Tom Gunning, "Le récit filmé et l'idéal theatral: Griffith et les 'films d'art' français," in Pierre Guibbert, ed., *Les premiers ans de cinéma français* (Paris: Collections des Cahiers de la Cinémathèque, 1985), pp. 123–129. Also see Davide Turconi, "From Stage to Screen: Notes for a Five-Year History of Famous Players Film Company, Jesse L. Lasky Feature Film Company and Triangle Film Corporation between 1912 and 1917," in Paolo Cherchi Usai and Lorenzo Codelli, eds., *Sulla via di Hollywood* (Pordenone: Edizioni Biblioteca dell'Immagine, 1988), pp. 16–131.

3. Richard H. Campbell and Michael R. Pitts, *The Bible on Film: A Checklist, 1897–1980* (Metuchen, N.J.: Scarecrow Press, 1981), pp. 73–93; 83. The structural parallel between *Intolerance* and *Satan* (four different narratives heading toward a devastating climax, though not intercut with each other) is pointed out by Edward

Wagenknecht, *The Movies in the Age of Innocence,* 2nd ed. (New York: Ballantine, 1971), p. 86.

4. "Five Dollar Movies Prophesied," *New York Times,* March 28, 1915.

5. Henabery assembled a scrapbook with reproductions from dozens of scholarly works on Babylonia and Assyria, though few of these sources are identified: Kevin Brownlow, *The Parade's Gone By . . .* (Berkeley: University of California Press, 1968), pp. 51–52; Bernard Hanson, "D. W. Griffith: Some Sources," *Art Bulletin* 54.4 (December 1972): 493–515. For a critique of the kind of art-historical source-hunting exemplified by Hanson's article, see Russell Merritt's interesting reading of the famous publicity still from *Intolerance,* "On first looking into Griffith's Babylon," *Wide Angle* 3.1 (1979): 13–21.

6. Roland Barthes, *S/Z,* trans. Richard Miller (New York: Hill & Wang, 1974), pp. 55.

7. Karl Brown, *Adventures with D. W. Griffith* (London: Secker & Warburg, 1973), p. 135. On Griffith's "approach to research," see William M. Drew, *D. W. Griffith's "Intolerance": Its Genesis and Its Vision* (Jefferson, NC: McFarland, 1986), ch. 3.

8. Brownlow, *Parade,* p. 53–54.

9. Barthes, "The Realistic Effect," trans. Gerald Mead, *Film Reader* 3 (February 1978): 131–35.

10. Hanson, "Some Sources," pp. 499–500. The legend has recently been further cultivated by the Taviani brothers' exercise in nostalgia, *Good Morning, Babylon* (1987).

11. Gian Piero Brunetta, "Constitution du récit et place du spectateur chez D. W. Griffith," in Mottet, ed., *Griffith* p. 249.

12. The problem of connotation as such challenges the signifier-signified distinction; see Christian Metz, "Connotation Reconsidered," *Discourse* 2 (Summer 1980): 18–31. Also cf. Barthes, *S/Z,* pp. 6–7.

13. This reading departs from Chateau, "Encyclopédie," p. 271. Chateau also notes the double inscription of the spectator that I am pursuing here but, remaining within a basically structuralist framework, ignores the stylistic peculiarities involved: "La double lecture, selon le thème et selon les genres, fait osciller le spectateur entre deux poles: la fusion idéologique qui suppose la continuité de l'illusionnisme narratif et la conscience métafilmique qui la brise" (p. 270). On alternation as a key figure in the development of narration, see Raymond Bellour's analysis of Griffith's *The Lonedale Operator* (1911), "Alterner/raconter," in *Le cinéma américain* (Paris: Flammarion, 1980), I, 68–88.

14. David Bordwell, Janet Staiger, Kristin Thompson, *Classical Hollywood Cinema: Film Style and Mode of Production to 1960* (New York: Columbia University Press, 1985), pp. 228–29.

15. Hanson, "Some Sources," p. 498, mentions the close-up of the puppies as an instance of historical detail, namely Catherine de Medici's notorious fondness for little dogs, even if Griffith may have used "one of his favorite devices" (close-ups of small animals, often attached to women and children) without being aware of that

particular source. The shot is overdetermined, but the more interesting aspect is the tension between its diegetic connotation of decadence and perversion (the puppies in the lap of the king's brother, who is shown adjusting his earring) and its discursive invocation of similar close-ups in other Griffith films—as part of the authorial signature that asserts itself even within the "foreign" sequence.

16. G. W. Bitzer, *Billy Bitzer: His Story* (New York: Farrar, Straus and Giroux, 1973), pp. 134–35. Also see Merritt's comment on this shot, "On First Looking into Griffith's Babylon," pp. 18–19.

17. Tom Gunning, "An Unseen Energy Swallows Space: The Space in Early Film and Its Relation to American Avant-Garde Film," in John L. Fell, ed., *Film Before Griffith* (Berkeley: University of California Press, 1983), p. 362. Also see Jon Gartenberg, "Camera Movement in Edison and Biograph Films: 1900–1906," *Cinema 1900–1906*, comp. Roger Holman (Brussels: FIAF, 1982), I: 169–80; and David Bordwell, "Camera Movement and Cinematic Space," *Ciné-Tracts* 1.2 (Summer 1977): 19–25; 23. Also see Chapter 1.

18. Will M. Ritchey, "Tricks of the Trade," *Motography* 16.10 (Sept. 2, 1916): 542, quoted in Bordwell, Staiger, and Thompson, *Classical Hollywood Cinema*, p. 229.

19. The barely concealed artificiality of the Babylonian narrative was first noted by Heywood Broun, "Babylon Caught on First Bounce: David Griffith Picks Up Well Known City Which Fell," *New York Tribune*, Sept. 7, 1916: "Griffith is tickled to death to learn that there was once a town called Babylon full of folk who loved and laughed and fought, with never a thought that they were ancients. He thrills with the poet's 'When I was a king in Babylon and you were a slapstick slave' and puts slave, slapstick and king into one picture." (The poet is W. Henley, and the poem was to play a major part, along with another Babylonian fantasy, in Cecil B. DeMille's *Male and Female* [1919].)

20. *San Francisco Chronicle*, Jan. 14, 1917; also see Julian Johnson, *Photoplay* (December 1916): "You were taught that the Jewish Jehovah traced destruction's warning in letters of fire on the wall of Belshazzar's palace . . . See this picture and get the facts" (p. 78). The major biblical references to the Fall of Babylon are: II Chronicles, 36; Ezra, ch. 1; Isiah, ch. 21; Jeremiah, chs. 50–51; Daniel, chs. 1–5; Revelation, 15. 8. For the film's use of Assyrio-Babylonian archaeology, see Hanson, "Some Sources," 502–04, and Drew, "Intolerance," pp. 42–62. On the figure of "Babylon the Great" in the tradition of American millennialism, see Ernest Lee Tuveson, *Redeemer Nation: The Idea of America's Millennial Role* (Chicago: University of Chicago Press, 1968) pp. 11, 18, 116–17.

21. Martin Christadler and Miriam Hansen, "D. W. Griffiths *Intolerance* (1916): Zum Verhältnis von Film und Geschichte in der Progressive Era," *Amerikastudien/American Studies* 21.1 (1976): 20–26, 29–34; Merritt, "On first looking into Griffith's Babylon" 20. On anti-Puritanism and the New Paganism, see Leslie Fishbein, *Rebels in Bohemia: The Radicals of The Masses, 1911–1917* (Chapel Hill: University of North Carolina Press, 1982), chs. 3–4.

22. Herodotus emphasizes the use of brick in Babylonian construction: *Histories*,

Book One (Harmondsworth: Penguin, 1972), pp. 113ff. On the archaeological search for the Biblical Tower of Babel, see James Wellard, *Babylon* (New York: Saturday Review Press, 1972), pp. 158–63; one of the keys to its discovery was a clay tablet containing a description of the Babylonian ziggurat dedicated to Bel-Mardouk. For centuries, the ruins of the legendary tower-temple "served as a brick-yard for the local peasants who built their huts out of the debris" (p. 161), an image that evokes another quarry more than two thousand years later: the Babylonian set of *Intolerance*, with its fragmentary, and legendary, reappearances in later Hollywood films, if not the metaphoric quarry of the film itself.

23. Whether the betrayal of Babylon has any possible historical source, as Mitry argues (*Histoire du cinéma*, II, 173), seems irrelevant in light of this parallel. The point is that the perpetrators are priests, that is, intellectuals, who are denounced as a self-serving, hypocritical caste, very much in the spirit of Julien Benda's later crusade in *The Treason of the Intellectuals* (*La traison des clercs*) (1928).

24. Jacques Derrida, "Des Tours de Babel," in Joseph F. Graham, ed., *Difference in Translation* (Ithaca, N.Y.: Cornell University Press, 1985), pp. 165–248; passage quoted on pp. 165–66. Also see *The Interpreter's Bible* (New York, Nashville: Abingdon-Cokesbury Press, 1952ff.), I: 562–65.

25. Metz, *Film Language: A Semiotics of the Cinema*, trans. Michael Taylor (New York: Oxford University Press, 1974), pp. 63–64. For an elaboration of problems raised by Metz and further perspectives on the relation between film and verbal language, see Stephen Heath and Patricia Mellencamp, eds., *Cinema and Language*, American Film Institute Monograph Series, vol. 1 (Frederick, Md.: University Publications of America, 1983).

26. The emphasis on figuration implies that rhetorical tropes and figures cannot be reduced to codes and system, nor to the crypto-structuralist binarism of meta-phor and metonymy (for example, Metz, *The Imaginary Signifier*, pt. IV). For an elucidation of the questions involved, see Paul de Man, "Semiology and Rhetoric," *Allegories of Reading* (New Haven and London: Yale University Press, 1979); Dudley Andrew, "Figuration," *Concepts in Film Theory* (New York: Oxford University Press, 1984), ch. 9; D. N. Rodowick, "The Figure and the Text" (on the work of Thierry Kuntzel and Marie-Claire Ropars-Wuilleumier), *Diacritics* 15.1 (Spring 1985): 34–50.

8. Hieroglyphics, Figurations of Writing

1. Béla Balázs, *Schriften zum Film* 1, ed. Helmut H. Diederichs (Munich: Carl Hanser Verlag, 1982), p. 57. As an example of the rebirth of a physiognomic, gestural language, Balázs cites the work of Ruth St. Denis, the American dancer who crucially inspired the choreography of the Babylonian narrative. For an extensive discussion of "Cinema and Writing," see Christian Metz, *Language and Cinema*, trans. Donna Jean Umiker-Sebeok (The Hague: Mouton, 1974), ch. 11.

2. In an essay which is not part of the book, "Physiognomie" (1923; *Schriften*, pp. 205–08), Balázs introduces dimensions of writing and reading with an interest-

ing reference to psychoanalysis, prefiguring Walter Benjamin's notion of the "optical unconscious." The ideal of a film with no intertitles had a vogue in the United States as early as 1913 but yielded, in 1916, "to an approach that emphasized cleverly written inter-titles" (David Bordwell, Janet Staiger, and Kristin Thompson, *The Classical Hollywood Cinema: Film Style and Mode of Production to 1960* [New York: Columbia University Press, 1985], p. 186).

3. D. W. Griffith, "The Motion Picture and Witch Burners," rpt. in Fred Silva, ed., *Focus on THE BIRTH OF A NATION* (Englewood Cliffs, N.J.: Prentice Hall, 1971), p. 96.

4. Concurrently with the emphasis on wit and self-consciousness, around 1916 intertitles began to show pictorial and graphically specific designs, so-called "art titles" (Bordwell, Thompson, and Staiger, *Classical Hollywood Cinema*, p. 187). For a film of comparable graphic diversity, both in the intertitles and in narratively motivated images of writing, see Murnau's *Nosferatu* (1921), restored version.

5. Max Horkheimer and Theodor W. Adorno, "Das Schema der Massenkultur" (1942), Adorno, *Gesammelte Schriften* 3 (Frankfurt am Main: Suhrkamp, 1981): 333. Sound films are just as much "written," but industrialized film practice amalgamates dialogue, image, and music into a fictive homogeneity which suppresses the antithetical and discursive quality of the filmic materials; Horkheimer and Adorno, *Dialectic of Enlightenment*, (New York: Seabury Press, 1972), p. 124; also see [Adorno and] Hanns Eisler, *Composing for the Films* (New York: Oxford University Press, 1947).

6. Jacques Derrida, *Of Grammatology*, trans. Gayatri Chakravorty Spivak (Baltimore: Johns Hopkins University Press, 1976), pp. 74–93; "Freud and the Scene of Writing," in *Writing and Difference*, trans. Alan Bass (Chicago: University of Chicago Press, 1978), pp. 207ff., 240–42; Sigmund Freud, *The Interpretation of Dreams* (1900), *Standard Edition* 4: 277–78; 5: 341; "The Claim of Psychoanalysis to Scientific Interest" (1913), *SE* 13: 177. The foremost proponent of Derridean film theory in France is Marie-Claire Ropars-Wuilleumier; see for example, "The Graphic in Filmic Writing: *A bout de souffle*, or The Erratic Alphabet," *Enclitic* 5.2/6.1 (Spring 1982): 147–61; *Le texte divisé* (Paris: PUF, 1981). An attempt to "apply" Derrida in an involuntarily McLuhanesque fashion is Gregory L. Ulmer's *Applied Grammatology* (Baltimore: Johns Hopkins University Press, 1985); ch. 9 deals explicitly with film, primarily Eisenstein.

7. Horkheimer and Adorno, "Schema der Massenkultur," pp. 332–35; Adorno, "Prolog zum Fernsehen," *Eingriffe* (Frankfurt am Main: Suhrkamp, 1963), pp. 77–79. Derrida focuses more explicitly on the politics of hieroglyphic encryptment and deciphering in "Scribble (writing-power)," *Yale French Studies* 58 (1979): 117–47.

8. Derrida, *Of Grammatology*, p. 89; Cyrus H. Gordon, *Forgotten Scripts: Their Ongoing Discovery and Decipherment*, rev. ed. (New York: Dorset, 1987), pp. 92ff.

9. John T. Irwin, *American Hieroglyphics: The Symbol of the Egyptian Hieroglyphics in the American Renaissance* (Baltimore: Johns Hopkins University Press, 1983).

10. Vachel Lindsay, *The Art of the Moving Picture*, 2nd ed. (New York: Liveright, 1970), pp. 152–53. Arthur Knight, *The Liveliest Art: A Panoramic History of the Movies*

(New York: New American Library, 1957), refers to the famous close-up of Mae Marsh's hands in the courtroom scene of *Intolerance* as a "visible hieroglyph," attributing the term to Horace M. Kallen who "once called such material, 'the visible hieroglyphs of the unseen dynamics of human relations'" (p. 33).

11. Derrida, *Of Grammatology*, pp. 75–81; Irwin, *American Hieroglyphics*, does not explicitly refer to the epistemological disjunction thrown into relief by Derrida, but the material he discusses clearly participates in both a theological (in a peculiarly American, not necessarily Christian sense) and a rhetorical conception of the hieroglyph.

12. In addition to the obvious parallels of narrative and character constellations, numerous details assume a transhistorical, 'hieroglyphic' quality, such as the close-ups of doves that appear in both Judean and Babylonian episodes, or the "candid" shots of the yawning page at the French court and of a yawning guard at Belshazzar's feast. More puzzling is the marked repetition of narrative situations within one and the same narrative, which should emerge more clearly in the restored print, such as the multiplication of incidents in which Belshazzar saves the Mountain Girl (1917 print and Huff, 373–390 [not included in standard MOMA prints]; also compare *The Fall of Babylon*). *The Mother and the Law* also has instances of undisguised repetition, especially of encounters between the Dear One and the Boy, including the motif of being interrupted by a stranger (eloquently described by Eisenstein). Karl Brown notes this tendency of repetition throughout his chapter on the making of *Intolerance*, *Adventures with D. W. Griffith* (London: Secker & Warburg, 1973), esp. p. 130, and, in true Griffith style, defends the "supposedly modern advertising saying that repetition is reputation" as an ancient device: "Nor would a single statue do. The more the merrier, so it was Ramses, Ramses, Ramses all over the Egyptian empire of three thousand years ago, just as it was Coca-Cola, Coca-Cola, Coca-Cola all over our present-day world" (pp. 145–46). On repetition as a principle of industrialized culture, see Horkheimer and Adorno, *Dialectic of Enlightenment*, pp. 134–36, "Schema der Massenkultur," pp. 305, 317, and, on its dialectical alterity, pp. 331. For an example of the classical tendency to mask repetition, see Bellour's reading of a sequence from *The Big Sleep*, trans. "The Obvious and the Code," *Screen* 15.4 (Winter 1974–75).

13. At the risk of stretching the analogy, one could extend it to the excessive use of vignetting throughout the film (excessive even compared to other Griffith films), especially when these techniques can in no way be construed to signal a subjective shot. Thus, the vignetting might be taken as an allusion to the figure of the cartouche, an oval ring used in hieroglyphics to enclose the characters of a royal name, a proper name. This discovery had been a key to Champollion's legendary deciphering of the Rosetta Stone and, according to Irwin, had come to symbolize the process of decipherment itself. In that sense the vignetted framing would stress the ideographic inscription of individual images and thereby underline not merely the memorability and uniqueness of the events depicted but, at the same time, their repeatability and interpretability.

14. Bishop William Warburton, *The Divine Legation of Moses Demonstrated* (1737–41); Derrida, "Scribble (writing-power)," p. 124.

15. During the prewar years Whitman had come to symbolize the hope for an integration of American culture, as in this well-known passage from Van Wyck Brooks, *America's Coming of Age* (New York: B. W. Huebsch, 1915): "But it happens that we have the rudiments of a middle tradition, a tradition which effectively combines theory and action, a tradition which is just as fundamentally American as either flag-waving or money-grabbing, one which is visibly growing but which has already been grossly abused; and this is the tradition which begins with Walt Whitman. The real significance of Walt Whitman is that he, for the first time, gave us the sense of something organic in American life" (p. 112).

16. Paul O'Dell, *Griffith and the Rise of Hollywood* (New York: A. S. Barnes; London: A. Zwemmer, 1970), p. 46, cites Seymour Stern's "commonly accepted" anecdote "that Griffith conceived the basic idea for the story of *Intolerance* when, traveling from California to New York for the premiere of *The Birth of a Nation*, he saw a billboard advertisement from a train window, with the words 'The Same Today as Yesterday.'" The fatalistic aspect of the inscription also ties in with the allegorical voice, discussed in Chapter 5 ("The Loom of Fate weaves death for The Boy's father") as an instance of disparate styles of narration.

17. D. N. Rodowick, "The Figure and the Text," *Diacritics* 15.1 (Spring 1985): 47.

18. Lindsay, "Photoplay Progress," *The New Republic* 10.120 (Feb. 17, 1917): 76.

9. Riddles of Maternity

1. Print variants are of considerable importance here. The tinted MOMA print has an unusually high number of Cradle shots (at one point, in the sequence showing the death of Modern heroine's father, the shot is even used intra-diegetically); in prints circulating in Europe the shot occurs only sixteen times.

2. See Chapter 2, at notes 9–11, and Chapter 5, before note 9. This tradition persists even in the postclassical Hollywood film, foregrounded to the point of involuntary self-parody in the pile-up of *Waste Land* "sources" in *Apocalypse Now!*. Also see David Bordwell, *The Films of Carl-Theodor Dreyer* (Berkeley: University of California Press, 1981), pp. 34–35.

3. Paul O'Dell, *Griffith and the Rise of Hollywood* (New York: A. S. Barnes, 1970), p. 42; Seymour Stern, "D. W. Griffith's *Intolerance*," *The Essential Cinema*, ed. P. Adams Sitney (New York: Anthology Film Archives and New York University Press, 1975): I, 18; Gerald Mast, *A Short History of the Movies*, 4th ed. (New York: Macmillan, 1986), p. 69; Christian Metz, *Language and Cinema*, trans. Donna Jean Umiker-Sebeok (The Hague: Mouton, 1974), p. 109; Edward Wagenknecht and Anthony Slide, *The Films of D. W. Griffith* (New York: Crown, 1975), p. 86; Marcel Oms, "Essai de lecture thématique de INTOLERANCE," *Les Cahiers de la Cinémathèque* 6 (Spring 1972): 34–35.

4. Sergei Eisenstein, "Dickens, Griffith, and the Film Today" (1944), *Film Form*, ed. and trans. Jay Leyda (New York: Harcourt Brace Jovanovich, 1949), pp. 240–44. Siegfried Kracauer notes an affinity between the "ludicrous recurrent image of the rocking cradle" and Eisenstein's own "lapses into pictorial symbolism": "out of this very cradle come many shots in Eisenstein's own films TEN DAYS THAT SHOOK THE WORLD and OLD AND NEW", *Theory of Film: The Redemption of Physical Reality* (New York: Oxford University Press, 1960), p. 208. For its even greater allegorical extravagance, *Strike* (1924) deserves to be added to that list.

5. Pierre Baudry, "Les aventures de l'Idée (sur *'Intolerance'*): 2," *Cahiers du Cinéma* 241 (September–October 1972): 36–37.

6. For these aspects of allegory as a rhetorical mode, I rely primarily on Angus Fletcher, *Allegory: The Theory of a Symbolic Mode* (Ithaca: Cornell University Press, 1964). Also see Joel Fineman, "The Structure of Allegorical Desire," *October* 12 (Spring 1980): 47–66, rpt. in Stephen Greenblatt, ed., *Allegory and Representation* (Baltimore: Johns Hopkins University Press, 1981), pp. 26–60.

7. Benjamin's notion of allegory is developed primarily in *The Origin of German Tragic Drama* (1919–1925), trans. John Osborne (London: New Left Books, 1977); *Das Passagen-Werk*, 2 vols. (Frankfurt am Main: Suhrkamp, 1983); "Central Park" (1938–39), trans. and intr. by Mark Harrington and Lloyd Spencer, *New German Critique* 34 (Winter 1985): 28–58; "The Work of Art in the Age of Mechanical Reproduction" (1935), *Illuminations*, trans. Harry Zohn (New York: Schocken, 1969), pp. 217–51; "Surrealism" (1929), *Reflections*, ed. and intr. by Peter Demetz, trans. Edmund Jephcott (New York: Harcourt Brace Jovanovich, 1978), pp. 177–92. Among the commentaries dealing with Benjamin's concept of allegory as a master trope of modernity, see especially Lloyd Spencer, "Allegory in the World of the Commodity: The Importance of *Central Park*," *New German Critique* 34 (Winter 1985): 59–77; Christine Buci-Glucksmann, "Catastrophic Utopia: The Feminine as Allegory of the Modern," *Representations* 14 (Spring 1986): 220–29; Ansgar Hillach, "Allegorie, Bildraum, Montage: Versuch, einen Begriff avantgardistischer Montage aus Benjamins Schriften zu begründen," in W. Martin Lüdke, ed., *'Theorie der Avantgarde': Antworten auf Peter Bürgers Bestimmung von Kunst und bürgerlicher Gesellschaft* (Frankfurt am Main: Suhrkamp, 1976), pp. 105–42; and, with some reservations, Craig Owens, "The Allegorical Impulse: Toward a Theory of Postmodernism [part 1]," *October* 12 (Spring 1980): 67–86. Benjamin's strategic transformation of myth into allegory clearly inspired the critical double vision of Adorno's concept of mass-cultural hieroglyphics (see Chapter 8).

8. Charles Musser, *Before the Nickelodeon: Edwin S. Porter and the Edison Manufacturing Company* (Berkeley: University of California Press, 1990). On the traditional linkage of allegory with femininity (Justice, Liberty, Industry, the Muses), see Cillie Rentmeister, "Berufsverbot für die Musen," *Ästhetik und Kommunikation* 25 (1976): 92–112.

9. Peter Bürger, *Theory of the Avantgarde* (1974), trans. Michael Shaw (Minneapolis: University of Minnesota Press, 1984), pp. 68–82, and Hillach's critique of Bürger in "Allegorie, Bildraum, Montage"; Owens, "The Allegorical Impulse."

10. Kevin Brownlow, *The War, the West, and the Wilderness* (New York: Knopf, 1979), p. 33. The sequel to *The Battle Cry of Peace* (retitled in 1917 as *The Battle Cry of War*) was released under the title *Womanhood, Glory of the Nation*. The traditional appeal to women's natural moral superiority and responsibility was mobilized by both interventionist and pacifist camps; as an example of the latter, see Thomas Ince's *Civilization* (1916) and Herbert Brenon's *War Brides* (1916), with Alla Nazimova and Richard Barthelmess. Griffith himself was planning to make, after *Hearts of the World* (1918), a film about rich women and the war effort titled *Women and the War* (Brownlow, 145). On the cradle image in the tradition of domesticity, see Dorothy Dinnerstein, *The Mermaid and the Minotaur* (New York: Harper & Row, 1976), pt. 2, "The Rocking of the Cradle and the Ruling of the World."

11. Henry Stephen Gordon, "The Story of David Wark Griffith: His Early Years: His Struggles: His Ambitions and Their Achievement," pt. 1, *Photoplay Magazine* 10.1 (June 1916): 31, 35.

12. See, for instance, John Spargo, *Socialism and Motherhood* (New York: B. W. Huebsch, 1914); Ellen Key, *Love and Marriage* (1911); Havelock Ellis, *Analysis of the Sexual Impulse, Love and Pain, the Sexual Impulse in Women* (1903), *Man and Woman: Study of Human Secondary Sexual Characters* (1904).

13. Ruth Rosen, *The Lost Sisterhood: Prostitution in America, 1900–1918* (Baltimore: Johns Hopkins University Press, 1982); William O'Neill, *Divorce in the Progressive Era* (New Haven: Yale University Press, 1967); Mary P. Ryan, *Womanhood in America*, 2nd ed. (New York: New Viewpoints, 1979), ch. 4; Linda Gordon, *Woman's Body, Woman's Right: A Social History of Birth Control in America* (1974; Harmondsworth: Penguin, 1977), esp. sec. II, chs. 5–9.

14. Even in the few films that ostensibly focus on mothers, the narratives have little to do with mother-child relations or the social problems of motherhood. In the 1911 Biograph film, *The Eternal Mother* (with Blanche Sweet), for instance, the plot revolves around marital fidelity and the wife's sacrifice, not around children; also see *The Mothering Heart* (1913, with Lillian Gish). On Griffith's female characters, see Molly Haskell, *From Reverence to Rape* (New York: Penguin, 1974), pp. 54–58; on representations of motherhood, E. Ann Kaplan, "Mothering, Feminism and Representation: The Maternal in Hollywood Melodrama, 1910–1940," in Christine Gledhill, ed., *Home is Where the Heart Is: Studies in Melodrama and the Woman's Film* (London: British Film Institute, 1987), pp. 113–37.

15. Fletcher, *Allegory*, pp. 224ff., 298–302.

16. *Complete Poetry and Selected Prose by Walt Whitman*, ed. James E. Miller, Jr. (Boston: Houghton Mifflin Co., 1959), pp. 181–184.

17. Commentators have consistently rationalized the excessive inscription of the Medici figure as an effect of Josephine Crowell's performance, dismissing the character as either "comically overplayed" (Schickel, *D. W. Griffith*, p. 314), or "positively grotesque" (William K. Everson, *American Silent Film* [New York: Oxford University Press, 1978], p. 96), "more demon than woman" (Wagenknecht and Slide, *The Films of D. W. Griffith*, p. 85).

18. Ezra Goodman, *The Fifty Year Decline and Fall of Hollywood* (New York: MacFad-

den, Bartell, 1957), p. 11. The surviving drafts of the play actually differ quite a bit from this summary, offering a rather wild phantasmagoria set, successively, in the Garden of Eden, Ancient Rome, the Middle Ages and the modern Jazz Age. In the key tableau the eponymic treadmill is envisioned center stage, a cage of monkeys and other animals next to it, and planets in space behind gauze in the background. The tableau involves a cast of Jesus Christ (seated on top of the treadmill), Buddha below him, and "crowds representing humanity" (their dress getting more modern the further down on the treadmill), passing "prostitutes flaunting their trade," "laborers with tool chests," and "a group of fairy like men"; among the supporting characters are three devils and three monkeys. Goodman's interview is notoriously unreliable and tendentious, but his clichés are distinguishable from Griffith's (the description of the play, for instance, is punctuated with the comment, "It is the greatest dream any man has had—ah, the superb egotism of this old man in a cheap hotel!"). Moreover, the hidden and perhaps unconscious parallel with *Intolerance*, and its particular neurotic slant make it unlikely that the fantasy was contrived by Goodman alone.

19. The terms are used in contemporary reformist discourse, for example, "Wayward Girls," *Survey* 25 (1911): 690–91; Ruth True, *The Neglected Girl* (New York: Russell Sage Foundation, 1914); "fallen woman" of course relates to an older, Victorian tradition that was displaced by Progressive reform.

10. Crisis of Femininity, Fantasies of Rescue

1. Gerald Mast is one of the few critics to note *Intolerance*'s preoccupation with women, especially the haunting close-ups of women's faces. But his analysis remains on the level of Griffith's chivalrous self-image: "*Intolerance* makes it perfectly clear that social chaos takes its toll on the women, who are the helpless sufferers of its violence." *A Short History of the Movies*, 4th ed. (New York: Macmillan, 1986), p. 69. Since I completed this book, Michael Rogin has published an essay that in many ways parallels and complements my reflections in this chapter: "The Great Mother Domesticated: Sexual Difference and Sexual Indifference in D. W. Griffith's *Intolerance*," *Critical Inquiry* 15.3 (Spring 1989): 510–55.

2. Michael Rogin, "'The Sword Became a Flashing Vision': D. W. Griffith's *The Birth of a Nation*," *Representations* 9 (Winter 1985): 150–95; 174–78.

3. Anthony Slide, *The Griffith Actresses* (South Brunswick, N.J., and New York: A. S. Barnes & Co.; London: Tantivy Press, 1973), p. 127. Slide also quotes Julian Johnson's eloquent comment on Cooper's performance, *Photoplay Magazine* 10.7 (December 1916): "All actresses who honestly provide for home and baby by the business of vamping and gunning, would do well to observe Miss Cooper's expressions and gestures. Miss Cooper is police dock—she is blotter transcript. Her face is what you *really* see some nights under the green lamps" (pp. 80–81).

4. The term "Friendless Girls" was used primarily by female reformers engaged in projects to rescue young women from prostitution. From the perspective of the

prostitute whose networks and livelihood was threatened by Progressive reform, it was just another expression of the condescension and ignorance of her middle-class sisters. Ruth Rosen, *The Lost Sisterhood: Prostitution in America, 1900–1918* (Baltimore: Johns Hopkins University Press, 1982), quotes from the letters of Maimie Pinzer: "The kind of girl—the human jelly fish—that is willing to be classed as 'friendless' I haven't much time for" (pp. 66). On the persistence of Victorian assumptions in Progressive discourse on prostitution, see Robert E. Riegel, "Changing American Attitudes Toward Prostitution (1800–1920)," *Journal of the History of Ideas* 29 (July–September 1968): 447.

5. For contemporary comparisons, see Leslie Fishbein, "The Fallen Woman As Victim in Early American Film: Soma Versus Psyche," *Film & History* 17.3 (September 1987): 50–61; Sumiko Higashi, *Virgins, Vamps, and Flappers: The American Silent Movie Heroine* (Montreal: Eden Press Women's Publications, 1978).

6. Addams not only signed the protest but also condemned the film in an interview to the *Evening Post*, which was reprinted in the New York *Post*, the only paper that refused to carry advertisements for the film. Fred Silva, ed., *Focus on "The Birth of a Nation"* (Englewood Cliffs, N.J.: Prentice Hall, 1971), pp. 67–68, 117. Addams herself invited discussion of the personal motives for reform with her 1892 address, "The Subjective Necessity for Social Settlements," reprinted in *Twenty Years at Hull-House* (1910), though hardly on the level proposed by Griffith and Loos. Also see Christopher Lasch, *The New Radicalism in America [1889–1963]: The Intellectual as a Social Type* (1965; New York, London: W. W. Norton, 1986) pp. 3–37; Rosen, *Lost Sisterhood*, pp. 60–62; Blanche Wiesen Cook, "Female Support Networks and Political Activism: Lillian Wald, Crystal Eastman, Emma Goldman," *Chrysalis* 3 (1977): 43–61; on Addams, pp. 44–48. On lesbianism in *Intolerance*, see Rogin, "Great Mother," pp. 543ff.

7. On the "abolitionist" position, see Rosen, *Lost Sisterhood*, pp. 9, 12, 17, esp. 30.

8. Ibid., p. xi. "By 1916, it appeared as though a national consensus had been reached. Although advocates of regulation and segregation continued to advance their positions, and although many Americans continued to believe privately that prostitution could not be eradicated, Progressive abolitionists had seemingly won the public's sympathy and support. 'Absolute annihilation of the Social Evil' was declared a national goal synonymous with the preservation of moral society" (p. 18). Rosen's study represents a break with the more traditional view that Progressive reform actually benefited the prostitute by shifting responsibility from individual moral depravity to her commercial exploiters; for an example of this view, see Roy Lubove, "The Progressives and the Prostitute," *The Historian* 24 (May 1962): 308–30: "Instead of the wicked symbol of disease and lust, she became a somewhat romantic object of charity, compassion, and sympathetic understanding" (p. 318).

9. Emma Goldman, "The Traffic in Women" (1917), repr. in *The Traffic in Women and Other Essays on Feminism* (New York: Times Change Reprint, 1970), pp. 19, 30–31; Brand Whitlock, former mayor of Toledo, "The White Slave," *Forum* 51 (1914): 193–216, quoted in Rosen, *Lost Sisterhood*, pp. 18, 31–32. Rosen also cites James

Rolph, mayor of San Francisco, as one who "challenged the 'humanitarian' motives of moral reformers. The campaign against prostitution, he argued, had become harsh and particularly harmed prostitutes and poor people. 'I reply to all the *self-advertising pharisees* and all who have been agitating so loudly to reform other people's morals—many who are calling for *intolerant* restriction would not be satisfied until they destroyed all the amusement and entertainment that have given San Francisco life and character. What will be done with all the women put out of work?'" (p. 28; emphasis mine). The defense of the prostitute against the Progressive crusade could also draw on a bohemian tradition of romanticizing the prostitute; for a contemporary example, see Hutchins Hapgood, *Types from City Streets* (New York: Funk & Wagnalls, 1910), pp. 125–41, esp. 138ff.

10. Egal Feldman, "Prostitution, the Alien Woman and the Progressive Imagination, 1910–1915," *American Quarterly* 19 (Summer 1967): 192–206; Rosen, *Lost Sisterhood*, ch. 7, "White Slavery: Myth or Reality." For a diverging analysis of white slavery as primarily an instance of mass hysteria, see Mark Thomas Connelly, *The Response to Prostitution in the Progressive Era* (Chapel Hill: University of North Carolina Press, 1980), ch. 6.

11. James Hart, ed., *The Man Who Invented Hollywood: The Autobiography of D. W. Griffith* (Louisville, Ky.: Touchstone, 1972), p. 56. On Griffith's fascination with prostitutes, also see Schickel, *D. W. Griffith: An American Life* (New York: Simon & Schuster, 1984), pp. 45, 55–58.

12. Erotic triangles involving "another woman" can be found in a number of Griffith's films, for example, *The Eternal Mother* (1911), *The Female of the Species* (1912), *Hearts of the World* (1918), *True-Heart Susie* (1919). The repressed ethnic connotations of the fear—and desire—of the "other" woman were more explicit (though still repressed) in the contemporary figure of the vamp, notably her personification by Theda Bara. On the appeal of transgressions of the sexual taboo on the ethnic-racial other also see Chapter 11.

13. Kathy Peiss, "'Charity Girls' and City Pleasures: Historical Notes on Working-Class Sexuality, 1880–1920," in Ann Snitow, Christine Stansell, and Sharon Thompson, eds., *Powers of Desire* (New York: Monthly Review Press, 1983), pp. 74–87; Griffith, *Autobiography*, p. 56. Also see Hapgood, *Types from City Streets*, pp. 125–38.

14. Rick Altman, "*The Lonely Villa* and Griffith's Paradigmatic Style," *Quarterly Review of Film Studies* 6.2 (Spring 1981): 123–34; also see Rogin, "Sword," 158–59.

15. The series of sequences beginning with the exodus of the modern protagonists after the strike can be read as a montage unit in a larger sense, presenting variations on the themes of courtship, marriage, jealousy, adultery, and prostitution; at least seven couples are formed—or fail to form—across centuries and classes. These sequences are, briefly: the Boy's first encounter with the Friendless One; both defeated by adversity (the Boy turns to crime and the Friendless One listens to the Musketeer); the Babylonian marriage market (the Mountain Girl exempted by Belshazzar, the effeminate rhapsode pining for her in vain); the highly

ritualized courtship between Belshazzar and the Princess Beloved; the Boy's second encounter with the Friendless One (confrontation with Musketeer); the Dear One's encounter with the Boy, followed by her father's death; the Marriage in Cana; Brown Eyes courted by Prosper (confrontation with the Mercenary); the end of a Coney Island day (the Dear One's virtuous refusal prompts the Boy to propose); the Woman Taken in Adultery; the Uplifters' report, including the flashback of the raid on a brothel; the Boy's decision to go straight (the Dear One, having domesticated him, gives credit to the statue of the Madonna).

16. The processes of condensation converging in the figure of the Friendless One altogether elude a structuralist attempt to systematize the characters in terms of essential qualities and basic oppositions. This is evidenced by Baudry's chart in "Les aventures de l'Idée (sur '*Intolerance*')," pt. 2, *Cahiers du Cinéma* 241 (September–October 1972): 38.

17. George Soule, "After the Play," *The New Republic* 8. 100 (Sept. 30, 1916): 225. I am grateful to Peter Williamson for alerting me to this important print variant and showing me the slide from the copyright deposit. *The Chicago Tribune* (Dec. 24, 1916), prints a still showing Olga Grey as Mary Magdalen. In the credits to the standard 1922 version (which omits the sequence), Grey is still listed as the Magdalen and no credit appears for The Woman Taken in Adultery, who is a much more haggard, guilt-ridden figure. Griffith's fascination with the Magdalen figure can also be seen in a Biograph film of 1910, *The Way of the World*, in which a young priest (Henry Walthall), trying to put the New Testament into practice, succeeds in doing so only in the last episode, a typological reenactment of the Magdalen story. On the Magdalen tradition in Victorian discourse on prostitution, see Riegel, "Changing American Attitudes Toward Prostitution," pp. 443–44.

18. See *The Philadelphia North American* (Dec. 30, 1916), a paper that called for a boycott of *Intolerance* on behalf of the Charity Trust, accusing the film of making the argument "for legalized and legally tolerated houses of prostitution." The reviewer seems particularly outraged about the way the "beautiful story" of the Woman Taken in Adultery is linked "with a police raid on a bevy of frowsy strumpets, the inference being that Christ's way of dealing with the modern social cesspool would be to let it go on unmolested."

19. Sigmund Freud, "A Special Type of Choice of Object Made by Men" (1910), *Standard Edition* 11: 164–75; also see "On the Universal Tendency to Debasement in the Sphere of Love" (1912), *SE* 11: 178–90; quotation in next paragraph, *SE* 11: 173. A classic example of an adolescent fantasy rehearsing the split analyzed by Freud and the concomitant turn to a prostitute figure can be found in a short story Griffith wrote in his later years, "It Never Happened" (Griffith Papers, reel 19).

20. Nick Browne, "Griffith's Family Discourse: Griffith and Freud," *Quarterly Review of Film Studies* 6. 1 (Winter 1981): 79.

21. Rogin elaborates on Sweet's role in *Judith* in a convincing argument as to why Griffith, in *Birth*, replaced her with Gish: "Blanche Sweet, in spite of her name, was neither white nor sweet enough to play Elsie Stoneman" ("Sword," pp. 159–60,

163–64). On the reversibility of Griffith's rescue scenario even with Gish, see ibid., p. 190.

22. Browne, "Griffith's Family Discourse," p. 79.

23. Harron was to play yet another role which emphasized the Oedipally defeated aspect of his persona. In *Hearts of the World* (1918), the Harron character is trapped inside with the helpless woman, this time in a romantic death pact with Gish; only in joint hysterical frenzy does he succeed in killing the Hun who is threatening from outside. In the prologue to *The Mother and the Law* (1919), Jenkins is equated with the German Kaiser.

24. Rogin, "Sword," pp. 173–74; Schickel, *Griffith*, ch. 1. Psychoanalytically inspired readings like Rogin's seize upon Griffith's obsession with his father's sword, first reported and embellished in great detail by Henry Stephen Gordon, "The Story of David Wark Griffith: His Early Years: His Struggles: His Ambitions and Their Achievement," pt. 1, *Photoplay Magazine* 10.1 (June 1916): 31, 35 (partly reprinted in *Focus on D. W. Griffith*, pp. 13ff.).

25. Gordon, "Story of Griffith," p. 35; Robert M. Henderson, *D. W. Griffith: His Life and Work* (New York: Oxford University Press, 1972), pp. 23–26 (also on Griffith's mother); Schickel, *Griffith*, pp. 24, 26, 34. Gordon registers that Mattie's choice was unusual for a young woman of her time and background: "Miss Griffith had herself fought for an education, and she in Griffith fashion obtained what she wanted, and gave it again to her slender, sensitive brother" (p. 31). Browne notes Mattie's significance, but then shifts his attention to the father's sword ("Griffith's Family Discourse," pp. 72–73).

26. Walter Benjamin, "Central Park" (1938–39), trans. Mark Harrington and Lloyd Spencer, *New German Critique* 34 (Winter 1985): 28–58; Walter Benjamin, "Paris—the Capital of the Nineteenth Century," trans. Quintin Hoare, in *Charles Baudelaire: A Lyric Poet in The Era of High Capitalism* (London: Verso, 1983), p. 171; Rosen, *Lost Sisterhood*, ch. 3, "Prostitution: Symbol of an Age."

27. Significantly, Biograph reissued the film 1917 under the title *Her Condoned Sin*.

28. Lary May, *Screening Out the Past: The Birth of Mass Culture and the Motion Picture Industry* (New York: Oxford University Press, 1980), gives a plot summary that still testifies to the repressed incestuous power of the Jenkins' sibling relationship: "Griffith shows a wealthy manufacturer and his reformer wife policing the innocent amusements of the workers" (p. 84).

29. Max Horkheimer and Theodor W. Adorno, *Dialectic of Enlightenment* (1947; New York: Seabury Press, 1972), pp. 32–34, 59–60.

30. Benjamin, "Paris," 170–71. Also see Susan Buck-Morss, "The Flaneur, the Sandwichman and the Whore: The Politics of Loitering," *New German Critique* 39 (Fall 1986): 99–140; 120ff.; and Christine Buci-Glucksmann, "Catastrophic Utopia: The Feminine as Allegory of the Modern," *Representations* 14 (Spring 1986): 220–29; 224.

31. Dudley Andrew, "BROKEN BLOSSOMS: The Art and the Eros of a Perverse Text," *Quarterly Review of Film Studies* 6.1 (Winter 1981): 83. The literal and meta-

phorical association of the cinema with the prostitute is somewhat more prominent in early German discourse on the cinema; see Miriam Hansen, "Early Silent Cinema: Whose Public Sphere?" *New German Critique* 29 (Spring–Summer 1983): 174–75.

32. Rogin, "Great Mother."

33. That this kind of symbolism was intended is suggested by Karl Brown's account of his initiation to the Griffith's crew's vernacular humor regarding phallic symbols, occasioned by his own time-lapse shot of a drooping lily, *Adventures*, pp. 39–42.

34. Bernard Hanson, "D. W. Griffith: Some Sources," *Art Bulletin* 54.4 (December 1972): 508–11; Herodotus, *The Histories* (Harmondsworth: Penguin, 1972), pp. 120–121, on the marriage market, prostitution, and other interesting sexual customs in ancient Babylon.

35. Sondra R. Herman, "Loving Courtship or the Marriage Market? The Ideal and Its Critics, 1871–1911," *American Quarterly* 25 (May 1973): 237.

36. Linda Williams, "Film Body: An Implantation of Perversions," *Ciné-Tracts*, 3.4 (Winter 1981): 19–35; 28ff.; Lucy Fisher, "The Lady Vanishes: Women, Magic, and the Movies," in John L. Fell, ed., *Film Before Griffith* (Berkeley: University of California Press, 1983), pp. 339–54. According to Joseph Henabery, after *Intolerance* was edited Griffith went back East to shoot additional footage for Belshazzar's Feast—of "some naked women he'd dug up from the red-light district"—because "some of the powers that be said, 'You ought to have more sex in it'" (Brownlow, *The Parade's Gone By. . .*, pp. 63–64). These seminude shots are missing in *The Fall of Babylon* and, since they were added after the New York premiere, are not included in the MOMA reconstruction.

37. Sigmund Freud, "Fetishism" (1927), *Standard Edition*, 21: 147–57; "The Splitting of the Ego in the Process of Defense" (1940 [1938]), *SE*, 23: 271–78; on the difference between the earlier and the later essay, see J. Laplanche and J.-B. Pontalis, *The Language of Psychoanalysis*, trans. Donald Nicholson-Smith (New York: W. W. Norton, 1973), p. 119.

38. Benjamin, "Paris," 164–66; *Das Passagen-Werk* 1 (Frankfurt am Main: Suhrkamp, 1983), sec. G: "Exhibitions, Advertising, Grandville." Benjamin elaborates the concept of "distraction," borrowed from Siegfried Kracauer, in "The Work of Art in the Age of Mechanical Reproduction" and "Some Motifs in Baudelaire," *Illuminations*, trans. Harry Zohn (New York: Schocken, 1969), pp. 234–41, 163–65, 174–76. Also see Robert W. Rydell, *All the World's a Fair: Visions of Empire at American International Expositions, 1876–1916* (Chicago: University of Chicago Press, 1984); and Reid Badger, *The Great American Fair: The World's Columbian Exposition and American Culture* (Chicago: Nelson Hall, 1979)

39. Brown, *Adventures*, p. 120. Also see Philippe Jullian, *The Orientalists: European Painters of Eastern Scenes*, trans. H. and D. Harrison (Oxford: Phaidon, 1977); on Orientalism in American dance, especially on Ruth St. Denis, see Elizabeth Kendall, *Where She Danced* (New York: Knopf, 1979).

40. On Griffith's resistance to the star system, see Chapter 5, at note 23.

41. "In contrast to the liberal era, industrialized culture, like its *völkisch* counterpart, may wax indignant at capitalism; but it cannot renounce the threat of castration. The latter, however, is fundamental to its existence." Horkheimer and Adorno, *Dialectic of Enlightenment*, p. 141 (trans. revised).

42. The phrase is from Benjamin, "Paris," 166; also see *Passagen-Werk* 1, section on "Fashion" convolutes B 3,8; B 9,1; B 9,3.

43. One might read the ideological ambiguity of the Babylonian narrative, its status as both Utopia and Whore (the decadence justly punished by the narrative), in terms of the ambivalence that Freud observed in behavior toward the fetish, as oscillating between tenderness and hostility; "Fetishism," *SE*, 21: 156–57.

11. Male Star, Female Fans

1. One such model is David Bordwell, Janet Staiger, and Kristin Thompson, *The Classical Hollywood Cinema: Film Style and Mode of Production to 1960* (New York: Columbia University Press, 1985). For a critique of that model, see Rick Altman, "Dickens, Griffith and Film Theory Today," *South Atlantic Quarterly* 88.2 (Spring 1989): 321–359. Also see Chapter 2, following note 81.

2. Richard Dyer, *Stars* (London: British Film Institute, 1979); Christine Gledhill, ed., *Star Signs: Papers from a Weekend Workshop* (London: British Film Institute, 1982) pp. 47–54; James Donald, "Stars," in Pam Cook, ed., *The Cinema Book* (New York: Pantheon, 1985), pp. 50–56.

3. Richard deCordova, "Dialogue" (reponse to my essay, "Pleasure, Ambivalence, Identification: Valentino and Female Spectatorship"), *Cinema Journal* 26.3 (Spring 1987): 55, 56. DeCordova also cites the cartoon reproduced here. Also see Lea Jacobs and Richard deCordova, "Spectacle and Narrative Theory," *Quarterly Review of Film Studies* 7.4 (Fall 1982): 293–303.

4. See Richard deCordova, "The Emergence of the Star System in America," *Wide Angle* 6.4 (1985): 4–13; and Janet Staiger, "Seeing Stars," *Velvet Light Trap* 20 (Summer 1983): 10–14, and *Classical Hollywood Cinema*, ch. 9; Tom Gunning, *D. W. Griffith and the Origins of American Narrative Film* (Urbana: University of Illinois Press, 1991), ch. 7.

5. See Tino Balio, *United Artists: The Company Built by the Stars* (Madison: University of Wisconsin Press, 1976); Richard Dyer, *Heavenly Bodies: Film Stars and Society* (New York: St. Martin's, 1986), pp. 6–7 and passim; Robert Sklar, *Movie-Made America* (New York: Random House, 1975), ch. 5.

6. Laura Mulvey, "Afterthoughts . . . Inspired by *Duel in the Sun*," *Framework* 15–17 (1981): 12; Laura Mulvey, "Visual Pleasure and Narrative Cinema" originally appeared in *Screen* 16.3 (Autumn 1977): 6–18.

7. For a still useful discussion of Mulvey in the larger context of recent film theory, see Christine Gledhill, "Developments in Feminist Film Criticism" (1978),

rpt. in Mary Ann Doane, Patricia Mellencamp, and Linda Williams, eds., *Re-Vision: Essays in Feminist Film Criticism*, AFI Monograph Series 3 (Frederick, Md.: University Publications of America, 1983), pp. 18–48. Among articles devoted primarily to a critique of Mulvey, see David Rodowick, "The Difficulty of Difference," *Wide Angle* 5.1 (1982): 4–15; Janet Walker, "Psychoanalysis and Feminist Film Theory," *Wide Angle* 6.3 (1984): 16–23. For discussions challenging the Metzian-Mulveyan paradigm of spectatorship altogether, see Gaylyn Studlar, "Masochism and the Perverse Pleasures of the Cinema," *Quarterly Review of Film Studies* 9.4 (Fall 1984): 267–82; Gertrud Koch, "Exchanging the Gaze: Re-Visioning Feminist Film Theory," *New German Critique* 34 (Winter 1985): 139–53.

8. "Afterthoughts," p. 12.

9. On the trope of transvestism, in particular its different uses by male and female writers, see Sandra M. Gilbert, "Costumes of the Mind: Transvestism as Metaphor in Modern Literature," *Critical Inquiry* 7.2 (Winter 1980): 391–417; esp. 404ff. On the theoretical significance of sexual mobility in a particular period of film history and mass culture, see Patrice Petro, *Joyless Streets: Women and Melodramatic Representation in Weimar Germany* (Princeton: Princeton University Press, 1989), pp. 221ff., 110ff.

10. Mary Ann Doane, "Film and the Masquerade: Theorising the Female Spectator," *Screen* 23.3–4 (September–October 1982): 81.

11. The question of temporality has been raised as a crucial aspect of female spectatorship by Teresa de Lauretis, *Alice Doesn't: Feminism, Semiotics, Cinema* (Bloomington: Indiana University Press, 1984), pp. 96ff.; also compare Tania Modleski, "Time and Desire in the Woman's Film," *Cinema Journal* 23.3 (Spring 1984): 19–30. Modleski refers to Julia Kristeva, "Women's Time," trans. Alice Jardine and Harry Blake, *Signs* 7.1 (1981): 13–35. For a discussion of the conflicting temporal registers of gendered areas of social experience, see Oskar Negt and Alexander Kluge, *Öffentlichkeit und Erfahrung* (Frankfurt am Main: Suhrkamp, 1972), pp. 45–74. Also see Chapter 3, at note 40.

12. Mary Ann Doane, *The Desire to Desire: The Woman's Film of the 1940s* (Bloomington: Indiana University Press, 1987), p. 13. Also see Doane, "The 'Woman's Film': Possession and Address," in Doane, Mellencamp, and Williams, *Re-Vision*, pp. 67–82.

13. Linda Williams, "'Something Else Besides a Mother': *Stella Dallas* and the Maternal Melodrama," *Cinema Journal* 24.1 (Fall 1984): 2–27; Tania Modleski, *Loving with a Vengeance: Mass Produced Fantasies for Women* (1982; New York: Methuen, 1984). Also see Annette Kuhn, "Women's Genres: Melodrama, Soap Opera and Theory," *Screen* 25.1 (January–February 1984): 18–28, rpt. in Christine Gledhill, ed., *Home Is Where the Heart Is: Studies in Melodrama and the Woman's Film* (London: BFI, 1987); and other essays in that collection.

14. Williams, "'Something Else,'" in part responds to E. Ann Kaplan, "The Case of the Missing Mother: Maternal Issues in Vidor's *Stella Dallas*," *Heresies* 16 (1983): 81–85; Kaplan's reply appeared in *Cinema Journal* 24.2 (Winter 1985): 40–43. The debate continued with contributions by Patrice Petro and Carol Flinn, *CJ* 25.1 (Fall

1985): 50–54; Tag Gallagher, Tania Modleski, and Linda Williams, *CJ* 25.2 (Winter 1986): 65–67; Christine Gledhill and E. Ann Kaplan, *CJ* 25.4 (Summer 1986): 44–53.

15. See Judith Mayne, "Feminist Film Theory and Women at the Movies," *Profession* 87 (New York: Modern Language Association of America, 1987), pp. 14–19; Tania Modleski, "Rape versus Mans/laughter: Hitchcock's *Blackmail* and Feminist Interpretation," *PMLA* 102.3 (May 1987): 304–15; Mary Ann Doane, "Masquerade Reconsidered: Further Thoughts on the Female Spectator," *Discourse* 11.1 (Fall–Winter 1988–89): 42–54, esp. 49ff.; and Diane Waldman, "Film Theory and the Gendered Spectator: The Female or the Feminist Reader," *Camera Obscura* 18 (1989): 80–94.

16. Doane, "Masquerade," 77; also see E. Ann Kaplan, *Women and Film: Both Sides of the Camera* (New York and London: Methuen, 1983), p. 29. A number of critics have focused on the representation of the male body and the question of masculinity, among them Pam Cook, "Masculinity in Crisis?" (on *Raging Bull*), *Screen* 23.3–4 (September–October 1982): 39–53; Richard Dyer, "Don't Look Now: The Male Pin-Up," ibid., 61–73; Steve Neale, "Masculinity as Spectacle," *Screen* 24.6 (November–December 1983): 2–16.

17. De Lauretis, *Alice Doesn't*, p. 83.

18. Much of this material is available in the Theatre collection, New York Public Library at Lincoln Center, clippings on microfilm and in scrapbooks (bibliographic information often incomplete). For a filmography and bibliography, compiled by Diane Kaiser Koszarski, see Eva Orbanz, ed., *There Is A New Star in Heaven. . .: Valentino* (Berlin: Volker Spiess, 1979); also Alexander Walker, *Rudolph Valentino* (Harmondsworth: Penguin, 1976). Among the slew of popular biographies, varying mostly in terms of the type of mythology that has become Valentino's life, see Brad Steiger and Chaw Mank, *Valentino: An Intimate and Shocking Exposé* (New York: MacFadden, 1966); Edouard Ramond, *La vie amoureuse de Rudolph Valentino* (Paris: Librairie Baudiniere, n.d.); Vincent Tajiri, *Valentino: The True Life Story* (New York: Bantam, 1977); Irving Shulman, *Valentino* (1967; New York: Pocket Books, 1968); Noel Botham and Peter Donnelly, *Valentino: The Love God* (New York: Ace Books, 1977). Sources I did not consult include internal studio communications, studio contracts, and court proceedings. Important insights might also be gained by pursuing the methods of oral history, especially in tracing Valentino's reception by nonwhite women or gay men.

19. I find this perspective elaborated in feminist terms in much of the German film journal *Frauen und Film*, edited by Gertrud Koch and Heide Schlüpmann. Also see Chapter 3, last paragraph.

20. Janes Gaines and Michael Renov, "Preface" to special issue on *Female Representation and Consumer Culture, Quarterly Review of Film and Video* 11.1 (1989): viii.

21. Gaylyn Studlar, "Discourses of Gender and Ethnicity: The Construction and De(con)struction of Rudolph Valentino as Other," *Film Criticism* 13.2 (1989): 19.

I am grateful to Gaylyn Studlar for letting me read a manuscript version of this article which in part responds to my earlier essay on Valentino: Miriam Hansen, *Cinema Journal* 25.4 (Summer 1986): 6–32.

22. John Higham, *Strangers in the Land: Patterns of American Nativism 1860–1925*, 2nd. ed. (New Brunswick, N.J.: Rutgers University Press, 1988), p. 169. For more on Valentino's reception in the context of 1920s nativism, see Studlar, "Gender and Ethnicity."

23. Michael Rogin, "'The Sword Became a Flashing Vision': D. W. Griffith's *The Birth of a Nation*," *Representations* 9 (Winter 1985): 150–95; Jacqueline Dowd Hall, "The Mind That Burns in Each Body: Women, Rape, and Racial Violence," in Ann Snitow et al., eds., *Powers of Desire* (New York: Monthly Review Press, 1983), p. 337; Homi K. Bhabha, "The Other Question: The Stereotype and Colonial Discourse," *Screen* 24.6 (November–December 1983): 18–36. On the problematic concept of the New Woman, see Estelle B. Freedman, "The New Woman: Changing Views of Women in the 1920s," *Journal of American History* 56.2 (September 1974): 372–93; Mary P. Ryan, *Womanhood in America*, 2nd ed. (New York: New Viewpoints, 1979), ch. 5; Julie Matthaei, *An Economic History of Women in America* (New York: Schocken, 1982), chs. 7–9.

24. Studlar, "Gender and Ethnicity," p. 23.

25. "A Latin Lover," *Photoplay* 20.4 (September 1921): 21; *Pantomime* (September 28, 1921).

26. McElliott [sic], *News* (November 8, 1921); the reviewer goes on to link the taming of the Sheik's "natural" qualities to the "unnatural" behavior of the female protagonist: "Where Mrs. Hull's Ahmed was bold, ruthless . . ., an 'I-take-what-I-will' person . . . Mr. Valentino's is gentle, thoughtful, more or less considerate of the 'defiant English beauty' whom he captures, as she indulges her wild whim to ride unchaperoned through the desert." On the relation between the film and the novel, see Sumiko Higashi, *Virgins, Vamps, and Flappers* (Montreal: Eden Press Women's Publications, 1978), pp. 114–16, 122–23. Valentino himself supposedly acknowledged his fear of skirting the color line in an interview with Gordon Gassaway, "The Erstwhile Landscape Gardner," *Motion Picture Magazine* (July 20, 1921).

27. Dick Dorgan, "A Song of Hate," *Photoplay* 22.1 (June 1922): 26. The litany that follows starts off with an eclectic volley of ethnic-racial stereotypes: "I hate Valentino! All men hate Valentino. I hate his oriental optics; I hate his classic nose; I hate his Roman face; . . . I hate his glistening teeth; . . . I hate his patent leather hair; . . . I hate his Svengali glare." Also see, by the same author, "Giving 'The Sheik' the Once Over from the Ringside," *Photoplay* 21.5 (April 1922): 90–92.

28. Adela Rogers St. Johns, "What Kind of Men Attract Women Most?" *Photoplay* 25.5 (April 1924): 110.

29. For example, *Detroit Times* (January 10, 1926): "Valentino will always remain what we call a Foreigner. . . . Awful? Not so awful after you meet Valentino." Also see Gassaway, "Erstwhile Landscape Gardener," *Motion Picture Magazine* (July 20,

1921); Dorothy Donnell, "Wanted: A Protective Tariff on Lovers," *Classic* (July 1924). The apologetic discourse on his ethnicity often was attributed to Valentino himself, as in "The Rise of Rudolph," *Pantomime* (February 11, 1922): 12.

30. Anne Jordan, "R Stands for Rudy and Romance," *Movie Magazine* (September 1925): 40.

31. Announcement for upcoming installments of Rudolph Valentino, "My Life Story," *Photoplay* 23.2 (January 1923): 34–35; syndicated story, *Evening Telegram* (New York), May 28, 1922. To the more highbrow critics of culture, Valentino came to symbolize the failure of the American Dream; see, for instance, H. L. Mencken, "On Hollywood—and Valentino," *Prejudices: Sixth Series* (New York: Knopf, 1927), pp. 290–311; rpt. *Cinema Journal* 9.2 (Spring 1970): 13–23, and John Dos Passos, *The Big Money* (1936). Ken Russell's film, *Valentino* (1977), based on the Steiger and Mank biography and starring Nureyev in the title role, articulates this theme through its pervasive references to *Citizen Kane*, such as the use of a post-mortem multiple flashback narration and other corny allusions.

32. Kaja Silverman, "Fragments of a Fashionable Discourse," in Tania Modleski, ed., *Studies in Entertainment: Critical Approaches to Mass Culture* (Bloomington: Indiana University Press, 1986), pp. 139–52; the phrase, "Great Masculine Renunciation," was introduced by J. C. Flugel, *The Psychology of Clothes* (London: Hogarth, 1930), see Silverman, "Fragments." pp. 140ff.

33. Lewis Erenberg, *Steppin' Out* (Chicago: University of Chicago Press, 1981), p. 84.

34. "The Sheik," *Globe*, November 1921; review of *The Young Rajah, Elmir*, Nov. 15, 1922; review of *A Sainted Devil, Sun*, Nov. 24, 1924. The article featuring the cartoon is Don Ryan, "Has the Great Lover Become Just a Celebrity?" *Classic* (May 1926): 20–21, 69, 78.

35. "Do Women Like Masterful Men?" *New Orleans Item*, Oct. 9, 1921. Also see *Baltimore News*, Oct. 22, 1922: "'No matter whether they are feminists, suffragettes, or so-called new women, they like to have a masterful man make them do things,' he asserts"; and *Examiner-New Era*, Sept. 29, 1921: "'She likes domination—perhaps secretly, but she likes it just the same.'"

36. Richard Dyer observes a similar dynamic of racial difference, fetishization, and feminization in representations of Paul Robeson, see *Heavenly Bodies: Film Stars and Society* (New York: St. Martin's Press, 1986), pp. 115ff.

37. Studlar, "Gender and Ethnicity," p. 21.

38. The *Boston Daily Advertiser*, for instance, ran sensationalist coverage of Valentino's visit to Boston along the lines of "10,000 Girls Mob 'World's Greatest Kisser': . . . At City Hall Police Battle Mad Wave of Femininity" (Jan. 16, 1923): 5. By contrast, the *Boston Post* (which sponsored Valentino's visit), covering the same events speaks of "men and women" involved in the mobbing of the star; women are singled out, along with children of course, in connection with safety concerns.

39. Ryan, "Great Lover," p. 78.

40. See, for example, "Over the Tea Cups," *Movie Weekly* (Dec. 17, 1921): 19 (a

writer eavesdropping on a conversation between three "girls" in a tea room); Gladys Hall, "Women I like to Dance With, by Rudolph Valentino," *Movie Weekly* (Jan. 27, 1923): 7; Gladys Hall and Adele Whitely Fletcher, "We Discover Who Discovered Valentino: A Playlet in One Act and Three Scenes," *Motion Picture* (June 1923). The collective aspect of women's reception of Valentino also emerged from some of the interviews I conducted with women who participated in the cult in their youth. On the homosocial dimension of "collective daydreams," see Hans Sachs (psychoanalytic advisor to G. W. Pabst on *Secrets of a Soul*), "Gemeinsame Tagträume," *Imago Bücher* 5 (1924): 3–36; 8–9.

41. James R. Quirk (Editor of *Photoplay*), "Presto Chango Valentino!" *Photoplay* 27.6 (May 1925): 36–37, 117. His destructive reputation notwithstanding, a remarkably high number of women actually participated in the production of Valentino's films (although this usually was more often the case in film production prior to 1930). His most important films had scripts written by women, in particular June Mathis and Frances Marion; many of the sets and costumes were designed by Rambova; and *Blood and Sand* was brilliantly edited by Dorothy Arzner.

42. "Are Wives of Screen Lovers Jealous?" *Motion Picture Stories* 25.268 (Jan. 6, 1925).

43. Among the numerous popular biographies, *Valentino* by Steiger and Mank specializes in rumors of this kind, as does Ken Russell's film, *Valentino* (1977). Also see Kenneth Anger, "Rudy's Rep," *Hollywood Babylon* (New York: Dell, 1981), pp. 155–70.

44. Review of *Cobra*, *Graphic* (Dec. 8, 1925); "Eyes of Valentino," no ref., scrapbook, New York Public Library, Lincoln Center; anonymous "psychologist," "The Vogue of Valentino," *Motion Picture Magazine* (February 1923): 27–28. On the pervasive comparison between Valentino and Theda Bara, see Robert C. Toll, *The Entertainment Machine: American Show Business in the Twentieth Century* (New York: Oxford University Press, 1982), pp. 190–91.

45. Mae Tinnee, "Come to Mother!" clipping (no ref.). Also see *Screenland* (January 1923): "Sometimes he looks exactly like a small boy who is being abused, so that every woman instinctively wants to pat his shiny black head and comfort him. Yet she knows perfectly well that he is not a small boy and that it would be rather like patting dynamite. Which, of course, makes him very *interesting*." And Winifred Van Duzer, "The Battle of the Male Beauties: Choose Your Favorites!" *Pittsburgh Times Gazette* (March 4, 1923): "Rodolph has been naughty; Rodolph must be spanked."

46. Both the Pink Powder Puff attack and Valentino's response are reprinted in Steiger and Mank, *Valentino*, pp. 167–70; also see Anger, "Rudy's Rep," and Mencken, "On Hollywood—and Valentino."

47. Dorgan, "Song of Hate."

48. Kenneth Anger, "Valentino Remembered, Valentino Discovered," in Orbanz, *A New Star in Heaven*, pp. 19–22, and Karsten Witte's discussion of Anger's Valentino worship in "Fetisch-Messen," *Frauen und Film* 38 (May 1985): 72–78. Elvis Presley was another avowed admirer of Valentino. On the significance of Valentino

for the tradition of gay male subculture, see interviews collected in *Before Stonewall* (Archive for Gay and Lesbian History, New York).

49. "Are You an Indifferent Husband?" Advertisement for "The Vogue of Valentino" (note 44), *Motion Picture Magazine* (January 1923).

50. Ryan, "Great Lover," p. 78.

51. Larzer Ziff, *The American 1890s* (1966; Lincoln: University of Nebraska Press, 1979), p. 273, quoted in Leonard Kriegel, *On Men and Manhood* (New York: Hawthorn Books, 1979), p. 78. Also see Peter Gabriel Filene, *Him/Her/Self: Sex Roles in Modern America* (New York: Harcourt Brace Jovanovich, 1974), pp. 77–104.

52. "Rodolph Valentino Blames Trust for Our Poor Movies: Champion Lover of the Screen Bemoans Triumph of Art over Industry," *Boston Telegram* (Jan. 26, 1923): "Seventy-five per cent of the motion pictures shown today are a brazen insult to human intelligence. This is because the trusts are producing pictures as a matter of industry—not art—and are employing factory methods." The most detailed version of this indictment seems to be "What's the Matter with the Movies?" *Illustrated World* (May 1923): 342–44, 422, 426ff. Invariably, this line of defense tries to distance Valentino from his erotic commodification in *The Sheik*: "Art, Not Film Profits, Lures Valentino in Legal Battle: Screen Actor Says He Hates Himself for Work He Did in 'The Sheik'; Wants a Chance to Show Public That He Can Do Greater Things," *Tribune* (Sept. 2, 1922); J. K. Winkler, "I'm Tired of Being a Sheik" (interview), *Colliers* (January 1926): 28.

53. Quirk, "Presto," pp. 36–37.

54. Rudolph Valentino, "Muscles in the Movies: How Physical Culture Made Me a Screen Star," *Muscle Builder* (August 1924); T. Howard Kelly, "Red Blood and Plenty of Sand," *Physical Culture* (February 1923): 27–29, 138–39; ads for the latter beckoned the reader with rhetorical questions like: "Do you know that Rudolph Valentino has the muscular development and chest expansion of a Roman gladiator?" Also see "Who Said Lounge Lizard?" *Screenland* (February 1923), as well as a lengthy article on Valentino's pipe, "Rodolph Valentino's Big Comfort," *Movie Weekly* 3.27 (Aug. 11, 1923). On the vicissitudes of representations of the male body, see Dyer, "Don't Leave Now," and Neale, "Masculinity as Spectacle." On the shift from moral to physical notions of selfhood in the historical construction of masculinity, see E. Anthony Rotundo, "Body and Soul: Changing Ideals of American Middle-Class Manhood, 1770–1920," *Journal of Social History* 16.4 (Summer 1983): 23–38.

55. Willene Taylor, "Rodolf Wants to Be a Cowboy," *Chicago Herald* (Sept. 8, 1922); anon., "No Woman Said Last Good-bye to Rudy—No Deathbed Kiss for Rudy," *Mirror* (Aug. 23, 1926).

56. "Rudolph Valentino to Change His Act? Advisers of the Film Star Would Make Him a Real He-Man," *World* (Nov. 22, 1925).

57. See Shulman, *Valentino*: "Act V: Cuckooland." The increased dissociation of the signifier Valentino from any empirical basis became itself a topic of discourse: "Valentino and Yellow Journalism," *The Nation* (Sept. 8, 1926): 207.

58. Lois Banner, *American Beauty* (Chicago and London: University of Chicago

Press, 1983), pp. 226–48. For an example of a contemporary writer noting Valentino's redefinition of the terms of masculinity, see the review of *Four Horsemen*, *Boston Evening Record* (April 28, 1921): "A wonderful portrayal of a real man subjecting to all the errors of a great love and committing none of the gaucheries."

12. *Patterns of Vision, Scenarios of Identification*

1. For a filmography, see works cited in Chapter 11, note 18.

2. Sigmund Freud, "Three Essays on the Theory of Sexuality" (1905), *Standard Edition*, 7: 182.

3. Laura Mulvey, "Visual Pleasure and Narrative Cinema," *Screen* 16.3 (1975): 11.

4. See Kaja Silverman, "Fragments of a Fashionable Discourse," in Tania Modleski, ed., *Studies in Entertainment: Critical Approaches to Mass Culture* (Bloomington: Indiana University Press, 1986), pp. 139–52.

5. A more misogynist version of the same pattern occurs in *Cobra* (1925), when a friend advises the unhappily courting but much pursued Valentino, "look at the woman with the torch: she is safe!"—cut to the Statue of Liberty. For an excellent reading of these "duels" and "ballets" of the gaze, see Karsten Witte, "Rudolph Valentino: Erotoman des Augenblicks," in Adolf Heinzlmeier et al., eds., *Die Unsterblichen des Kinos* (Frankfurt am Main: Fischer, 1982), I, 29–35.

6. Sigmund Freud, "Instincts and their Vicissitudes," trans. James Strachey, *Standard Edition*, 14: 128ff.; "Three Essays," *SE*, 7: 156ff., 199–200, and passim.

7. I am much indebted here to Gertrud Koch, "Why Women Go to the Movies," *Jump Cut* 27 (July 1982), and "Von der weiblichen Sinnlichkeit und ihrer Lust und Unlust am Kino: Mutmaßungen über vergangene Freuden und neue Hoffnungen," in Gabriele Dietze, ed., *Die Überwindung der Sprachlosigkeit* (Darmstadt: Luchterhand, 1979), pp. 116–38.

8. Sigmund Freud, "The Psycho-Analytic View of Psychogenic Disturbance of Vision" (1910), *Standard Edition*, 11: 216–17.

9. For an elaboration of this aspect of Freud's essay, see Stephen Heath, "Difference," *Screen* 19.3 (Autumn 1978): 86–87.

10. Christa Karpenstein, "Bald führt der Blick das Wort ein, bald leitet das Wort den Blick," *Kursbuch* 49 (1977): 62. Also see Jutta Brückner's important essay on pornography, "Der Blutfleck im Auge der Kamera," *Frauen und Film* 30 (December 1981): 13–23; Brückner links the historical "underdevelopment" of women's vision with the modality of dreams, as a more archaic form of consciousness: "This female gaze, which is so precise precisely because it is not too precise, because it also has this inward turn, opening itself to phantasy images which it melts with the more literal images on the screen, this gaze is the basis for a kind of identification which women in particular tend to seek in the cinema" (p. 19).

11. The discrepancy between the advertising pitch and Valentino's actual lack of orientation and focus is obvious in the promotional short *Rudolph Valentino and His Eighty-Eight American Beauties* (1923), which shows him as a somewhat halfhearted

arbiter in a beauty contest. Even Roland Barthes's compelling reading of the Valentinian face emphasizes the aggressive aspect of his gaze: "The face is mysterious, full of exotic splendor, of an inaccessible, Baudelairean beauty, undoubtedly made of exquisite dough; but one knows all too well that this cold glistening of make-up, this delicate, dark line under the animal eye, the black mouth—all this betrays a mineral substance, a cruel statue which comes to life only to thrust forth." ("Le visage est arcane, splendeur exotique, beauté baudelairienne, inaccessible, d'une pâte exquise sans doute, mais on sait bien que cette froid luisance du fard, ce mince trait sombre sous l'oeil d'animal, cette bouche noire, tout cela est d'un être minéral, d'une statue cruelle qui ne s'anime que pour percer" ["Visages et figures," *Esprit* 204 (July 1953): 7]). The metaphor of piercing or thrusting, however, only confirms the suspicion that the Valentinian gaze is a substitute for phallic potency, hence the fetishistic cult surrounding it.

12. Two of Valentino's most popular films, *The Four Horsemen* and *Blood and Sand*, actually culminate in the protagonist's death, bringing into play the deep affinity of eros and death drive that Freud observes in his fascinating paper on "The Theme of the Three Caskets" (1913), SE 12: 289–301. According to Enno Patalas, Valentino identified much more strongly with these two roles than with the superficial heroism of the Sheik, *Sozialgeschichte der Stars* (Hamburg: Marion von Schröder Verlag, 1963) pp. 96–97.

13. See, for example, Janet Walker, "Psychoanalysis and Feminist Film Theory," *Wide Angle* 6.3 (1984): 20ff.; Teresa de Lauretis, "Aesthetic and Feminist Theory," *New German Critique* 34 (Winter 1985): 154–75; 164ff.

14. Mary Ann Doane, "Misrecognition and Identity," *Ciné-Tracts* 3.3 (Fall 1980): 25; Metz, *The Imaginary Signifier*, pp. 46ff., 56–57, and passim.

15. Suffice it here to invoke the work of Stephen Heath, Raymond Bellour, and Thierry Kuntzel; also compare the section on Point of View in *Film Reader* 4 (1979).

16. This option actually prevails in contemporary statements of female spectators; see Herbert Blumer, *Movies and Conduct* (New York: MacMillan, 1933), pp. 69–70. In retrospect, however, as I frequently found in conversations with women who were in their teens at the time, the female star has faded into oblivion as much as the narrative, whereas Valentino himself is remembered with great enthusiasm and vividness of detail.

17. John Pratt, "Notes on Commercial Movie Technique," *International Journal of Psycho-Analysis* 34.3–4 (1943): 186, quoted and elaborated in Harriet E. Margolis, *The Cinema Ideal: An Introduction to Psychoanalytic Studies of the Film Spectator* (New York and London: Garland, 1988), pp. 148–49. On the theoretical blind spot of Metz's concept of primary identification, see Doane, "Misrecognition and Identity," pp. 28ff.; Doane's major objection is that since this concept is based on the analogy with the Lacanian mirror stage and hence the hypothetical constitution of the male subject, on a theoretical level the notion of primary identification perpetuates, the patriarchal exclusion of female spectatorship.

18. See Richard Dyer, *Stars* (London: British Film Institute, 1979).

19. This pattern of combining dark and light oppositions in one and the same character must have been perceived as typical of the Valentino text; thus, Dubrovsky's alias in *The Eagle* was changed from Pushkin's Monsieur Deforge to Valentino's Monsieur LeBlanc.

20. *Sun*, Nov. 24, 1924.

21. Dressing up Valentino is a major theme in *Rudy: An Intimate Portrait of Rudolph Valentino by his Wife Natacha Rambova* (London: Hutchinson, 1926). Given his own sartorial extravagance as well as his being a phenomenon of fashion, it is curious how little the films participated in the promotion of contemporary clothing styles. Only three of Valentino's major films, as far as I can tell, cast him in modern dress. In this context, one might also consider the link between transsexual and transhistorical changes of costumes in Virginia Woolf's *Orlando* (1928); compare Sandra M. Gilbert, "Costumes of the Mind: Transvestism as Metaphor in Modern Literature," *Critical Inquiry* 7.2 (Winter 1980): 406.

22. Sigmund Freud, *Group Psychology and The Analysis of the Ego* (1921), *Standard Edition*, 18: 108. Also see Margolis, *Cinema Ideal*, pp. 148–49, and ch. 5, and Anne Friedberg, "A Denial of Difference: Theories of Cinematic Identification," in E. Ann Kaplan, ed., *Psychoanalysis and Cinema* (London: Routledge, 1990).

23. A number of critics have commented recently upon the role of sadomasochistic structures in cinematic identification, for instance, D. N. Rodowick, "The Difficulty of Difference," *Wide Angle* 5.1 (1982): 4–15; Mary Ann Doane, "The Woman's Film: Possession and Address," in Mary Ann Doane, Patricia Mellencamp, Linda Williams eds., *Re-Vision: Essays in Feminist Film Criticism* (Frederick, Md.: University Publications of America, 1983), pp. 67–82; Kaja Silverman, "Masochism and Subjectivity" (on Cavani's *Portiere di Notte*), *Framework* 12 (1980): 2–9. Also compare Jessica Benjamin, "Master and Slave: The Fantasy of Erotic Domination," in Ann Snitow et al., eds., *Powers of Desire: The Politics of Sexuality*, (New York: Monthly Review Press, 1983), pp. 280–99.

24. Gertrud Koch, "Schattenreich der Körper: Zum pornographischen Kino," *Lust und Elend: Das erotische Kino* (Munich: Bucher, 1981), p. 35; trans. "The Body's Shadow Realm," *October* 50 (Fall 1989): 3–29. The investment in eros as a negation of the principle of social identity is of course a topos of the Frankfurt School, especially in the work of Theodor W. Adorno; see his and Max Horkheimer's critique of the subject under patriarchy and monopoly capitalism in *Dialectic of Enlightenment* (1947); his fragments, dating back to the period of exile, in *Minima Moralia* (1951), as well as later essays in cultural criticism such as "Sexualtabus und Recht heute," *Eingriffe* (Frankfurt am Main: Suhrkamp, 1963), p. 104.

25. Vincent Tajiri, *Valentino: The True Life Story* (New York: Bantam, 1977), p. 63.

26. Consider, for instance, a sequence early on in the Pickford vehicle, *Sparrows* (1926), in which the villain (Gustav von Seyffertitz) crushes a doll sent by an absent mother to one of the children he keeps as slaves; the camera lingers, close-up, on the remnants of the doll as it slowly dissappears in the swamp. The fascination deployed in such a shot far exceeds narrative motivation, that is, its function for establishing

Mr. Grimes as irredeemably evil. Gaylyn Studlar makes a case for an association of the eroticized male body with suffering similar to Valentino in films starring John Barrymore, specifically *Beloved Rogue*: "When a Man Loves: Male Spectacle and Female Pleasure in Romantic Melodramas of the 1920s," paper delivered at the annual convention of the Society for Cinema Studies, Iowa City, April 1989.

27. Sigmund Freud, "Three Essays," *Standard Edition*, 7: 160; also "Instincts," *SE*, 14: 126.

28. Most notably in "The Economic Problem of Masochism" (1924), *SE* 19: 155–70, where Freud develops the notion of a "primary" masochism linked to the death instinct; this notion is already present though rejected in "Instincts and Their Vicissitudes" (1915), *SE* 14: 127, but resumed as early as 1920, in *Beyond the Pleasure Principle, SE*, 18: 55.

29. Gaylyn Studlar, "Masochism and the Perverse Pleasures of the Cinema," *Quarterly Review of Film Studies* 9.4 (Fall 1984): 267–82; Gilles Deleuze, *Masochism: An Interpretation of Coldness and Cruelty* (France 1967; New York: George Braziller, 1971), pp. 21, 37–38. Studlar acknowledges the problem of the male perspective of the Sacher-Masoch fantasy in passing (p. 270 and n. 27). The reason why Deleuze's model seems to work so surprisingly well for the Sternberg-Dietrich films might have less to do with the validity of the model than with Sternberg's endebtedness to the same cultural background that gave us *Venus in Furs*.

30. The essay has been much discussed in recent film theory, for example, Rodowick, "The Difficulty of Difference," and Doane, "The Woman's Film." On the beating fantasy in the context of "daydreaming," see Anna Freud, "Schlagephantasie und Tagtraum," *Imago* 8 (1922): 317–33.

31. Sigmund Freud, "A Child Is Being Beaten," *Standard Edition*, 17: 186. The English spelling distinguishes between "phantasy" (referring to a scenario of the unconscious, as in recurring types of "primal phantasies") and "fantasy" (referring to the process of fiction-making on a more conscious level, as in daydreaming), but the distinction is a sliding one because the two terms are epistemologically inseparable. See Jean Laplanche and J. B. Pontalis, *The Language of Psychoanalysis*, trans. Donald Nicholson-Smith (New York: W. W. Norton, 1973), pp. 316–19.

32. This incestuous-narcissistic aura is encapsulated in a portrait showing Valentino and Rambova in profile and, obviously, in the nude; rpt. in Walker, *Valentino*, p. 73, and Kenneth Anger, *Hollywood Babylon* (New York: Dell, 1981), pp. 160–161.

33. The radiant quality of the visual style of Valentino's films is singled out as an important "spiritual" dimension by one of the female fans overheard by a reporter in "Over the Tea Cups," *Movie Weekly* (Dec. 17, 1921): 19

34. Williams, "When the Woman Looks," in Doane, Mellencamp, and Williams, *Re-Vision*, pp. 83–96. The point Williams makes with regard to a number of classic horror films also elucidates the function of the dark-light split in the Valentino character: "the power and potency of the monster body . . . should not be interpreted as an eruption of the normally repressed animal sexuality of the civilized male

(the monster as double for the male viewer and characters in the film), but as feared power and potency of a different kind of sexuality (the monster as double for the woman)" (p. 87).

35. Adorno, "Sexualtabus," pp. 104–05; the phrase is used in English and without quotation marks; also see "This Side of the Pleasure Principle," *Minima Moralia: Reflections from Damaged Life* (London: NLB, 1974). Marcuse's plea for polymorphous perversity in *Eros and Civilization* (1955; Boston: Beacon Press, 1966) is more problematic, especially in light of the Foucauldian analysis of the "perverse implantation" (*The History of Sexuality* 1); Marcuse himself takes a more pessimistic view in his "Political Preface 1966," while maintaining a utopian distinction between sexual liberty and erotic-political freedom (pp. xiv–xv). The prophets of a "healthy sex life" already were numerous in the 1920s, drawing on the essentialist sexual psychology of Havelock Ellis, on the newly discovered "doctrine" of psychoanalysis, as well as libertarian positions developed among the Greenwich Village bohemians, though not necessarily all that liberating for women; see writings by Hutchins Hapgood, Max Eastman, V. F. Calverton, and, probably the single most repressive instance of sexual hygiene, Floyd Dell, *Love in the Machine Age: A Psychological Study of the Transition from Patriarchal Society* (1930).

36. Michel Foucault, *The History of Sexuality* I, trans. Robert Hurley (New York: Vintage, 1980), pt. two.

37. Walker, *Rudolph Valentino*, pp. 8, 47, and passim.

38. See Estelle B. Freedman, "The New Woman: Changing Views of Women in the 1920s," *Journal of American History* 56.2 (September 1974): 372–93; Mary P. Ryan, *Womanhood in America*, 2nd ed. (New York: New Viewpoints, 1979), ch. 5; Julie Matthaei, *An Economic History of Women in America* (New York: Schocken, 1982), esp. chs. 7–9.

39. *Blood and Sand*, closest to the melodramatic matrix, is the only film that makes Valentino's mate a mother. Most female characters opposite Valentino have tomboyish qualities (especially Moran in *Moran of the Lady Letty*), an air of independence, owing to either a superior social status or work, and, above all, a certain "mischievous vivacity" associated with the Flapper; see Mary Ryan, "The Projection of a New Womanhood: The Movie Moderns in the 1920s," in Jean E. Friedman and William G. Shade, eds., *Our American Sisters: Women in American Life and Thought*, 2nd ed. (Boston: Allyn & Bacon, 1976), pp. 366–84.

40. Elinor Glyn actually endorsed Valentino's sex appeal, and he starred in *Beyond the Rocks* (1922), based on one of her novels. Still, the focus on a male star distinguishes the Valentino films from films that more immediately functioned to train their audiences in "fashionable femininity"; Ryan, "Projection," pp. 370–71.

41. Barthes, "Visages et figures," p. 6.

Illustration Credits

1.1, page 26, *Uncle Josh at the Moving Picture Show* (Library of Congress / Pat Loughney)

1.2, page 27, *Uncle Josh at the Moving Picture Show* (Library of Congress / Pat Loughney)

1.3, page 50, *The "Teddy" Bears* (Edison National Historic Site / Charles Musser)

1.4, page 50, *The "Teddy" Bears* (Edison National Historic Site / Charles Musser)

1.5, page 52, *The "Teddy" Bears* (Edison National Historic Site / Charles Musser)

1.6, page 53, *The "Teddy" Bears* (Edison National Historic Site / Charles Musser)

2.1, page 72, *Romance of a Jewess* (Joyce Jesionowski)

2.2, page 75, *The Musketeers of Pig Alley* (Museum of Modern Art, Film Stills Archive)

5.1, page 144, *Intolerance* (unless noted otherwise, all frame enlargements of *Intolerance* and *The Birth of a Nation* were done by Joyce Jesionowski, courtesy of the Museum of Modern Art)

5.2, page 145, *Intolerance*

5.3, page 145, *Intolerance*

5.4, page 147, *Intolerance*

5.5, page 148, *Intolerance*

5.6, page 152, *The Birth of a Nation*

5.7, page 152, *The Birth of a Nation*

5.8, page 156, *Intolerance* (Museum of Modern Art / Film Stills Archive)

5.9, page 156, *Intolerance*

5.10, page 157, *Intolerance*

5.11, page 157, *Intolerance*

5.12, page 160, *Intolerance*

7.1, page 176, *Intolerance* (Museum of Modern Art / Film Stills Archive)

7.2, page 177, *Cabiria* (Museum of Modern Art / Film Stills Archive)

8.1, page 189, *Intolerance*

8.2, page 190, *Intolerance*

8.3, page 191, *Intolerance*

8.4, page 196, *Intolerance*

9.1, page 200, *Intolerance*

9.2, page 200, *Intolerance*

9.3, page 201, *Intolerance*

9.4, page 201, *Intolerance*

9.5, page 206, *Intolerance*

9.6, page 208, *Intolerance*

9.7, page 208, *Intolerance*

9.8, page 209, *Intolerance* (Museum of Modern Art / Film Stills Archive)

9.9, page 210, *Intolerance*

9.10, page 210, *Intolerance*

10.1, page 219, *Intolerance* (Museum of Modern Art / Film Stills Archive)

10.2, page 224, *Intolerance* (Courtesy of *Film Comment*)

10.3, page 234, *Intolerance*

10.4, page 235, *Intolerance*

11.1, page 247, *Photoplay* 15.4 (March 1919)

11.2, page 258, *Photoplay* 22.1 (June 1922)

12.1, page 270, *The Eagle*

12.2, page 270, *The Eagle*

12.3, page 271, *The Eagle*

12.4, page 272, *The Eagle*

12.5, page 273, *Blood and Sand*

12.6, page 274, *Blood and Sand*

12.7, page 275, *Blood and Sand*

12.8, page 276, *Blood and Sand*

12.9, page 277, *Monsieur Beaucaire* (Museum of Modern Art/Film Stills Archive)

12.10, page 284, *The Eagle*

12.11, page 284, *The Eagle*

12.12, page 289, *The Son of the Sheik*

12.13, page 289, *The Son of the Sheik*

12.14, page 290, *The Son of the Sheik* (Museum of Modern Art / Film Stills Archive).

Index

Abolitionism, 165, 221
Acculturation, 68. *See also* Ethnic groups;
  Working class and immigrants
Acker, Jean, 261
Acting styles, 64, 74, 80, 82, 148, 219,
  334
Actualities, 30, 44, 46, 47, 69, 96. *See also*
  Documentaries
Adaptations, 45, 48, 63–64, 256–257, 276
Addams, Jane, 65, 184, 220, 221
Address, direct, 37–39, 59, 82, 142, 157,
  282
Adorno, Theodor W., 8, 11, 12, 110,
  190–192, 198, 231, 313, 316, 325, 338,
  343, 354, 365
Advertising, 31, 85, 100, 112, 186; women
  as target of, 122, 123, 256. *See also* Con-
  sumer culture; Marketing; Publicity; Star
  system
African-Americans, 51, 71, 257, 311. See
  also *Birth of a Nation*, racist ideology of;
  Black culture; Race and racism
Aiken, George, 45
Akerman, Chantal, 132
Allegory, 56, 204–205, 213, 346; in *Intol-
  erance*, 143, 147, 149, 150–151, 160–
  161, 169, 171, 184, 206–207, 213, 241;
  Babel in Babylon, 194
Allen, Jeanne, 85
Allen, Robert, 5, 31, 62, 115
Allen, Woody, 3
All on Account of the Milk, 79
Alpine Echo, The, 70

Altenloh, Emilie, 124–125
Althusser, Louis, 3, 4, 249
Altman, Rick, 223
Ambiguity. *See* Sexual ambiguity
Ambivalence, 40–41, 48, 56, 161; psycho-
  sexual, 39, 213, 215, 256, 276–277,
  279, 354
American Mutoscope & Biograph Co., 32,
  64, 70, 71, 72, 74, 164, 223, 247, 315
Americanization. *See* Acculturation;
  Upward mobility
Amusement parks, fairs, traveling shows,
  16, 29, 30, 60, 61, 62, 108–109;
  women and, 104
Andrew, Dudley, 231–232
Androgyny. *See* Sexual ambiguity
Anger, Kenneth, 18, 263, 359
Antifilm movement, 95. *See also* Censorship
Anti-Semitism, 70, 71
Appointment by Telephone, 31
Arbuckle, Fatty, 248
Archaeology, 181, 183–184, 187, 189–
  190, 233, 342
Arendt, Hannah, 8, 299
Art films, 6. *See also* Film d'Art
Arzner, Dorothy, 359
Assassinat du Duc de Guise, L', 173
As Seen through a Telescope, 33, 39
Audience, 2, 5, 16, 62, 88, 240; women
  in, 1, 2, 17, 18, 57, 65, 86, 91, 92,
  103, 105–106, 115, 240, 248, 312;
  social composition of, 16, 59, 60–61,
  65, 66, 86–87, 90, 96, 103–104, 105,

Audience (continued)
312; foreknowledge of, 48, 51, 79, 94;
participation of, 59, 66, 95, 104, 106,
113, 240, 248, 325; upward mobility of,
58–59, 61, 62–63; children in, 65, 119;
theater experience vs. film experience,
93–101, 123, 245. See also Nickelodeon,
audience composition; Social function of
cinema, for women; Valentino, Rudolph,
female reception of; Vaudeville,
audience composition; Working class
and immigrants, as audience
Audience research, 567, 298, 313
Avant-garde films, 24. See also Modernism
Avenging Conscience, The, 193
Ayres, Agnes, 288

Babel, Tower of Babel, 16–17, 19, 77, 183,
184–188, 192, 239
Babylon, theme in Intolerance, 161, 172,
174, 176, 180–182, 183–186, 190, 192,
194–195, 197, 221, 228, 234, 236, 238,
239, 341, 342; Hollywood, 182; Whore
of, 183, 232–233, 238
Balázs, Béla, 188–189, 325
Banky, Vilma, 269, 288
Bara, Theda, 123, 262, 350, 359
Bargain, The, 149
Barry, Iris, 125, 131
Barrymore, John, 254, 364
Barthelmess, Richard, 254
Barthes, Roland, 75, 175, 282, 293
Battle Cry of Peace, The, 120, 206, 347
Baudry, Jean-Louis, 3, 81, 203–204
Baudry, Pierre, 203–204, 351
Beheading the Chinese Prisoner, 31
Bellamy, Madge, 120
Bellour, Raymond, 4, 282, 332
Benjamin, Walter, 12, 13, 29, 31, 109,
110–112, 171, 172, 192, 231, 237, 239,
253, 300; on allegory, 204–205, 346,
352; on "optical unconscious," 110–111,
124, 343
Benvenist, Emile, 4
Berkeley, Bishop George, 338
Bernhardt, Sarah, 63, 173
Bettelheim, Bruno, 51, 52
Biograph Company. See American Muto-
scope & Biograph Company

Birth of a Nation, The, 64, 130–131, 137,
142, 150–151, 164–168, 175, 225; cen-
sorship and, 15, 165; racist ideology of,
52, 77, 158, 159, 165, 166, 167, 168,
184, 218–219, 220, 338; reception and
public controversy, 129, 164, 165
Bisexuality. See Sexual ambiguity
Bitzer, G. W., 164, 180, 237
Blaché, Alice Guy, 120
Black culture, 15, 54, 71, 100
Black Diamond Express, The, 25, 26
Blackton, John Stuart, 70, 206
Blasco-Ináñez, Vicente, 257
Bloch, Ernst, 300, 320
Blood and Sand, 266, 271–272, 279, 281
Booth, Elmer, 75
Bordwell, David, 6, 87, 134, 329
Bow, Clara, 120, 220
Bowser, Eileen, 79, 313
Brecht, Bertolt, 106, 307, 336
Brewster, Ben, 58
Bricolage, 29, 47–48
Broken Blossoms, 158, 229
Brooks, Louise, 220
Brooks, Van Wyck, 182
Brown, Karl, 164, 166, 175, 237
Browne, Nick, 218
Brownlow, Kevin, 206
Burch, Noël, 42, 43, 56, 57, 87, 97
Burlesque, 29, 38, 59, 104, 115, 119
Burlesque Suicide, The, 37
Bush, W. Stephen, 97
Bushman, Francis X., 254

Cabiria, 174, 177, 234
Cahiers du Cinéma, 171
Camera movement, 31–32, 33, 35, 54,
179, 180, 237, 276
Carbine, Mary, 100
Casting, 74, 159, 218, 246, 247, 255, 257
Castration, 233, 239, 266, 290. See also
Fetishism
Censorship, 15, 42, 63, 66, 76, 95–96,
119, 165–166, 220, 336
Ce que l'on voit de mon sixième, 39
Chanan, Michael, 57
Chaplin, Charlie, 42, 75–76, 248, 264
Chartism, 12
Chase comedies, 46, 49, 69

Cheat, The, 149
Child of the Ghetto, A, 73, 74
Children as audience, 65, 119
Cinema of attractions, 34, 56, 100, 109, 111, 238, 247, 282, 331
Cinematic apparatus, 4, 36, 41, 82, 90, 246
Civilization, 120, 130
Classic fan magazine, 259–260
Cobra, 361
Cohen, Lizabeth, 100, 113
Cohen's Advertising Scheme, 71
Cohen's Fire Sale, 55, 71
Comedy, 37, 39, 44, 45; slapstick, 71, 113, 236; sexual deviation and, 236. *See also* Chase comedies
Comic strips, 25, 35, 45, 58
Comolli, Jean-Louis, 81
Comstock, Anthony, 182
Coney Island, 16, 30, 116, 222
Consumer culture and consumption, 3, 8, 12, 16, 17, 30, 53–54, 55, 59, 63, 76, 77, 85–86, 92, 112, 113, 123, 191–192, 239; women as target of, 11, 18, 116, 121, 122, 231, 240, 241, 248, 254; domesticity and, 52–53, 120, 326
Continuity editing, 24, 42, 44, 80, 81, 148, 232
Cooper, Miriam, 159, 218–219, 222
Corbett-Fitzsimmons Fight, The, 1, 2, 6, 92, 119
Corner in Wheat, A, 137, 205
Costello, Maurice, 254
Country Couple, The, 25
Countryman's First Sight of the Animated Pictures, The, 25
Crosscutting. *See* Parallel editing
Crowd, The, 74
Crowell, Josephine, 154
Cup of Life, The, 74

Dadaism, 205
Dance halls, 104, 105, 118
Darling, J. C. ("Ding"), 77
Davis, Michael, 66
deCordova, Richard, 246
de Grasse, Sam, 143
de Lauretis, Teresa, 282
Deleuze, Gilles, 286, 287, 364

de Man, Paul, 204
DeMille, Cecil B., 120, 341
Derrida, Jacques, 184–185, 191–192
Dewey, John, 8
Dickens, Charles, 143, 207
Diegesis, 17, 23, 37, 44, 82–84, 97, 149, 246
Dioramas, 30
Distraction, 29, 100, 237, 239, 353
Distribution, 17, 23–24, 93, 245
Doane, Mary Ann, 5, 38, 121, 124, 250, 251, 280
Documentary, 30–31, 34, 44, 74. *See also* Actualities
Domesticity, 10, 11, 18, 52–53, 114, 117, 120–121, 206, 212, 261, 326, 347
Donnelly, Ignatius, 170
Dos Passos, John, 358
Douglas, Ann, 326
Dresser, Louise, 269
Drunkard's Reformation, A, 41–42
Duchamp, Marcel, 205
Dumb Girl of Portici, The, 130

Eagle, The, 267, 269–271, 274, 281, 283
Edison, Thomas Alva, 25, 47, 63
Edison Trust, 62, 69, 70, 79
Editing, 34, 42, 44, 79, 80, 81. *See also* Continuity editing; Parallelism, Parallel editing; Point of view
Eisenstein, Sergei, 132, 136, 143, 149, 203–204, 206
Electrocuting an Elephant, 31
Electronic media, 3, 13
Eliot, George, 143
Eliot, T. S., 330
Ellis, Havelock, 365
Emerson, Ralph Waldo, 167–168, 193, 239
Empire State Express, 25
Enlightenment, 9, 11, 76
Enunciation, 4–5, 332–333
Epstein, Jean, 325
Erens, Patricia, 71, 73
Erotic films, 30, 38–39, 282
Esperanto, 76, 77, 186. *See also* Language, film as/and
Ethnic groups, ethnicity, 14–15, 16, 18, 39, 54, 59, 60–61, 70–71, 88, 91–92,

Ethnic groups, ethnicity (*continued*)
95, 100, 101, 103, 105, 107, 113, 125,
222, 255, 267, 314–315; Italian, 71,
100, 102, 113, 118, 255, 322; Jewish,
69, 71–76, 77, 103, 108, 113, 118,
255, 314, 322; Polish, 100, 113. *See also*
Nativism; Race, racism; Working class
and immigrants
Ethnic theater, 103, 115
European Rest Cure, 55
Ewen, Elizabeth, 91, 110
Execution by Hanging, 31
Execution of Czolgoscz, The, 31, 47
Execution of Mary Queen of Scots, The, 31
Exhibition: modes and contexts, 7, 14, 17,
24, 29–30, 32, 34, 36, 42–44, 54, 60–
63, 76, 87, 93–101, 123, 245. *See also*
Kinetoscope; Nickelodeon; Variety for-
mat; Vaudeville
Exhibitionism, 33, 35–36, 39–41, 42, 238,
259, 273, 276–277
Experience, 12–13, 44, 90, 91, 92, 101–
102, 109, 111, 125, 139
Expositions. *See* World's Fairs and Exposi-
tions
Eyeline match. *See* Sight link

Fairbanks, Douglas, Sr., 248, 264, 269
Fairs. *See* Amusement parks, fairs, traveling
shows; World Fairs and Expositions
Fairy-tale films, 48–57, 68
Fall of Babylon, The, 133, 174, 180, 233,
245, 334, 353
Fandom, 260–261. *See also* Star system
Fan magazines and clubs, 123, 248, 253,
279
Feature film, 44, 84, 87, 98, 165
Female impersonators. *See* Impersonators
Female spectator. *See* Spectator
Fetishism, 33, 121, 219, 249, 252, 354; in
Intolerance, 175, 180, 214, 219, 233–234,
236–239; Valentino and, 260, 266,
293–294
Figure/figuration, 191, 197–198, 203,
207–209, 213, 226, 231, 241, 342. *See
also* Allegory
Film criticism, as institution, 24, 64, 251,
253. See also *Intolerance*, reception and
critical response

Film d'Art Company, 173, 179
Fletcher, Angus, 212
Fool's Revenge, The, 173
Ford, John, 131, 171, 339
Foucault, Michel, 107, 108–109, 292, 365
Four Horsemen of the Apocalypse, The, 256, 257,
259, 269, 362
Fox, William, 69
Framing, 34, 35, 44, 64, 74, 79, 80. *See
also* Camera movement; Tableau shot
Freud, Sigmund, 4, 39, 57, 130–131, 191,
214, 225, 230, 233, 237, 272, 276,
277–278, 283, 285–287, 337
From Showgirl to Burlesque Queen, 38
From the Manger to the Cross, 174, 178
Frye, Northrop, 204

Gangster films, 74, 249
Gay Shoe Clerk, The, 33
Genre, 25, 28, 30, 44, 47–48, 69, 337. *See
also* Actualities; Chase comedies; Com-
edy; Documentary; Erotic films; Ghetto
films; Horror films; Melodrama; Musi-
cals; "Peeping Tom" films; Pornography;
Reenactments; Scenics; Travelogues;
Trick films; Westerns; Woman's film
Ghetto films, 71–75, 76, 86, 94, 98
Ghetto Seamstress, The, 71
Gilbert, John, 254
Gish, Lillian, 74, 77, 120, 142, 150–151,
162, 207, 233, 351–352
Glyn, Elinor, 293
Godard, Jean-Luc, 132
Gold Is Not All, 58, 137
Gomery, Douglas, 5
Grandma's Reading Glass, 33
Great Train Robbery, The, 37, 42, 47, 69
Grey, Olga, 351
Griffith, D. W., 15–16, 17, 23, 41, 64,
71–73, 74–75, 77, 80, 129–130, 132,
137–138, 141–143, 148, 162–163,
164–172, 173–177, 179–182, 185, 189,
193–195, 203, 206, 218–223, 228–232,
237, 239–241, 264; Biograph films, 41,
58, 64, 71–75, 164, 167, 223, 225,
226; rescue races and fantasies, 46, 223,
225–226, 228, 230, 232, 240; racial ideology, 52, 77, 155, 158, 165, 168, 221,
255, 336–337; classical cinema and, 64,

131–132, 137, 139–140, 141–143, 148, 162–163, 174, 211, 240–241, 245; universal language myth, 77, 130, 183–186; star system and, 137, 162, 238; literary tradition and ambitions, 142–144, 166–167, 193, 195, 201, 211, 214–216. See also *Birth of a Nation, The; Broken Blossoms; Fall of Babylon, The; Hearts of the World; Mother and the Law, The; Musketeers of Pig Alley, The*

Griffith, Jake, 228

Griffith, Mattie, 226, 228, 229, 230

Gunning, Tom, 24, 33, 34–35, 40, 79, 96–97, 141–142

Gutman, Herbert, 102, 103, 300

Habermas, Jürgen, 8, 9, 10, 11, 12, 111

Hale's Tours, 32, 307

Hampton, Benjamin, 67, 68

Hapgood, Hutchins, 74, 312, 350

Happy Hooligan series, 58

Haraway, Donna, 52

Harrison, Louis Reeves, 66–67

Harron, Robert, 143, 227, 352

Hayakawa, Sessue, 255

Hazards of Helen, The, 120

Heartfield, John, 205

Heart of a Jewess, The, 71

Hearts of the World, 347, 350, 352

Heath, Stephen, 4, 81, 133, 282

Hegel, G. W. F., 8

Henabery, Joseph, 164, 166, 175–176, 177

Heterotopia, 107–108, 118

Hieroglyphics, film as, 77–78, 191–194; in *Intolerance,* 17, 180–181, 190, 192, 193–195, 197–198, 214, 215, 232, 233, 239

Hitchcock, Alfred, 131, 142

Homosexuality, 157, 266–267. See also Lesbianism and lesbians

Hold-Up of the Rocky Mountain Express, The, 47, 55

Hooligans of the West, The, 55

Horkheimer, Max, 8, 11, 110, 190–191, 198, 231, 316, 338, 343, 354

Horror films, 251, 292

How a French Nobleman Got a Wife Through the New York Herald "Personal" Columns, 46

Howe, Frederic, 184

Howe, Irving, 103

How the Other Half Lives, 74

Hudnut, Richard, 261

Hull, E. M., 256, 357

Identification, 31–32, 35, 57–58, 75, 80–81, 84, 85, 121, 124–125, 137, 142, 149, 161–163, 276, 280–283, 304, 337; star system and, 246, 281–283; female, 250–252, 280, 287; transsexual, 251, 280–281

Immigrant, The, 76

Immigrants. See Working class and immigrants

Impersonators, 46, 253, 266, 294

Independents (producers), 62, 79, 99

Indiscreet Bathroom Maid, The, 40

Industrialization, 102–103, 169

Ingram, Rex, 256

Inner speech, 332

Inquisitive Boots, 39, 40

Intellectuals, 106, 184, 194–195, 312, 342

Interior N.Y. Subway, 14th Street to 42nd Street, 32

Intolerance, 15, 17–19, 24, 77, 82, 122, 129–241, 264; reception and critical response, 17, 129–130, 133, 134–135, 136, 138–139, 162–163, 194, 201–202; articulation of vision and space, 17, 132, 141, 143–163, 178–180, 194; film/viewer relations in, 17, 129, 132, 139–140, 141, 149–150, 161–163, 194, 232; femininity, figurations of, 18, 122, 123, 146–147, 151, 154–160, 169, 198, 206–207, 211–236, 240–241, 264; concept of (universal) language and, 77, 129, 130, 166, 183–189, 192; classical paradigm and, 129, 131–132, 136–137, 139–140, 142, 174–175; print history and variants, 133, 199, 224–225, 330; parallel design/narration/editing, 133–141, 143, 148–149, 162, 169–172, 184, 197, 201, 209, 214, 223; concept of representation, 166–167, 175–178; concepts of history, 166–172, 174, 181–182, 195; camera movement, 179, 180, 237, 276; race and ethnicity, 221, 222. See also Babylon; Hieroglyphics; Prostitu-

Intolerance (*continued*)
   tion, Prostitute, in *Intolerance;* Writing
Iron Heel, The, 170
Irwin, John, 193
Irwin, May, 35

Jack and the Beanstalk, 49
Jacobs, Lewis, 58, 68, 69, 70
Jean and the Waif, 70
Jew's Christmas, The, 72, 73
Jews/Jewish: immigrant producers and per-
   formers, 69, 71, 255; as subject of films,
   71–76; millennialism, 77; Yiddish the-
   ater, 103; as audience, 108, 113
Johnson, Julian, 162, 173, 348
Judith of Bethulia, 185, 226, 229

Kalem Film Manufacturing Company, 70,
   74, 174
Kaplan, E. Ann, 251–252
Karpenstein, Christa, 279
Keaton, Buster, 23
Keats, John, 228, 238
Kellerman, Annette, 138
Kinetoscope, 36, 40. *See also* Peep shows
King Lear, 64
Kiss, The, 35
Klein, Melanie, 57
Kleptomaniac, The, 34, 56, 69, 137, 205
Kluge, Alexander, 8, 11–14, 48, 91, 92,
   108, 132, 139
Koster and Bial's Music Hall, 27
Koszarski, Richard, 99
Kracauer, Siegfried, 12, 29, 109, 112, 121,
   339, 346

Lacan, Jacques, 3, 122, 125, 280
Laemmle, Carl, 69, 73
Landis, Joan, 10
Language, film as/and, 24, 130, 186, 188–
   189; universal, 16, 17, 18, 55, 76–80,
   166, 183–187, 188, 192, 193. *See also*
   Inner speech; Writing
Last Days of Pompeii, The, 174
Last Laugh, The, 188
Leach, William, 85
Lears, Jackson, 123
Lecturers, on-stage, 42, 43, 45, 79, 93,
   96–98, 142, 306

Lee, Lila, 271
Lennig, Arthur, 164–165
Lesbianism and lesbians, 157, 221, 261,
   264, 285
Levine, Lawrence, 95
Lewis, Vera, 145
Life of an American Fireman, 47, 69, 306
Life of Moses, The, 70, 113
Lighting, 80, 85, 135, 259
Lightning Sketches, 71
Lindsay, Vachel, 77–78, 138, 139, 193,
   198
Lippmann, Walter, 15
Literature, as institution, 11, 64, 74, 97,
   142, 144, 166, 193, 195, 202, 216. *See
   also* Adaptations
Loew, Marcus, 98
London, Jack, 170
Lonely Villa, The, 223
Long, Edwin, 234
Long, Walter, 159, 218–219
Loos, Anita, 155
Lubin, Sigmund, 46, 70
Lukács, Georg, 167
Lumière Brothers, 25, 30, 77

Magdalen, Mary, 221, 224–225, 229, 351
Maggi, Luigi, 174
Magic films, 68. *See also* Trick films
Magic lantern shows, 25, 29, 35, 42, 43;
   biblical, 175
Manifest Destiny, 171, 172
Marcuse, Herbert, 365
Marion, Frances, 359
Marketing of films, 63–65, 67, 248, 249,
   256. *See also* Publicity, Star system
Marsh, Mae, 151, 154, 161, 172, 212, 223
Masochism, 251, 262, 277, 285–287. *See
   also* Sadomasochism
Masquerade, 39, 283, 285
Mast, Gerald, 203, 348
Mathis, June, 261, 359
Matinee-idol tradition, 2, 253, 254, 264.
   see also Star system; Valentino, Rudolph
Mayne, Judith, 68, 146
McCutcheon, Wallace, 46
Meet Me at the Fountain, 46
Meighan, Thomas, 254
Méliès, Georges, 34, 48, 236

Melodrama, 44, 69–70, 71–75, 76, 251
Mencken, H. L., 182, 358
Metapsychology, 4
Metz, Christian, 3, 35–36, 38–39, 81, 186, 203, 280, 332–333; on *Intolerance*, 134, 135, 136
Millennialism, 76, 77, 169, 170, 185, 191
Mill Girl: A Story of Factory Life, 70
Mills, C. Wright, 8
Miscegenation, 255–256
Mise-en-scène, 28, 31, 54–55, 79, 159, 214, 276, 281, 289
Mitry, Jean, 34
Modernism, 6, 30, 132, 205, 218, 323, 330, 335
Modern Times, 76
Modleski, Tania, 251
Monsieur Beaucaire, 2, 266, 274–276, 282
Montage, 131; in *Intolerance*, 134, 135, 149, 178, 201, 203, 223. *See also* Parallelism; Parallel editing
Moran of the Lady Letty, 2, 282
Moreno, Antonio, 254, 264
Mother and the Law, The, 133, 153, 154, 160, 164–165, 166, 207, 237, 245; sexual themes, 223, 225
Mother Goose in Hieroglyphics, 193
Mother Goose's Fairy Tales, 50
Motherhood/maternal figure: as theme in *Intolerance*, 199–200, 201–204, 211–217; and Valentino, 262, 359, 365
Motion Picture magazine, 263
Motion Picture Patents Company, 63, 98
Moving Picture World, The, 62, 79, 80, 97
Mulvey, Laura, 5, 38, 246, 249–250, 272, 280, 292
Munsterberg, Hugo, 83, 138–139, 246, 318
Murnau, F. W., 188, 343
Museum of Modern Art Film Library, 131, 133
Music accompanying films, 42, 43, 44, 93; in nickelodeons, 66; ethnic, 100
Musicals, 24, 37
Musketeers of Pig Alley, The, 74–75, 174
Musser, Charles, 34–35, 50, 54, 98, 205
Mutoscope, 40
Mutual Film Corporation, 71
Mutual Film Corporation v. Industrial Commission of Ohio, 15

NAACP, 184
Naldi, Nita, 271
Napoleon, Man of Destiny, 64
Narcissism, 249, 250, 275, 276
Narration, 6–7, 16, 17, 23, 28, 45, 54, 58, 60, 79–82, 85, 97, 89, 90, 97, 141–146, 154, 162, 173. *See also* Enunciation; Parallelism
Narrative film, 33, 44–48, 51, 54, 56–57, 64, 69, 74, 79, 174, 210; industry's shift to, 33, 44–45, 69, 96, 306; history and, 167–169
National Association of the Motion Picture Industry, 165
National Board of Censorship, 63
Nativism, 222, 255, 256, 262
Nazimova, Alla, 261
Negt, Oskar, 8, 11, 12, 14, 91, 92
Neptune's Daughter, 138
New Woman, 117, 120, 212, 220, 255, 292
Newsreel, 54, 69. *See also* Actualities
Nickelodeon, 16, 29, 44, 61–63, 65–66, 68, 70, 84, 86, 88, 94, 108, 113; audiences, 53, 61–68, 70, 73, 86, 95, 103, 119, 225; censorship and, 63, 95, 119; as public sphere, 93, 94–95, 97; star system and, 247
Nonsynchronism, 93, 94, 132, 251, 300, 320, 330, 333, 337
Norman, Mabel, 42
Novarro, Ramon, 254, 264
Novello, Ivor, 254

Oedipus/Oedipal scenarios, 51–52, 57, 162, 215; in *Intolerance*, 226, 227, 230, 233; in Valentino films, 277, 282, 286, 288, 289, 291
Olcott, Sidney, 174
Old Isaacs, the Pawnbroker, 71
Oms, Marcel, 203
100 to 1 Shot, The, 70
Orientalism, 177, 237–238, 239, 255–256, 292

Pan-American Exposition at Night, 47
Panoramas, 30
Parallelism, Parallel editing, 58, 64, 80, 135, 137–138, 141, 142, 143, 148–149,

Parallelism, Parallel editing (*continued*)
 169–172, 201, 211, 223, 225. *See also*
 Intolerance, parallel design
Parisian Dancer, 25
Park, Ida May, 120
Parker, Dorothy, 278
Passion Plays, 173
Passover Miracle, A, 71, 73
Pastor, Tony, 115
Pastrone, Giovanni, 174
Paul, Robert, 25
Peeping Tom, 39
"Peeping Tom" films, 39–41, 56. *See also*
 Voyeurism
Peep shows, 36, 38, 40, 119. *See also*
 Pornography
Peiss, Kathy, 91, 104, 117
People's Institute, 63
Personal, 46
Phantom rides, 32, 33, 35
Phonograph, 113
Photoplay: A Psychological Study (Munster-
 berg), 83
Pickford, Mary, 120, 248, 264, 363
Poe, Edgar Allan, 193
Point of view, 24, 33, 39–41, 55, 81, 149,
 150–154, 158, 159, 214, 251, 269, 271,
 274–275, 288, 334. *See also* Sight link
Political cartoons, 35, 45, 49, 51
Pornography, 29, 38, 40, 283, 353
Porter, Edwin S., 25, 31, 33, 34, 45, 46,
 47, 48–57, 123, 205
Pound, Ezra, 136, 330, 338
Private/Public, 8–11, 52, 74; gendered
 hierarchy of, 10, 40, 114–116, 118,
 121, 122, 240, 248. *See also* Public
 sphere
Progressive Era/Progressivism, 76, 167,
 182, 212, 220
Prostitution, Prostitute, 115, 156, 157,
 159, 212, 217, 220, 221–222, 225, 226,
 231, 348–350; in *Intolerance*, 156, 221–
 225, 229–232, 351; ethnicity and, 222;
 rescue fantasy, 225
Psychology of the Photoplay, 138
Publicity: star, 18, 246–248, 253, 260. *See
 also* Star system; Valentino, Rudolph,
 star persona and publicity discourse
Public sphere: transformation of, 2, 14,

91, 115–116, 121, 240, 292; cinema
 and/as, 3, 7–8, 13–16, 43–44, 48, 52,
 62–64, 90–95, 103–105, 108, 114,
 123–124, 125, 165–166, 240, 248,
 260–261, 292; concept(s) of, 7–15;
 European, 8, 14, 114; bourgeois, 8–12,
 14, 15, 64, 92, 114; vs. private sphere,
 8, 11, 74, 102, 248; industrial-
 commercial, 11–12, 60–61, 92, 112,
 114, 123, 247, 248; American, 14, 114,
 240; and ethnicity, 62, 103–104, 114;
 and gender, 114–124, 215, 240, 248,
 254, 293
Public Sphere and Experience, The (Negt/Kluge),
 11
Purple Rose of Cairo, The, 3
Purviance, Edna, 76

"Quality" films, 64, 70, 87
Queen Elizabeth, 123
Quintilian, 204
Quirk, James R., 264
Quo Vadis?, 113–114, 174

Race, racism, 39, 51–54, 59, 61, 107, 221,
 255, 257, 311, 336–337. *See also*
 African-Americans; *Birth of a Nation, The*,
 racist ideology of; Black culture
Rambova, Natacha, 261, 264, 265
Ramsaye, Terry, 68
Ray, Man, 205
Reading public, 10, 11, 16, 118
Realism, 4, 68–76, 81–83, 167, 175–178
Reenactments, 30–31, 35, 46, 47, 119
Reid, Wallace, 254, 257
Rescue plots, 46, 223; in *Intolerance*, 170–
 171, 172, 174, 225–227. *See also*
 Griffith, D. W., rescue races and
 fantasies
Resurrection, 173
Rice, John C., 35
Richardson, Dorothy, 327
Riis, Jacob, 74, 75
Rise and Fall of Free Speech in America, The
 (Griffith), 165, 207
Rise of the American Film, The (Jacobs), 68
Robeson, Paul, 358
Rogers, Will, 245, 262
Rogin, Michael, 219, 229, 233

Rolph, James, 350
Romance of a Jewess, 71, 72–73, 308–309
Roosevelt, Theodore, 49, 56, 255
Rosalie et Léonce à théâtre, 124
Rosen, Philip, 130
Rosen, Ruth, 221
Rosenzweig, Roy, 91, 103, 109
Rube and Mandy at Coney Island, 25
Russell, Ken, 358, 359
Russell Sage Foundation, 29, 66
Ryan, Mary, 120

Sacher-Masoch, Leopold von, 286
Sadism, 31, 41, 56, 58, 277; in Valentino
  films, 1–2, 283–288; in *Intolerance*, 158,
  228, 239. *See also* Masochism;
  Sadomasochism
Sadomasochism, 283, 285–288, 292
St. Denis, Ruth, 342, 353
Sainted Devil, A, 282
St. Johns, Adela Rogers, 257
Saint-Louis Exposition, 32
Salome, 64
Sampson-Schley Controversy, The, 46
Satan, 174
Scenics, 44, 46, 47, 54, 69, 96, 113
Scopophilia, 259, 276–277; in *Intolerance*,
  239; female, 277, 278. *See also*
  Voyeurism
Scott, Sir Walter, 142, 167
Search for Evidence, A, 40, 41
Sennett, Richard, 8, 9, 13, 95, 105
Sexual ambiguity, 233, 236, 252, 259,
  262, 267–268, 269, 276
Sheik, The, 256–257, 259, 261, 282, 285,
  288, 360
Sherlock, Jr., 23
Sight link, 146–147, 149, 179, 334
Slapstick. *See* Comedy
Slide, Anthony, 220
Smalley, Phillips, 72
Smith, Frederick James, 138
Smith, G. A., 33, 48–49
Song of the Shirt, The, 137
Son of the Sheik, The, 1, 287, 292
Sound: effects, 42, 43, 44, 79, 93; syn-
  chronized, 43, 99, 190, 343
Southey, Robert, 49
Sparrows, 363

Spectator: as concept, 2–7, 13–14, 16–
  17, 23–24, 25–26, 28, 35, 38–39, 43,
  56–57, 59, 66, 84–85, 121, 129, 136,
  139, 216, 246, 249; female, 2, 5, 18,
  39, 121–125, 240–241, 249–252, 276–
  279, 288. *See also* Audience;
  Identification
Staiger, Janet, 87
Star system, 24, 93, 123–125, 246–248,
  267, 269; Griffith and, 162, 238. *See also*
  Fandom; Publicity; Valentino, Rudolph
Stella Dallas, 58, 251
Stereopticon shows, 25, 29, 30, 43
Stern, Seymour, 131, 165, 339
Sternberg, Josef von, 364
Story films, 44, 55, 68, 69–70, 96
Story the Biograph Told, The, 41
Structural Transformation of the Public Sphere, The
  (Habermas), 8
Studlar, Gaylyn, 254, 256, 260, 364
Swanson, Gloria, 120
Sweet, Blanche, 226, 351

Tableau shot, 28, 34–35, 45, 54; in *Intol-
erance*, 149, 178, 179, 180, 194, 198,
  199
Talmadge, Norma, 236
"Teddy" Bears, The, 48–49, 50–56, 94
Tellegen, Lou, 254
Terrible Ted, 56
Terrible Teddy, the Grizzly King, 49–50
Thanhouser Company, 70
Theater(s): location of, 54, 60–62, 100,
  245, 311; as social space, 61, 63, 65,
  105, 109, 117–118; closing of, 63, 95;
  experience, 93, 95, 99–100, 245;
  chains, 98–99. *See also* Ethnic theater;
  Exhibition; Heterotopia; Nickelodeon;
  Variety format; Vaudeville; Working
  class and immigrants, as audience
Thief of Bagdad, The, 239
Thomas, William Isaac, 109
Thompson, Kristin, 79, 87, 136, 142, 329
Those Awful Hats, 124
Tillie's Punctured Romance, 42
Tower of Babel. *See* Babel, Tower of Babel
Traffic in Souls, 137, 221
Tramp figure, 58, 76
Tramp's Dream, The, 58

Transvestism and cross-dressing, 250, 280–281, 287. *See also* Impersonators
Travelogues, 30, 31–32, 42, 55, 96
Treadmill, The (Griffith), 214–215, 227, 348
Trick films, 31, 44, 45, 54, 69, 309
Tucker, George Loane, 137

Uncle Josh at the Moving Picture Show, 25–28, 30, 35, 40, 43, 57, 59, 160
Uncle Tom's Cabin, 45–46, 94, 287
United Artists, 248
Universal language. *See* Language, film as/and
Universal Film Manufacturing Company, 70, 71, 73, 74
Unwritten Law, The, 119
Upward mobility: of audiences, 58–59, 61, 62–63, 68, 74, 86, 88, 114, 309–310; vaudeville and, 91, 115

Valentino, Rudolph, 1–2, 7, 18, 24, 93, 120, 124, 239, 245, 248, 252–294; female address and reception, 1–2, 18, 93, 124, 253, 254–255, 257, 260, 293–294; star persona and publicity discourse, 120, 124, 248, 253–254, 256–267; ethnic-racial otherness of, 253, 254–257, 260, 263, 264, 267, 282, 292, 293; sexual ambiguity, 254, 259–268, 275–276, 279, 285, 287; male reception of, 257, 259–261, 262, 263, 267, 285, 293; articulation of vision in films, 269–276, 279–280, 288; identification, 276, 280–283, 287
Valentino, 358, 359
Vamp figure, 123, 266, 269, 274, 281, 283, 292
Vampire, The, 41–42
Variety format, 29–30, 43, 93, 94; in nickelodeons, 29, 59, 61, 108, 113
Variety show. *See* Burlesque
Vaudeville, 45, 59, 71, 91; exhibition outlet for films, 1, 28, 29, 43, 59, 60–61; audience composition, 16, 59, 61, 62, 94; as model for film genres and characters, 25, 30, 58; gentrification of, 95, 115, 119; ethnic, 95, 103; gender segregation and, 115–116, 117
Vernet, Marc, 37

Vertov, Dziga, 132
Virgin/virginal figure, 120, 152–153, 158, 212, 225–226, 227
Vitagraph Company of America, 64, 70, 174, 206
Vorse, Mary Heaton, 104, 105–106, 107, 110, 119, 312
Voyeurism, 28, 34–42, 65, 75, 121, 153, 161, 238, 239, 249, 252, 277, 294. *See also* Scopophilia

Wagenknecht, Edward, 203
Wald, Lillian, 220, 221
Walker, Alexander, 292
War Brides, 120
Warburton, Bishop, 194
Way of the World, The, 351
Weary Willie series, 58
Weber, Lois, 72, 120
Welles, Orson, 131
West, Mae, 260
Westerns, 48, 249
What Happened in the Tunnel, 39
What Happened on Twenty-Third Street, New York City, 39
White Slavery, 221–222
Whitman, Walt, 77, 166, 170, 193, 195, 199, 201, 206, 207, 212, 214, 216–217, 218
Widow Jones, The, 35
Wilkins, John, 317
Williams, Alan, 29
Williams, Linda, 251, 252, 292
Wine Opener, The, 38
Wise, Rabbi, 184
Woman's film, 249, 251, 287
Woods, Frank, 37, 64, 67, 82–83, 84, 97
Woolf, Virginia, 125
Woollcott, Alexander, 129, 138
Working class and immigrants, 15, 51–52, 101–114, 255; as audience, 16, 60, 61–63, 65–68, 69, 70, 76, 85, 87–89, 91–92, 104–107, 113–114, 118, 123, 255; racism and, 54, 107; as subject of films, 69–76; gender segregation in, 115, 117, 118; sexual culture of, 118, 222–223; women, 119–120, 211, 215. *See also* African-Americans; Ethnic groups, ethnicity; Nativism

World's Fairs and Expositions, 30, 47, 237.
See also Amusement parks, fairs, traveling
shows
Writing, 188–190, 194–197, 202; femi-
ninity and, 158, 207, 215–216. *See also*
Hieroglyphics; Language; Literature

Yankee production company, 70
Young Mr. Lincoln, 171
Young Rajah, The, 260

Zamenhof, Ludwig, 77
Zukor, Adolph, 64, 69, 173